DOUBLE
CROSSED

Also by Matthew Avery Sutton

American Apocalypse: A History of Modern Evangelicalism
Aimee Semple McPherson and the Resurrection of Christian America

DOUBLE CROSSED

THE MISSIONARIES WHO SPIED FOR THE UNITED STATES DURING THE SECOND WORLD WAR

MATTHEW AVERY SUTTON

BASIC BOOKS

New York

Basic Books
Hachette Book Group
1290 Avenue of the Americas, New York, NY 10104
www.basicbooks.com

Printed in the United States of America
First Edition: September 2019

Published by Basic Books, an imprint of Perseus Books, LLC, a subsidiary of Hachette
Book Group, Inc. The Basic Books name and logo is a trademark of the Hachette Book
Group.

The Hachette Speakers Bureau provides a wide range of authors for speaking events. To
find out more, go to www.hachettespeakersbureau.com or call (866) 376-6591.

The publisher is not responsible for websites (or their content) that are not owned by the
publisher.

Print book interior design by Amy Quinn.

Library of Congress Cataloging-in-Publication Data has been applied for.

ISBNs: 978-0-4650-5266-0 (hardcover), 978-1-5416-9967-0 (ebook)

LSC-C

10 9 8 7 6 5 4 3 2 1

For Kristen, Jackson, and Nathan

AND YE SHALL KNOW THE TRUTH,
AND THE TRUTH SHALL MAKE YOU FREE.

John 8:32

*Inscribed on the lobby wall at CIA headquarters,
Langley, Virginia, by order of Allen Dulles*

CONTENTS

Contents

INTRODUCTION

WILLIAM ALFRED EDDY DID NOT LOOK THE PART OF SUPER SPY. NO MOVIE mogul would have cast him as a James Bond or a Jason Bourne. The middle-aged professor had a limp, a receding hairline, a pudgy face, and an expanding waist. He also had a disarming smile, a deep laugh, and an eternally delightful sparkle in his eye. He served as a marine in World War I, and after the war, he dedicated his life to the cause of peace. He became a missionary, sharing the Christian gospel with students in the Muslim world. When the United States returned to war in the early 1940s, he again responded to his nation's call to serve.

Eddy joined a ragtag group of men and women who launched the United States' first foreign intelligence agency, the Office of Strategic Services. Leading the OSS was William "Wild Bill" Donovan, an irascible Irishman who had gone from marine to lawyer to politician to spymaster. Donovan sent Eddy to North Africa, where the missionary could put his knowledge of the Koran, years of practice speaking Arabic, and partnerships with Muslim leaders to good use.

Not long after hitting the ground in Tangier, Morocco, Eddy became the target of Axis intelligence agents. The skills he had honed as a missionary made him a marked man. An Italian spy tried to plant a bomb in his car, but Eddy's chauffeur was vigilant and kept him safe. A few weeks later, Eddy learned from a double agent working for the British that Axis spies were again scheming to "unobtrusively" slip a bomb into his vehicle. Eddy's American bosses warned him to take the "greatest precautions" or he would be returning home in a box.[1]

Eddy was one of the OSS's most effective field operatives. Donovan had sent him to prepare the way for Operation Torch, the 1942 Allied invasion of North Africa, which was central to American and British plans for taking control of the Mediterranean. Eddy advised Generals George Patton and Dwight Eisenhower on the incursion strategy. He also recruited a secret network of local agents on the ground in North Africa. His most audacious undertaking included a plot to "kill," as he described it, "all members of the German and Italian Armistice Commission in Morocco and in Algeria the moment the landing takes place." In a straightforward and matter-of-fact memo, he told Donovan that he was targeting dozens of people. He additionally ordered the executions of "all known agents of German and Italian nationality." Never one to mince words, he called the proposal an "assassination program."[2]

To orchestrate the daring and ambitious plot, Eddy hired a team of Frenchmen. His "principal" hired gun was the father of a boy who had been imprisoned in Paris by the Germans. "The father," he noted, "is impatiently awaiting permission to carry out this assignment." Eddy wanted to ensure that no one could trace the assassinations back to him or the OSS. He planned to frame the executions as a "French revolt against Axis domination." "In other words," he explained to Donovan, "it should appear" that the dead Germans and Italians were "the victims" of a French "reprisal against shooting of hostages by the Germans and other acts of German terror," and not an OSS operation.[3]

Assassination plots were not the only thing on Eddy's mind. At about the same time that he was recruiting French hit men, he wrote to his family about the sacrifices he was making for Lent. He described the Easter season as "abnormal" this year. "I am certainly abstaining from wickedness of the flesh," he confessed. With his wife thousands of miles away, that was not too difficult. "I haven't even been to a movie since Lisbon, I don't overeat any more, and I allow myself a cocktail at night, but never before work is all done." At the time, he was attending services at the local Anglican church. The "small community" of congregants, he wrote home, knew that fellow believers around the world were joining with them in "the act of consecration and penance." He told his family he was thinking of them and that he was praying that "all of us come through to better days when mercy and charity again return to the earth."[4]

The calculus was clear for Eddy. To honor the death and resurrection of his Lord and Savior, no movies, no fleshly wickedness, and not much booze. Pray for mercy and charity to return to earth. And in the meantime, covertly arrange for the murders of Germans, Japanese, and Italians.

The war, the assassination plot revealed, seemingly changed everything for religious activists turned spies like Eddy. Or maybe it didn't. Maybe assassinating those who did the devil's handiwork represented the logical culmination of their sense of global Christian mission, how they planned to bring peace and charity back to earth. If they hoped to restart their religious work after the war, they first had to defeat the evil that blocked their path. Perhaps for Eddy and dozens of other holy spies, serving a secretive, clandestine US wartime agency tasked with defeating German and Italian fascism and Japanese militarism was another way, maybe the best way, to serve the very same Jesus they sought to emulate as missionaries.

They were never quite sure.

The US government closely guarded the secret that missionaries and religious activists had become spies and assassins. The cover-up began with William Donovan. At the end of the war, the general pivoted from battling Germans and Japanese to planning for the postwar world. The OSS leader hoped that the United States would establish a permanent foreign intelligence agency. After the ticker-tape parades and impromptu street-corner kisses had ended, he took to the pages of *Life* to make his case. He highlighted how his organization had used hard work and old-fashioned American virtues to contribute to the Allied victory. His "amateurs in intelligence," he boasted, "showed what intellect, diligence, courage and willingness to get around can accomplish in a supposedly esoteric realm." Donovan worked to reassure readers that his operatives were good, patriotic, respectable Americans and not the liars, cheats, and scoundrels many people at the time associated with spy craft and secret police like the Gestapo. "The heart of American wartime intelligence," he surmised, included a "collection of highly implausible 'operators.'" Then he named them: scholars, researchers, economists, engineers, historians, sociologists, linguists, anthropologists, and experts on labor movements. In other words, everyday professionals populated the OSS, people just like you and me. He recruited his officers from universities, private research institutions, commercial businesses, law firms, and labor organizations. They included many of the nation's best and brightest men and women.[5]

But these were not the only people Donovan had recruited. The spymaster intentionally hid the fact that another group of Americans had played a substantial role in wartime intelligence gathering, espionage, and covert operations. Dozens of missionaries, missionary executives, priests, religious activists, and at least one rabbi also worked for the OSS. These operatives exchanged their calling to serve God for a more temporal and temporary duty.

As Donovan made the case for what was to become the Central Intelligence Agency (CIA), he ensured that the stories of the OSS's godly spooks remained top secret. He and his missionary operatives went to great lengths to hide, obfuscate, and sometimes outright deny their collaborations. Neither the missionaries nor their religious agencies nor American military leaders felt comfortable acknowledging the wartime lying, deceiving, manipulating, and even killing that these religious activist operatives engaged in. Donovan's godly crusaders did what they did because they needed the United States to win the war in order to guarantee their freedom to work around the globe. But they did not want to bring any attention to their wartime actions. If native peoples knew that some missionaries had worked as government spies, how could they ever trust the ones who insisted they were only doing the Lord's work? They couldn't. As a result, the wartime stories of Wild Bill's religious operatives have remained almost entirely hidden.

Until now.

This book tells the story of a secret army of holy spies who fought around the globe for the sake of their God and their country. None of them had ever imagined that this was the work they would do. But Japan's surprise attack on the United States on December 7, 1941, changed everything. Americans from all walks of life heeded the call to serve. For many, this meant enlisting in the armed forces or going to work in munitions factories. For a handful of people whose religious activities had inadvertently provided them with a unique and valuable skill set, a different opportunity arose. Donovan and other American intelligence officers realized that they could send missionaries and priests back to their foreign posts as secret agents.

Donovan's religious operatives had good precedents for their actions. Spying is one of humankind's oldest professions. In the Old Testament book of Numbers, twelve spies scouted the promised land and reported back to Moses. A little later, Joshua dispatched spies to Jericho. Although Donovan was no Moses, he knew that American missionaries were keen to secure access to what they envisioned as their own promised lands.

In the nineteenth century, missionaries often worked at the vanguard of American imperialism. They were frequently the first Americans whom foreign people encountered, and they routinely influenced foreigners' views of the United States. In China, India, Hawaii, the Philippines, the Middle East, and many other places, missionaries served as cultural mediators, helping bring diverse peoples and regions into contact with one another. Their work forced American diplomats to engage with other governments, and they represented an unofficial foreign service. Theirs was an imperialism not of armies and force but of ideas and humanitarian-oriented institutions. These ambassadors hoped to spread American values, ideas about human rights, and democracy to all who would open their doors to them. They rarely used weapons to accomplish their work.

Things were different under Donovan during World War II. The actions of missionary operatives made overt and explicit what had in earlier generations been subtle and implicit. The cross and the flag, missionaries and the military, were building, expanding, and defending the American empire together. Religious activists collaborated closely with the US government, wielding along with their Bibles everything from poison pills to dung bombs. The differences between sinners and saints, missionaries and mercenaries, were no longer distinguishable, at least not for the duration.

Although missionary operatives believed in the Allied cause, most were not proud of their wartime actions or the choices and compromises the conflict forced upon them. Men of great faith became men of great doubt. "We deserve to go to hell when we die," Eddy later lamented. "It is still an open question," he continued, "whether an operator in OSS or in CIA can ever again become a wholly honorable man." Distinguished journalist and religion writer Malcolm Muggeridge, an agent for the British Secret Intelligence Service, agreed. "Intelligence work," he insisted, "necessarily involves such cheating, lying and betraying" that it destroys one's character. "I never met anyone professionally engaged in it," he concluded, "whom I should care to trust in any capacity." They both agreed with Joseph Stalin's adage: "A spy should be like the devil; no one can trust him, not even himself."[6]

Espionage is not like most occupations. It is not even like serving in the military. An operative's success is often proportional to his ability to bend the rules, to fix the game, to load the dice. Operatives and agents betray, bluff, bribe, cheat, con, dupe, fake, forge, hoodwink, and manipulate. Covert actions are always about ends; they are never about means. Evangelism is not like most other jobs, either. Preachers and missionaries usually believe that God has called them specifically to their work. They embark on their careers with a sense of divine mission. They seek to build up the kingdom of God, not dismantle kingdoms of man. They seek the protection of the cross; they do not expect to double-cross.

Excavating the stories of the United States' clandestine missionary spies is difficult. Muggeridge insisted that scholars would never be able to tell the full story of what happened during the war. "Secrecy," he resolved, "is as essential to Intelligence as vestments and incense to a Mass, or darkness to a Spiritualist séance." Historians trying to write about wartime spies, he argued, were on a fool's errand. And he was right that the OSS, and later the CIA, did not make it easy to recover the histories of their religious operatives. Yet despite Muggeridge's warnings, we can glimpse into the shadows to trace the actions and contributions of at least a few of the most important religious activists who went to work for Donovan. This book centers primarily on the wartime careers of William Eddy, John Birch, Stephen Penrose, and Stewart Herman. They served around the globe, from North Africa to Europe, from the Middle East to Asia. They left a trail of letters, diaries, and other personal documents, which when read in the light of recently declassified government records and sources obtained through the Freedom of Information Act illuminate their wartime actions and the challenges they faced. They did their part and more to ensure that the Allies won the war. Their lives show us how World War II became for some Americans as much a crusade for expanding American power in the name of religious liberty as a war to avenge Pearl Harbor.[7]

William Eddy was working for the US government as an attaché when President Franklin Roosevelt took the United States to war. The Beirut-born child of missionaries, decorated World War I marine, and Episcopalian educator had spent the 1920s and 1930s trying to make the case for Protestant Christianity as the solution to the world's problems. With American participation in the growing conflict looking inevitable, he volunteered for a temporary job working under the director of naval intelligence. The navy sent him to Cairo in the summer of 1941. "So far as I can work out," he wrote his wife, Mary, "I am to be a...'Lawrence in Arabia' to promote Allied propaganda among the natives, and a reporter on politics of the Arabs and Egyptians. At least it will be a creative job, not stereotyped." Military leaders hoped that Eddy could convince Muslim leaders to support the Allies. Eddy was one of the few Americans with the requisite skills to do the job right. His missionary background, fluent Arabic, and knowledge of the Koran prepared him for intelligence and diplomatic work in a way that almost nothing else could. Worried that the US government had too few people who understood Muslim cultures, Eddy promised to do the best he could for both his homeland and the Arab peoples he had long served. He had just returned to Washington, DC, for new orders when the Japanese struck the American base on Oahu that December.[8]

The American entry into the war meant less to John Birch, a missionary working in China. He was already essentially at war with Japan as he labored to build a small community of Chinese Christians near the front lines of the latest Sino-Japanese conflict, which had been raging for years. In 1940 Birch established a mission at Hangzhou, a major city in Southeast China, a little more than one hundred miles from Shanghai, but he suspected that death and destruction would soon overshadow his work. Shortly before the Pearl Harbor attack, the Japanese launched an offensive in the area. Birch had to abandon the church. He fled the front to Shangrao, a couple hundred miles into the interior of China, where he established a new mission. It too soon fell to the Japanese.

Stephen B. L. Penrose Jr. felt shocked by the news that the United States was now at war. He was living with his young family in New York while working as the assistant director of the Near East College Association (NECA). The association oversaw a handful of Protestant missionary schools in Turkey, Greece, Syria, and Egypt. Its board of directors included numerous prominent Americans, including corporate attorney Allen Dulles. Penrose also served as a member of the American Board of Commissioners for Foreign Missions (ABCFM), the oldest and most heralded foreign missionary agency in the United States. "The whole thing," he wrote his parents about the American declaration of war, "seems so utterly fantastic that I have difficulty in taking it seriously, which may of course be a great mistake on my part. We shall see." Once the news settled in, Penrose decided that he needed to find a way to support the American war effort. He told his parents that he was letting a few people in Washington know that he was ready to take "a defense job if a reasonably urgent demand arises."[9]

Stewart Herman Jr. was affected most directly and most immediately by the American entry into the war. The young Lutheran minister, who had worked for the previous six years as the pastor of the American Church in Berlin, was rounded up by the Nazis and interned right after Germany declared war on the United States in the days after Pearl Harbor. With that his pastoral work on the Continent came to an end, at least for the duration of the war. Over the previous half decade, he had developed close alliances with the leaders of the Confessing Church, one of the strongest anti-Nazi movements in the Third Reich. Herman's knowledge of the German underground would prove extremely valuable, not just for the perpetuation of Christianity in Europe, but for waging an American war.

Little did any of these religious activists, missionaries, and missionary executives know that their lives were about to intersect. During the war, all four served in the Office of Strategic Services. Many missionaries and former missionaries worked in the OSS's Research and Analysis Branch, safe in offices located in Washington, DC, and New York. Eddy, Birch, Penrose, and Herman, in contrast, all served in the field. In China, Germany, the United Kingdom, North Africa, Greece, Italy, France, the Balkans, and the Middle East, they made significant contributions to the nation's war effort. They had many different reasons and motives for exchanging the cross for the sword, but each hoped that in working for the United States, he was working for God. They all shared a commitment to supporting American leaders' efforts to build a better postwar world. They sought a new global order that blended a generic, inclusive Protestant Christianity with American power. But they had to win the war first. They had to defeat the evil that threatened them before they could get back to the good work of expanding God's kingdom. "To make the devil flee," Eddy had decided years earlier, "it is sometimes necessary to resist him." Resist him they would.[10]

But resistance has consequences. What happens when missionaries become spies? What happens when they trade one calling for another or supplement one with a second? As they embraced their new vocation, most wrestled with difficult questions. How far should they go in service to country? How much of their character and values should they compromise? Should they lie and deceive? Use force? Kill enemies? At what point would their wartime choices smother their religious convictions? Would the war change the nature of their faith? Did they risk trading their eternal souls for the sake of temporal gains? Could missionary work and skullduggery mix? They could boil these questions down to one: Could a person faithfully serve God and the Office of Strategic Services at the same time?

The four spies also wrestled with less esoteric challenges. Eddy and Penrose, who had families, both desperately wanted to return home alive. If they died on the front lines, their children would grow up without fathers and their wives would have to survive without a breadwinner in the house. And if they did make it home, they wondered what normal life would be like after serving as professional liars and masters of deceit. For Birch and Herman, the issues were different. Younger men, they were both eager to settle into permanent careers and to live a life that had purpose and meaning. They sought to understand what they thought God had called them to do and what role the war played in God's divine plans for them. They also wondered if they would have families of their own. Both began the war with few close relationships. They sometimes doubted if they would ever find love. Could they simultaneously wage covert war while opening their hearts to another person? For one group of operatives, the question was whether they could walk back from the abyss and return to trusting relationships. For the other, the question was whether clandestine work made trusting relationships impossible. *Double Crossed* examines how some of the United States' first professional intelligence operatives wrestled with these questions and many more while winning the world's most horrific war.

During the 1940s, American leaders came to understand in deeper and more explicit ways how central religion was to crafting a successful foreign policy. But historians, for the most part, have overlooked the role of religion in the war. Religion helped shape the work, policies, and ideology of President Roosevelt and many members of his administration. The president insisted that religious convictions and beliefs provided the foundation for healthy, secure democratic governments, and he defended "freedom of worship" around the globe. He made the fight against Germany and Japan in part a religious crusade, which is why missionaries, priests, religious activists, and a rabbi proved so eager to enlist in Donovan's secret army. They believed they could serve God and country since American wartime policy objectives were so closely entwined with the aims of religious activists.[11]

Roosevelt's goals and those of missionary activists blended seamlessly in the execution of the war. The OSS's holy spooks fought to implement FDR's religious ideals and commitments as they engaged in their clandestine work. They wanted the war to end not just because they hated the death and destruction that it generated, but because they also longed to get on with their real business of promoting Christianity and American interests abroad. They believed that what was good for the United States was good for Christianity and that what was good for Christianity was good for the United States. They were true believers in the old Puritan notion that God has chosen the United States to serve as his "city on a hill," transforming the world through its example and its actions.

They shared a vision for the future best articulated by China-born missionary son and publishing mogul Henry Luce, who in 1941 took to the pages of *Life* to call on readers to make the twentieth century the "American Century." Luce, like the OSS's missionary operatives, called on Americans to accept "wholeheartedly" their duty, responsibility, and opportunity as citizens of the most powerful nation in the world. This meant, he insisted, that Americans must "exert upon the world the full impact" of their influence. The publisher demanded that the United States take a bold new place on the world stage. OSS religious activists believed that expanding American power and influence would enhance their efforts to build the kingdom of God around the globe.[12]

The United States' victory in World War II, facilitated in part by missionaries and religious operatives, allowed the nation to claim global supremacy and a divine commission to export Americans ideals and values. Many Americans had long believed that God had destined the United

States to lead the world, and the war provided them with the opportunity to fulfill what they saw as their holy mandate. Victory over Japan and Germany seemingly verified what Americans had long thought—that their nation was the new chosen land and they were the new chosen people. They saw in their past and in their wartime success the hand of God shaping history. They believed that their country was walking with the Almighty, called to share his truth. World War II spurred Americans to make the world more American, and with it, they hoped, to make it more Christian.

Americans came out of the war believing that they had a divine obligation to expand their nation's influence and power. The work of Donovan's holy spies supported this mission in at least three ways. First, two of the OSS's missionary recruits helped create and launch the Central Intelligence Agency, and they built into the CIA's charter some of the spy agency's most controversial characteristics. In so doing, the OSS missionaries thought they were doing the right thing. History teaches us that perhaps they were wrong. Second, Donovan's spies provided American leaders, from the president to some of the future directors of the CIA, with a playbook for using religious activists on an operational level to help meet foreign policy objectives. Missionaries, foreign religious agents, and both real and fake religious organizations became tools of the American foreign intelligence apparatus. Finally, the OSS's missionary spies crafted new and important partnerships for the United States with the foreign leaders overseeing Mecca, the Vatican, and Palestine. FDR's successors from Truman to Trump depended on these relationships as they crafted their foreign policies. OSS operatives established important bonds that allowed postwar American leaders to rally global leaders around the cause of religious freedom in ways that benefited the United States and its missionary empire. We cannot fully understand the Cold War crusade against "godless communism," nor can we understand the religious foundations of the war on terror, without understanding religion's prominent role in American intelligence and foreign policy during World War II and its immediate aftermath.[13]

Double Crossed recounts the sometimes comic, sometimes tragic, and sometimes profound ways that the founders of the United States' pioneering foreign intelligence agency tried to use humans' deep spirituality as a tool for war. American leaders discovered that the religious commitments of individuals, groups, and nations were rarely shallow or ephemeral. Rather, they intersected with global politics in powerful ways to motivate people to act toward many different goals. Modern American leaders are still struggling—and oftentimes failing—to understand this simple reality.

PART I

BEFORE THEY WERE
SPIES (1883–1941)

ONE

"The Moral and Spiritual Defenses of a Nation"

FRANKLIN DELANO ROOSEVELT WANTED HELP. A LOT OF IT. AS HE watched the unfolding wars in Europe and Asia in the late 1930s, he determined that the United States needed a first-rate intelligence-gathering agency. The Federal Bureau of Investigation (FBI) focused mostly on domestic threats, and although the army, navy, and State Department each had intelligence divisions, collecting information was not their primary mission and they did not coordinate their efforts. Moreover, many American leaders felt ambivalent about spy craft. Herbert Hoover's secretary of state summed up the traditional American attitude when he allegedly quipped, "Gentlemen do not read each other's mail." When it came to understanding events happening abroad, the president felt like a man making his way in the dark.

Mounting conflict around the globe inspired Roosevelt to act. On September 1, 1939, the German military invaded Poland. Tanks ripped over Polish terrain, while planes provided air cover. The German strategy of blitzkrieg, or lighting war, had begun. Within days of the invasion, Great Britain and France declared war on the Third Reich. Over the coming months, Hitler moved against Denmark and Norway and then Luxembourg, Holland, and Belgium. In May 1940 the Nazis invaded France. Facing annihilation, the French surrendered the next month. The Germans occupied northern France, including Paris, and allowed those in the southern part of the country to set up a new government located in the city of Vichy, a couple of hundred miles south of Paris. Its leaders claimed neutrality but collaborated extensively with the Nazis. A "Free French" contingent fled to the United Kingdom to join the British. Winston Churchill, the new prime minister of Great Britain, pledged never to surrender, but he confided to FDR that without American help, the British would soon suffer the same fate as their continental allies.

Germany was not Churchill's or Roosevelt's only fear. In 1939 the Italian fascist Benito Mussolini had joined forces with Hitler. Then in 1940 the Japanese government signed the Tripartite Pact with the Germans and Italians, establishing a powerful, new global alliance. It was past time, Roosevelt concluded, for the Americans to start reading other gentlemen's mail.

FDR and Secretary of the Navy Frank Knox, both hungry for information, sent army veteran and successful corporate lawyer William "Wild Bill" Donovan on a trip to the United Kingdom in the summer of 1940. The president wanted an analysis from Donovan of Britain's defenses. Could the British, Roosevelt asked Donovan, hold out against the Nazi onslaught? And if so, for how long? He hoped that Donovan, after seeing conditions in Europe firsthand, would encourage his fellow Republicans to support increased American aid to the British. The president believed that the United States' entry into the war was inevitable, but he knew that the American people were not yet ready. During the 1940 presidential campaign, FDR even pledged never to send American "boys" into foreign wars.

The British leadership embraced Donovan, recognizing that he could help them make the case for American intervention in the European struggle. The Germans had just forced the British and French to retreat to Dunkirk, and the Allies wanted all the help they could get. They courted and flattered the World War I hero and arranged meetings for him with Churchill as well as with "C," Stewart Menzies. Menzies directed Britain's foreign intelligence agency, the Secret Intelligence Service (SIS), also known as MI6. Menzies shared his agency's mission and strategies with Donovan and showed him top-secret intelligence reports. The British spymaster wanted the Americans to help him win the espionage game, and he suspected that Donovan did, too.

Roosevelt was so pleased with Donovan's work that just a few months later he approved another trip abroad. Having recently won an unprecedented third term in the Oval Office, the president dispatched the veteran officer in the last weeks of 1940 on a tour of the United Kingdom, the Balkans, the Middle East, and Ireland. This time the British paid the bills for much of Donovan's mission. He met again with Churchill and again with "C." He also met a rising star in the British Secret Intelligence Service, Ian Fleming, who later created the character James Bond. Fleming served briefly as Donovan's handler, helping him navigate the complicated world of British intelligence.

After debriefing Wild Bill on his latest travels abroad, Roosevelt tasked Donovan with an important assignment. The president wanted Donovan to draw up plans for a new central intelligence agency. On June 10, 1941, Donovan delivered his memo to the president. "Strategy," he began, "without information upon which it can rely, is helpless. Likewise, information is useless unless it is intelligently directed to the strategic purpose." Donovan worried that although the nation was "facing imminent peril," it lacked an "effective service for analyzing, comprehending, and appraising" information, especially regarding the power of potential enemies. American methods of collecting intelligence to date, he asserted, were "inadequate." He counseled the president that modern total war required information not just on armaments and troop strength, but also on economics, industry, communications, and civilian morale. Nor was that all. "There is another element in modern warfare," he advised the president, "and that is the psychological attack against the moral and spiritual defenses of a nation." The colonel recognized that religion mattered. He planned from the very moment of the OSS's inception to use religion as a weapon in the fight against the nation's enemies.[1]

Roosevelt agreed. In the margins of Donovan's proposal, he scribbled a note to an aide: "Please set this up confidentially." With those simple words, the United States' first foreign spy agency was born. The president did it without consulting Congress, he sent no inquiries to the military leadership, and he entertained no discussions of the move's constitutionality. The man who had created the Civilian Conservation Corps (CCC), the Public Works Administration (PWA), the Social Security Administration (SSA), the Rural Electrification Administration (REA), and much more now had a new alphabet agency in the works, one that would change the course of America's role in the world in ways that he could not have imagined.[2]

On July 11, 1941, FDR announced via executive order his establishment of the office of the Coordinator of Information (COI), which he charged with keeping the White House abreast of the latest developments as war raged in Europe and Asia. He appointed Donovan as the agency's new director. He authorized Wild Bill to collect data for the commander in chief and to carry out "such supplementary activities as may facilitate the securing of information important for national security." What those supplementary activities were, the president never explained. Donovan planned to interpret the president's order as liberally as possible. He had no intention of just sitting back and passively collecting data. The open-ended COI mandate gave Donovan carte blanche to build a covert intelligence network that operated around much of the world.[3]

Donovan set up the COI's headquarters on E Street, near the Lincoln Memorial, in Washington, DC. Once the United States officially entered the war after Pearl Harbor, Donovan's vast mandate expanded further. The nation needed a first-rate intelligence-gathering agency more than ever. In June 1942, FDR redesignated Donovan's agency as the Office of Strategic Services and put it under the authority of the Joint Chiefs of Staff, which was also a new wartime creation. (To avoid confusion, I will refer to both the OSS and its COI predecessor as the OSS hereafter.) Donovan hoped that the OSS would function as an independent but essential part of the US military, on equal footing with the army and navy. "We have succeeded," he boasted to a friend, in organizing "under one tent" three core units within the OSS, each with its own mission and function: "special intelligence, special operations and psychological warfare." His mission was to corral these three units into an effective team that could generate wartime victories in partnership with the military.[4]

Donovan was not an obvious choice for the job of top American spymaster. Born to a working-class family in Buffalo, New York, on New Year's Day 1883, Donovan spent his life fighting for respect. His parents, the children of Irish immigrants, worked hard to give their sons and daughters a good life. They raised their children in the Catholic Church, and Bill served as an altar boy. According to a biographer, Bill thought seriously about training for the priesthood. He graduated from parochial school and then went to Niagara University, a Catholic college in upstate New

York. There the Vincentian Fathers indoctrinated young Donovan in the importance of the Catholic faith and pushed him to wrestle over its application to real-world issues. He excelled at debate and even delivered a much-lauded speech titled "Religion: The Need of the Hour."

The Irishman eventually decided on law school instead of the priesthood and transferred to Columbia University. It was the right choice, allowing Donovan to parley his charisma, wit, and smarts into a successful career. At Columbia he overlapped with another New Yorker, Franklin Roosevelt. Donovan played quarterback for the school's varsity football team at a time when players wore few pads and men at his position often took substantial hits. Yet he always wanted the ball in his hands. When he finished law school, Donovan returned to Buffalo, where he launched a career in corporate law. He fell in love with and married Ruth Rumsey, a wealthy Protestant and a member of the Buffalo elite. She would not be the only woman smitten by Wild Bill's good looks, athletic physique, adventurous spirit, and Irish charms. Boasting a law degree and married to a woman from a respected family, this ambitious grandson of immigrants gained entrée into the most exclusive of social circles.[5]

In 1912 Donovan joined the New York National Guard as a captain. His unit essentially served as a gentlemen's club for playing soldier. The members of the guard, businessmen and bankers and lawyers, drank, gossiped, marched, and rode together, all under the pretext of protecting the Empire State. But the party ended in 1916 when the army ordered Donovan's unit to the southern border separating the United States from Mexico. Mexico was embroiled in a brutal civil war, and it was starting to spill into the American Southwest. Donovan was excited to have the chance to distinguish himself on the battlefield as he had on the football field. Under the command of General John Pershing, the attorney saw action in a skirmish with Pancho Villa, a Mexican revolutionary who had launched a raid into the United States that resulted in the deaths of some Americans. Military prowess, Donovan realized, was perhaps the ultimate way to prove himself as a man and as a patriotic American. Some people cowered and hid from danger. Not Donovan. He loved the rush of battle.

While the lawyer turned soldier was fighting with Pershing, Europe was embroiled in a major war. The German army had marched in 1914 almost to Paris before the French and their British allies stopped the advance. Then, slowly, the French and British began pushing the Germans back. Soon the warring factions established a western front in the form of a long line of trenches that ran from the coast of Belgium through France to Switzerland. They settled in for what became a long, bloody, horrific struggle.

President Woodrow Wilson had pledged the United States to neutrality, but staying out of the conflict eventually proved impossible. On April 2, 1917, Wilson appeared before Congress to read a list of German atrocities and call for a declaration of war. Building to the lines that would define the rest of the war, he demanded that the world "be made safe for democracy. Its peace," he pledged, "must be planted upon the tested foundations of political liberty." He insisted that Americans were ready to fight not for spoils, but for seemingly inalienable truths. "We must have no selfish ends to serve. We desire no conquest, no dominion. We seek no indemnities for ourselves, no material compensation for the sacrifices we shall freely make. We are but one of the champions of the rights of mankind."[6]

When the United States entered the war, Donovan and his national guard unit joined the famous 69th "Fighting Irish" Infantry Regiment (redesignated the 165th), where he commanded the first battalion. By his side was Father Francis P. Duffy. The priest constantly prodded Donovan and the rest of the 69th to draw on the Catholic faith for strength. And he required everyone to take regular communion. "I have no place for backwardness or politeness about this matter of the sacraments over here," Duffy confessed from the front. And "that policy suits Bill." Duffy's service during the war, blending faith and action, led New Yorkers to erect a statue in his honor in Times Square, where tens of thousands of locals and tourists see it every day.[7]

Donovan and his battalion arrived in France in late 1917. Early the next year they were at the front and engaged in the fight. Donovan wrote his wife as often as possible from the trenches, where he again dove into the center of the action. His letters detail numerous harrowing events. "I do not know why I was not killed," he revealed in one note. "I had previously been hit on the head with a piece of stone or shell which ripped my gas mask." As the battle continued, "another piece of shell had hit me on the left heel tearing my shoe and throwing me off my balance, while somehow I got some shrapnel in my leg." He made light of the onslaught, which he was surprised to have lived through. "I guess I have been born to be hanged," he quipped. Without his mask he inhaled mouthfuls of gas as soldiers fell all around him. But he knew he had a job to do leading those men who could still fight. "It was a real test," he admitted, "to keep these youngsters, who were game, but nervous, up to their jobs and make everyone feel that no matter how bad everything looked, we were going to hold on."[8]

Donovan was injured twice more, earning the Medal of Honor and many other commendations, and he became one of the most highly decorated American soldiers of the war. Whether he acquired the nickname "Wild Bill" on the football field or the battlefield is a matter of debate, but no one questioned its applicability. Father Duffy told Donovan that when he died, his men had an epitaph ready for him: "He was a son of a bitch, but a game one."[9]

After the war, Donovan resumed his law career. Major firms were eager for the services of this much-heralded war hero. His work for various corporate clients, including J. P. Morgan, required him to travel extensively around the world, where he crafted deals with European governments, banks, and businesses to help the Morgan company break into new markets. His foreign negotiations taught him the significance of the United States' relationships abroad and heightened his awareness of emerging threats.

Donovan's travels also exposed him to the ever-increasing role of religion on the world stage. During a Mediterranean cruise in 1923, the attorney read James Frazer's *The Golden Bough*, a pioneering book on comparative religion. He called it "very difficult reading" but kept at it over the length of the cruise, thinking about how religion was shaping geopolitics. Blending theory with experience, he used his time in port to study the religions on the ground wherever he was. In Algiers he visited numerous mosques. Throughout his time abroad, he noticed the growing influence of Islam on global politics.

Donovan never let his curiosity about competing faiths take all of his attention, however. After a long day visiting religious sites, he and his cruise mates went to a "dancing place." The group was unimpressed with the tourist trap, so they headed upstairs to watch dancing "au nature." "Only one dancer," he recorded in his diary, "had any kind of a figure and any kind of good looks." In Carthage he had a similar experience. During the day he wrestled with the religious history of the region and the intermingling of so many different peoples. That night he "went to a den of iniquity," where he claimed to have only "talked" to the French "girls" who "had been traveling in their trade all over the French possessions."[10]

That FDR would one day tap Donovan to lead his new spy agency would have surprised anyone who knew of the men's political rivalry in New York. Republican leaders in the early 1920s had identified the war veteran and successful attorney as a rising star in the party, and in 1924 President Calvin Coolidge made Donovan an assistant attorney general. He gained national fame for his raids on speakeasies and elite social clubs that served liquor during Prohibition. Wild Bill had hoped that President Herbert Hoover would nominate him in 1929 for attorney general, but the new president went in a different direction. So did Donovan. The veteran moved to Manhattan and opened a successful law firm on Wall Street, which made him a wealthy man.

In 1932 Donovan ran for governor of New York. On the campaign trail, he traveled with a personal trainer and emphasized his vigor by boxing for exercise. The colonel wanted to be sure that the voters of New York understood that he was the most manly of men, in contrast to the current governor, Franklin Roosevelt, who was now running for president. While FDR was privileged and effete and spent most of his day in a wheelchair as a result of his bout with polio, Donovan tossed heavy medicine balls and showed that he was a scrappy fighter who could both take and land a punch. If war is the continuation of politics by other means, for Donovan politics was becoming war by other means.

Roosevelt did not want to see his home state's highest office turned over to a Republican. He tried to neutralize Wild Bill by plugging his opponent while also referring to Donovan as his "good friend" since the two had overlapped at Columbia Law School. But Donovan would have none of it. "I happened to be in the same class in law school that he was," the Irishman responded, "but I was a youngster earning my way through law school and he never knew me." The Democratic leader, Donovan claimed, "holds out his right hand" in friendship, while he "socks with his left." He knew that FDR was no friend of his or of any other Wall Street corporate attorney. In the end, Donovan lost the gubernatorial campaign to his Democratic opponent, while Roosevelt won the presidency.[11]

During FDR's first few years in the White House, Donovan fired a steady barrage of insults at the president. He told a Republican women's club that "there is a moral as well as a material side" to the economic depression, "a side resting on spiritual values and human interests." He and his fellow Republicans, Catholics and Protestants and Jews, he argued, were on the right side; Roosevelt and his Democratic allies were on the wrong side. "This country," he harangued, has to "come to grips with an issue which reaches down to the very foundations, not only of its government, but of its moral and spiritual life." Roosevelt, he asserted, had forced a choice on all Americans. Either the people would embrace "collectivism" and from there "dictatorship," or they would remain true to their foundations. He worried that FDR was driving them to "abandon the principles and ideals on which not only our government but our various codes of human relationship are founded." Roosevelt, like Stalin, Hitler, and Mussolini, he feared, coveted total power. He hoped that his fellow Republicans would stop the president's "wild and reckless career" before it was too late.[12]

When FDR called on Donovan in 1940 to visit the United Kingdom on his behalf, the president knew exactly what he was doing. FDR chose influential Republicans for top assignments to demonstrate the bipartisan nature of his foreign policy. He recognized that a war hero and longtime critic of the administration was exactly the kind of person who could help him sell American intervention to the nation's isolationists. This task was especially urgent given that FDR's ambassador to the United Kingdom was Joseph P. Kennedy, who believed that the British were destined to lose and that the Americans should steer clear of the conflict. Who better to challenge Kennedy's assessment than another prominent Irish American Catholic?

Choosing Donovan to lead the OSS was another strategic choice. FBI director J. Edgar Hoover feared any challenge to his authority and worried that the creation of the OSS might reduce his power and that of the bureau. Hoover thought the FBI should serve as the center of US intelligence, not just at home but also abroad. When FDR established the OSS, Hoover was determined to make operating the new organization as difficult as possible. By choosing a Republican critic for the post, Roosevelt hoped to avoid the appearance that the OSS was his personal partisan spy school. Hoover still didn't like it.

Donovan understood the role he needed to play in the unfolding wartime drama. A good soldier, he could serve under those with whom he sometimes disagreed. And, perhaps just as important, he knew how to flatter FDR. He loved hand-delivering to the president the latest gadgets his team had invented. On one memorable afternoon, he brought a silent gun to the White House. Showing off for his boss, he nonchalantly emptied the entire clip, firing repeatedly into a sandbag he had lugged to the Oval Office for the occasion, all while Roosevelt dictated a letter to his secretary. This stunt was the perfect metaphor for the OSS's wartime actions—an agency officer fires a new and mysterious weapon, while the president pays scant attention. Wild Bill regularly sent the president rare and exotic stamps for his collection from everywhere the OSS had operatives posted around the globe. One senior OSS operative went to great lengths to obtain a rare German stamp depicting Schutzstaffel (SS) leader Heinrich Himmler. He did not realize at the time that the stamp was a fake—the British had printed and circulated it to try to play up a rivalry between Himmler and Hitler. In return for Donovan's loyalty and service, FDR regularly invited Wild Bill to be his guest at prayer and communion services marking important occasions.[13]

In some ways, Donovan was a perfect choice for the spymaster job. An experienced war veteran, a seasoned political operative, and a successful lawyer, he knew how to work the levers of power. Yet Donovan was no bureaucrat suited to a desk. He always wanted to be in on the action. Arthur Schlesinger Jr., a historian who worked for the OSS during the war and later an aide to President John F. Kennedy, captured Donovan's strengths and weaknesses. Donovan, he wrote, was "in his eccentric way a remarkable man, a winning combination of charm, audacity, imagination, optimism, and energy—above all, energy." But that was not all. "He was a disorderly administrator and an impetuous policymaker, racing from here to there, coming up with ideas and initiatives and then cheerfully moving on to something else." He was both the OSS's greatest asset and its greatest liability.[14]

Donovan stacked his agency with dozens of prominent and skilled Americans. Most of the key players Donovan brought to the OSS were men. Women served in the agency as secretaries and clerks and sometimes as analysts, but not in leadership and only in rare exceptions as operatives in the field. "It was evident from the start," one OSS woman recalled, that agency leaders "meant the women to be at the headquarters stations, and the men to go out in the field." One of the OSS's female office staffers, Julia Child, later gained fame for her French cooking. Most senior-level OSS officers came from elite social circles and included intellectuals, businessmen, and soldiers, many with blue-blood backgrounds. Both critics and spies jokingly referred to the "OSS" as "Oh, So Social" because of its elite membership. OSS leaders' myopic views about who made the best operatives limited the agency's effectiveness. There is no doubt that had they put a more diverse set of operatives into the field they could have accomplished even more.[15]

Early on the OSS established a set of terms to clarify who was who. Agency leaders called Americans employed by the OSS and sent into the field on specific assignments "operatives" and sometimes "officers." They referred to those they recruited in the field, usually foreign nationals, as "agents." This is a practice that has continued into the modern CIA, which causes some confusion, since the FBI often refers to its own American employees as "agents" and the CIA does not.

One of Donovan's most important operative recruits was Allen Dulles, a well-connected attorney with a passion for alcohol, espionage, and extramarital sex. Serving as Donovan's right-hand man, Dulles enlisted many of the initial officers of the OSS. Like Donovan, he was a Republican and a very successful corporate lawyer. Unlike Donovan, he had an excellent pedigree. His grandfather served as secretary of state for Benjamin Harrison, and his uncle held the same job for Woodrow Wilson. His father was a powerful Presbyterian minister who ensured that his children knew the old faith and the old creeds, as well as their relevance to contemporary life. He was an active church member, with connections to religious leaders, missionary boards, and leading ecumenists around the globe. As a young man, Dulles saw the world, working as a diplomat after graduating from Princeton. Then he joined the law firm where his older brother, John Foster Dulles, was a partner. During the 1930s Allen continued to travel while practicing law. He consulted occasionally with the US government and foreign leaders, and he met both Mussolini and Hitler.[16]

Donovan put businessman and chemist Stanley Lovell in charge of developing gadgets and counterfeit items for the OSS. Donovan dubbed Lovell "Professor Moriarty," after the criminal genius of Sir Arthur Conan Doyle's Sherlock Holmes novels. He later called Lovell "a villain, a scientific thug with a sense of humor," for the creative lethal devices he engineered. The colonel didn't mind having a bad guy or two on his side, and he even counseled Lovell not to let old moral qualms get in the way of his work. This was war, he reminded his mad scientist, total war.[17]

Lovell's team came up with many schemes, some of them harebrained and others more legitimate. "We had to 'play it by ear' or not at all," Lovell recalled about his new job. "Like a pianist, improvising his melodies and rhythms, the chords had to be found and the dissonances corrected or ignored. No one could tell us how to do our job." They needed to learn how to counterfeit documents and uniforms—passports, traveling papers, money, military orders, clothes, and any number of other things. If the OSS intended to send operatives into foreign territories, they needed to look right. Their lives depended on it. For some of this work, Lovell recruited forgers and safe crackers from local jails.[18]

Lovell also developed deadly devices and other tools to equip those operatives. Like James Bond's "Q," the professor put no limits on what they could do. OSS "toys" included a uniform button that hid a compass, a camera that looked like a matchbox, a dagger concealed inside a pencil, and a candle that, when the wick burned down, exploded. Another instrument kept getting pinched by Lovell's own men. Called "Who? Me?" it was a small bottle that contained a potion intended for use on Japanese officers. When casually sprayed on a person's clothes, it gave off an odor mimicking the smell of someone who had soiled his pants. Lovell's scientists also developed a white substance called "Aunt Jemima" that they could camouflage as flour and that agents could even bake into bread or biscuits. It could also be used to form an explosive. Another Lovell device simulated the roar of a falling bomb. Its purpose was to incite chaos if an operative or agent needed to leave an area fast. Lovell named it the "Hedy" after actress Hedy Lamarr because, he explained, "my lusty young officers said she created panic wherever she went." One afternoon he and Donovan demonstrated the Hedy for a group of generals. When the roar began, the military brass all scrabbled for the doors and windows. "Professor Moriarty," Donovan quipped, "we overdid that one, I think."[19]

While Lovell's team worked on gadgets, weapons, and counterfeits, officers in the OSS's psychological warfare unit sought ways to gain an advantage by manipulating their enemies' traditional beliefs. This was something Donovan encouraged. Issues of religious difference had piqued Donovan's curiosity in the past, especially while he was abroad, and they would shape his tenure as leader of the OSS. To wage war against the Japanese, the OSS developed numerous schemes revolving around foxes, magical and powerful creatures in Japanese religious life. "The fox," according to an OSS report, "is the oldest and most potent fear-producing demon in Japan. It is believed to have the power of bewitching and possessing people. The fox must therefore be propitiated." Propitiating the fox led to numerous innovative—and amusing—OSS strategies.[20]

One proposal, code-named "Fantasia" after the 1940 animated Disney movie, began with the construction of a giant, glowing fox-like creature, which was supposed to rise about two thousand feet above Japanese lines with the aid of black helium balloons. The OSS floated a trial version of the creature over Rock Creek Park in Washington, DC. According to a journalist, "horrified citizens" fled the park with the "screaming jeemies." The trial looked like a success. After all, if Americans who had no fear of foxes felt terrified by the glowing creature over the nation's capital, how would Japanese soldiers in the midst of battle react to such a horrible omen? Ultimately, the project proved too risky and too expensive to execute.[21]

The OSS also developed plans for using live foxes. In order to keep things simple during trials, operatives borrowed raccoons from the zoo. They shaved them and coated them with radium paint in order to make them glow. They hoped to release the foxes toward enemy lines during nighttime battles. Luminous foxes, the OSS believed, would portend disaster in the minds of Japanese troops, driving them to retreat. But a fatal flaw doomed the plan. The OSS never figured out how to get either the trial raccoons or real foxes to charge the Japanese rather than simply sprinting off in whatever direction they pleased.

The fox projects, and many more like them, reveal the ways in which the OSS hoped to make the most of folk religious beliefs. They also reveal how far American operatives were from understanding those beliefs. They were like tourists who put ketchup on their tacos—they had clearly lost something in translation. It did not take long for Donovan and other OSS leaders to realize that they needed experts who were truly versed in foreign cultures to help them best exploit and manipulate those cultures.

*

To lead the OSS's efforts to understand, use, and manipulate religion for the purposes of war, Donovan and Allen Dulles secretly put another group of operatives to work. They recruited dozens of missionaries and religious activists, people who knew more than how to shave a fox and make it glow. Although missionary work had long been one of the few areas in which women could escape the male-dominated hierarchies of US church structures, the OSS hired mostly male missionaries, missing the opportunity to build on a century of women's work and knowledge among foreign cultures.

As missionaries labored to spread their faiths and to make them relevant to people living around the globe, they developed a particular skill set that during wartime was both much needed and in short supply. They were fluent in numerous languages; they worked closely with foreign peoples; they knew the geographies of many parts of the world; they understood competing beliefs, religions, and cultures; and they learned how to totally immerse themselves in alien societies. As missionaries and ministers, they mastered the skill of analyzing foreign groups and conveying that information back to the United States—to their mission boards, their boosters, other missionaries, and the government. Most important, they worked to effect change abroad. They became masters at infiltrating other cultures in order to transform them from the inside out. They believed that this was their God-given duty. By their very nature, missionaries represented a sort of fifth column. Their skills proved to be extremely

William "Wild Bill" Donovan drew on the talents of Americans from many different walks of life as he built the OSS. Little did he know when he accepted President Roosevelt's call to launch the nation's first foreign intelligence agency that missionaries and religious activists would be central to his plans.
Courtesy of National Archives and Records Administration, College Park, Maryland.

valuable not just in the domain of missionary activity, but also in the world of espionage and covert operations.

OSS leaders did not plan or centrally coordinate their recruitment of missionaries. Instead, through a series of fits and starts, OSS leaders stumbled upon the powerful ways that they could mobilize religious people, ideas, and organizations in the pursuit of wartime objectives. They sometimes tried to make distinctions between religious work and secular work, insisting that they were using missionaries for only the latter. But separating the sacred from the profane was and is often impossible. For some OSS leaders, religion and religious activists represented little more than tools that could be effectively—even cynically—wielded to gain an advantage over the enemy. For others, however, using true believers perfectly embodied their faith in their nation's history and role in the modern world. Winning the war would guarantee that they could extend Americans' First Amendment liberties to Europe and Asia. The United States could become what Puritan John Winthrop had imagined in 1620: a shining city upon a hill, bringing God's light to all. Whether OSS leaders believed in the existence of a true, objective, transcendent faith that could lead a person to God or instead thought that all religions were simply human-made myths created to make sense of the world and humans' place in it, the results were the same. Almost no one in the spy agency denied the power of religion as a tool for intelligence and espionage.

Missionaries and other religious activists realized what they stood to gain by working with the government during the war. The State Department strictly controlled Americans' ability to travel abroad, and the War Department controlled most overseas transportation. Missionaries and religious activists were particularly committed to this war because of the ways in which Roosevelt framed its purpose and goals. In 1939 the president had affirmed his confidence in the power of religion to secure global peace. "Storms from abroad," the president boldly warned during his State of the Union address, "directly challenge three institutions indispensable to Americans, now as always. The first is religion." Religion, he continued, "is the source" of the second two indispensable American institutions—"democracy and international good faith." Roosevelt insisted that religion had shaped the American character, laid the foundations for democratic government, and provided the hope for international peace.[22]

Roosevelt believed that in some ways, this was a religious war, and his staff encouraged him to make religion central to his framing of the conflict. Donovan, citing the example of Thomas Jefferson, encouraged the president to call for a day of fasting, humiliation, and prayer. Archibald MacLeish, the librarian of Congress whom Donovan recruited to help organize the OSS's Research and Analysis Branch, peppered the president with advice about how to define the war in religious terms. He wanted to ensure that the nation's churches were fully on board. Harold Ickes, the secretary of the interior and a close adviser to Roosevelt, wrote an unsolicited letter to the president. "Formerly there were more wars for religion than for anything else and the religious conviction is a deep one." He suggested that the government lead "a carefully planned campaign . . . to explain the religious implications of this war." FDR's staff forwarded a copy of Ickes's message to Donovan.[23]

The president understood what his advisers had long been telling him. In 1941 he identified "freedom of worship" as one of four essential universal values at the core of the Allies' cause, one of his famous "Four Freedoms." Building on and expanding Woodrow Wilson's vision of the United States as the hope and salvation of the world, Roosevelt established a powerful religious rationale that helped shape the United States' global role into the twenty-first century. Securing freedom of religion around the world became a justification for American intervention abroad. American missionaries wanted and expected to be on the front lines of this new crusade. Yet when William Eddy, Stephen Penrose, John Birch, and Stewart Herman enlisted in Donovan's upstart spy agency, none of them had any idea what the war would bring. Nor did they know how dramatically it would change them and the world around them.

TWO

"Between Hope and Despair"

WITH THE UNITED STATES FINALLY IN THE WAR, AMERICAN LEADERS needed as much intelligence as they could get from inside the Third Reich. Wild Bill Donovan wanted to infiltrate Germany and to connect with the anti-Nazi underground. But how? Perhaps religious activists, he realized, could help him meet his objectives.

Shortly after Pearl Harbor, Donovan met with Father Paul Schulte. The Catholic priest was one of a handful of people pitching Donovan on the benefits of using religion and religious activists for spy craft. Schulte had served as a pilot in the German army during World War I and then entered the Catholic priesthood. Combining his training as an aviator with his religious calling, the "Flying Priest" moved to Canada, where he flew doctors and other emergency aid personnel to isolated missionaries working among indigenous peoples in remote locations in North America and the Arctic. In the late 1930s, the Royal Canadian Mounted Police feared that Schulte was using his mission as cover for photographing and mapping North America for the Germans in anticipation of an invasion. The tools central to his work, including airplanes, fuel reserves, cameras, and radios, could also support intelligence gathering. The Canadian government expelled him from the country.

Schulte moved to the United States, where he sought out fellow Catholic Bill Donovan. Church leaders in New York, many of whom knew the OSS director, may have facilitated the meeting. Schulte convinced the spymaster over breakfast that he could return to Germany and serve as a high-ranking chaplain in the Wehrmacht, the German military, where he would secretly spy for the OSS. Schulte claimed that a cardinal had even offered him the position of bishop in the army. The plan Schulte and Donovan drew up had two parts: first, the priest would pass information to the Americans through Switzerland, and, second, he vowed to "bring about a break between the army and Hitler, so as to cause dissention and an overthrow of Hitler." Where Canadian authorities saw intolerable risk in the priest's German background, Donovan saw opportunity. But before he could dispatch the missionary aviator, he had to deal with the constant interagency battle raging in Washington and the suspicions of J. Edgar Hoover.[1]

FBI agents had been watching Schulte since his arrival in the United States. Although their evidence was thin, they concluded that Schulte was actually a Nazi spy who had no intention of serving the United States. A top-secret FBI report claimed that Schulte had joined the Nazi Party; that Hermann Göring, a close ally of Hitler and the leader of the Luftwaffe (German air force), had given Schulte two planes and a car for his supposed missionary work; that Schulte constructed a secret radio network to signal and guide Nazi bombers over North America; and that the German government considered him "one of the most important and influential Catholic Priests" in the United States. The FBI also believed that rescuing the priest from the United States was a high priority for the Nazis.[2]

In the end, one of Wild Bill's most promising foreign recruits became one of J. Edgar Hoover's holiest political prisoners. Just months after the United States entered the war, Hoover confined Father Schulte to the campus of St. Henry's Seminary in Bellevue, Illinois. There agents kept him under continuous surveillance. G-men submitted regular reports covering such things as his phone calls, the contents of all his mail, and the actions of visitors who came to see him. They even recorded other priests' drunken conversations with the father during dinners at his private residence on campus. FBI agents spent countless hours trying to decode prayer requests and other letters, looking for secret Nazi messages. They never found any. Sometimes, the FBI learned, a prayer request to an alleged Nazi agent was simply a prayer request. Schulte spent the war in exile at the Catholic seminary, where he raised money for a shrine to Our

Lady of the Snows. It was not the first time, nor would it be the last time, that Hoover outmaneuvered Donovan.[3]

The tug-of-war between the OSS and the FBI over the priest early in the conflict demonstrated the importance of religion and religious activists to the war. Government leaders knew that the cloth provided excellent cover for conducting espionage. But with the Schulte project dead, Donovan had to find other ways to infiltrate the Reich. Eventually, he discovered another religious activist, one whose knowledge of the current German religious scene and the anti-Nazi underground far exceeded Schulte's. He was the young pastor of the American Church in Berlin.

Stewart Herman Jr. was born in Harrisburg, Pennsylvania, on August 4, 1909. His father served as the pastor of the city's historic Zion Lutheran Church in the state's capital and as the head of the United Lutheran Church's Foreign Missions Board. Stewart went to Gettysburg College and then Gettysburg Seminary. After graduation he was ordained in the United Lutheran synod. Filled with both academic aspirations and a deep commitment to global ecumenical Christianity, he decided to study more and to travel before settling down to a permanent job. The Herman family was financially well off, and Stewart never really had to worry about money, even during the Depression.

Herman was an excellent student who believed that God had called him to help build the global Protestant faith. He was eager and ambitious, but he could also be stoic, cold, and uncaring, which he sometimes regretted. Herman's parents rarely expressed much warmth or affection, and the young minister had a hard time acting any differently. Nor was he very self-reflective. Nevertheless, he had many friends.

In 1934 Herman earned a fellowship to do graduate work in France at the University of Strasbourg in Alsace-Lorraine on the French-German border. As he embarked on this new adventure, he wondered what the future held. What was he going to do with his life? What plans did the God he had promised to serve have for him? He was eager to analyze conditions in Europe. The study of religion on the Continent, he knew, was somewhat different compared to in the United States. And what to make of Europe's politics? Hitler was garnering international headlines. Was the führer the savior of Germany or a threat to the world? He had no idea how challenging the next few years would be or how they would inadvertently make him an expert on the Nazi regime and on Germany's dissident underground.

In Alsace-Lorraine Herman honed both his French- and his German-language skills. He described his days there as "splendid," although not all of his new experiences were equally profitable. When he had the chance to eat some cat, he balked. He tried a piece but decided it was a "bit more" than he could "relish in the way of exotic foods." He later learned to his great relief that it was actually rabbit and not cat. In Strasbourg he immersed himself in the foreign world of European theology. He encountered many new ideas and studied how Christianity was evolving in a very different context compared to in the seminaries back home. He also realized that although theology interested him, he was not cut out to be an academic theologian. Building and strengthening the church, the real-world application of theology, was far more interesting to him. Nevertheless, he treasured the time he spent debating the contours of the faith with fellow students and professors, and especially with famed theologian Albert Schweitzer. Their liveliest discussions happened over meals of sausage, sauerkraut, and beer.[4]

Hitler had been in power for more than a year when Herman began his studies at Strasbourg. The young American was curious about changes occurring just over the border. He did not want to make any rash judgments until he understood the world as Europeans, and especially as Germans, saw it. Initially, he went over the border a few times for beer and tobacco—both were cheaper and better on the German side. In early 1935 he and some friends decided to take a weekend trip into the Third Reich to really check things out. Arriving in Saarbrücken by train, they noticed Nazi soldiers patrolling the streets, pro-Hitler propaganda papered all over the town, and that "Heil Hitler" had become the official greeting. Herman was impressed by the hypernationalist celebration that marked voting day and then the passage of a referendum that brought the Saar territory on the German-French border back under German administration. "The spirit was so contagious that even such good Americans as we could not desist from flinging up our arms in the Roman salute and yelling 'Heil' (although we did not add 'Hitler!')." Herman saw the Nazi leader as a curiosity. He was cautiously sympathetic with some of what Hitler seemed to be trying to accomplish and was skeptical of other moves that the German leader was making. When Germany renounced the terms of the Treaty of Versailles in the spring of 1935, Herman lauded the move for its boldness and honesty. "It's a relief," he felt, "to see someone like Hitler cut a clean line for once, even though he may be half-crazy." He opened his next letter home to his parents with a tongue-in-cheek "Heil Hitler!"[5]

Unwilling to separate theology from current events, Herman and his fellow students in Strasbourg debated the strengths and weaknesses of different forms of government and the church's proper role within them. For the young Lutheran, American theologian Reinhold Niebuhr's groundbreaking 1932 book, *Moral Man and Immoral Society*, best outlined how Christians should make sense of and respond to the rise of fascism. Herman devoured the book and bought copies for friends, including Albert Schweitzer.

Niebuhr was becoming one of the United States' most prominent theologians. In the aftermath of World War I, Niebuhr, like many other social gospel–oriented Protestants, championed pacifism. But as he became more aware of injustice in the United States and around the world, he rethought his presuppositions. He took seriously the idea of original sin and believed that humans could never eradicate it completely from their own lives or their communities. The best they could hope for was to mitigate it. In this he drew on the neo-orthodox ideas of Swiss German theologian Karl Barth, another man whose life would soon intersect with Stewart Herman's.

Niebuhr argued that at the heart of Christianity and its relationship to the real world was a distinction between individuals and groups, a distinction between what he called moral men and immoral society. Individuals could be redeemed, but they could never fully redeem their broader communities. Individuals could be "moral," but their communities could not. To believe otherwise was naive and lacked any sense of history or an awareness of modern conditions. Rejecting generations of social gospel thinking, Niebuhr insisted that Christians could not build the kingdom of God on earth. He criticized much of liberal Protestantism for its impotence and lack of relevance to current issues and problems, and he called on fellow believers to recognize the enduring presence of real evil in the world.

If the world was an evil place and sin was rampant, how should Christians then live? Bringing about positive social change sometimes required the use of political force, Niebuhr determined. An end to class conflict, the establishment of racial justice, or the securing of human rights for those living under repressive regimes were all goals worth pursuing through the coercive power of the state. And sometimes establishing a more just world even required the use of violent force. Although individuals should not use violence to solve problems, at times a nation must. Niebuhr argued that nations sometimes had to act in ways that "a purely individualistic ethic must always find embarrassing." Christians, he continued, should be able to make a distinction between the two. They should know when they were acting selfishly as individuals and when they were serving a state that was working toward peace and justice. It did not matter, he concluded, if the state's path to peace and justice was ugly, as long as that path led to righteous conclusions. The job of the Christian was to help the state determine whether it was acting toward just ends. True believers were not to withdraw from positions of power, but to ensure that power was used toward the proper goals. "If a season of violence," Niebuhr wrote, "can establish a just social system and can create the possibilities of its preservation, there is no purely ethical ground upon which violence and revolution can be ruled out." He told Christians that "the real question is: what are the political possibilities of establishing justice through violence?"[6]

Many of Wild Bill's Christian covert operatives could answer this question with confidence. They knew that using violence to stop fascism would help bring about a more just world. They found in Niebuhr's theology justification for rejecting an idealistic, uncompromised Christian ethics and instead embraced a sort of pragmatism that acknowledged that evil was present in all of us and that sometimes states had to use force to defend the defenseless. Some readers of the theologian took this a step further, believing that Christians sometimes needed to do bad for good to prevail. The concept of "Christian realism," developed and articulated by Niebuhr, directly or indirectly shaped the thinking of almost all of the major religious activists working in and for the OSS. Niebuhr gave them some of the language and the theology for understanding why they felt compelled to get their hands dirty in this war. He also gave them the biblical justification to come out of the war believing that they had not violated their calling as missionaries, pastors, and priests. But the ideas of an insightful theologian, no matter how persuasive, were not enough for some of the OSS's missionary spies to feel that God sanctified all of their nefarious wartime deeds.

The growing international Christian student movement also had a major impact on Herman and more than anything else defined the trajectory of his developing career. The 1920s and 1930s was the high point in Christian, ecumenical international activity. Liberal Protestants in the United States and Europe believed that together they could separate sincere faith from crass nationalism and imperialism and in so doing lead the way forward toward establishing something that better approximated a universal kingdom of God on earth. In the United States, the Federal Council of Churches (FCC), which was founded in 1908, became the leading organization pushing Protestant internationalism as a tool for peace. Despite Herman's curiosity about German hypernationalism, he wanted to be a part of this work, which was in many ways the antithesis to Nazism. He viewed ecumenical Christianity as the best hope for the future.[7]

During Herman's first spring break, in 1935, he went to Marseilles where he met with some of the regional leaders of the international student movement, including Willem A. Visser 't Hooft. The energetic Dutchman, who later served as the founding secretary-general of the World Council of Churches (WCC), was among the vanguard of North American and European religious leaders working to train a new generation of students in an engaged, relevant form of ecumenical Protestantism. Herman could not have imagined at the time that exactly ten years later, he and Visser 't Hooft would serve together on a secret mission into Germany for Allen Dulles and the OSS.[8]

As the school year neared its end, Herman had no desire to leave Europe. He confessed to his parents that he was rejecting a "conventional" life, at least for now. Yet he remained "in a quandary" about how to live the rest of his "mortal days." He believed God had plans for him, somehow. He recognized that the world's leading nations had arrived at a momentous point in history, and no one knew what might follow. "The next couple of decades," he presciently predicted, "are going to be very important for religion (and theology). I feel like a small boy behind his fort in a snowball battle. I haven't, even now, nearly enough 'ammunition.' And what I should like to do above everything else is to put in a 'few good licks' for the spiritual side when the occasion occurs." Then, he noted, "if the battle becomes another 'World War,' perhaps these languages that I am learning will be of invaluable service." The war was indeed coming, and, thanks to Wild Bill, Herman was going to have more than languages and snowballs in his arsenal.[9]

To Herman's great relief, he received fellowships to study in Germany at Göttingen for the fall of 1935 and at the University of Tübingen the following spring. He was determined, he insisted, "to see the rest of Europe and study people as well as theology." His fellowships paid for his housing and university costs, but he depended on regular cash from his parents to cover extra fees as well as to fund his many excursions. Though Herman was in his midtwenties, he had no problem sponging off his mother and father.[10]

Before settling into his studies at Göttingen, Herman went to Berlin for a few weeks of intensive language training. On the way he stopped in enchanting Heidelberg. He loved the castle ruin, which "really is all that advertisements say," as well as the Heidelberg Tun, an enormous cask that held almost sixty thousand gallons of wine. To Herman, even more interesting than old wine were the responses of religious leaders to the growing power of the Nazi regime.[11]

In Berlin, Herman met some pastors who supported the Nazi government. After hearing one sermon, the American concluded that German religious leaders could walk a fine line between supporting the Nazis and remaining faithful to the Christian gospel. "As a matter of fact," he reflected, "I am beginning to see how a preacher can be whole-heartedly in favor of this government and be absolutely sincere in his homiletic and pastoral work—taking it for granted that he is German. But—more of that when I know more about it." Herman was an outsider, new to Germany. He wanted to learn more in order to be sure he fully understood what was happening before drawing any hard conclusions.[12]

Herman felt especially excited to meet Martin Niemöller and to see him preach. A U-boat commander during the Great War and now a minister, Niemöller had earned a reputation as a critic of the Nazi regime and fierce advocate for clerical independence. He was also a leader in the Confessing Church, a movement of pastors who opposed Nazi efforts to infringe on their autonomy and religious freedoms. Though not necessarily anti-Nazi, they defended a clear separation between church and state—churches should not serve as tools of Hitler or any other political leader. In 1934 they adopted the Barmen Declaration, a statement penned primarily by Swiss German theologian Karl Barth, which exalted the lordship of Christ over all things, including the state. Barth had taught for many years at the University of Bonn, but he left Germany for Switzerland as the Nazis began to crack down on religious dissenters. Some of the more radical members of the Confessing Church movement, including Dietrich Bonhoeffer, who had studied with Niebuhr in the United States, spoke out against Hitler's persecution of Jews. Others, including Niemöller, felt little concern for any Jews besides those who had converted to Christianity.[13]

Niemöller, whose church was located in the Berlin suburbs, was not exactly what Herman had expected. He had, Herman observed, a "rather small, serious, and monastic face entirely dissociated from submarines. But his voice was deep and clear." The service impressed the young American. The minister preached that the essence of Christianity was not in "race or blood," and he warned that the devil might grab hold of the church if parishioners allowed "specious economic and social arguments" that promised "to solve all financial and employment difficulties" to lure them away from the faith. Herman thought the not-so-subtle critique of National Socialism was "really strong stuff." If Niemöller was "not exceptional," he concluded, "his sermon was and I am still impressed that he can speak the way he does, draw the audiences he does, and still remain unmolested."[14]

In early November Herman finally settled in Göttingen for the semester. From the very start, he recognized the religious divisions that were beginning to split Germany's church communities. Just as in Berlin, he attended different churches and saw different approaches to negotiating church life under the Nazi regime. On his first Sunday morning, he attended a sermon in honor of Protestant reformer Martin Luther's birthday that included a "pulpit-pounding, political discourse on German Christianity and the beauty of dying as a soldier for the Vaterland." The German minister worked to reconcile the Christian faith with Nazi aspirations. Then that night Herman experienced something entirely different. He went to the first meeting of the students' *Bekenntnisgemeinschaft*, a branch of the Confessing Church movement.[15]

With a new moon cutting the darkness, Herman entered a medieval chapel hidden inside an old monastery. The setting gave the service a feel of authenticity. "Candles," he observed, "were placed on the back of the plain old pews in order that we might see. And they supplied the only heat there as well. The Roman arches . . . reflected the dim light and our breath hung in the frosty air." The service was primitive but powerful. The true German church, as Herman understood it, was being reborn in these meetings. "It was as though a group of early Christians were gathering in the Roman catacombs," he wrote his parents. But Herman, rather than see Hitler as a modern Nero ready to sacrifice Christians at the stake, still viewed the fascist leader neutrally. Perhaps, he hoped, Hitler could potentially combine political leadership with Christian revival. "Here," he thought, "is Germany's salvation if Hitler is only wise enough to combine this awakening religious spirit with his own best principles." He had not given up hope that Hitler could be a force for good.

The meeting was a life-changing event, exposing Herman to a movement that he eventually came to see as Germany's only chance for redemption. His new friends, he decided, were the "real <u>Protestants</u>." They were the only people protesting the degradation of the church in the Third Reich. Herman concluded his thoughts about the experience on a note more ominous than he could have realized at the time: "The moon was riding high when we came out of the church and strode down over the mountain into Göttingen. Our shadows were thrown on the road as though a searchlight were above us." Indeed, the Nazi regime would soon point its searchlights at the Confessing Church. And at Herman.[16]

In early 1936 Herman received a surprising invitation. The council overseeing the American Church in Berlin wanted to know if Herman could fill the church's pulpit that spring. He was familiar with the church and had visited it the last time he was in the German capital. The church sanctuary was inviting and had a pipe organ, beautiful stained-glass windows, and wooden pews that seated a few hundred people. Adjoining the sanctuary were a library and a fellowship hall. It was "a nice church in a good section" of town, he recorded after his initial visit, "a little wind-blown and dirty" perhaps, but with a "<u>very nice</u>" auditorium. The congregation was a different matter. The prior minister, a young American, had driven away most expats by preaching "hellfire and damnation," leaving behind only Germans wanting to practice their English. The "aged

Episcopalian" who replaced him had done little to repair the damage. Herman reckoned at the time that the church "won't last much longer." In fact, rumor had it that the Church of Jesus Christ of Latter-day Saints was likely going to take over the building.[17]

Herman was not sure how to respond to the invitation. "Well," he wrote his family, "perhaps you can guess the sort of turmoil I have been in for the last two days. Endless arguments have crossed and re-crossed my mind until my hair looks like a rabbit warren." Taking the position would mean interrupting his studies and spending four months in "disagreeable Berlin," rather than spending Easter break exploring Switzerland. But he found the opportunity of "preaching and doing some real work" "exceedingly attractive." He joked that if this was to be his first crack at a pastorate, it would be good to "make all my worst mistakes over here where no one will ever hear about them." Yet preaching in Nazi Germany was not exactly a fool-proof way to avoid attention.[18]

The church council invited Herman to Berlin to give a guest sermon and to discuss potential terms for a contract. If all went well, he told his family, he planned to send a one-word cablegram: "Suits." They should interpret this to mean, "I suits their need and needs my suit"—that is, ship it at once. The interview was a success and the terms reasonable. Herman had a job that would end up lasting far beyond the few months he was initially expecting. Rather than watch how German pastors negotiated their responsibilities to their congregations and their obligations to the state, he would have to determine for himself how to relate to German authorities, how far he was willing to go in speaking out against unjust policies, and how much aid to offer those who came to him for help.[19]

In February 1936 Herman packed up to move from Göttingen to Berlin. But before settling in the capital, he decided to go on another quick adventure. He took a trip to Garmisch-Partenkirchen to visit the Winter Olympic Games where he attended some sporting events, toured the Olympic Village, and went to numerous parties. Over the course of the Games, he met Reinhold Niebuhr and Sherwood Eddy (a leader of the international ecumenical movement). He invited Niebuhr to preach at the American Church, but the theologian declined. He feared that he would not be free to speak his mind in Berlin.

At the Olympics, Herman got a good look at Hitler. "I must say that I was impressed by his appearance—not as a true-leader-of-men sort but as a sincere and simple man full of honest effort and good intentions." The Nazi regime proved endlessly fascinating to the American. "There is something splendid, inspiring . . . and dumb about it all." Herman, at this point, still did not anticipate the horrors that Hitler would unleash on the world. The fascist dictator used the Games as propaganda to sell the world on his supposed good intentions. Like so many others, Herman had been duped. Had he really studied the growing evidence of Hitler's suppression of dissenters, he would not have given Hitler the benefit of the doubt. But like many other Americans living in or visiting Germany, he refused to believe that Hitler was the devil that the fascist leader's staunchest opponents claimed.[20]

As Herman's first official duty in Berlin, he gave the opening prayer at a luncheon in honor of George Washington's birthday. He sat by Ernst Hanfstängl, a close friend and confidant of Hitler, who compared the Nazi leader to George Washington. He also met American ambassador William Dodd. "I have not stepped gingerly, toe by toe, into the social whirl of Berlin's public life," he told his parents. "I have been tossed headlong into the deep waters and left to swim for myself, gasping and choking as unbelievably 'big fish' glided up and away again." The *New York Times* speculated that his prayer was perhaps the first "at any official Nazi meal." The event was a challenge for the young minister and a taste of what was to come as he navigated his new position in the heart of the Third Reich. "The day has been too much," Herman recorded in his diary that night. "Hard walking on diplomatic ice especially when Hitler is compared to Washington."[21]

The churchman had ambitious plans for the American Church in Berlin. The pipe-smoking, determined young man wanted the church to serve as the social center for English-speaking expatriates in Berlin. When Herman accepted the congregation's call, he identified two goals: "First, to preserve and foster this lovely church as the heart and center of our American community here in Berlin. That is our social task." And second, "as a community of Christian Americans, to maintain and continue the work begun by our Lord Jesus Christ, namely the extension of the Kingdom of God." He aspired to have an impact on Nazi Germany as well. He later reflected that in the era of Hitler's reign, he hoped that the church had served as a light to the local Germans "who, directly or indirectly, came into contact with it, a reminder, however modest, of an unbreakable faith in the super-national power of Christian love and brotherhood."[22]

Herman came to occupy a prominent role in the American expatriate colony, where he established networks that would serve him well in future years. As Herman began the task of church building, he courted all of the elite Americans in the city, from the ambassador to business leaders to bankers to movie people, including Jews. He asked the most important and influential men among them to serve on his church board. He knew he needed to "cater" to the tastes of "an extremely diversified and cosmopolitan group" if the church was to have any real influence. Ambassador Dodd, a historian before FDR dispatched him to Germany, agreed to serve as the honorary chairman of the church board. Herman found Dodd useful but not particularly interesting. Students in Dodd's history classes at the University of Chicago probably had had the same reaction. Herman joked that when he approached Dodd about serving the church, the ambassador "enlightened" him "on many obscure points in American history" before the preacher sprang the "invitation and secured his willing acceptance." Later that year, the ambassador offered the opening words at a Thanksgiving service. Unfortunately, the ambassador mumbled through his remarks, and most of the audience could not hear him. No matter. Herman reported that the historian-diplomat had simply "recommended a

In the social hall at the American Church in Berlin, Stewart Herman (*standing*) counseled, advised, and taught American and British expats that a thriving international ecumenical church was the key to global peace and security. He also partnered with members of Germany's Confessing Church, which grew into one of the strongest anti-Nazi groups in the nation.
Courtesy of Stewart Herman III.

few more good history books for us to read." Later, when FDR replaced Dodd with Ambassador Hugh R. Wilson, Herman ensured that the tight relationship between the church and the embassy continued. The church board rewarded Herman for his hard work and the good results it produced by regularly renewing his contract.[23]

Only a few months into the job, Herman had his first real problem regarding his lack of enthusiasm for Hitler. He emerged from a subway in the midst of a Nazi rally, on his way to the church office. His hands were full, but everyone else raised their arms in the Nazi salute. He kept walking. Feeling conspicuous, he finally stopped at the curb. At that point, he later recalled, "something crashed down" between his shoulders, and "an angry voice" asked him why he hadn't saluted. "'Why should I?' I said, 'I'm an American.'" Other bystanders joined in, verbally attacking him. He argued right back. "Fuming" by the time he got to the church, he shared the story with a member of the council who happened to be at the office. The councilman worked in journalism and relayed Herman's account to the Associated Press, which ran the story of the American pastor "accosted" at a Nazi rally. The event, and the media interest it provoked, earned Herman his first visit from agents of the Gestapo, the Nazis' secret police, who apologized for the incident. Hitler did not want to provoke the United States.

Having finally felt the power of the Nazi regime firsthand and its hold over the German people, the minister started to realize that Hitler might not be the fascinating, eccentric figure who might do some good for his country as Herman initially thought, but instead was an ever more threatening autocrat. He understood that he had to be careful criticizing the regime if he planned to remain in Germany. Herman learned from a friend at about that time that the Gestapo was reading his mail, and, when he started noticing strange sounds on his phone line in his church-owned apartment, he concluded that it was tapped. Although the Germans' clandestine foreign operations were never as successful as those of the other major powers, the Germans had an effective domestic intelligence service that quashed dissent and intimidated foreigners like Herman.[24]

Nor were Nazis the only ones Herman sometimes inadvertently offended. He delivered a Fourth of July message titled "Marble and Mud," in which he emphasized the importance of living a full life. Herman thought the message had gone over well, until an incensed visitor met him at the door and exclaimed, "Preach Jesus, young man, nothing but Jesus." The unhappy churchgoer was a preacher from the fundamentalist Moody Bible Institute in Chicago. He incredulously asked Herman if he realized that every person in the church that day was "lost." Then, "with growing suspicion," he asked Herman, "Are you saved?" Herman felt devastated. "So that's the way it is," he confessed to his parents, "between those who are convinced that I'm a lost soul and those who think I'm a bulwark of faith. I myself rattle around like a dry pea in a pod and only wish I could be as sure about myself, either way, as they are." This criticism forced the young churchman to reevaluate what he was trying to accomplish through this work.[25]

Herman's early years at the church were filled with self-doubt. He was working hard but did not seem to be making any real progress in improving the spiritual lives of those in the church community. "I wonder why I am in the ministry at all?" he wrote in his diary. "I haven't experienced any notable spiritual influence in the colony." One friend who attended the church told him that as a minister, he seemed "cold." Perhaps he began to work on that, because a few months later, one of his sermons brought the congregation to tears, which raised a new problem. "Are revival tent qualities entering my preaching?" he wondered and worried. Herman declined various offers to return home for permanent preaching jobs. He couldn't quite understand why he felt such a strong desire to stay in Europe, but he believed that he needed to be in Germany.[26]

The 1936 Summer Olympic Games, held in Berlin, provided new opportunities for Herman to connect his current work to broader ecumenical activities. Herman met German boxer Max Schmeling and African American track star Jesse Owens. Confessing Church activists used the Games to bring attention to their work. They held nightly services to spread their message as widely as possible. Herman heard Dietrich Bonhoeffer, Martin Niemöller, and others preach. He felt inspired by their unequivocal, unapologetic assertion of the lordship of Jesus over all things. One evening he went to a closed meeting with about a dozen Confessing pastors, where he heard tales of Nazi searches, confiscation of church property, and arrests of church leaders. But Herman was skeptical of their stories, and he found several of the ministers' accounts "scarcely credible." Herman feared that more radical members of the Confessing Church might tear German Protestantism apart. He wondered if their refusal to compromise with moderates was a sign not of their Christian integrity but of their intractable Germanness. Throughout his career Herman would fight to protect the integrity of the Christian church. Anything that seemed likely to lead to schism troubled the young pastor.[27]

Over the next couple of years, Herman came to understand that he should never have doubted the stories he had heard about how perilous life in Germany had become for nonconforming religious activists. His own experiences, and what he witnessed around him, increased his sympathy and respect for the Confessing Church. He quietly and secretly studied and discussed the church situation in Germany with Confessing Church activists as well as with other religious leaders in Europe, seeking ways to support the religious rebels. At one point, Herman noted in his diary, he had to hide some Christian papers "for fear of confiscation." When he could get away from his own church, he went to hear the leaders of the Confessing movement speak. He was constantly impressed by their boldness and their willingness to call a "spade a spade," although he feared doing so was "dangerous." Indeed, it was. At one service, Niemöller read a long list of names of pastors who had been imprisoned. "Strange to think of this happening in Berlin today!" Herman remarked. Another time when he stopped by Niemöller's church, he could not get in. Local police had surrounded the building to prevent parishioners from entering it. A week later, at the beginning of July 1937, the famed German pastor and former U-boat commander was arrested for treason. "Things look bad," Herman noted.[28]

During Herman's time in Berlin, the pastor witnessed firsthand Hitler's unprecedented, extraordinary persecution of Jews. But he had little interest in getting involved. Although Jews often came to him for help, the churchman felt little compulsion to assist them. He feared that if he aided Jews, local authorities would crack down on him and on the church. Instead, he compartmentalized. He convinced himself that he was in Berlin primarily to serve the Anglo-American Christian expat community, and he refused to jeopardize that mission by getting involved with Hitler's victims. He believed that the German government and the US embassy should deal with such problems. Not him.

Herman received many different kinds of requests from Berlin's Jews. Some, raised as Christians, asked the minister to baptize them, hoping this would give them a little more cover from persecution. The American told them that they had waited too long. He even refused to baptize one whom he had converted and mentored, fearing reprisals. "How often we compromise our Christianity," he lamented about his own reluctance to act. Another Jew admitted to Herman that he had been "too busy" to keep attending church. For seeking help without a clean church record, Herman "bawled him out." "That," he recorded in his diary, "gave me some pleasure." Others asked for help with visa applications for the United States. They think, he wrote, that "America owes them a way out." They were "the refugees" whom he felt "least anxious to help," although his impotence sometimes made him feel "very helpless." When one Jew asked Herman if he could join the church, hoping that doing so might help facilitate travel to the United States, Herman lost his temper. "I proceeded to tell him that church-joining for political reasons has been largely the cause of the present Jewish-Christian trouble today."[29]

Herman's response implied that Jews themselves deserved some of the blame for the persecution they were experiencing, and he seemed oblivious to the fact that "Christian" governments had for generations forced Jews to join churches. Furthermore, church joining for political reasons was exactly what Herman tried to sell to the members of the American diplomatic legation (including prominent American Jews) as he built his church. "These panic-stricken people," Herman coldly continued, "even while I feel sorry for them—remind me of a rat I once caught and threw in the ashcan before he was quite dead. His terror-struck, beady eyes and his babyish squeal almost made me forget for a moment that he was a rat to whom I must give the coup de grace." In comparing Jews to nearly dead rats, Herman was drawing on common anti-Semitic, Jews-as-vermin tropes. He implied that although he might feel sorry for persecuted Jews, this particular group of people deserved what they got no matter how plaintively they squealed.[30]

Herman's indifference to the Jews who sought him out was consistent with how he dealt with other people in need. He had little patience for beggars who came by the church for aid, and when a Syrian refugee stranded in Berlin came to him for help, Herman called him "a baby" and other names. When an African had trouble filling out relief forms and sought Herman's assistance, the pastor "blew up" at him until he realized the man could not read or write.[31]

The pastor's lack of sympathy was not unique. His actions and attitude toward refugees and especially Jews matched that of many Americans back home. In the 1930s the number of anti-Semitic political and religious groups in the United States surged. Henry Ford had promoted anti-Semitic conspiracies, and popular radio priest Father Charles Coughlin, who had an audience that numbered in the millions, accused Jews of bringing financial ruin to the nation and the international economy. Some Americans saw anti-Semitism as a real problem in the United States, similar to racism against African Americans, but most did not.

Few Jews made it to the United States from Germany. A majority of Americans opposed opening immigration restrictions to allow more than a handful of refugee Jews to settle in the United States. American officials would not allow immigrants to come to the United States unless they could demonstrate financial self-sufficiency, while the German government would not let Jews leave with anything more than a few dollars. As a result, most Jews seeking sanctuary in the United States were out of luck. President Roosevelt, although sympathetic to the plight of Europe's Jews, mostly chose not to act, fearing that to do so would arouse opposition and make it more difficult to move the United States toward intervention in Europe's growing crisis. Nor were leaders in the State Department, where numerous top officials had track records of anti-Semitism, interested in making the rescue of European Jews a priority. Congress even killed a bill in 1939 that would have brought German refugee children to the United States. After the war, many Americans regretted that their nation had not done more to rescue Europe's Jews. By then it was too late.[32]

Although Herman refused to help most of the Jews who came to him, he privately criticized the growing number of Nazi laws and regulations targeting Jews. He described a Nazi rally that included a raving anti-Semitic speech by Nazi minister of propaganda Joseph Goebbels as "revolting, and even sickening, almost obscene." He had numerous arguments with Germans, insisting that Jesus was a Jew, despite what the Nazis claimed. Yet he also accused Jews of sometimes exaggerating the discrimination and persecution they faced, just as he had earlier accused Confessing churchmen of exaggerating the Nazi threat. He complained when some American rabbis came to town with an ecumenical religious group sponsored by the American Protestant internationalist Sherwood Eddy. He described the American rabbis in the group as "venomous with a hatred that the Nazis come no where near duplicating." Perhaps he had been "corrupted" by the Germans, he mused (apparently he had), but he couldn't "stomach so much pure poison as these Jews were spouting." He worried that American Jews were spreading too much exaggerated propaganda about Germany, that they were "taking advantage of their persecution." In the summer of 1938, he returned to the United States for a brief vacation and to visit family. The trip further convinced him that Jews in the United States were painting an unfair picture of the Nazi regime.[33]

Late on the night of November 9, 1938, Hitler's paramilitary troops and members of the Hitler Youth launched a new pogrom. They went on a rampage, harassing, beating, and murdering Jews. They also destroyed as much Jewish property—homes, businesses, and synagogues—as they could. The night came to be remembered as Kristallnacht, or the Night of Broken Glass, for all of the shop-window glass that littered the streets after the riot. Hitler responded by levying a new tax on Jews, forcing them to pay for the damage they had supposedly caused in their communities. In the days that followed, more Jews came to Herman for help, only to be turned away. He was, at the time, working hard to learn the Hebrew language for his continuing graduate work in theology. He sensed no irony in the fact that he was studying Hebrew to bring himself closer to God's holy book while ignoring the pain of the very people to whom his God had chosen to reveal himself and to trust with his words.

Herman nevertheless realized that he could no longer deny or excuse the evil around him. "Aside from feeling sick in the stomach from the signs of murderous vandalism," he wrote his parents, "I feel as though all my effort to paint a fair picture of Germany while I was at home has been cold-bloodedly sabotaged." Herman fretted over how Kristallnacht undermined his defense of average Germans. He had worked hard to make the case that not all Germans were pro-Nazi or supporters of the regime's racial policies. Kristallnacht seemed to prove otherwise. "These are days of tears and despair for thousands of Jews," he observed, "and days full of bitterness and disgust and shame for many thousands of Germans." He believed this event marked the "final capitulation of the Jew."[34]

Roosevelt was furious about the Germans' overt persecution of Jews. In protest of Kristallnacht, he recalled Ambassador Hugh R. Wilson. Herman had come to know Wilson fairly well. The ambassador, Herman noted, was very interested in the "church situation" in Germany and had been eager to pick Herman's brain about it. However, Herman was disappointed that Wilson was not a regular churchgoer himself. "It is rather discouraging," he wrote home, "to buck up against indifference thru out our whole foreign service. The pretense of being a Christian country is very hollow." Although Wilson's lack of personal spirituality disappointed Herman, the ambassador understood, perhaps better than Herman, the role that religion played in geopolitics. The two men would eventually cross paths again in the OSS.[35]

Herman worried that FDR's recall of the ambassador, and the other ways in which American leaders threatened to retaliate against Germany for the horrors that Hitler had unleashed, would "backfire" on the Americans still abroad. As various other nations recalled their diplomats, the minister fretted that "soon all diplomats will be sitting at home letting the world go wild."[36]

Only after Kristallnacht did the young churchman finally start to recognize where Hitler's policies toward Jews were headed. He reported to his parents that Joseph Goebbels had pledged that the Nazis would drive all Jews out of German territory. "In the meantime, there are all sorts of rumors," he wrote, "to the effect that huge concentration camps will be constructed to house all Jews. This seems impossible when one only thinks of the sheer number—500,000—who are eligible for this honor." Time and again, Herman underestimated Hitler's hatred for Jews and the scope of Nazi terror.[37]

Herman hoped that Jews might find Jesus or at least a revitalized version of the Hebrew faith. Religious revival, he suggested, might be their salvation. They should adopt a "far-sighted plan," the churchman suggested, that aimed for the "very regeneration of the Jewish race itself." Until then, he believed, the persecution they faced was not going to subside. He must have known that religious revitalization would not have changed anything in the eyes of the German authorities, yet that did not keep him from speculating about how Jews had brought persecution upon themselves and how he thought they should change.

"Sorry as I must feel for those who come sniveling to me in their extremity," Herman continued, "I cannot look upon them as desirable spiritual neighbors." But he offered a caveat. "<u>Unless</u> (here is the point!) some effort is made to give their own prophetic religion back to them." In other words, if Jews embraced the religion that Herman wanted them to embrace, they might deserve his help. Otherwise, better to not have them as neighbors. In the meantime, he had grown "tired of them coming and crying" about their hardships, "with their fatty, flabby hands which haven't done a day of manual labor." Strong words from a man who still asked his parents for money to fund his European vacations. Then he returned again to the varmint metaphors. "While making protestations and asking for special favors they look at me in a way which I can compare only to the terrified, glistening glance of a mouse which I once had to kill." Once again, in this metaphor Herman inadvertently adopted the role of executioner of Jews. Perhaps Herman knew, at least subconsciously, that his inaction and that of many other churchmen relegated the fate of Germany's Jews to a murderous regime.[38]

Kristallnacht inspired an uptick in the number of German Jewish Christians attending the American Church. Herman considered their presence "a delicate problem which needs Jesuitical casuistry to be neatly answered." While he recognized that he had an opportunity through them to bring more Jews into the Christian fold, he feared that if he welcomed them he might embarrass the US embassy and his congregation. "Our only reason for being here," he claimed at the time, "is to bring Americans into the church, not Germans." He hoped that some of the local German churches would step into the breach, taking the problem off his hands. Slowly, the gravity of the situation finally started to sink in. By late 1938, Herman acknowledged that the "eventual fate" of those Jews who did not flee Germany was "death."[39]

Modern Americans often ask how the German people could have let this happen. How could they have failed to realize what Hitler was doing? How could they have let the Holocaust occur? They often wonder—we often wonder—would we have acted any differently? Would I have risked my life to challenge Hitler's regime for the sake of Jews and other targets of the Nazis? Herman provides one opportunity to see how a young, idealistic American committed to establishing a more charitable, peaceful world reacted to the horrific events occurring right before his eyes. He did and said things that were anti-Semitic. But he never saw himself as an anti-Semite. By his reasoning, he was just saying no to impossible requests and focusing on what he could do, which was ministering to German Christians and American and British expats. But the consequences of his indifference and that of so many others were becoming clearer every day.

*

While Hitler was cracking down on the rights and liberties of those in Germany, he was also looking to expand the Third Reich. The führer had long claimed that the German people needed *Lebensraum*, or more room for growth. Germany annexed its neighbor Austria in 1938. Then Hitler turned to the Sudetenland, a region of Czechoslovakia where several million ethnic Germans lived. Knowing that Western democracies seemed increasingly concerned with his many violations of the Versailles Treaty that ended World War I, the German leader met with British prime minister Neville Chamberlain in Munich in late September 1938 to cut a deal. He promised that if the British did not oppose his seizure of the Sudetenland, his territorial aggression would stop. Chamberlain, along with the French and the Italians, agreed. On his return to London, the British prime minister proclaimed that the meeting with the Nazi dictator guaranteed "peace for our time."

But Hitler was not done. On August 23, 1939, the Soviets and the Nazis stunned the world by signing a nonaggression pact. Hitler had made fighting communism a priority during his rise to power. That the German dictator signed a peace treaty with his seeming archenemy could mean only one thing—that he planned to go to war and didn't want an enemy on his eastern flank. The American government instructed all US citizens to leave Germany, and many did, as did many other non-Germans. Herman refused to go. As much as he failed the German Jews who sought his help, he wanted to do everything he could to support the German Christians he had come to know. "The air," he felt, "is heavily charged with serious preparation." He was praying "night and morning" for "peace for today," believing that he could plan only one day at a time. He anticipated that the world's response to the nonaggression pact would prove to be "a turning point in modern history."[40]

On September 1, 1939, the German military invaded Poland. Two days later, Poland's allies, France and the United Kingdom, responded by declaring war on Germany. The outbreak of full-scale war in Europe inspired Herman. His work in Berlin, he realized, really mattered. In his first service after the start of the blitzkrieg, he noted in his diary, "I let myself go! For the first time in the pulpit, I felt I was <u>preaching</u>!" He also sent off a letter to his parents. He observed that for the most part, little had directly changed, other than the fact that the number of expatriates in Berlin was fast declining. Herman said he planned to stay, however, because he had plenty of work to do. "It is said that war is the best occasion for doctors to learn how to be surgeons; it is, I find, a great occasion for clergymen to learn how to become preachers and pastors." He was maturing quickly, yet he knew his parents would worry. "You should know by this time that, like a cat, I always seem to land on my feet." He attended a communion service with Confessing Church students to mark the start of the war. They said prayers, he reported, "for all in danger of death 'in prison, at the front, or against a wall.' It was pretty grim. And it left me with feelings badly mixed."[41]

The onset of war provided Herman with another new opportunity. With Europe plunging into chaos, the American embassy needed skilled translators, and in the fall of 1939 Herman joined the embassy staff. His new government salary exceeded what the church paid. The church was suffering financially as many American business leaders, whose finances kept the church afloat, left Germany or planned to leave soon. For Herman, going to work for the embassy was the perfect solution to the financial problem raised by the war. He could keep working at the church, free it from paying his salary, and stay in Berlin at the center of the action. The government job also gave him a layer of diplomatic protection from the German government, should any problems arise. "I feel rather like the pioneer preachers," he wrote his parents, "who ploughed the fields or conducted a business venture as a sideline." Usually, however, those pioneer preachers were not working under the protection of a powerful government like the United States. The new job came with another benefit—he could now send letters home via the embassy's diplomatic pouch. He no longer had to worry about Nazi censors reading his mail.[42]

Herman's responsibilities at the embassy grew and evolved as the war progressed. Initially, he helped translate documents for government officials, and each day he dealt with stranded foreigners seeking American aid. A few months into the war, embassy and American Church leaders created what they called the American Emergency Relief Committee, and they made Herman its chair. The committee provided various services to those in German prisoner-of-war (POW) and internment camps. The latter were not death camps, which had not yet begun operating. The job allowed Herman to investigate wartime conditions around the country. At the camps he distributed supplies and held church and communion services. He also came to appreciate what he could learn from prisoners of war, who often had excellent knowledge of the governments, militaries, and cultures that they had served.

Dealing with air raids became another routine part of Herman's life in wartime Berlin. As he grew increasingly used to the incessant warning sirens, he stopped getting out of bed for them. He also continued to badger his parents, as he had so often, for supplies. He especially desired soap and shaving cream, two items that were hard to come by in wartime Berlin. The lack of shaving cream had inspired him to grow a wild John the Baptist–style beard, although it did not last. He later groused to a friend about how hard it was to get materials from his parents when he was abroad. "My family," he wrote, "is never prompt at executing requests to send parcels by mail. It involves wrapping them up, taking them to the post-office, and putting stamps on them—all of which require a long, long, period of preparation and mental adjustment." He also noted another consequence of wartime rationing—one evening he had to go to four different cafés in search of a pint of beer.[43]

As the Nazi regime tightened its control over its citizens, it grew less tolerant of dissenting churchmen. Fewer and fewer leaders of the Confessing Church remained in their pulpits, and many including Niemöller went to jail. Herman kept in touch with the dissident pastor through his wife, who occasionally attended services at the American Church. Herman also heard that the Gestapo arrested two German pastors who had been aiding Jews and who "took too great an interest" in the Nazis' anti-Semitic purges.[44]

Herman did what he could to support the Confessing Church without sticking his neck out too far. The minister routinely received documents and tracts that were illegally circulating among the church leaders. One, slipped into his mailbox at night, pleaded, "Can't you help your German brethren?" The American minister later accepted an invitation to hold a secret service in an air-raid shelter for twenty young members. Although the "lads" looked like "the usual Hitler youth," he thought he had never "heard such evidences of splendid faith as these boys presented." They wanted the minister to convey to Americans that such a "remnant" still existed in Berlin. Yet he exercised caution. The American pastor told his parents that he remained "non-committal on every subject" they raised that "could be considered political or dangerous." But "I longed," he continued, "to open up my heart to those boys and give them the encouragement they need." Yet he couldn't muster the courage to do it.[45]

Herman had good reason to exercise caution. Members of both the Schutzstaffel and the Gestapo occasionally attended Herman's services and monitored the American's actions. The Gestapo on multiple occasions also picked up Herman's German housekeeper for questioning. They quizzed her about his preaching, how the Americans treated her, and how many Jews attended church services. Herman heard from a friend that Gestapo agents had identified the pastor as one of the first Americans they would arrest if the United States entered the war. They believed he was anti-Nazi and anti-German.[46]

In April 1941 the police did arrest and briefly detain the churchman, sparking outrage in the United States. American leaders suspected that the Germans were harassing American citizens in response to the US seizure a week earlier of German commercial ships docked in US ports. The Americans feared that the ships might be used for sabotage. After the arrest Herman continued to work not only with expats and students but also with those Confessing Church religious leaders whom the secret police had not jailed, including Eugen Gerstenmaier. Herman described the minister as "an unshake-off-able bulldog" who refused to give up his work on behalf of the German church. Their ongoing discussions about the state of Christianity in Germany, Herman noted, "hangs a conscientious person between hope and despair." Gerstenmaier would later play a role in an attempted assassination of Hitler.[47]

As summer turned to fall in 1941, Herman faced another crisis in the American Church. Despite his private misgivings, a number of Christian Jews had been regularly attending his services. Once Hitler started requiring all Jews to wear yellow armbands and prohibited them from joining public gatherings, they stopped coming. The churchman despised the new policy. "I feel like beginning to take action in this business," he recorded in his diary, "which is going one step too far for my 'objective mentality.'" But he did not act. Once things settled down, some Jewish converts tried to come back to the church. Even though they were fellow Christians, Herman didn't want them worshipping at the American Church. "I've had the unpleasant task of being oily and diplomatic on several occasions when these non-Aryan Christians called up or wrote to us about permission to continue attending." He told them that their presence endangered the congregation.[48]

That October, word came that the Nazis planned to transport those Jews still left in Berlin to Poland. Once again, some came to Herman for help. Their efforts were mostly in vain. "As I can do nothing for them," he admitted, "I am probably unnecessarily gruff and ungracious." Unable to empathize, he failed to understand how desperate and terrifying the situation had become for Germany's Jews. His primary complaint was having "to listen helplessly to their whining, moaning, hand-wringing despair." Although Herman did not know it at the time, German Jews' impending deportation to Poland eventually meant almost certain death. But he was not completely immune to their pleas for help. He vacillated as his frustration over his impotence grew. The Sunday following the deportation order, he gave an especially powerful sermon, inspired, he claimed, by his anger over various German policies, including the "anti-semitic plague." Herman was more comfortable talking right and wrong, justice and injustice in an abstract sense, rather than dealing with actual people.[49]

Herman was somewhat aware of other American Christian activists in Europe working to rescue Jews, and on a few occasions he tried to offer a little help. He supported a project led by Adolph Kurtz, a German pastor and member of the Confessing Church who had married a Jewish Christian. Kurtz had helped Christian Jews escape Germany in the early years of Nazi rule, and now he covertly assisted those Jews who had defied the deportation order. Herman helped Kurtz hide at least one elderly couple who had been on the run. He also secretly supported an endeavor launched by German Christians to rescue Jewish Christian children. He approached George Kennan, a leading American diplomat posted to the embassy, about the project and also reached out to the Federal Council of Churches. He soon decided, however, that the plan was doomed and that these "troubles . . . need not concern me." Yet his guilt mounted. One local Jew even confronted the pastor directly, asking Herman if he was an anti-Semite. "It struck me that there are probably a lot of Berlin Jews who think that I am unsympathetic," he wrote his parents, "simply because I brace myself to refuse their impossible pleas for help."[50]

On December 6, 1941, as Japanese ships sailed toward Hawaii, Stewart Herman decided he had had enough. He had built up a vibrant church only to see it decline as Berlin's expat community shrank. He had be-friended Confessing churchmen and then watched as they went to jail. He had disagreed with Germany's anti-Semitic policies but then stood by as Jews reached out to him for help. He had gone from being curious about Hitler to realizing how dangerous the German leader was. Through it all, he had remained in Berlin, at the center of the war, at a time when just about every other American who could leave had done so. As he sat in his church office not far from the Tiergarten, the five-hundred-acre forested park in the heart of Germany's capital, he noted that his "abnormal ex-istence" in Nazi Germany had given him "the willies." He felt "just about done in." He was having the kind of week, he groused, that "makes strong men weep or get drunk or smash everything in sight." He dreamed of hav-ing "a sparring partner" to punch whenever "some harmless little old lady" came to him with an "abysmally stupid question."[51]

Nothing frustrated him more than the United States' partial commit-ment to helping the Allies win the war. Like many of his friends in Ber-lin, he wanted the United States to intervene fully. They all agreed that American involvement would speed the war to its end, whatever that end might be. The next day the Japanese attacked the American naval base at Pearl Harbor. On December 11 Hitler declared war on the United States. The German authorities gave Herman, the staff at the American embassy, and the American journalists still in town two days to pack their things. "Except for my last brief and lonely visit into the church auditorium my eye remained quite dry," he told his parents. He would never preach from its pulpit again. On the fourteenth, Herman and the rest of the Ameri-cans, led by George Kennan, the embassy's first secretary, boarded a train for the Grand Hotel in the German resort town of Bad Nauheim. Rather than serving interned prisoners of war, they were now the internees.[52]

THREE

"A Conquering Faith"

WILLIAM EDDY'S RELIGIOUS BACKGROUND AND MISSIONARY EXPERIENCES had shaped his life, his intellect, and his values. They had also prepared him for clandestine work in ways that almost nothing else could. He was exactly the kind of person Donovan needed for the OSS, not to share the love of Christ, but to orchestrate assassination plots and foment uprisings at the fringes of the war. His skills, his commitment to helping build a more just and peaceful world, and his pragmatic willingness to carry both Bibles and bombs made him one of the war's most important covert operatives.[1]

William Alfred Eddy, who usually went by Bill, was born March 9, 1896. He spent the first fifteen years of his life in Syria, where his parents worked as Presbyterian missionaries. Bill's grandparents had helped found the American University in Beirut, which was originally called the Syrian Protestant College, and their children, including Bill's father, followed in their footsteps at AUB. The school eventually became one of the most prestigious universities in the Middle East.

The Eddy family along with their missionary partners helped to establish a Protestant presence in the Middle East in an era when most Americans, including government officials, had little interest in the region. In the second half of the nineteenth century, missionaries opened schools, built printing presses, and learned local languages. Eddy grew up speaking both Arabic and English, and he mastered the Koran and the Bible and could recite from memory large chunks of both. He returned to the

United States for preparatory school and then went to college at Princeton, where he played basketball. He planned to train as a minister but ended up answering a different kind of call. When President Woodrow Wilson beckoned the United States to war, Eddy joined the US Marines.

Eddy began his service in Quantico, Virginia, where he trained as an intelligence officer. Just before departing for the front in France in late 1917, he telegrammed his girlfriend, Mary Garvin, another missionary child who was born and raised in Chile. He wanted her on the first train to Washington, DC, he told her, so he could see her once more before he sailed for Europe. He instructed her to "borrow money for ticket come at once with suitcase wait for me at Union Station." The next day, he realized, was "the only day we can have together." Mary went. She sent a telegram the following day to her brother. "Married tonight seven oclock will stay until Bill sails possibly one week tell mother and the rest."[2]

Eddy, like Donovan, proved to be a born leader and an excellent warrior. As the marines prepared for the battle of Belleau Wood, he led reconnaissance patrols near German lines. He risked his life by studying and analyzing enemy movements at close range. When Eddy's thoughts were not on Mary or the war, they were often on theology. He developed a close friendship with his marine bunkmate Francis Patrick Mulcahy. He later recalled that they "used to sit out under the stars and talk theology" all night long. Eddy noted that his Roman Catholic friend was "equally competent with hard liquor," which probably enhanced all of the God talk. Mulcahy went on to have a distinguished career in World War II.[3]

Near the end of the fierce battle of Belleau Wood, shrapnel tore into Eddy's leg. After he recovered from his injuries, he became the aide-de-camp to a brigadier general, and he expertly organized intelligence work for the division. Then he came down with pneumonia and probably the Spanish flu, a devastating epidemic that killed more people in 1918 and 1919 than the war. While in the hospital, Eddy developed an infection in his hip and an abscess in his groin. Too weak to write, Eddy dictated letters to Red Cross nurses to mail to Mary. He feared that his new bride would not want him back after the war, especially if he was damaged. "My life's ambition," he wrote her, "is to work for you—to secure for you and to throw around you all the comforts that I can—to make you happy even as you have made me happy." Would he be able to do that? What if the hip infection and abscess left him an invalid? Eddy's greatest fear, the thing that kept him awake at night, was that he might prove unable to support his family. But he would not give up. In another letter, he wrote Mary that he had "fought away the grave time and time again—all that I may see you again." Eddy's hip joint was permanently damaged, but he otherwise recovered, and he earned numerous accolades for his distinguished service record.[4]

The terror of war and Eddy's reflections on it reinforced for the marine the importance of faith—real, thorough, unapologetic faith. As the world recovered from the conflict, veterans and ministers debated the significance of religion in warfare and the proper role of military chaplains. Eddy, in a letter published in the *New York Times*, criticized those who believed that chaplains should simply be friends to soldiers and not serious about living the Christian life. "Let me state emphatically that the only ones that were worth their salt to the man in the trenches were the ones who believed in 'miracles and superstitions,'" that is, in the resurrection of Jesus. "What we were grateful for was a priest who was not ashamed of his ministry, who did not camouflage his job, but frankly brought the power of Christ to hungry souls." The war, he concluded, had tested religion, separating the true from the false. "It proved once and for all that Christianity based on a man's eloquence and smiling face is superfluous in the face of death, and that the 'miracle,' the supernatural power of Christ working through his priests, is the most important fact that religion has to offer to men."[5]

After the war Eddy went back to school. He earned a PhD in literature from Princeton and became an expert on the works of Jonathan Swift, especially *Gulliver's Travels*. Like Gulliver, he too would regularly be a stranger in a strange land. Then, following in his missionary parents' footsteps, he took a teaching job at the American University in Cairo (AUC), a mission school founded by Presbyterians. While there he wrote what may be the first Arabic-language basketball rule book. Although he had decided not to become a minister, he still dedicated his life to serving God. He and Mary spent most of the 1920s at AUC, where Eddy thought of himself as a missionary, working to build and expand the kingdom of God by living and modeling the Christian faith.

Living in Cairo gave Eddy the opportunity to find new ways to apply his religious convictions in a context that was very different from the United States, and he sought common ground with those whose beliefs diverged from his own. He continued to study the Koran and to improve his Arabic. He even occasionally joined local religious leaders to chant passages from the Muslim holy book on street corners. "No outsider can 'argue' intelligent men of any faith out of their religion," Eddy discovered during his time in Cairo. "The reform must come from within, from enlightened believers" of other faiths who become "friends of the Nazarene," that is, Jesus, through their exposure to real, lived Christianity.[6]

Eddy's theology, unlike that of more fundamentalist-leaning missionaries, was not grounded in absolutist doctrine. He thought true faith was about a relationship with Jesus and not about creeds. "The early disciples agreed about nothing," he insisted. "Christianity meant and means, not agreement in views about Jesus, but only a desire to see Him, to follow Him, and to be made whole. The common language of our common Christian life, is not opinion, but experience shared." He wanted to draw others in to experience that faith.[7]

Faculty members at AUC, including Eddy, usually did not directly proselytize. They sought to foster better interreligious understanding and dialogue, based on the conviction that Christianity was the superior religion and that once a nonbeliever saw it for him- or herself, he or she would be more likely to embrace it. Eddy laid out the role that "mission" colleges like AUC played in the Muslim world in a 1928 article in the *Christian Century*, the flagship journal of mainstream liberal American Protestantism. He believed that such schools and their faculty needed to remain explicitly and passionately Christian to the core. "Let it be understood," he insisted, "once and for all, that we who have worked abroad do not subscribe to the absurdity that all religions are equally good, any more than all automobiles." The key to winning over Muslims, he argued, was to demonstrate that "the seeds of Christianity are not in ethical culture but in Christ." How was this best done? By bringing Muslim students into Christian communities like the one missionaries established at AUC. "As they move in and out of Christian homes, see Christian family life which is as different from theirs as light from dark . . . they will be attracted to the spirit of Jesus."[8]

In other words, the stated goal of schools like the American University in Beirut and American University in Cairo was to provide a top-tier education to the most elite members of Middle Eastern societies. The unstated goal was to make Christians out of these Arab leaders, hoping that they would then take the Christian faith to their countrymen. Just before the United States entered the Second World War, missionary executive Stephen Penrose summed up the purpose of the American University in Beirut, which mirrored that of AUC. "It was and is a missionary institution," he wrote, "in the sense that it has always sought to create in its students an appreciation of and devotion to the values of the Christian life."[9]

Eddy returned to the United States in 1928 and took a job at Dartmouth College, where he taught English. In 1936 he accepted a call to serve as the president of the Episcopalian Hobart and William Smith Colleges in upstate New York. As Europe plunged into war in the late 1930s, the war veteran made it his mission to train Hobart and William Smith students to become global Christian citizens capable of changing a dangerous and seemingly imploding world. He believed that the United States was becoming too secular and that students were losing their understanding of the Bible and the Christian faith. Knowing the Bible was essential to making sense of the past, of the "poets, philosophers, saints, and artists" that had come before them. A deep understanding of the Bible was also necessary for living a meaningful life and building a successful career. Eddy hoped to mold a new army of "laymen who go into politics, journalism, and the professions as others go into the ministry—with a sense of awful responsibility as citizens in the kingdom of God." To make this happen, one of his first initiatives at Hobart was a controversial plan to require every student to take a four-year course in "responsible citizenship." He intended the course to serve as the foundation for students' general education. Eddy wanted his school to produce practical Christians who could go out into the professions and use them to transform humanity by embodying the Christian faith, thereby drawing others to it.[10]

To train his Christian global-citizen students, Eddy sought to hire laypeople, not priests. He wanted professors at Hobart to approach religion "through the door of history, philosophy, art, or science"—not through a narrow theological window. In Eddy's mind, all Christians were missionaries regardless of their jobs. Christianity was not something that one performed on Sundays, but something that infused every part of life. While priests and theologians played an important role in the church, they were not the church. Laypeople, like Jesus's disciples, represented God's real army of faith.[11]

*

Eddy's work at Hobart derived from his conviction that new threats to the Christian faith were materializing around the world. Nor was he the only one worried. In 1938 Eddy accepted an intriguing invitation from Assistant Secretary of State Francis B. Sayre to attend a secret meeting in Washington, DC. Sayre, who came from a prominent religious family, laid out in the invitation his reasons for calling the meeting. The world, he told Eddy and a handful of others, was in the midst of change. "Titanic forces"—communism, fascism, and Nazism—were in "irreconcilable conflict with the fundamental teachings of Christ and with many of the most precious values of Western civilization." These godless forces threatened "to sweep across and dominate large areas of the world." Sayre insisted that "those who profoundly believe in Christ and in the Christian way" needed to meet to "take stock of their own beliefs, to evaluate and formulate their own faith and, if theirs is to be a conquering faith, to reach some kind of agreement on a program for action." He hoped that these influential Christian leaders would settle on a "feasible" and "practical" plan to "make our Christianity more virile and dominant in the world today."[12]

In hindsight, it is perhaps stunning that a US government official would sponsor such an overtly religious secret meeting with the purpose of shaping foreign policy through a form of "conquering" Christian faith. But this was the world that Roosevelt was creating and the one that Eddy wanted to help mold. Leaders like Roosevelt and Sayre, much like Woodrow Wilson before them, believed that spreading Christian values and Americans ideals abroad would produce a safer, better, more peaceful world. They mostly refused to force their faith and ideals on others, at least not at the point of a gun, but they expected that Christianity, when given a fair hearing, would win the world over. In many ways, they saw the war as an opportunity to secure a global victory for the Christian faith. As Niebuhr and other Christian realists argued, sometimes Christians needed to use violent force so that justice and righteousness would prevail.

Eddy agreed with Sayre's assessment of the problems that they were facing as Americans and as Christians. In his estimation, strengthening and expanding American power was nearly the same thing as strengthening and expanding Christian power. In a letter to a friend in the State Department in 1939, Eddy laid out his hope for American foreign policy. The college president envisioned "a popular front of all liberal and democratic communities throughout the world," stemming "the tide of fanatical nationalism whose success is breeding success all over the map." However, he was not sure such a front would succeed. As he watched what was unfolding all around him, he thought it might already be too late. The fall of the Republican government in Spain, "the break-down of the popular front in France," and "the virtual disappearance of the liberal party in England" worried the World War I veteran. Democracy was at risk all over Europe. Eddy fretted about changes at home as well. "I am also fearful," he admitted, of the "tremendous influence" of the fascist-leaning, popular American Catholic priest Father Coughlin; "the danger of anti-semitism," which was growing not just in Europe but also in the United States; "and aggressive efforts" by right-wing "patrioteering societies in this country to restrict freedom of speech."[13]

Over the next two years, Eddy did what he could at Hobart, and through various writing opportunities and speaking engagements, to apply faith to the conflict, to encourage the rise of a "conquering" Christianity that would remake the world. He believed that the Christian church—and for Eddy "Christian church" always meant the ecumenical Protestant church—offered the only real solution to the political and social problems that rankled the globe. "The Church alone knows that the disease is universal and the cure 'Ye must be born again.'" Liberty, he contended, "is truly realized only in the Church of God." The church was his hope for the future. "The only culture that is really as wide as humanity in its sympathy and understanding is the Christian Church," he asserted, "which claims all peoples, all national flags, and all races and breeds of mankind. The Church brings us freedom, not by taking cities, but by helping us rule our spirit in tolerance and Christian love. This is the only road to freedom."[14]

The spread of Christian freedom, Eddy contended, was possible only if the United States stopped fascism and militarism in its tracks, if his nation intervened around the world. Such views pitted the college president against isolationists, including aviator Charles Lindbergh and those leading the America First Committee, who claimed that the United States should focus on building a strong national defense while letting Europeans fend for themselves. Eddy and other mission-minded Christians thought that the United States isolating itself from the world's problems was immoral and selfish. "I am ashamed," he acknowledged, "of the caution and compromise and fear for security which control so many of our fellow countrymen." He warned Hobart students not to "believe the defeatists or the isolationists." The fight for faith and freedom "will go on as long as there is one square foot of ground or one man of courage alive." Eddy and his like-minded friends in the State Department felt confident that the spread of freedom, the spread of American values, and the spread of Christianity were interrelated. They also agreed that they could achieve none of their goals by standing aside while fascism rolled over the earth.[15]

As the war worsened in Europe, Eddy decided that he could best effect change not at Hobart, where he thought he wasted too much time dealing with inane faculty squabbles, but by serving his government. In the early summer of 1941, Eddy took a leave from Hobart and reenlisted in the Department of the Navy. His age and bad hip ensured that he would not serve as a conventional sailor or marine. Excited to have someone of Eddy's caliber yearning to go abroad, naval officers planned to dispatch him to the American legation in Cairo as an attaché. When State Department leaders learned of the navy's plans for Eddy, they too wanted the benefit of his skills. Wallace Murray, the State Department's director of Near East affairs, confided to the US ambassador in Egypt that he hoped to use "Major Eddy not only in Egypt but in nearby Arabic speaking countries such as Saudi Arabia, Palestine, Syria and Iraq." He knew that diplomats in Cairo would soon discover that Eddy was an exceptional officer. Eddy, Murray continued, "has many close friends among high-placed Arab officials and Arab families throughout these territories." This was all due to his missionary work at AUC and his connections through his parents' earlier missionary work. The State Department expected the major to develop contacts among influential Arabs, which "would be impossible for almost any other American." Eddy, Murray summarized, should have "as much opportunity as possible to travel around freely, make contacts and observations and submit reports."[16]

Eddy's orders were clear. He was still seeking converts, but now of another sort. Rather than labor to make Muslims Christian, he aspired to turn Muslims skeptical of colonial empires into freedom fighters for the Allies. This new mission was no easier than his earlier one.

Eddy left San Francisco for Egypt in July 1941. The missionary son was not nervous about heading into a war zone, but he was nervous about leaving his family. He adored his wife, Mary, of twenty-four years. He was also a proud father, and worried about his children as they moved toward adulthood. Bill Jr. was twenty, Mary Garvin (Marycita) was nineteen, John was sixteen, and Carmen, the baby of the family and light of her father's life, was nine. Eddy had almost died in the last war, and he realized that the stakes now were much higher. If he did not return from the war, the trajectory of the kids' lives would change dramatically. Bill Jr.'s plans to attend Princeton seminary, Mary's matriculation at Vassar, and whatever opportunities John and Carmen might have down the road could be lost. Eddy had to survive.

The trip to Cairo took almost two weeks by a relatively new, luxurious, and thrilling form of transportation. The navy reserved a seat for Eddy on a Pan American Clipper, a long-range "flying boat" made by Boeing. He landed first in Hawaii, where he wrote a friend from the Outrigger Canoe Club in Waikiki. The "Honolulu gals," he observed, "are overrated, but the swimming is not." While relaxing on the beach, he enjoyed watching surfing, an increasingly popular sport. He told his wife, Mary, who loved outdoor recreation, that he was sure she would enjoy surfing if she had the chance. He felt less enamored with the leis people kept ringing around

William Eddy was a missionary, a marine, a spy, and an architect of assassination plots. He was also a wonderful, loving husband and father whose greatest joy in life was his wife and children.
Courtesy of Seeley G. Mudd Manuscript Library, Princeton University.

his neck. He always "ditched" his "right away." Apparently, the marine veteran was too manly to wear flowers.[17]

The rest of the trip was not as relaxing as Hawaii. The clipper touched down at Wake Island, Guam, Manila, Singapore, Bangkok, Calcutta, Karachi, Basra, and then, finally, Cairo. While Eddy was swimming off Midway during a layover, a Portuguese man-of-war stung him. His departure from Guam proved harrowing—a brewing storm generated high winds and waves, and the pilot could not initially get the plane into the air. Finally, when a break came, he managed to lift the flying ship off the water just as it reached a massive coral reef, which would have torn the clipper to shreds. "It was really an exciting adventure," Eddy reported, "one I would not have missed for anything."[18]

The importance of Cairo, and Egypt more generally, was growing as the European war progressed. Egypt had won its independence from Great Britain after World War I, but the British maintained a military presence in the country to protect and control the Suez Canal, which they needed in order to keep oil flowing in from the Middle East. The Axis powers coveted that oil, and they recognized that taking Egypt could pave the way for them to conquer the entire Middle East. Hitler sent forces under the command of Erwin Rommel to Egypt in early 1941 to try to secure North Africa for the Third Reich. The Nazis drove the British back to within about 150 miles of Cairo, where the British stopped the attack. But the Nazis were not yet done in the region.

Eddy's daily routine in Cairo was harried and intense. He knew that at any moment, the Nazis might launch an offensive in the region. He read the local Arab press each morning, listened to news of the war, scanned reports for the legation and other attachés, attended meetings with British military leaders, worked with Egyptian intelligence operatives, led or participated in investigations into regional military actions, and wrote descriptions for US military leaders narrating what he observed and heard.

Eddy also got out into the field as often as he could. In addition to his regular attaché duties and the work that the State Department asked of him, Eddy had secret "other instructions" from the man he called his "primary boss," the director of naval intelligence. Most of the career diplomats at the legation were unaware that Eddy was using the diplomatic post as cover for intelligence work. Eddy's secret boss tasked the missionary with collecting as much information as possible. Eddy used his knowledge of Arabic and his local connections to acquire a membership in the Royal Egyptian Club, which he called "a hot-bed of pro-German propaganda . . . and meetings of fifth columnists." The Americans worried that the local Arabs, still smarting over their recent colonial past, would rather see a German victory than a British one. Although Eddy's citizenship and government affiliation prevented him from gaining access to the club's inner circles, he "did enough 'agreeing' and 'cursing the British and the Jews,'" he reported, "to get quite a bit of information." He also developed contacts in several cities in the region. Most of the career diplomats at the legation didn't know quite what to make of Eddy or why he was mixing so much with local Arab leaders. They feared that his secretive work with foreigners, whatever its purpose, could endanger their diplomatic immunity.[19]

Work was not all that Eddy did. The Mediterranean could be the sight of horrific violence, but it could also be the source of new pleasures. Eddy took a few days off for some recreation, where he became "a convert to fishing as a sport." Such little escapes helped Eddy and others maintain a sense of sanity in an insane world.[20]

The rigors of the new job, especially in comparison to life in the ivory tower, made the former college president acutely aware that in his mid-forties, he was no longer a young man. One morning "I intended to go to early communion," he confessed to Mary, "but was too tired." He was actually getting sick. A few days later, he was in the hospital with bronchitis and slight pneumonia. He belatedly recognized that as hard as he was trying to keep up with the younger officers, those days were over. "My eager efforts to condition myself and harden up look silly now. I guess perhaps I am just a fat old fool who cannot recover his earlier rigor." He fretted about his weight, too. He regularly wrote Mary with his latest plans for shedding pounds, from skipping meals to taking sweat baths. He hoped that when he next saw his wife, she would hardly recognize him as the "old indoor softy with the two stomachs separated by a belt to whom you said goodbye in San Francisco." However, he was not yet ready to show off his legs, not even in the Cairo heat. "I do not wear shorts," which most members of the legation did, "for the good reason that the distribution of my anatomy leaves much to be desired." Nevertheless, his years would never limit his ability to contribute to this—or any—mission in important and substantial ways.[21]

During Eddy's Cairo adventure, his lifelong partner was never far from his thoughts. As a member of the legation, the attaché was able to send confidential letters home to his wife via the State Department's diplomatic pouch. He shared his work with Mary but reminded her that it was top secret. "Nothing on this sheet should ever appear in print unless you are in a hurry to become a widow." That Eddy's secret work might get him killed was a constant and legitimate fear.[22]

He especially missed Mary as he reflected on their recent time in San Francisco as he was preparing to leave for Egypt. "I am more than ever convinced," he wrote his bride, "that the very heart of living is found only in love such as you and I have developed for each other." For the attaché, getting to know his spouse intimately was one of the real benefits of aging. "It isn't all there at the beginning, is it?" he realized. The trials and triumphs of life, the years of "sharing, suffering, home and children," had made their marriage real. He knew that their love would grow only deeper over time. "All I know is that I want you," he told Mary, and "you completely, with every shade and mood of love from the tenderest caress to the supreme ecstasy of passion."[23]

Indeed, Eddy really missed his wife. A few years earlier, he expressed his feelings to her while on another trip abroad. He claimed to be on one of his "naughty" streaks, writing his wife about his dreams in the middle of the night. He hoped, he told her, to "press your swelling breasts where my fingers would encircle your nipples and coax them to become hard. Would my mouth water then?" As his trip was winding down, seemingly all he could think about was seeing Mary when he docked in New York, "and especially to the minute we are alone in the hotel. We will lie together naked, won't we darling, and you will let me love you long and fiercely till we dissolve together in passion." In the first decades of the twentieth century, many Americans still did not acknowledge that women had sexual desires and passions or that a partner's job was to cater to them. But Bill treated Mary as his equal in all ways.[24]

Eddy sometimes begged Mary to "write naughty love letters" to him and to help fuel his "sex passion" for her while he was away. He craved his wife's companionship and affection but also her touch. He worried, though, that perhaps his obsession with sex with Mary was abnormal. "I wonder whether it's those early experiences in Syria as a boy of ten, watching our servants caress and have intercourse, which fixed my interest so permanently in the primary sex acts and organs. To me it is merely the most intense and exciting of all the experiences of our married life." He hoped Mary agreed, but he feared that she seemed less interested in "'loving' parties" and more interested in the "more refined" things. "Do you think I am abnormal?" he asked. Apparently, she did not. She offered him enough tantalizing teases in her letters to keep him fully enraptured with her. In return, Eddy vowed always to be faithful—and it seems that indeed he was—something of a rarity among married men of his class working abroad in the war years.[25]

In late October 1941, Eddy went on a cruise in the Mediterranean with Britain's Royal Navy. For the first time in this war, which the United States had not yet officially entered, Eddy saw the front lines. His ship shelled enemy installations on the coast, and then he helped the crew rescue sailors from a sinking British minelayer. The minelayer was supposed to have had air cover provided by the Royal Air Force (RAF), but planes were nowhere to be seen when the Germans attacked. The rescue was a "shambles," Eddy wrote home, "with 84 dead, and 150 terribly burned of whom 18 died of burns on our way back to Alexandria." But like others in wartime, Eddy and the rescued crew used humor to lighten the situation. The sailors joked that RAF must stand for "Royal Advertising Force." Eddy and the naval crew also went on a "gratifying" and successful hunt for a U-boat. Eddy loved the experience at sea. "I would go again anytime to share the life of the navy boys in action. There is nothing like their teamwork and quiet courage."[26]

Eddy's experience with the British navy convinced him that the United States needed to get into the war, and fast. "There is no hope for the future," he wrote his children after returning from sea, "except as Hitler is first utterly crushed and the Germans prevented from ever again building a war machine." He was not confident, based on his work with the British in Egypt, that they could do the job alone. He thought the "muddle-headed" decision makers in London were incapable of adapting "the historic empire defenses to modern Blitzkrieg necessities." Quelling native uprisings was not the same thing as stopping the Wehrmacht.[27]

When the attaché returned to Cairo after his stint with the Royal Navy, he found what he considered "a bombshell in the form of telegraphic orders" waiting for him. The director of naval intelligence wanted Eddy to return immediately to Washington "for instructions regarding other foreign duty." He had no idea what this meant. "Absolutely no clue," he told his family. Perhaps, he speculated, he'd be returning to some new job in the Middle East. Regardless, he felt happy he would be seeing everyone soon. What he would discover as soon as he got home was that Donovan wanted to enlist him in the United States' new foreign intelligence agency.[28]

On his way back to Washington in November 1941, Eddy passed through Lagos, Nigeria, awaiting transport once again by Pan Am Clipper to Brazil and then up the Americas to the United States. Between rounds of whiskey (he assured his family that the locals used the spirits to "ward off snake bites"), Eddy went on a brief trip into the interior of Africa, where he visited with American missionaries.

While waiting for his flight home, Eddy met with King Ademola II of Nigeria at a lunch hosted by British officials. "Thinking he might be fed up with flattery," Eddy reported, "I tried him out at lunch and found he had a sense of humor, so I got going with funny stories and all but got to slapping His Majesty on the back." Eddy always treated those around him, no matter how rich and powerful, as real people, thereby (usually) winning their friendship and respect.[29]

The lunch had gone so well that Ademola invited Eddy to his palace, where, according to Eddy, the king offered the major a position as chief of staff of the small Nigerian army. "Think of it," Eddy wrote his children, "promotion to Four-Star rank, a power behind the throne, slaves and concubines galore, no income-tax collector, easy work. Of course my conscience might trouble me for deserting wife and children." It would, and so Eddy decided he had better decline. Instead, all he got was a photo of the king inscribed, "To my Friend, Major Eddy." He also picked up presents for his children, including two boa-constrictor skins for his sons. "It is understood of course," he wrote in a note about the present, "that I strangled these two boas myself with my own little hands. It was nothing, don't mention it."[30]

Just days after the attack on Pearl Harbor, Eddy received his new orders. The secretary of the navy wanted the missionary to relocate to Tangier, Morocco, again as a naval attaché. But this was simply his cover. Eddy's real job was to serve as Donovan's chief OSS officer in North Africa and to coordinate "all propaganda activities." This included recruiting and training a network of local agents and establishing a clandestine radio network. The American military had not yet settled on their strategy for North Africa. If the Axis invaded, Eddy would leave his recruits behind to organize a resistance movement. If the Allies decided to invade North Africa, Eddy's agents would lay the groundwork.[31]

Before Eddy returned to North Africa, he completed a brief OSS training regimen. Although it is not clear what exercises OSS leaders put the missionary through, some of their drills were brutal. One participant described being "taught hand-to-hand combat: how to garrot a man with piano wire, how to break his shins, how to rip his groin with a trench knife." They also had to stab a pig "to get used to" warm blood running over their hands. As an OSS operative, Eddy was reentering a world of horror and violence, one he thought he had put behind him at the end of the last world war. While dealing with insubordinate faculty at Hobart and William Smith had its downsides, no disgruntled professors had ever tried to rip his groin.[32]

Eddy's new responsibilities were part of a larger strategy Donovan had mapped out for the OSS. Operatives deployed around the globe, the spymaster reported to President Roosevelt, were organizing guerrilla armies and resistance fighters in neutral territories that might not remain neutral for long. He wanted the Americans to sow "the dragon's teeth," he said, meaning to lay the foundations for later wreaking havoc. The native teams that the OSS trained, he reckoned, could strike "the enemy where he least expects it and yet where he is most vulnerable."[33]

On a cold January morning in 1942, just one month after Roosevelt asked Congress for a declaration of war, Mary drove her husband to La Guardia field in New York. At 8:30 AM, Eddy again boarded a Pan Am Clipper. He wore civilian clothes despite his new rank of lieutenant colonel. He did not want to attract any attention on his travels abroad. Mary hoped he would be back to the States within a few months.[34]

Bad weather delayed the plane in Bermuda, so Eddy got some days of vacation as he anticipated what was to come in North Africa. Donovan personally wrote to Mary, assuring her that although Eddy "was having difficulty in sending the usual messages," her husband was well and sent his love. Eddy was clearly one of Wild Bill's top priorities. When Eddy's letters did finally make it home, he caught Mary up on his temporary island adventure. "Bermuda looked so balmy and inviting we all agreed it was a good place to get stuck if get stuck we must," he quipped. He did not know at that point that he would be in Bermuda for almost two weeks. He explored the island, swam in the ocean, sunbathed, and got to know those stranded with him as well as the locals. He met one eighty-year-old American multimillionaire and his "fifth wife—a gold digging young thing who takes her pleasure where she finds it, which is everywhere he is not." Before long Eddy grew bored of the island paradise.[35]

As Eddy lounged on the beach, he wondered about the cause of the delay. He later learned that the Pan Am Clippers were transferred into the service of another important asset, one with a higher rank than Eddy. Winston Churchill and his entourage were flying through Bermuda as they made their way back home after three weeks of meetings with Franklin Roosevelt and US leaders. "No wonder we had no news in advance of the whereabouts of the planes," Eddy noted. "I would have liked to have gotten a glimpse of W.C. but no luck." Nor did Eddy know that his fate had just been decided by Churchill and FDR. As the family man worked on his tan, the Allied leaders had decided to focus their military operations first on North Africa. The Axis powers and the missionary son were now on paths certain to collide. The only question was when.[36]

FOUR

"Prophecies Yet to Be Fulfilled"

THE WAR WAS NOT GOING WELL IN THE PACIFIC. AFTER SURPRISING THE US Navy at Pearl Harbor on December 7, 1941, Japan attacked Allied forces in Guam, Wake Island, the Philippines, Malaya, and Hong Kong. Japanese military planners believed that they had to act quickly and decisively. The more time they gave the United States, the greater the challenge they would face. They also captured British Singapore as well as the Dutch East Indies, getting the valuable oil reserves they had long coveted. The Japanese claimed to be securing Asia for the Asians, but having been at war with China for most of a decade, the reality was that they wanted Asia for themselves. Missionary John Birch, preaching and working near the front lines in Shangrao, a few hundred miles inland from the East China Sea, knew that if the Japanese took control of much more Chinese territory, his work, along with that of generations of other missionaries, would probably be wiped out. He decided to do whatever was necessary to keep the Japanese from choking the seeds of the Christian faith that he and other missionaries had planted in China.

John Birch was born in Landour, India, on May 28, 1918, to Presbyterian missionaries George and Ethel Birch. The Birches embraced a form of apocalyptic, millennialist Christianity. They believed that time was short and that the world was madly careening toward a great cataclysm that would culminate in the rapture of all true Christians from the earth, the battle of Armageddon, and the Second Coming of Christ. World War I seemed to confirm both their theology and their fears. Such convictions inspired the rise of the fundamentalist movement within American Protestantism.

Convinced that time was running out and judgment was coming, George and Ethel Birch decided to go abroad in late 1917 to evangelize. George, on his missionary application, vacillated from acknowledging the hard time he had controlling his temper and his "sex passion" to acknowledging how he had come to recognize "the coming of Christ" as "a vital reality" to his life and work. For Ethel, a course in Bible prophecy, and "especially the prophecies yet to be fulfilled," led to her religious transformation and her new missionary impulse. However, their commitment to saving as many foreign souls as possible lasted fewer than three years. India was not for them.[1]

John, the oldest of seven children, spent most of his childhood in rural New Jersey. He apparently accepted Jesus as his savior at age twelve and believed that God had called him then to the mission field. When John was in high school, the Birches moved to Georgia, where they established a family farm near Macon on land inherited from John's grandfather. They called their property Birchwood. Like so many Americans, they struggled to make ends meet during the Great Depression. John attended small country schools and learned to be creative with the family's few resources.[2]

Birch noticed the racial dynamics at play in the Jim Crow South. In describing Macon to a friend, the missionary son noted that all the white "Birches" in the region were relatives of his, and all African American Birches "descended from the family's slaves." He had racial prejudices, he admitted, but was self-aware enough to fret over them.[3]

The Birch family worshipped in a small Baptist church. On Sundays John learned about the major theological currents and controversies of the day, including the rise of the fundamentalist faith that his parents had made their own. In school Birch wrote a paper arguing against evolutionary theory based on his understanding of the Bible. In the years following the infamous 1925 Scopes anti-evolution trial, fundamentalists like Birch continued to battle against Darwinian theories of evolution. Humans, he believed, could not be the product of natural selection and random chance but were made in the image of God and in desperate need of a savior to redeem them. John graduated from high school in 1933, the class valedictorian.[4]

*

In 1934 Birch enrolled at Mercer University, a nearby Baptist school. The seventeen-year-old was a joiner, and he leaped into the vibrant student life in Macon. He demonstrated some talent for theater and appeared in numerous university productions. Learning how to play a variety of roles would serve him well in the years to come. He also joined the debate team, where he honed his public speaking skills and his ability to make persuasive arguments, another skill that served him well for the rest of his life. He participated in Sigma Upsilon, Mercer's literary club, where he shared original pieces of writing with classmates. His experience on the student newspaper proved more frustrating. Birch tried with little success to convince editors to include more articles on religion. Despite all of these activities, Birch never let his class work suffer. He earned good grades and routinely made the dean's list. While a junior, Birch accepted a call to pastor the nearby Benevolence Baptist Church and made plans to be a missionary after he graduated.

Although Birch enjoyed most of his courses, the work of some of his professors troubled him. He and a few other students believed that some of the ideas taught in class violated the school's mission and especially its Baptist commitments, and so they lodged complaints and publicized their concerns. School administrators took the students' assertions seriously and launched an investigation. Birch and twelve other students signed affidavits outlining their concerns against five professors. Birch claimed that John Freeman, a religion and philosophy professor and the students' main target, seemed to indicate during a class discussion that souls were not immortal. Birch pursued the professor after class, seeking further clarification, but was not satisfied with the professor's response. The professor simply asked questions of his inquirer, refusing to take a clear position on what Birch saw as a core doctrine of the Christian faith. This was a tried-and-true tactic among professors dating back to Socrates who want to teach students to think for themselves rather than to tell them what to think. Birch, accustomed to seeing the world in black-and-white, wanted a straight answer from his instructor: either Freeman was a heretic, or he was not.[5]

In another class session, the same professor implied that the New Testament story in which Jesus seemed to heal a demon-possessed man reflected first-century understandings of mental illness. According to some modern interpretations, demons had not actually possessed people but instead served as a means of making sense of psychological problems in the premodern world. Birch vehemently disagreed with this theory. "I denounce as slander against my Lord and Savior," he proclaimed, "the insinuation that He would perpetuate a misconception in the minds of his disciples and in the divine record, simply because He might have found it inconvenient to explain the true nature of a psychosis."[6]

One final issue troubled Birch. The professor had indicated to his students that Christ's death symbolically cleansed humans' sins, but that Jesus's literal loss of blood did not wash away the sins of those who believed in him. This too ran against fundamentalist interpretations of the scriptures. And for John it represented more heresy.

Ultimately, the Mercer administration charged five faculty members with "un-Christian" teaching and decided to put them on trial. Most Mercer students denounced the inquisition. A fundamentalist minister who came to encourage Birch and his allies complained that a "mob" of students had "hurled rocks against" his car "with murderous force." "Had it not been for the grace of God," the minister melodramatically claimed, "I would have been killed or seriously injured." The angry students also went after Birch, and one posted a sign that read, "Lynch St. Birch."[7]

When Birch took the witness stand during the trial, students jeered at him. It didn't matter. Birch, never one to cower or be intimidated, testified against the content of Professor Freeman's teaching and questioned the state of the teacher's soul. Despite Birch's young age and inexperience, he thought he was capable of judging his teacher. He believed that the path to truth and righteousness was easily discernible. Once he had fixed upon it, there was nothing that would dissuade him. Birch's confidence and his total commitment to his beliefs could be interpreted as arrogance and close-mindedness. Such traits are common in a theology classroom, but they become a hindrance for religious leaders once they step out of school and into the real world. On the mission field, and on the battlefield, flexibility and openness are often more effective than dogmatism. Birch was young and would learn.[8]

Adding fuel to the heresy trial fire was J. Frank Norris, one of the South's leading fundamentalist firebrands. A decade earlier, when a man barged into the minister's church office to criticize him, Norris calmly opened his desk drawer, pulled out a loaded revolver, and emptied the chambers. Three bullets slammed into the chest of the unarmed man. In the spectacular murder trial that followed, the jury affirmed the minister's claim of self-defense. Norris apparently saw a kindred spirit in Birch. The radical preacher admired Birch's intellect and his uncompromising stand for the fundamentalist faith. Through Norris's magazine the *Fundamentalist*, the minister ensured that the Mercer heresy trial received substantial attention outside the region.[9]

To an outsider, the theological issues that animated people like Birch and Norris might seem relatively insignificant. But they emerged in the context of the fundamentalist-modernist controversy, which since the 1910s had torn churches, denominations, and seminaries asunder. Different interpretative methods led to different conclusions about the historical and scientific accuracy of the scriptures, the literalness of Jesus's miracles, and the nature of human sin. What may have begun as seemingly esoteric questions about theological nuances led to major differences in determining how one should live the Christian life. At the heart of the fundamentalist controversy was a debate about the future of the world and Christians' role within it. When Birch and other fundamentalists read the Bible, they reached dire conclusions about time, history, and the future compared with their liberal counterparts. This would directly influence how they saw the war, their role in it, and postwar reconstruction.

In the 1940s many fundamentalists began calling themselves "evangelicals." They reappropriated the historical term to mark their renewed commitment to fully engaging with the world around them. More mainstream Protestants rejected fundamentalists' and evangelicals' apocalyptic ideas. Stewart Herman once quipped that those Christians obsessed with the imminent "rapture" must be struggling with "inverted sexuality!"—a phrase used at the time to describe people attracted to those of the same gender.[10]

Birch, like his parents, took biblical prophecy about an imminent apocalypse seriously and literally. He believed that humankind was nearing the great apocalypse described in the book of Revelation. Heresy was on the rise, the devil was working harder than ever to deceive the faithful, and the earth, beyond redemption, would soon be enveloped in flames. The Christian's job was to pluck as many people as possible off the conveyor belt to hell before time ran out. Explicit and direct evangelism became Birch's focus.

For liberals, the future looked much brighter. They believed that God had called them to build his kingdom or some approximation of it on earth. They worked toward establishing an earthly paradise. They had the benefit of time, which is why missionaries working at universities in the Middle East, for example, sought to transform Muslim culture through Christian influences rather than through direct proselytization. Had William Eddy been teaching at Mercer, he would have been on the wrong side of the heresy controversy for Birch. So too would Stephen Penrose and Stewart Herman. Theological liberals all, Eddy, Penrose, and Herman expressed little interest in the issues that shaped the fundamentalist and later the evangelical movement and that drove Birch's college-era concerns. Yet the war would unite these unlikely religious activists behind a single cause. Whatever nuances separated fundamentalists from moderates and liberals in the United States, the Christian faith was at stake in Europe and Asia. They shared a common mission: win the war in order to expand Christendom.

The Mercer heresy trial did not end as Birch had hoped. The three Baptist ministers and three attorneys overseeing the hearing cleared the professors of all charges. Birch moved on. He graduated magna cum laude with degrees in English and the Bible. During his senior year, 1938, college administrators nominated the stellar student for a prestigious Rhodes scholarship. Although he did not get one, the nomination served as a sign of the respect he had earned from both faculty and students, despite the heresy controversy.

After graduation the lanky young man with cropped hair and hollow eyes moved to Texas to enroll in Frank Norris's new seminary, the Fundamental Bible Baptist Institute. He wanted additional, explicitly fundamentalist, theological training. The goals of Norris's missionary group aligned perfectly with Birch's views at the time. "We have the deep conviction that no nation around the globe today can save civilization except America," Norris's mission statement affirmed, "and America cannot save civilization except through Jesus Christ, and Jesus Christ can't save civilization except through the preaching of His Gospel." Birch took classes for one year and was a member of the institute's first graduating class. Then he decided to travel to China under the auspices of Norris's fledgling World Fundamental Baptist Missionary Fellowship. Seamlessly embodying faith and American exceptionalism, Birch had a clear mission. The dour young evangelist hoped to bring the lost to a saving faith in Christianity and American values, thereby to save the world.[11]

Birch sailed in 1940 from Seattle to Japan en route to China aboard the *Hie Maru*, a Japanese cargo and passenger ship. It offered the cheapest fare that he could find. The ship took Birch near the Aleutian Islands and on to Yokohama. By the time he arrived, he looked like he hailed from a Florida retirement community—too much shuffleboard on deck left him thoroughly sunburned. He had refused, however, to attend any dances on the ship. Like telephone poles, good Baptists didn't dance. Once in Japan, Birch had a few days free before continuing on to China. While touring historic sites, he worked to share the Christian faith with as many people as he could. He had brought dozens of religious tracts with him, which he distributed liberally. For the moment he was more focused on converting Japanese souls than on the empire's military aggressiveness or the death and destruction it was inflicting on China.[12]

A few days later, Birch continued on to Shanghai. He spent the next few months in the region, immersing himself in the language and culture of his new homeland. While some missionaries focused simply on preaching the gospel while separating themselves from the native culture in just about every other way, Birch jumped into his new environs with abandon. He had every intention of following the biblical adage "I am made all things to all men, that I might by all means save some." To win the Chinese, he was going to become like the Chinese. The transition from one culture to another was not always smooth. At one memorable communion service, Birch, while preparing the elements, meant to say "let us pray" in Mandarin. Apparently, he actually said, "I will now take the knife." Some people in the congregation, fearing that he was planning a human sacrifice, left quickly.[13]

Birch chose a difficult time to start a missionary career in China. Japan had invaded Manchuria in 1931, and in 1937 a full-scale war broke out between the two nations. The missionary enterprise, difficult even in the best of circumstances, grew substantially harder for those like Birch laboring in one of the world's hot spots. When Birch arrived, conditions had deteriorated to the point that most other missionaries were leaving. Not Birch. He proved as stubborn in his commitments as in his theology. He redoubled his efforts to master Mandarin and the nuances of regional dialects.

John Birch (*right*) arrived in Shanghai ready to convert the Chinese to a fundamentalist form of the Christian faith. Just a few years into his work, he became an intelligence officer, but he never stopped evangelizing.
Courtesy of Arlington Baptist College Heritage Collection.

Birch set up his first mission in the fall of 1940, in Hangzhou, one of China's largest and most impressive cities. He preached, worked with local communities, and supported existing Christian ministries. Sometimes he even slept. But the project was short-lived. When the Japanese launched a new offensive in the area in the fall of 1941, the missionary had no choice but to abandon the work. His retreat away from enemy lines was not easy. As Birch and his traveling companions moved out of Japanese-controlled territory, they had to evade enemy patrols. At one point Japanese soldiers nearly caught them. They spent almost an entire day hiding among bamboo. To pass the time, Birch ate persimmon and read the book of Ezekiel, a fitting choice. Ezekiel is one of the Bible's more apocalyptic books, so while the evangelist was eluding enemy troops, he was studying the strange hallucinations of an Old Testament prophet who forecast God's damning judgment of the nations for their sins.

Church leaders shared the stories of missionaries like Birch with supporters back home, allowing them to feel like they were part of the great missionary projects from the safety of their Sunday-morning pews. Norris dramatized Birch's Hangzhou saga for his tens of thousands of followers, and he hyperbolically called the missionary's successful flight another "act of the apostles." Like the disciples struggling to build the early church in the face of a hostile Roman empire, Birch was working to establish a Christian foothold in the face of an equally oppressive regime. Norris printed Birch's "thrilling" account of his escape in the *Fundamentalist*, read it over his radio broadcasts, and made sure that it circulated throughout his network. In this way, the heroic and sometimes dangerous work of missionaries became something for American Christians to celebrate. They were essentially witnessing a continuation of the work of the New Testament apostles who spread Jesus's gospel around the world.[14]

After fleeing Hangzhou, Birch settled in Shangrao, deeper into the interior and farther from the Japanese lines, where he established a new mission. But rather than limit his work to the city, he regularly rode his bike to nearby villages to share the gospel with all who would listen. Over the coming months, as the Japanese once again closed in, he converted dozens of people and baptized a handful of Chinese men and women in local rivers. At one point a military leader in the region invited Birch to preach to a company of Chinese soldiers, who listened attentively to his message. This was the first but not the last time that Birch received a warm welcome from the Chinese military. He also traveled up and down nearby rivers, dodging bombing raids while supporting local "country" churches on the edge of the Japanese lines. Despite the inherent danger in working so near a war zone, the missionary loved the adventure. He wrote his parents that he was having the time of his life and hoped that they too were experiencing the "blessings" of God as "richly" as he was.[15]

But he was rich in spiritual blessings only. The US declaration of war against Japan in December 1941 had a direct impact on Birch. The conflict severed most foreign communications systems, and the next few months passed without any money from his agency or news from his family. The missionary started to feel marooned.

Cut off from financial support from US churches, the fundamentalist offered his services to the US Army in early 1942. While he planned to continue preaching, he noted on his enlistment application that he found missionary work "increasingly hard to do on an empty stomach." He believed in "God," he confessed, and "His Son, in America, and in freedom." In that order. He wanted to serve as a chaplain but offered to work wherever the army most needed him. The army did need him, and in ways that he could not have anticipated.[16]

FIVE

"What a Fine Schooling You Are Having"

ANGERED BY THE ATTACK ON PEARL HARBOR, STEPHEN B. L. PENROSE JR. wanted to do something to support his country. He asked US Supreme Court justice William O. Douglas, an old family friend, if he had any ideas how Penrose might contribute to the war effort. Douglas had an idea. The justice saw something in Penrose, a missionary and missionary executive, that he thought OSS director Wild Bill Donovan would like. He was right. Penrose was a faithful Christian and a staunch advocate for American foreign missions. But he was no naive idealist focused only on spiritual things. He was innovative and pragmatic and sought real-world solutions to religious problems. In other words, he was perfect for the United States' new intelligence agency.

Penrose, whom friends called "Binks," took the justice's advice and filled out an application for the OSS. The government bureaucrats who met with Penrose described him as "a very likeable chap, with quite a sense of humor." They also noted that he was fluent in French and spoke some German and Arabic. Then they realized he had something even more valuable. Penrose's work on various missionary boards, and especially his administrative position with the Near East College Association, made him the perfect conduit for building new networks for the OSS abroad. Penrose had the education, the refinement, and the connections that Donovan would find invaluable.[1]

Stephen B. L. Penrose Jr., with his daughter Dale celebrating Christmas a couple of weeks after the United States entered the war against Japan. Penrose had just let some friends know that he was interested in war work if the right opportunity arose.
Courtesy of Dale Penrose Harrell.

Penrose, however, felt less certain about his potential than did his OSS recruiters. "A certain government agency," he confided to his parents, had sounded him out about the possibility of "going abroad, possibly to the Near East, as an agent for them." He noted that if he was still single and did not have children, he would have jumped at the chance. But in light of his family obligations, he was not initially sure about the job. When he learned that Donovan's people were running background checks on him, he told his parents not to tell them about his "communistic tendencies." He was joking. Penrose, like many of the leaders of the OSS, was no radical.[2]

Things moved much more quickly than Penrose expected. Just days after the interview, he told his parents that he had quit his job in New York and was immediately moving to Washington, DC, to go to work for Donovan. He could not, he explained, share any details about what he was going to be doing, since "of all the confidential sections" of the OSS, "this is about the most so." He worried that his wife, Peggy, would not like living in the capital, but Justice Douglas promised to help them find a house and did his best to make them feel comfortable in their new hometown.[3]

*

Penrose was born on March 19, 1908, in rural eastern Washington State. His father, Stephen B. L. Penrose, had attended Yale Divinity School, where he joined the Yale Band, a small group of students who pledged to serve as missionaries wherever they were most needed. The American Board of Commissioners for Foreign Missions assigned the elder Penrose to a "home missions" position and shipped him off to the "frontier"—to Walla Walla, a longtime center of missionary work among Native Americans now better known for its excellent wines. Penrose initially pastored a church, but in 1894 he accepted a call to serve as the president of the Congregational Church–affiliated Whitman College. Over the next few decades, he helped transform it into a respected liberal arts college.

Penrose Jr. grew up in Walla Walla and graduated from Whitman. Like his father, Penrose was a devout Congregationalist—a member of one of the more diverse Protestant denominations in the United States that had substantially evolved from its Puritan roots. After graduating with a bachelor's degree in 1928, Penrose went to Beirut, where he taught physics at the American University. "He just loved the life out there," his wife told an interviewer years later. Penrose's experience in the Middle East nurtured in him a deep empathy for Arabs. It also convinced him that trouble was looming, at least in regard to the Holy Land.[4]

Penrose's official job at the university was teaching math and science. But that was not his primary purpose. Like Eddy in Cairo, he hoped to turn Muslims into Christians. He believed that the best way to do this was through humanitarian educational institutions like the American University. He did not want to force his faith on others, nor did he threaten them with the fires of hell. Instead, he patiently modeled the Christian faith for all whom he encountered in his classes and around the region. For local Arabs, the university provided substantial opportunities. It offered the children of elite Arabs a first-class Western education. Yet it also threatened to undermine their religious and cultural values. American schools in the Middle East were (and are) in a precarious position. They did a lot of good, but they also served as symbols of American, and Christian, imperialism.

Penrose was a faithful churchgoer throughout his life. When he missed a Sunday-morning service in Beirut, only the second one he had missed all year, his conscience "hurt" him "badly." But he had a good reason. He was going on a long day trip up into the hills of Lebanon on a double date with two British women and Lewis Leary, a friend and colleague from the American University. They did their "best as males, which was pretty good," Penrose noted. The young missionary tried to be chivalrous and not to be a boring date. He and Leary could not have imagined as they wooed young women, met Arab villagers, visited old palaces, explored ruins, and sought out cedar trees that a decade later they would work together as spies based out of the OSS's Cairo field station. Leary, like Penrose, would play a key role in shaping American policy in the Middle East.[5]

While teaching in Beirut, Penrose used his summers to see as much of the world as possible. Just weeks before the stock market crashed in October 1929, he went on a European tour. "What a fine schooling you are having," his father wrote, "getting acquainted with different sorts of people, and learning that they are not so different after all." Penrose Sr. had worked with missionaries for years and understood how getting outside of the United States could reshape a person's understanding of people and religion. He hoped that as his son encountered different cultures, he would grow more tolerant and empathetic.[6]

Sometimes, however, Penrose's parents worried that their son was going too far in his self-directed cultural education. Like John Birch, Penrose had no trouble slumming it. He purposely chose lower-class accommodations when traveling. "You have plenty of money available here," his father chastised, "and unless you take pride in seeing how economical you can be I do not see the use in subjecting yourself to all sorts of hardships and dirt and the danger of disease." His father feared that Penrose would get smallpox or typhoid fever from the world's downtrodden. While Stewart Herman, pastor of the American Church in Berlin, constantly begged his parents for money and often complained about his accommodations, Penrose enjoyed the experience of mixing with and learning from other social classes.[7]

Americans paying attention to world events at the time could sense darkness on the horizon. The Nazi Party was gaining ground in Germany and in 1930 had just picked up about one hundred seats in the Reichstag. Others worried about the changes enveloping Italy. Benito Mussolini had risen to power in the 1920s by championing Italian nationalism. He was creating a fascist state, and he demanded the loyalty of his people. Penrose was eager to visit Italy and to see what was going on. When his letters to his family were slow to reach the United States, the elder Penroses worried. "We did not know but what Mussolini had taken a fancy to you," his father joked, "or perhaps had overheard some rash remark of yours and had shut you up in an Italian dungeon."[8]

Tensions were also growing in the Middle East. From Penrose's position in Beirut, the missionary-teacher witnessed the ongoing debate about the future of Palestine. The Arabs he worked with had hopes and dreams for Jerusalem and especially the ancient city's holy sites, which were coveted by the world's Jews, Christians, and Muslims. He also knew that the Zionist movement was growing, both in the United States and in Europe. He discussed the question of Palestine with his father many times. The elder Penrose was not optimistic. "I suspect," he wrote, "that the last people to get together will be the Arabs and the Jew, at least in Palestine." Penrose agreed. If the two groups were not going to be able to work out a compromise, Penrose would have to choose a side. For the young missionary working in the Middle East, it was an easy decision. He supported Arab claims to Palestine and rejected Zionism.[9]

In 1932 Penrose returned to the United States to attend graduate school at Columbia University, where he studied philosophy. He was twenty-four years old. His father continued to pepper him with a steady stream of advice, some of which would serve him well in the intelligence business. The elder Penrose encouraged his son to understand competing religions. He worried that the current generation of young people could not see beyond their own little worlds, even as the globe shrank and more and more people from different tribes and cultures crossed paths. His Whitman students, he lamented, are startled to "discover that other religions are worth studying besides Christianity."[10]

Religion was not all Penrose Sr. worried about. His son, he feared, was not taking his studies seriously enough. "Girls and scholarship," he warned Penrose, "do not mix well." He suggested that Penrose spend no more than two evenings a week socializing. "One has to be practical as well as romantic" and should not "burn" his "candle freely." That Penrose was popular with the ladies was a bit surprising. He was no Clark Gable, nor was he even a Bill Donovan. With his dark hair parted down the middle, accentuating his oversize ears, he had a bit of a goofy look. Although his dad advised him to "remember that you are in New York to make a great scholar of yourself and not a social butterfly," Stephen managed to become both.[11]

While at Columbia, Penrose met Margaret "Peggy" Dale, a missionary daughter born in Mexico. They quickly fell in love and in the fall of 1934 decided to get married. They held their wedding at the Dales' home in Mexico. "Senorita Perez," a guest at the wedding, described the bride as "beautiful: blue eyes and golden hair." A "grace and charm of spirit," she continued, seemed to "emanate from her." Peggy's mother was a medical doctor who worked among the poor, and her father was a minister. They raised Peggy in a family that was unusually egalitarian for the time. Her mother and father never insisted on maintaining clear roles for home and work but, as Peggy later recalled, instead "worked together in whatever they were doing." She and Stephen aspired to do the same.[12]

The same year that Penrose married, he graduated from Columbia with a PhD in philosophy. His dissertation, "The Reputation and Influence of Francis Bacon in the Seventeenth Century," analyzed Bacon's religious, philosophical, and scientific ideas and how European thinkers perceived them in the 1600s. He then took a teaching job at Whitman. Back in the Pacific Northwest, Penrose became the moderator of the Eastern Washington–Northern Idaho Association of Congregational Churches, an important position for a layman within the denomination. He helped organize and coordinate projects to bolster struggling churches and oversaw the denomination's annual summer camps. Although he never pastored a congregation, his work always focused on supporting and building the Christian church. He also welcomed a new member into the family. Peggy gave birth to a daughter, Dale, in 1937.

The elder Stephen Penrose had big plans for keeping his son, daughter-in-law, and new grandchild nearby. He and Stephen Jr. schemed to position the latter to take over the presidency of Whitman College when Stephen Sr. retired. But when the position opened up, the board of trustees went another direction. Disappointed and a bit discouraged, Penrose inquired about returning to the American University in Beirut. The Middle East continued to fascinate him, and especially AUB. But with his family to think about, he took a job instead with the Near East College Association, the umbrella agency based in New York that oversaw a half dozen missionary schools, including AUB. He also tried out his skills as a writer. In 1941 he published *That They May Have Life*, an excellent history of the American University in Beirut, the school where he had taught and that William Eddy's family had helped build. Influential Protestant leader Henry Sloane Coffin called it "one of the best pieces of missionary literature of modern times." The book received a positive review in the *Christian Science Monitor*, inspiring Penrose to joke that he might become a Christian Scientist.[13]

A few years into his tenure at the NECA, Penrose again started looking for a new job. He still hoped to be a university president—if not at Whitman, then somewhere else. Then the war interrupted his plans. When Penrose told his wife, Peggy, that he had taken a new job with a secretive government agency and that they were moving to Washington, DC, she asked what he was going to be doing. "Do you really want to know?" he queried. She decided that she did not: "I don't want to know and I never want to know, don't tell me." The necessary secrecy would place a tremendous burden on his marriage and family, but Penrose believed the sacrifice was necessary. He was now a covert operative, working for the Office of Strategic Services, leading a double life. Over the course of the war, he would shift from strategically sending missionaries into carefully selected parts of the world to dropping spies and hired hit men to their deaths in enemy territory.[14]

PART II

GOING TO WAR
(1941–1943)

SIX

"Converted to Our Service"

JUST A LITTLE MORE THAN A MONTH INTO THE WAR, PRESIDENT FRANKLIN Delano Roosevelt received a thank-you note from the leader of the Foreign Missions Conference of North America. So did William Donovan. The president had allocated $36,000 from a government emergency fund to support one of the ecumenical religious organization's projects. The purpose of the money was to support the conference's College of Chinese Studies, which had relocated from the Far East to the University of California at Berkeley. In the days immediately after Pearl Harbor, Wild Bill had badgered the president for the money. Donovan clearly had a plan, and he needed the president's cash to implement it.[1]

Roosevelt's investment in the college soon paid off. Like many other institutions, the College of Chinese Studies shifted its operations toward supporting the war effort. It provided expert training for government operatives and soldiers preparing to go to China.

But that was not the real reason that Donovan wanted to channel money to the missionary organization. A few months into the war, OSS officer Stephen B. L. Penrose Jr. received a list from the Foreign Missions Conference with the names of more than a dozen missionaries who were ready to return to the field. To dispatch these men and women around the globe, church leaders wanted the OSS's help securing visas and transportation. In return for OSS support, the missionaries agreed to serve two masters—their churches and Donovan. When Roosevelt sent money to the foreign missions group, he was buying more than the goodwill of

God. He was gaining access to a new and untapped source of covert intelligence, men and women who would be central to plans Penrose was developing for the OSS. FDR's money did more than help American missionaries continue their work; it also subsidized the rise of a new global covert operations network.[2]

Like John Birch, William Eddy, and Stewart Herman, Penrose eventually made it to the field, but not before helping Allen Dulles get the OSS running smoothly in Washington. During the first year of American participation in the war, he had to plan "from scratch" intelligence coverage of the Middle East. Penrose located, trained, and recruited agents; developed their covers; and equipped them for the various foreign operations that he was devising. He also identified potential bases for action, established methods of communicating with field agents, and drew up and oversaw budgets. And he did a lot of paperwork, documenting the office's work and responding to queries from the Research and Analysis Branch.[3]

Penrose sent a memo to Dulles in May 1942 laying out an ambitious and original two-part strategy for expanding the reach and influence of the OSS. First, Penrose wanted the OSS to hire missionaries to work as operatives. And second, he believed that the OSS should create fake missionary covers under which to dispatch operatives. In other words, he wanted both real missionaries working for the OSS and OSS operatives in the field to pose as missionaries.[4]

Not all spies thought using missionaries was a good idea. Carleton Coon, who worked closely with Eddy, wrote about the strengths and weaknesses of various "covers" in North Africa and the Middle East. He noted that using a business operation as a cover created problems if the agent became embroiled in too much actual business. "Archaeologist" had become an awful cover because it had been so routinely used, especially in the previous world war. "To be an archeologist is silly," Coon insisted, "even if the agent is really a well known professional archeologist in peace time." Then he came to the agents of God. "The only other cover I can think of in these countries would be that of a missionary, but this seems impossible." He doubted that any mission boards would allow their people to become intelligence agents. And if they did, he feared that their cover would be blown. "Missionaries are a special breed and they could smell imposters a hundred miles away." Penrose proved Coon wrong on every front. He oversaw the work of an excellent archaeologist turned secret agent, Rabbi Nelson Glueck, and he implemented a missionary-spy plan around the Middle East.[5]

Penrose was not the only person thinking about OSS-missionary partnerships. Multiple people inside and outside the OSS pitched ideas for new collaborations. Hugh Wilson, the career diplomat who had briefly served as ambassador to Germany where he worked with Stewart Herman, asked Dulles if they might locate missionaries "still residing in remote places . . . who might be helpful to us." He hoped that Allen could ask his brother, John Foster Dulles, an influential Presbyterian laymen and leading ecumenist, how to access information on Christian workers in foreign fields. Missionaries, Allen Dulles realized, could serve as excellent OSS agents.[6]

Developing a clandestine army of missionaries turned spies became one of Penrose's most important early jobs with the OSS. Through his work at the Near East College Association and with his position on the American Board of Commissioners for Foreign Missions, Penrose knew many of the leaders of the nation's largest missionary agencies. He recommended to Dulles, a Presbyterian, that they approach the Presbyterian Board of Foreign Missions, one of the largest and most respected missionary agencies in the world, to see if the board would allow the OSS to send out operatives under its auspices. Perhaps, he suggested, they could convince the Presbyterians to replicate the "laymen's inquiry" that had investigated missionary conditions a decade earlier. This time, however, instead of sending mission executives around the world, the inquiry would simply serve as a front for OSS operatives to travel from mission station to mission station.[7]

Although the OSS never launched the new laymen's inquiry, the agency did partner with the Presbyterians. Shortly after Penrose began his new job, J. L. Dodds, the secretary for the Presbyterian Board of Foreign Missions, approached Allen Dulles about getting three missionaries back into the field. Sensing an opportunity, Penrose reached out to Dodds. The Presbyterian executive knew Penrose from the latter's work with the NECA, and he also knew that Penrose was working for the new, secretive government agency, but he had little idea what his work entailed. Nevertheless, Dodds hoped that Penrose and Dulles could help get Presbyterian missionaries who had returned to the United States, either on furlough or fleeing war zones, back to work. "There will be no difficulty at all from this end," Penrose promised Dodds, "in giving you help towards returning certain of your men to the field."[8]

Penrose's aid came with strings attached. When Penrose met with Dodds, he brought a list of Presbyterian missionaries he wanted help evaluating. Penrose was open with Dodds about his plans. Who, he asked Dodds, could do the kinds of work the OSS needed? Who had the moxie and the discretion? Who had the right skills? Perhaps most important, who might be willing to serve two masters? Penrose also quizzed the church leader about the various Presbyterian schools located in the Middle East. Would the schools have native employees on site who might work with the OSS? Anybody worth recruiting?

Dodds was happy to help. He confirmed that some of the missionaries on Penrose's list could easily toggle between serving God and serving Wild Bill. Others, he feared, would view espionage as compromising their religious calling. William Miller, for example, a Tehran-based "enthusiastic" missionary, was "such a keen evangelist," Dodds explained, "that he sometimes gets in difficulties with the authorities." Singularly focused on making converts, Miller had neither the discretion, the skills, nor the poise to serve in the OSS. Penrose needed religious workers who understood that the world was a fallen place and that compromises were sometimes required. He needed Niebuhrians, even if they didn't recognize themselves as such. Purists like Miller, focused assiduously on their religious calling, could never envision engaging in the kind of duplicity that working for the OSS required.[9]

Most if not all of the missionaries Penrose and Dodds discussed for the Middle East were men. Elsewhere, such as in West Africa, OSS operatives recruited some women missionaries for intelligence fieldwork. An OSS leader described Frances Jolly and Mildred Black, for example, as "agents" working under the "cover" of missionary. The two women were missionaries who were moonlighting for the OSS. Black had traveled to Liberia in 1938, where she taught local children at a mission school, developed a written form of a local tribal language, and worked in the local medical clinic. When she wrote her memoirs covering her thirty-seven years in Africa, she said nothing about her wartime activities with the OSS and almost nothing about the war at all. For those missionaries who were willing to serve two masters, the compromises and deception involved were not something most felt willing to share.[10]

Jolly and Black were important because OSS leaders believed that the Germans had possibly established a network of locals and foreigners in West Africa to engage in subversive activities, to help with Axis communications, and to assist the German submarine fleet operating off the coast. To track German activities in 1942, the OSS employed multiple agents who, according to an internal OSS report, "have all been carefully selected and possess exactly the qualifications necessary to accomplish this task." They included two people who served in mission hospitals and a third missionary who ran schools in the region (this may have been Mildred Black). The missionary agents got results. One of the agents, the report continued, "recently uncovered the fact that an obscure native Liberian preacher working among the Kru tribe is in the pay of the Germans." The OSS also partnered with the Assemblies of God, an American evangelical denomination. Assemblies leaders allowed OSS operatives to use their mission facilities, which included more than a dozen houses scattered throughout West Africa, for intelligence work.[11]

As Dodds and Penrose began to identify possible operatives for the Middle East, Penrose told an OSS colleague that the project was extremely sensitive. Most of the members of the missionary boards did not know that a small number of their colleagues were partnering with the intelligence agency. "Our dealings with the Presbyterian Board have been limited to two men," Penrose acknowledged, "because it is quite certain that very great objection might be raised by other Presbyterians if they knew of the cooperation between the Board and ourselves." This would remain true for the duration. Only a handful of people among the many denominations that worked with the OSS knew about these government-missionary collaborations. The OSS needed to protect its clandestine agents, and few people were comfortable with the idea of using missionaries as spies, which is why their stories remained hidden for so long. When church leaders and missionary boards sent men and women out to the field, they expected them to be solely focused on expanding the kingdom of God. It would have surprised many of them, and probably troubled them as well, to know that their godly evangelists were also

With a background as a missionary executive and member of the American Board of Commissioners for Foreign Missions, Stephen Penrose brought a unique knowledge and skill set to the OSS. It did not take him long to begin recruiting missionaries for OSS fieldwork.
Courtesy of the American University of Beirut.

acting as wartime intelligence operatives on behalf of the United States and its allies. Many would have perceived an inherent conflict between serving the kingdom of God and serving the kingdom of man.[12]

Although Penrose spent most of his time in the early months of the war identifying potential missionary operatives, he did not give up on the idea of sending out OSS men under the cover of a missionary agency. Medical missions provided one such opportunity. Dodds desperately needed doctors for the Presbyterian hospitals in the Middle East, which had lost staff since the onset of war. Hospitals, like missionary-founded American universities, grew out of the Presbyterians' efforts to spread their religion around the world by living the Christian faith rather than by directly proselytizing. If Penrose could rustle up OSS agents with medical training, "who are willing to organize or operate mission hospitals for the Presbyterians," he explained to a fellow operative, "the Board will be exceedingly grateful and will be glad to take them under Presbyterian auspices." They need not be missionaries or even Presbyterians, he decided, though they should at least be Christians. The effort was a success, and Penrose was able to place a few doctors turned missionaries turned spies in key posts in the Middle East.[13]

*

Penrose also worked with F. M. Potter from the Board of Foreign Missions of the Reformed Church in America. Potter, like Dodds, had approached Penrose in June 1942 for help in dispatching missionaries abroad. "I hope," Penrose wrote Potter after their first meeting, "it may be possible for us to be of assistance to you" in getting evangelists back to their posts. "I feel sure that we can give you assistance and trust that you will not hesitate to get in touch with us if circumstances seem to warrant."[14]

It didn't take long for Potter to think that circumstances warranted a request for assistance. He wrote Penrose back right away, asking if he could help the missionary board deliver two large shipments of supplies to its hospital on the Persian Gulf. Penrose thought this was possible and then mentioned "confidentially" that the army needed a good map of Kuwait. Perhaps Potter's missionaries could help? "This is a peculiar form of mutual back-scratching in which Government offices are apt to indulge," he acknowledged. Potter immediately sent a map recommended by one of his missionaries. A week later, the War Department delivered the missionary agency's boxes to the Gulf. Penrose had executed the quid pro quo perfectly.[15]

Penrose propositioned the American Board of Commissioners for Foreign Missions as well, an organization that he had long supported. He promised Fred Goodsell, the executive vice president of the heralded missionary agency, that he had a plan for getting missionaries back to their posts. When Goodsell took the bait, Penrose reeled him in. So long as "a few of your field staff members can prove useful to the Government," Penrose promised, "it will not be difficult to arrange for them and others to be sent out."[16]

Penrose believed that OSS-missionary partnerships required discretion. As he made final arrangements with Goodsell regarding a missionary named Henry H. Riggs, he warned him to keep the OSS's relationship with the missionaries secret. "I know that you understand our desire to be left entirely out of any explanations regarding the departure of Mr. Riggs or any others. It would be unfortunate both for the individuals and for the American Board if any reference to our assistance were made in reports of their return to the field. I know that I can rely upon you to keep us anonymous." The OSS-ABCFM partnership was probably particularly uncomfortable for Penrose, since he was recruiting operatives from the very missionary board on which he served.[17]

Administering the OSS-missionary relationships required the naviga-tion of various obstacles. In one case, a missionary posted to West Africa resigned on the basis of "conscience" rather than work for the govern-ment's spy agency. A famous missionary who had spent decades in Iraq, John Van Ness, also refused to work for the OSS. To avoid having more of these kinds of problems, Penrose and missionary executives limited how much they revealed about their overall plans to the missionaries they were evaluating. Some, they knew, wanted to work with the OSS and would do so directly and explicitly. Others would likely have qualms about the deception involved in intelligence work. Penrose suggested they keep mis-sionaries who might express reservations somewhat in the dark about who they were serving and how they were helping. The missionary, Penrose decided in one case, "will not be a regular agent for O.S.S. but will coop-erate in supplying whatever information he is able to secure. He will not be on our payroll nor will he be informed of our field organization. His communications will be through the Consulate or possibly through our chief agent in Tehran of whose real activities he will know nothing." But most OSS missionaries knew exactly what they were doing and for whom they were working. Like Penrose, they believed in the cause.[18]

The OSS's missionary executive contacts had a few stipulations of their own. Dodds did not want his Presbyterian missionaries getting infor-mation "surreptitiously or by subterfuge," and he clarified that any infor-mation "of a confidential nature, secured by virtue of a person's religious position and work, would not be included" in OSS reports. A leader from the fundamentalist Christian and Missionary Alliance (CMA), another group that the OSS mined for missionary recruits, also expressed some res-ervations. He "strongly stated that none of the Mission's members would be available for any work to do with espionage or sabotage on the grounds that their work was solely of a missionary character." Nevertheless, this executive was eager to share any intelligence with the OSS he received from his people in the field in exchange for OSS travel support. Maintain-ing distinctions between these types of assistance, however, was easier said than done. In the end, the missionary executives probably sought to ease their own consciences by establishing some parameters around the work of their men and women in the field, no matter how impossible those pa-rameters may have been to maintain once the work began.[19]

Penrose and his missionary executive partners had the more obvious problem of keeping their cooperation covert once missionaries were recruited and preparing to go abroad. In the early months of the war, the government directed all available resources to the military. That a handful of missionaries could get priority travel authorization from the State Department and transportation aboard military ships or aircraft raised suspicions. Penrose had a quick answer to this problem. He suggested that the missionaries simply say as little as possible and credit their mission boards with finding a way. "The Board is great," he exclaimed, "praise ye the Board."[20]

Another problem had to do with how to pay the missionaries for their OSS work. Penrose noted that in dealing with the mission boards, "it will be necessary for our connection with men in their employ to remain unofficial and, if possible, secret." This required mission boards to sometimes take "anonymous" cash from the OSS. Missionary executives would essentially launder government money through their mission boards to their agents. In other cases, mission leaders suggested that the OSS simply give money to their missionary agents in the field directly, keeping administrators stateside ignorant about their missionaries' second careers.[21]

Penrose usually offered positive incentives to missionaries for collaborating with the OSS. But he sometimes used other forms of leverage. The army was pressuring a medical missionary who had returned to the United States to take a commission. When Penrose got wind of this through his Presbyterian contacts, he tried to snap up the missionary for the OSS instead.[22]

Once Penrose had secured the support of mission leaders and identified missionary operatives, he needed State Department help. Foggy Bottom's cooperation on visas, passports, and various other services necessary for getting missionaries into foreign territories proved indispensable. However, the State Department, like many other established government agencies, wanted to have as little to do with Donovan's upstart group as possible. Longtime diplomats viewed OSS men as naive troublemakers who rarely understood the art of diplomacy or the complexity of the United States' foreign relations.

To soften State Department leaders' resistance, Penrose emphasized the seemingly benevolent side of the OSS's work with American missionary organizations. He wanted to convince the State Department that "our hearts are in the right place." He assured State Department bureaucrats that they were helping out missionaries for the good of the world. He laid out the many ways that the American missionary presence in the Middle East had benefited the United States and the various countries in which Americans were working. Protestant-founded institutions like the American University in Beirut (where Penrose had worked), Robert College in Turkey (which would later invite Penrose to serve as its president), and the American hospital in Beirut all enhanced the image of the United States in this increasingly strategic part of the world. Penrose also singled out three missionary groups—the Presbyterian Board, the ABCFM, and the Dutch Reformed Board—that had "gained the favor of the people they attempt to serve, both as regards the activities themselves and the country of their ultimate origin."[23]

It was certainly no coincidence that Penrose was working with all three agencies to enlist their missionaries at the time. "It would be a strategic psychological blunder on the part of the United States," he lectured his colleagues at State, to allow the humanitarian work of these mission organizations to wane during the war. And this was sure to happen unless government agencies worked to ensure that "staff replacements now ready to serve can reach their posts." In other words, the State Department needed to understand that despite the war crisis, it was essential that missionaries receive all the support they could get from the government. The missionaries had to get back to work, Penrose insisted, for the good of the country and for the strengthening of US foreign relations.[24]

Yet Penrose was telling the State Department only part of the story. He hinted just once at the real purpose behind the OSS's lobbying efforts. Missionaries, he explained, were valuable to the government because they were "familiar with the country, the people, the languages" and had proved to be very self-reliant. Furthermore, they understood and accepted the risk that their work entailed. Penrose was describing not just good religious workers to the State Department, but ideal agents as well. "I have gently insinuated the suggestion of intelligence work," he confided to Dulles, "putting it in as innocuous a form as possible." The State Department promised to cooperate with Penrose, as did the War Department.[25]

While working on recruitment, Penrose carefully obscured the number of deals the OSS cut with missionary agencies and the total number of missionary spies serving in World War II. "For various reasons," Penrose disclosed in one note to a missionary executive, "it is not possible for me to discuss the matter" of OSS-missionary partnerships "in a letter." In addition, most of the missionary agencies seem to have wiped their records clean of any cooperation with the OSS. Dodds's correspondence with Penrose is missing from his papers at the Presbyterian Historical Society, nor does the Christian and Missionary Alliance hold any records of its mission board's work with the OSS. The whole story may never be known. There seem to have been other OSS leaders recruiting missionaries. We know for certain that Penrose passed on the names of missionaries seeking to return to regions outside of his supervision to other OSS station chiefs, and the records from many stations identify various missionaries on the OSS payroll.[26]

Penrose had managed to build a small army of Protestant spies, but what of the Catholics? Donovan wanted to establish an intelligence network within the worldwide Roman Catholic Church too, and for reasons beyond his own Catholic faith. The Catholic Church was the largest, most powerful, and most diffuse religious institution in the world. It was certainly going to play an important role in the war, but to what end remained a mystery to President Roosevelt and many of the OSS's leaders. Donovan's faith in the church, however, never wavered. Wild Bill was ready to use his power and influence to ensure that his church landed on the right side of the war. William Eddy summarized the stakes involved. "The Vatican may be a small temporal city," the missionary admitted, "but the Pope rules an empire unequalled in the world today. His dynasty is older than any other extant, he rules more subjects, and has more power than any living king. Most remarkable of all is the fact that their allegiance is freely given."[27]

While Penrose was recruiting Protestant missionaries, OSS operative Arthur Goldberg suggested to Allen Dulles that the agency develop a comprehensive strategy for building a Catholic intelligence network. An invaluable contributor to the nascent spy agency, Goldberg would later serve on the United States Supreme Court and as President Lyndon Johnson's ambassador to the United Nations. He was also one of the OSS's few Jews. He brought to the OSS a very different sensitivity to what was happening to the Jews of Europe, and in contrast to his Republican counterparts, he had a far more liberal, pro–New Deal political perspective. Like Donovan, Dulles, and Penrose, he recognized that religion could serve as a valuable tool in an intelligence war.[28]

Before Pope Pius XII's ascension to the papacy in 1939, he had criticized the Nazi regime and especially its crackdown on the independence of the church. As pontiff, however, he initially refused to issue any public criticism of aggressor nations. But as the war continued, he began condemning Nazi persecution of Christians and Jews. Donovan was optimistic, telling the president that the pope was "very anxious, unofficially, to help in every way possible." Although the church had to remain officially neutral, Donovan believed that the pope recognized that its "position must be beside us."[29]

The pope's commitment to finding a peaceful resolution to the war meant that diplomats from the warring powers, Axis and Allied, were always around. Donovan wanted, needed, to know what was happening in Vatican City, where these diplomats worshipped, schmoozed, and strategized. Donovan also wanted access to the pope's worldwide network of Catholic activists. But he knew penetrating the Catholic Church would be difficult. The church's international character and extensive bureaucratic hierarchies made recruiting rogue religious activists challenging—until an ideal, well-connected source fell into the spymaster's lap.

Just after the United States declared war, Father Felix Morlion walked into Donovan's Washington, DC, office. For Donovan, it probably felt like Christmas morning. A Belgian Dominican, journalist, and activist, Morlion had connections with the Catholic underground all over Europe, and he was willing to share what his sources knew with American leaders. He was living at the time in the Dominican House of Studies, an impressive Catholic compound near the Capitol.

In the early 1930s Morlion had established the Committee for Information Pro Deo (CIP) in Brussels, and by the start of the war the organization had offices throughout Europe. He believed that the Catholic Church needed to make better use of media to revive democracy and Christianity in Europe. He published numerous stories about Nazi atrocities as well as Hitler's crackdown on the church in Germany in more than 1,750 newspapers in thirty countries. As Nazi agents went on the hunt for CIP leaders, Morlion fled first to Lisbon, then to South America, and then in October 1941 to the United States. One of his partners was not so lucky—he ended up dying in a German labor camp.[30]

Morlion's Pro Deo network provided OSS leaders with their best early opportunity to tap into the network of European Catholics resisting Hitler. The priest's journalist/activist partners made excellent covert intelligence agents, and they sent Morlion a steady flow of information on resistance movements, popular sentiments, and conditions on the ground. He then passed the relevant material on to the OSS. But the priest needed something in return. The Belgian government in exile, based in London, had called Morlion up for active duty, and the priest was supposed to return to join his fellow countrymen in 1942. If he did, the CIP would fold. Then Dulles intervened, asking the Belgians to allow the priest to remain with the OSS in the United States. "It would be difficult to replace him," Dulles told the Belgian ambassador, "as his background and experience in this field is almost impossible to duplicate." The information and reports that Morlion provided to the agency, Dulles continued, were "necessary to the war effort." The Belgians agreed. They released the priest to the OSS for the duration. Morlion, still a man of the cloth, was now an OSS man, too.[31]

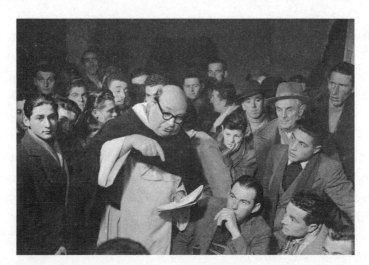

Father Felix Morlion, a Dominican priest from Belgium and master propogandist, could always hold an audience's attention. He helped the OSS launch a Catholic intelligence network throughout Europe before heading to Rome to be the OSS's eyes and ears in the Vatican. *Sueddeutsche Zeitung Photo / Alamy Stock Photo.*

Morlion's presence in the United States caught the attention of J. Edgar Hoover. The FBI had been keeping tabs on the Dominican since he entered the country. Hoover was not sure he could trust the tall and "semi-corpulent" priest. Nevertheless, the G-men couldn't dig up "anything derogatory" on the Flemish cleric, despite their best efforts. The Office of Naval Intelligence was also investigating Morlion and sharing the results with the FBI. Their investigation revealed that Morlion had been acting as a "propogandist" on behalf of the United States and other democratic nations in his travels abroad. It's not clear from Morlion's FBI file if Hoover realized that Morlion was secretly working for the OSS (parts of Morlion's FBI file are still redacted and may relate to his OSS activities).[32]

Morlion moved to New York, where he essentially ran his own intelligence agency through his Catholic networks. He recruited spies, solicited information, and issued propaganda to be distributed in Europe. He also secretly shared what he learned with the OSS, but never revealed to his contacts scattered around Europe that he was on the American government's payroll. Nor did he inform his Dominican superiors about his extracurricular activities, though they sometimes feared he was up to no good. But Morlion knew he was working for God, not the Dominican fathers. And perhaps working for Wild Bill was part of working for God too.[33]

One of Morlion's most prolific sources was J. C. Maier-Hultschin, code-named Henry Judah. OSS analysts felt enthusiastic about this source. Judah had run one of the strongest anti-Nazi German-language newspapers in eastern Europe, an affiliate of Morlion's CIP. He had fled the Nazi invasion of Poland and made it to London, where he stayed in touch with central and eastern European dissidents. He claimed to have no interest in political propaganda, but, according to OSS officers, he wanted to serve "purely religious aims." OSS leaders saw him as an ideal source nevertheless because of what they identified as "the importance of the religious effort in the anti-Nazi struggle."[34]

The OSS's partnerships with missionaries and priests was one of the agency's most closely guarded secrets. Nobody wanted to publicly acknowledge that the government was turning religious activists into covert agents. Agency leaders believed that the humanitarian work performed by missionaries abroad was good for the nation during the war and that it would be especially important when the hostilities ceased. They did not want to blow the cover of their missionary spies, nor did they want to taint the work of the United States' international missionary organizations.

As operatives successfully brought religious activists into the OSS, the work of Allen Dulles, Stephen Penrose, and Felix Morlion became one of the agency's burgeoning success stories. One operative, without any sense of irony, reported to Donovan that two American missionaries had been "converted to our service and sent back" into the field. Whose gospel they were preaching was never entirely clear. Wild Bill even bragged to Roosevelt about the positive results his agency was getting from its missionaries. For Penrose, this was just the beginning, not the end, of his work tying the OSS to all things religious.[35]

SEVEN

"Spies and Lies in Tangier"

DURING THE FIRST YEAR OF US INVOLVEMENT IN THE WAR, THE ALLIES remained on the defensive. In Europe the British hoped to survive long enough for the Americans to get their military battle-ready and their factories regeared toward making war matériel. In Asia and the Pacific, the Japanese continued conquering more territory. The United States needed a victory, a way to begin to stem the tide. Donovan needed something as well. The military brass and much of Washington had greeted the creation of the OSS with skepticism, and sometimes even hostility. Wild Bill needed to demonstrate that his spy agency was capable of more than developing fanciful weapons and irritating DC police by running simulated commando training missions around the capital. With Churchill and Roosevelt focused on North Africa and the Mediterranean, Donovan sensed an opportunity to demonstrate the OSS's potential. But his success depended primarily on the work of one of his best new recruits, former missionary William Eddy.

Colonel Eddy arrived in Tangier in late January 1942, his North African base of operations. Tangier is a bustling city located on Morocco's Atlantic coast, just west of the Strait of Gibraltar. During the 1940s, the city was part of an international zone that France, Spain, and Great Britain oversaw together, with Spain running its political administration. Its inhabitants included Africans, Arabs, French, and expats from all over Europe and even North America. The rest of Morocco was controlled by

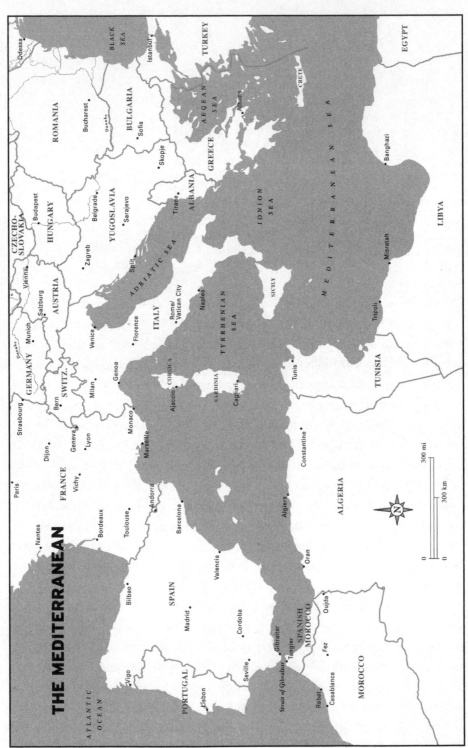

The MEDITERRANEAN. From William Eddy's base in Tangier, he helped secure North Africa and then the entire Mediterranean for the Allies.

the ostensibly neutral Vichy French government, and Spain and France had carved much of the surrounding region into colonies.

In Tangier Eddy encountered a world that looked remarkably like the one depicted a few months after his arrival in the hit film *Casablanca*. Humphrey Bogart's Rick Blaine would have fit right in on Tangier's streets and in the cafés teeming with spies, traitors, and political intrigue. Eddy loved the "white washed mosques and Moorish residences," and he compared the city to "a cute, compact, musical comedy set." He believed that most of the people who settled there had run away from something. He described Tangier as an "escape hatch from prison, banking laws, justice, persecution, morality." Its inhabitants were as "strange" a "crowd as ever gathered on an opera stage." He hoped to serve as their director, ushering men and women on and off the platform and in and out of a series of roles to suit his purposes.[1]

Eddy was feeling confident after his first full day on the ground in Morocco. "In spite of local colloquialisms and differences in pronunciation," he wrote his wife, Mary, "I have no trouble with my Arabic." He came to love the region and especially Casablanca. "Some day," he promised his family, "we must all come here for a trip when people can again travel for pleasure and not for murder."[2]

To maintain his attaché cover, Eddy had an office at the American Legation, a striking building of white adobe walls, curving archways, mosaic floors, redbrick stairways, fine woodworking, and a courtyard fountain. The sultan of Morocco had given the property to the United States in 1821, making it the oldest US diplomatic post in the world. Eddy described it as beautiful and, drawing on orientalist stereotypes, speculated that "dancing girls" had probably done the "Harem rhumba" there in earlier times. The legation was near the old city and just blocks away from the Grand Socco, a market where tourists, locals, and spies alike could find everything from vegetables to prostitutes to snake charmers. From the roof of the legation, Eddy could see much of the city, and on clear days Gibraltar and Spain as well.[3]

The OSS operative had other spaces for orchestrating his clandestine work. Eddy rented rooms in the Mitzah Hotel in the old town in Tangier where he sometimes stayed when he needed to remain in the city overnight. But he mostly lived and worked in a villa outside of town that overlooked the sea. "The location is so remote," he reported home, "that we can lose any watchers who try to follow us, and the spot will also be guarded."[4]

Axis agents noted Eddy's arrival in Tangier, and they immediately started tracking his movements. "I know the boys who usually do the following," he reported to his family, "and I have some fun with them every now and then." When he stayed at the Mitzah, German spies regularly posted agents in the room next to his. Sometimes he would snag a key from a chambermaid and sneak in to surprise them. The Nazis, in turn, did what they could to expose and embarrass the American. At one point they mocked the attaché in a newspaper article, claiming that his "big" dinners and "sumptuous champagne parties" were actually covert meetings. They also called him "fat"—perhaps he had hosted too many such parties. Eddy enjoyed toying with his enemies and wrote cavalierly about it to family members, probably in an effort to keep them from worrying. "The greatest heat here now," he wrote in a tantalizing note to his son Bill, "is the rage of the Germans who had the safe in their consulate cracked and robbed of its secret papers a few days ago. It was a beautiful job well done; and some day I'll tell you by whom." Eddy never told them that he was also dodging attempted car bombings.[5]

American political and military leaders had not yet established a complete strategy for the region, but Eddy knew what Donovan wanted from him. First, he needed to set up a secret radio network to keep Britain's Royal Air Force informed of enemy movements. Second, he needed to build relationships with various local groups in order to persuade them to support the Allies should the war come in earnest to this part of North Africa. And third, OSS leaders wanted him to consider orchestrating coups against the less sympathetic governments in the region, such as in Tunisia. Foreshadowing practices later employed by the CIA, an OSS leader recommended that Eddy use "corruption and bribery" to help bring pro-American leaders to power. He asked Eddy to consider "supplying the sinews of war for such a purpose." The OSS expected a lot of the missionary turned spy.[6]

Eddy got the radio network for communications with the RAF working relatively quickly. He and his small team began communicating with the British with almost immediate results. In a letter to his daughter Marycita, Eddy reported that he had transmitted a message to the RAF "about the departure for Berlin of a plane carrying nine German officers. The plane did not reach its destination." Such actions did not initially bother him—in fact, he told his daughter how pleased he was with his work. "We cannot win the war by typewriters," he wrote, "but we can win it by killing Germans and Japs." Having seen extensive action in World War I, Eddy understood that war meant death—either his or his enemies'. He did not reflect until after the war on what this pivot from laboring to build the kingdom of God to killing others meant for his life and his religious work.[7]

Eddy's second task, recruiting a pro-Allied clandestine army, was much more difficult and time-consuming. For this job, he had an excellent partner, Carleton Coon, a successful Harvard anthropologist turned OSS spook. "It is probably the secret ambition of every boy," Coon confessed, "to travel in strange mountains, stir up tribes, and destroy the enemy by secret and unorthodox means." As boys become men, such juvenile fantasies usually fade. But not for Coon; they became his reality. He and Eddy developed a close relationship, forged in the embers of war. Coon called the missionary "one of the greatest men I have ever met" and described their friendship as "one of the happiest associations of my life." Eddy described Coon to his family as a man "with whom I have had the most intimate collaboration for the past twelve months." Coon, he continued, was not what people might think. "For a Harvard prof . . . he is the most unacademic, profane, and idiomatic American you ever saw. Very refreshing." He later called Coon a "fearless organizer of homicidal guerrillas." Among Coon's many contributions to the war was his mastering the ability to make effective dung bombs, "explosive turds" that looked like mule droppings commonly found in the area.[8]

By the time Eddy arrived in Tangier, the OSS already had agents on the ground in Africa collecting intelligence. They included businessmen, employees of Pan American Airlines, and also missionaries. The work of the fundamentalist group the Christian and Missionary Alliance was typical. Under what an OSS operative referred to as "missionary cover,"

CMA evangelists provided "several outstanding pieces of intelligence work." They exposed "an Axis communications system between Liberia and the Ivory Coast" and tabulated for the OSS "unfriendly individuals and groups from Dakar to Nigeria."[9]

Eddy and Coon's job was to expand the existing network. One of their targets was Reverend Isaac Dunbar, who had been laboring to convert Jews in Tunis before Eddy recruited him for the OSS. The minister had already developed his own amateur intelligence network among locals, and he shared what he learned with Eddy and helped the agency identify and enlist members of the French resistance. Another OSS recruit was "Father Levy," whose real name was O'Shannahan. He served as a member of the Catholic order "White Fathers" (the Society of the Missionaries of Africa). Eddy put him to work collecting information and spying on enemy agents. Unfortunately, the priest got around in more ways than one. "So unclerical was his behavior," Coon recorded in a top-secret history of the unit, that the locals "soon decided he was a phony despite his clerical garments and his long black bathing suit. Strangely enough, he was a genuine White Father, but since no one would believe it . . . he had to go." Local residents did not believe that a real priest could be having so much sex.[10]

Eddy also put an African American expatriate named Henry Perkins to work for him. Perkins ran a restaurant on the beach called Uncle Tom's Cabin. "Uncle Tom," Coon reported, "explained to me that it was a great advantage for him to be black; people of all nationalities confided in him, and no one considered him an American, despite his prominent display of the flag on flagpole and lapel." The OSS would have been wise to employ more African Americans like Perkins, but during World War II the military was still segregated and few of the elite men running the OSS considered black Americans their equals. African Americans could not serve in the marines at the start of the war, and they received only menial jobs in the navy. Racism was just as prominent in the OSS as in many other branches of the US government.[11]

A top priority for Eddy was recruiting local Frenchmen and -women. Here he had to tread especially carefully. The Nazis had invaded France in 1940, and the French, facing annihilation, surrendered. Per the terms of the armistice, they set up a new government located in Vichy. Despite leaders' claim of neutrality, they routinely collaborated with the Nazis. Roosevelt wanted to convince the Vichy government to break from Hitler, so the United States had not yet cut off relations with Vichy. Furthermore, Vichy controlled the French navy, and the Americans did not want Hitler to seize it. The British, meanwhile, supported Charles de Gaulle's Free French movement, headquartered in London. Eddy's primary contact among the Free French was Henry Bourgoin, whom Coon described as "an incredible bouncing ball of French vitality. He is a militant French Protestant." The Frenchman had "very strict ideas about drinking and smoking," but was "interested chiefly in murder." Despite Bourgoin's penchant for killing, Coon called him "one of the most pleasant, colorful and amusing operatives whom we have recruited overseas."[12]

Agents like Bourgoin, Perkins, and Dunbar were not the only kind of people Eddy and Coon recruited. For Eddy to do his job effectively, he had to spend substantial time with exactly the opposite sorts of people he preferred in normal life. "The secret service," he lamented, "makes strange bedfellows. One must at times consort with scoundrels, and ostracize one's own ilk." Rather than socialize with what he called "a good family man," such as the German vice counsel and his "charming" wife, Eddy had to eat and drink with "wife-beaters and perverts."[13]

He also lamented how far some of the locals would go for money. "The Moors, the depressed have-nots of Tangier," he fretted, "would sell anything to anybody. When you stepped out of the hotel any morning, a tout would whisper, 'You want nice, girl, very cheap, I bring my sister?'" Eddy had no interest in the women. He would, however, "rent his brother as an informer." He did not think he had any choice. "The OSS was in a death struggle with the Gestapo," and the OSS—and Eddy as an operative of the OSS—"had no conscience." These were unusual days, he later reflected. "It is permitted to walk with the devil," he told himself, "until you have crossed the bridge." Eddy was doing on a small scale what Roosevelt was doing on a large scale with Stalin, making questionable alliances for the sake of defeating the Germans. If Donovan wanted Eddy to lay a solid foundation for future action, he had to recruit not just businessmen and missionaries, but also knaves.[14]

There were limits, however, to how much Eddy could stomach. He despised the psychopathic Toby Ellis, the head of the British Secret Intelligence Service in Tangier. "His sunken eyes," Eddy recalled, "receding, balding brow, corpselike cheeks and protruding gold tooth, bared when he grinned, made up the skull of Mephistopheles resurrected from the grave.

He was repulsive, yet he must have been useful." When Eddy later learned that Ellis had died, he noted that the British spy, if in hell, would not suffer since he would be among friends.[15]

If Coon had had his way, Ellis would have joined his friends in hell sooner. Coon claimed that Ellis needed two "golden rings" in his nostrils to keep his "large and fleshy nose" in shape and his airway open. "We often thought an excellent . . . operation would be to remove these rings in his sleep, thus suffocating Dr. Ellis in the fleshly collapse." Throughout the region the natives, Coon noted, "hate Dr. Ellis and refer to him as that English Jew, which I believe is ethnically inaccurate and libel to the Jews as a people." Coon saw Ellis as a threat to the joint US-British partnership. The Secret Intelligence Service agent was "a dangerous enemy and a serious impediment to our mission," he wrote. "The thought occurred to us several times that he would have to be destroyed, but Colonel Eddy, perhaps in the long run wisely, forbade this."[16]

Recruiting excellent field agents was a challenge for any OSS officer; ensuring that their team was not infiltrated by an enemy agent was another. Eddy constantly had to guard against this. One operative, Sidney Bartlett, attached to the American legation, established a relationship with a woman Coon described as a "luscious and untidy blond" named Nikki. She was actually a German spy. Bartlett had a photographic memory and would recite to Nikki "verbatim on the pillow" some of the information he read in incoming cables, hoping to impress her. The information then reappeared in messages sent from the German headquarters at Casablanca, which the OSS intercepted. Apparently, Nikki also had a photographic memory. Eddy sent Bartlett home.[17]

Yet another minor character in Eddy's operation was a Sergeant Force. The sergeant, Coon recalled, "lolled around the military attaché's office," smoking and mostly screwing up whatever minor jobs he was assigned. That did not stop him from bragging within earshot of enemy agents at the local bars that he was a secret operative. As a result, they identified the American as a prime source to exploit. The Spaniards and Hungarians spent a lot of cash hiring various women "to consort with him" and to ply him for information. While the Axis got little useful intelligence from Force, the sergeant enjoyed the attention. He did not know that his enemies had paid for it. "He formed a high opinion of his ability with women," Coon noted, "and served as a useful decoy for the rest of us." He was not smart enough for the OSS to ever trust with any real intelligence or to realize how he was being used by both his allies and his enemies.[18]

The final group that Eddy hoped to ally with was Muslims. His expatriate informants and spies, Americans and Europeans, saints and sinners, could only do so much. The main reason Donovan had chosen Eddy for this job was to rally Muslims to the Allied cause. Donovan thought the missionary's language skills, past experiences, and understanding of Islam made him the perfect operative for the job. Most Muslims in North Africa expressed little interest in risking their lives to join the Allies. If they were going to fight at all, they wanted independence from their Spanish and French colonizers. At the same time, the Americans could not afford to alienate the ostensibly neutral Spanish or the Vichy French. Eddy had to walk a diplomatic tightrope as he sought to get local tribal leaders on board with the Americans without promising them too much.

At a diplomatic party hosted by the Spanish, Eddy met the Khalifa, the man he identified as "the actual Sultan" of the province. They enjoyed a twenty-minute talk in Arabic. The sultan, Eddy observed, "was so obviously pleased with an American who talked Arabic easily that he kept me talking to the annoyance of some Spaniards who do not like to see us friendly with the Moorish leaders." Eddy believed that the Muslim "would probably hold the balance of power if there were ever any European strife in the Spanish Moroccan Zone." He did his best to ensure that the leader would line up with him and the Americans.[19]

OSS leaders instructed Eddy to assure the tribal groups that if they partnered with the Allies, the Americans would do what they could to support their aspirations for independence in return. Eddy knew this was not true, but he made the promises just the same. He told similar lies to Spanish communists who hoped that the United States would help them overthrow Franco. Eddy implied that the Americans would and that Roosevelt had all fascists in his sights. But he knew this was not true either. He was asking people to put their lives on the line for him and for the Allies on the basis of false promises.

Eddy convinced both French and Muslim leaders to partner with the Americans in exchange for US goods. They mostly needed what Eddy and his associates called "toys"—weapons. But Donovan was hesitant to arm non-Americans. Perhaps the OSS director and the State Department saw a bigger picture than Eddy did on the ground. Eddy might have been suffering from what Robert Murphy, FDR's envoy to French North Africa, called "localitis," a condition in which agents, operatives, and diplomats think that plans in their little part of the world are the most important things happening and cannot understand why Washington bureaucrats don't recognize their "earth-shaking importance." Donovan did not want to force a break with Vichy by arming Free French exiles, and he was probably very leery of arming anticolonial Muslim revolutionaries.[20]

Eddy was angry that the United States refused to provide as much matériel as he wanted. "They are taking all the risk," he told Donovan. "They will receive, distribute, and use the supplies" with "every step being taken with the threat of execution as traitors if they are uncovered. The least we can do is to help supply them on their own terms which are generous and gallant." Eddy pointed out to his boss that the weapons would go to good use no matter who invaded. If the Axis launched an attack, which he thought was imminent, the locals would wreak havoc on the invading force. And if the Allies stormed the region, his rebel groups would play a supporting role. "We need speed," he insisted. "Time is short."[21]

While Donovan continued to balk, Eddy refused to back down. In another memo to OSS headquarters, the colonel requested five hundred tommy guns, two thousand revolvers, two thousand rifles, ten thousand hand grenades, ten thousand spring coshes (a type of baton), five thousand commando knives, and five thousand fighting knives. He also wanted cash. He had just spent $50,000 to finance Arab and French resistance movements, and he wanted a half-million dollars more—huge sums in this era. Donovan forwarded Eddy's request directly to the president, asking Roosevelt for the money. Donovan intended to leave the use of the money completely to Eddy's discretion. There were few people Donovan trusted more. But the government denied the missionary son's proposal. Eddy felt disappointed. "You must not be discouraged," Wild Bill counseled. "If we are right it will work out right." But it did not. Eddy's allies did not get the weapons they hoped for or the independence they sought. Eddy had misled and used his allies, and he was not happy about it.[22]

*

Despite Eddy's busy schedule, he rarely missed church. God seemed to be as much a presence in his life during the war as ever, despite his nefarious deeds and double-dealing. Or perhaps because of it. But the Episcopalian was not too impressed with the local Anglican congregation. "The Church is a rather ugly little affair," he wrote, "the congregation usually twenty odd (very odd) coupon clipping ladies stranded here with the war." Nevertheless, Eddy believed in his work and saw it as part of his Christian duty. One Sunday service, he wrote, "gave me a marvelous lift—to feel that I should in my small and temporary deprivations be asked to do what He did on the Cross, be utterly willing to endure all for the sake of humanity." For Eddy, winning the war was not just about serving the Allies, but also about serving God, even if serving God meant martyrdom.[23]

Other services were less inspiring but sometimes more entertaining. Eddy attended a solemn High Mass in honor of the anniversary of the pope's inauguration. The German diplomatic envoys showed up at the last minute, but because the local church leaders did not like them, no one had saved them seats. Eddy and his colleagues watched in silent amusement as the German officers argued over seating arrangements with the Spanish consul. The local bishop's secretary, who had made the initial seating assignments, was conspicuously absent. The Germans ended up stomping out of the church and skipping the Mass. Eddy reported that although he did not like the "subordination of the Church to politics," he had nevertheless been "chuckling" "rather profanely" over the Germans' embarrassment. This was yet another example, he noted, of how the war was perverting his "normal standards." Having a good laugh at the expense of the Nazis was fun, no matter if it was a bit sacrilegious.[24]

Muslim holidays also mattered to Eddy and his work, and sometimes they offered a little amusement, too. Marking the start of the Muslim holy month of Ramadan, the Spanish fired a series of artillery shells after dark just outside of town. Meanwhile, Muslims poured out into the streets to celebrate. Two OSS men, stationed with Eddy at the villa, heard what Eddy described as the "ominous sound of tom-toms and beating on brass pots and shrill cries" that "began to mount in crescendo." They grew terrified, "quite convinced now that the end of the world was at hand." Eddy, who knew it was the first night of Ramadan, found the whole incident entertaining. "It all goes to show," Eddy concluded, "how unreliable circumstantial evidence is."[25]

While implementing OSS orders, Eddy eagerly sought updates from family members about their lives back home. He had missed their annual winter ski trip, which was fine by him. That nobody had been hurt on the vacation "annoyed" Eddy, he joked, because their positive reports of health and happiness robbed him of an "argument to sabotage that vicious sport." He would have to resort to other measures, using tactics that were becoming all too common for the missionary. "I shall bring home with me," he threatened, "several pull switches, booby traps, time bombs, limpets, and lethal tablets (my present stock in trade) to blow up all the handsome ski instructors with dimples and cute accents." He worried, though, when he discovered that his boys had just taught his wife to shoot a gun. Mary's new skills, he told his son Jack, might "make life more dangerous for me when I return."[26]

As the former college president continued to build a multiethnic resistance on the margins of the war, he hoped the United States would go after Hitler in earnest. In the summer of 1942, German field marshal Erwin Rommel, a.k.a. the "Desert Fox," led his forces almost to Alexandria. Eddy fretted that if Egypt fell, Palestine, Syria, and Turkey would be next. Then perhaps Spain. "As you can imagine," he wrote home, "things are not going any too well for us in this part of the world."[27]

Conditions on the ground were about to change. Defeating Hitler was the Allies' shared goal for the war in Europe. But how best to do it divided Roosevelt, Churchill, and Stalin. The Soviet leader insisted that the United States and the United Kingdom launch a major land invasion in western Europe as soon as possible in order to divert Hitler's forces from the eastern front. Many Americans, including naval leaders, wanted to focus primarily on Japan and on Hitler only after the threat in the Pacific had subsided. FDR believed the United States needed to battle on both fronts. He was already taking the war to the Japanese, and he wanted to get Americans into the European fight, too, both to show Stalin he was serious and to ensure that the American people felt that they had skin in the game. The British, meanwhile, wanted to put off a land invasion into western Europe for as long as possible. Churchill remembered the horrors of trench warfare during World War I and did not want to send major ground forces onto the Continent before he could guarantee success. Furthermore, the British knew the Americans needed more time to mobilize, and they didn't want to fight a western offensive alone.

Churchill convinced Roosevelt that the Mediterranean Sea should be a top priority. Taking control of the Mediterranean would allow the Allies to challenge Hitler's periphery, protect British holdings in the Middle East and Southeast Asia, and maintain access to the natural resources coming from the colonies that the British desperately needed. He and Roosevelt agreed that they would first move in 1942 against Hitler in North Africa, which would serve as a base for additional action in the Mediterranean. Donovan summoned Eddy to Washington and gave him the news that the Anglo-American operation was in the works. Wild Bill put the missionary son at the center of the first major American land incursion since World War I.

In the late summer of 1942, Eddy joined OSS and military leaders for meetings in London and New York to discuss objectives for the operation they code-named "Torch." Eddy proved essential to the mission's planning. He met with, briefed, and strategized with Generals George Patton, Dwight Eisenhower, and James Doolittle. Eddy entered the room in London for his first conference with Patton wearing his full marine uniform, complete with World War I decorations, which included five rows of ribbons (more than Patton had at the time). Another OSS leader asked Patton if he knew the colonel. "Never seen him before in my life," Patton responded. "But the son of a bitch's been shot at enough, hasn't he?"[28]

Eddy had plenty of specific advice and insights for Patton, Eisenhower, and other army leaders. He was responsible for ensuring that those on the ground did not offer any serious resistance to the Americans and British landing in North Africa. The generals needed him to vouch for the French military leaders in the region still under the command of the Vichy government. Eddy assured them that some would cooperate, and the rest would simply stay out of the conflict. But he insisted that Torch had to look like an American operation—if the British seemed to be orchestrating the invasion, the French would resist, fearing that the British might claim the French colonial possession of Tunisia and possibly additional French colonial holdings in the Middle East. At the same time, Eddy feared British double-dealing. He warned Eisenhower that they might try to manipulate him, making "him think he is running the show," while they got "what they want." Finally, Eddy warned the generals not to "rouse" the local Moors without offering them support. "We should," he suggested, "tell them that we will see that they get a fair deal at the peace table and promise to keep them supplied with food for themselves and their stock." On the location for the landings, Eddy offered numerous suggestions. Patton had other ideas, and the two debated the merits of the various options. Eddy also told Patton that he was wrong to think that he should soften the area for the invasion by bombing it. If any Free French were killed, Eddy warned, the rest would have a harder time allying with the American invading forces.[29]

Military planners also asked Eddy to locate an experienced boatman. They needed someone they could trust to navigate the tortuous harbor of Port Lyautey in northern Morocco during the Allied landings. Eddy thought that the best man for the job was a local Frenchman named René Malevergne. The difficulty was getting Malevergne into Tangier and then out to the fleet without neighbors, spies, or local authorities noticing. To pull this off, Malevergne developed an elaborate cover, which his wife helped authenticate. They pretended to be having marriage troubles, and his wife told neighbors she feared that he was seeing another woman. He started coming home late at night and then began spending nights away from home. Eventually, he disappeared altogether, and his wife hysterically told the neighbors that he had run off to Casablanca with a lover. In fact, he had spent eight hours in the trunk of a Dodge car, breathing carbon monoxide as he sneaked across borders and passed checkpoints to eventually reach the boat waiting for him on the coast. To get him out to sea without being observed, Eddy's men had to distract the local Spanish sentry. They knew what to do. Whenever they needed to lure a sentry away from his post, they hired a prostitute for the job. They paid her well for her expertise and then for her silence. As far as Eddy was concerned, everyone came out ahead from this arrangement.[30]

Eddy's meetings with the American generals represented a substantial success for the operative and the OSS. The top American military leaders in the European theater were "all very much impressed with Eddy," US Army general Lucian Truscott noted. They "thought he was a man of intelligence and character, and were disposed to rely upon him." The generals asked the former missionary to remain on the ground to "start the fireworks before or at the time of the invasion."[31]

*

Back in Tangier, Eddy prepared for the invasion. To do the job right, Eddy asked for more toys, including ten thousand each of Sten guns (British-made machine guns), tommy guns, pistols, and antitank mines. Although he never received as many weapons as he thought he needed, he did not give up on his dream of arming his local allies.[32]

He also continued to seek alliances among Muslim groups. He and Coon believed that during the Allied incursion, the Spanish might try to blockade the Strait of Gibraltar. If this should happen, they wanted to have Muslim tribal groups organized on the west side of the strait to sabotage the Spanish army. To help motivate them, Eddy suggested that the OSS rescue two exiled tribal leaders and use them for propaganda purposes as the invasion unfolded. He hoped they would broadcast pro-Allied messages from Eddy's clandestine radio station on Gibraltar.

Eddy informed Donovan that one of the Muslims he wanted to partner with was Abd el-Krim. In the early 1920s, Abd el-Krim had fought to unify the Rifian people of northern Morocco against their European colonizers and to modernize politics in the region. His revolt had some early success, driving back the Spanish. Then the French intervened. The combined Spanish and French forces ultimately compelled the Muslim leader to surrender and go into exile. Eddy knew that bringing el-Krim back to North Africa would enrage the French and especially the Spanish, which is why Eddy proceeded very cautiously with this plan. "I hardly need to add," he reminded Donovan, "that the Chief of Mission here and our British colleagues, as well as other representatives of your Office, have not been informed of our activities with the Natives."[33]

Eddy also knew that the Rifians would "rise to a man with tremendous enthusiasm" if the Americans produced Abd el-Krim. "The natives may well hold the balance of power in the event of crisis," Eddy and Coon concluded. "They form the majority of the population, and include the best fighting men in North Africa . . . men who know how to handle arms and to conduct guerrilla warfare in difficult terrain."[34]

Eddy's schemes reflected his personal beliefs and commitments. He loathed colonialism and wanted the United States to do more for Rifian and Arab independence than American diplomats back in Washington realized or intended. He knew, he confessed to Donovan, that the report of his and Coon's work mobilizing Muslims was "dynamite." The missionary's actions should not have surprised Wild Bill. Eddy was doing exactly what he had predicted a year earlier. He was doing his best Lawrence of Arabia act—rousing the Muslims to defeat evil while simultaneously helping them throw off the yoke of their colonial oppressors.[35]

Donovan instructed Eddy to develop propaganda for the invasion as well. Eddy's team crafted a leaflet in Arabic for American planes to drop across North Africa in conjunction with the Allied invasion. "Behold! We the American Holy Warriors have arrived!" it began in the English version. "We have come here to fight the great Jihad of freedom! We have come to set you free!" Muslims, the writers hoped, would find that they had much in common with the American Christian invaders. "Look upon our fighting men and you will find them pleasing to the eye and gladdening to the heart. We are not as some other Christians whom you have known, and who trample you under feet. Our soldiers," the flyer continued, "consider you as their brothers and will treat you as brothers, for we have been reared in the way of free men. Our soldiers have been told about your country and about their Moslem brothers and they will treat you with respect and with a friendly spirit in the eyes of God. . . . They are Holy Warriors happy in their holy work." As over-the-top as this pamphlet was, Eddy believed in the sentiments behind it. His ecumenical Protestantism and anticolonialism allowed him to think and hope that American Christians could find common ground with Muslims for the greater good of the world. His childhood in Beirut and his work in the 1920s at the American University in Cairo had taught him to aim for nothing less.[36]

The pamphlet also asked local Muslims to assist the Americans. If the soldiers needed water, share some. If they needed directions, show them where to go. If they lost their unit, help them locate it. "And if you see our enemies, the Germans or Italians, making trouble for us, kill them with knives or with stones or with any other weapon that you may set your hand upon." Yet Eddy still hoped the locals would not need stones. He continued pleading for American weapons with which to arm Muslim tribes on the eve of the invasion. "Help us," the American leaflet concluded, "as we have come to help you, and rich will be the reward unto you as unto all who love justice and righteousness and freedom."[37]

*

On November 8, 1942, Americans under the command of Generals Dwight D. Eisenhower and George Patton launched Operation Torch. Roosevelt had jested that the invasion had better happen before the midterm elections. War, he knew, could never be separated from politics. Eddy and Coon, following orders from headquarters, sailed across the strait to Gibraltar. While they waited for the radio to announce that the battle had commenced, they ate ham sandwiches and drank beer. Meanwhile, René Malevergne, the local man that the OSS had sneaked out to sea, piloted the USS *Dallas* into Port Lyautey. He would become the first Frenchman during the war to earn the US Silver Star. When Eddy received word that the invasion had begun, he telegrammed Donovan. Then he slept. His job was done, and it was now up to Eisenhower and Patton to secure the region.[38]

The next morning, at 9:00 AM, Mary Eddy received a telegram from Donovan, reading: "Colonel Eddy well and safe. Sends his love." Three hours later, Eddy sent his own cable: "Well and very happy. Love to all the family. Three cheers." Donovan also personally called Mary to assure her that her husband was in no danger. The OSS director, who was not all that committed to his own wife, recognized that things were different for the Eddys. For Bill Eddy, the sun rose and set with Mary. A week and a half into Operation Torch, Eddy gleefully reported that "the main facts are causes of jubilation all around."[39]

Despite numerous challenges and a few missteps, Operation Torch was a major success for the Allies. The Americans and British invaded from the West, penetrating the territory Eddy had softened. Meanwhile, the British Eighth Army under the command of General Bernard Montgomery landed farther east, where they faced Rommel's forces. The French, as American leaders had feared, resisted for the first couple of days, but eventually laid down their arms. After a few months of intense fighting, the Anglo-American forces drove the Axis powers out of North Africa. The southern Mediterranean was theirs.

Eddy was thrilled with the reception that the American soldiers received on the ground in North Africa. "Everywhere you see little French kids hobnobbing with them, trying to bum souvenirs. They generously give away cigarettes or share a meal unnecessarily just to be good sports. It is the best kind of propaganda and I am sure wholly spontaneous and unpremeditated." Eddy had worked hard to win hearts and minds, and he was ecstatic that American troops did the same. But he felt a little guilty about his nice accommodations compared to those of the average GI. "What I really need is to sleep on the ground under a pup tent and hike miles a day on iron rations, instead of living comfortably" in an apartment, "sleeping on a soft bed, and riding in a car whenever I go any distance." The Torch experience, he confessed to Wild Bill, had taught him that he preferred "the overalls to the white collars." But he didn't really mean it. After watching some paratroopers practice, he wrote his son Bill that he was happy to have been born "much too early for aerial life, and am quite content to use my two feet on the ground."[40]

Eddy's contributions raised both his own star as well as that of the OSS. His team had effectively coordinated the work of the State Department, British intelligence, the French resistance, dissidents working through the Catholic and Episcopal Churches, Jewish agents, Spanish communists, and various local Muslim groups. "The fact also remains that Americans, the least experienced great nation in the world in intrigue, espionage, and sabotage," Coon summarized, "pulled off one of the greatest . . . jobs in the history of the world." In summarizing the project, Coon perpetuated a myth of American innocence, one that he likely believed. But the people of Hawaii and the Philippines, territories that the United States had previously invaded, knew that the United States was not as inexperienced in the arts of intrigue, espionage, and sabotage as Coon claimed.[41]

Many operatives and agents lavished praise on Colonel Eddy. Coon, a cynic by nature who embodied all of the humility of the tenured Harvard academic that he was, could not say enough about his friend. "Eddy's performance of his duties in North Africa was brilliant; he was able to inspire his men with enthusiasm and complete loyalty, to see that security was maintained, to keep the regular State Department happy, and, above all, to see that the work was done and that the show came off." Donovan agreed. "I selected" Eddy, he recalled, "for this task because of his character, his training, his knowledge of French and Arabian people and their languages. . . . Without his inspired leadership it is doubtful if the work could have progressed to successful completion." His prior work as a missionary provided him with much of the necessary training to accomplish this.[42]

Eddy was proud of what he and his team accomplished, and he treated the whole episode when writing his family like it was all a big game. But privately, he sometimes worried about the moral implications of his actions. The constant lies and half-truths that he told during the war, to Muslims and Spaniards and others, haunted him to no end. In an unpublished memoir Eddy started drafting near the end of his life, he called this chapter "Spies and Lies in Tangier." In it he acknowledged that when he dreamed of his wartime service, he awoke "in a sweat." "I try to alibi," he confessed, "to curse and swear, saying, I know not this man of whom ye speak." The words he chose for this confession were particularly poignant. They parroted those used by Peter when he denied Jesus. No religious phrase better invokes treachery and regret. But would Eddy do it again? "Yes, in wartime, I would, but that melancholy conviction does not make it easier for me to live with myself." For people like Eddy, turning the skills that he had honed for doing good for God into weapons of death was unsettling. He had mastered foreign languages and intimate knowledge of other cultures to win the world for Christ, not to vanquish his enemies to hell. During the war, however, he believed that evil had to be done for good to prevail.[43]

After the successful invasion, Eddy reminisced about what the future might hold for his family. Their security, and what he could do to help support them, remained constant preoccupations. He imagined Bill in seminary training to be a priest, Marycita serving as assistant secretary of state, Carmen landing "on the stage in Hollywood," and Jack ending up "in the Brig." He had different plans for himself and his love. He and Mary, he dreamed, might soon be "manning a Naval Attaché Post or a lighthouse abroad." But Donovan had other ideas for Eddy's immediate future.[44]

EIGHT

"The Double Opportunity to Serve God and Country"

WHILE WILLIAM EDDY WAS RUNNING ALL OVER NORTH AFRICA DODGING Nazi agents, John Birch was trying to survive in China. The two men seemingly could not have been any more different. Eddy was middle-aged and had a family. Birch was young and single. Eddy was a self-effacing liberal ecumenist who believed that demonstrating Christ's love, not arguments, would bring people to Jesus. Birch was an angry crusader for a doctrinally uncompromising, fundamentalist version of the Christian faith. Eddy drank and smoked. Birch did neither. Eddy had attended elite boarding schools. Birch was the product of a southern Jim Crow public school system. Eddy had earned a PhD at Princeton. Birch did minimal graduate work at a small, radical, unaccredited fundamentalist seminary in Texas.

But the two had much in common as well. Both had been born to missionaries living in foreign lands. Both spoke several languages—Birch, Mandarin and local Chinese dialects; Eddy, French, German, and Arabic. Both had dedicated their lives to spreading the Christian faith. And both were the kinds of men you would want by your side in the heat of battle. They were missionaries who knew how to wield a gun and, if necessary, kill an enemy.

On April 18, 1942, just days after Birch submitted his application for duty in the US army, sixteen B-25 bombers and their crews led by James Doolittle secretly catapulted off aircraft carriers hidden in the vast Pacific.

They rained down bombs on the Japanese homeland. Then, because the planes were too large to land on the carriers that launched them, the crews flew as far west as their fuel would take them. Unable to locate secure landing strips, they had to bail out. Some made it to safety among the Chinese, but others dropped from the sky behind Japanese lines on the Chinese mainland.

The Doolittle raiders facing the threat of capture had to make their way to freedom. Birch, at the time, was working just inland from the East China Sea. He was moving from village to village preaching the gospel near occupied territory on the Qiantang River in Zhejiang Province, near Hangzhou. The Japanese had interned most of the remaining Protestant missionaries in the region, and Birch wanted to ensure that their work continued. While traveling the region, he observed Japanese planes on surveillance missions. He didn't know they were looking for the downed American airmen. Birch stopped in a small village on the river for a meal. A Chinese army officer came in and began speaking in English to the Baptist. Birch assumed the officer simply wanted to practice his language skills. In the midst of the conversation, the officer mentioned that there were Americans hiding in a boat anchored on the river below the restaurant. Birch felt sure he had misunderstood the officer. Nevertheless, he went down to check things out.

When Birch got to the dock, he shouted, "Are there any Americans in there?" Scared, the men hiding below remained quiet. Then Birch asked again: "Are there any Americans in there?" Finally, one of the men, catching Birch's southern drawl, exclaimed, "Hell, no Japanese can talk American like that." Then another quipped, "Well, Jesus Christ."[1]

"That's an awfully good name," Birch responded, "but I am not he." When Birch climbed into the ship's cabin, he discovered James Doolittle and his crew. "They didn't know what the score was," Birch realized, or where they were. The local Chinese were aiding them, but they were not sure whom they could trust.[2]

The missionary promised to help. He agreed to lead the men up the Qiantang to safety. Birch, Doolittle later recalled, "had been living off the cuff and was having a rough go of it." The missionary, still hoping to secure a job as an army chaplain, offered his services to Doolittle. Doolittle, in return, offered to put in a good word for Birch. Nevertheless, Birch had no intention of enlisting at the cost of his evangelistic work. He told

Doolittle that whatever happened, he "expected to continue preaching the Gospel."[3]

Birch safely delivered the men to the nearest US Army base, where he found a telegram waiting for him. General Clayton Lawrence Bissell, one of the primary American military leaders in East Asia, had read the missionary's army application and sent him a note asking him to help locate the rest of the missing American airmen in the region. Birch requested a uniform and a Colt .45. Doolittle, who had carried $2,000 on him for bribes and emergencies, gave his cash to Birch. The missionary then returned to the countryside for about a month to work with local Chinese in ushering the raiders to safety, locating their gear, and salvaging what he could from their B-25s. He also buried one of the airmen who had died. The missionary's skill in working with the local population proved essential to this work. His "ability to obtain information from Chinese sources," Doolittle reported, made him "extremely valuable to our forces in China."[4]

Birch's work was often dangerous. On his birthday, May 28, he narrowly escaped a Japanese bombing run. Enemy planes destroyed the house where Birch had been staying, killing four people. Birch believed that God had spared him. "How wonderful to be under the protection and guidance of our all-seeing Heavenly Father." Birch's faith in the sovereignty of God was typical of fundamentalists. So was his reluctance to think about the implications of his theological assumptions. If God had spared the missionary, does that mean God had killed his housemates? Or at least allowed them to die? Was he more valuable in God's eyes? If so, why?[5]

After Birch demonstrated his usefulness to the army by rescuing Doolittle raiders, Bissell ordered the missionary to Chongqing, the center of American military operations in the region. While Birch was en route, he learned that the Japanese had burned his mission station in Shangjao. "When I got to" Chongqing, Birch confessed, "I was both angry and discouraged—I didn't feel like doing much more mission work." There he officially joined the army air force as an intelligence officer. At the time, the air force was not an independent branch of the military but was part of the army. According to army records, he began active duty on July 4, 1942, although he had actually been working for the military since Doolittle's raid. He was five foot ten and weighed 150 pounds. On Birch's army application, he listed as references Doolittle; famed aviator Claire Chennault, whom he had recently met; and fundamentalist preacher

J. Frank Norris. That he could count all three as staunch supporters illustrates Birch's unusual ability to get along with people from very different worlds. On that same day, Birch attended a barbecue celebrating American Independence Day where he met the wife of Chinese leader Chiang Kai-shek. The American-educated Madame Chiang Kai-shek (Soong May-ling), a convert to Christianity, was a woman whom American missionaries had long revered. She had helped ensure that evangelists like Birch had the freedom to work in China.[6]

In joining the army, Birch told his parents he had "the double opportunity to serve God and country." It was a double challenge as well. For the next three years, Birch's religious convictions wavered as he sought to apply his fundamentalist convictions to an ever-changing and extremely complex world. By the end of the conflict, his faith would be deeper, but also softer. During those first days as a missionary in China, he believed he could almost single-handedly save the world for God and for the United States. His experience in the war, however, killed Birch's naiveté and some of his idealism. It made him a far more empathetic person. As he came to understand his own weaknesses, he grew more tolerant of those in others—a hard but important lesson that many young fundamentalists learned when they left their comfortable and sequestered subcultures for missionary ventures abroad.[7]

Birch was the perfect candidate for intelligence work. During his previous two years in China, the Baptist had fully immersed himself in the native culture, studying and practicing the language and living like a local. According to one report, he could disguise himself "as a Chinese coolie, even carrying a load from a bamboo pole across his shoulders. He spoke Chinese so perfectly that the natives all thought he was a Chinese from another province. Very few Americans could get away with this." If his southern accent and fundamentalist Christianity made it harder for Birch to pass in the halls of power in his own country, his ability to blend among Chinese laborers made it easier for him to do the kind of work his country needed. In fact, part of why he never managed to secure a chaplaincy was his lack of a degree from an accredited theological seminary. He had no legitimate church credentials. But nothing could keep him from fulfilling what he understood to be his calling from God.[8]

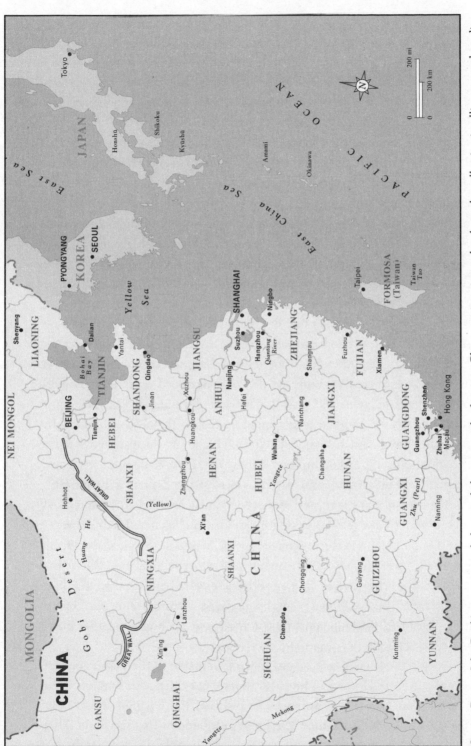

CHINA. During John Birch's wartime work, he traveled across much of eastern China, ministering to local people, collecting intelligence, and evading enemy Japanese troops.

Birch's wartime adventure took another turn under the direction of General Claire Chennault, who became one of Birch's heroes. Chennault went to China in the late 1930s to train native Chinese pilots to take on the Japanese. In 1940 and 1941, he expanded his mission. He recruited a ragtag group of American volunteers dubbed the "Flying Tigers" who battled the Japanese in the sky and provided support to the Chinese air force. When the United States officially entered the war in December 1941, Chennault returned to active duty, and he and the Flying Tigers disbanded and reorganized as the China Air Task Force. Chennault became the commanding general of the US Army Air Force in China, and in 1943 the CATF was incorporated into the newly organized Fourteenth Air Force. The Flying Tigers, and then the Fourteenth Air Force, were headquartered in Kunming, the capital of Yunnan Province in the South of China. The city served as an important base for Chinese and American political and military operations during the war.

Even before Chennault met Birch, he recognized the value of employing missionaries. While he was organizing the Flying Tigers, he recruited Paul Frillmann, a Lutheran missionary who had worked in China, to serve as the chaplain for the group. As the war expanded, so did Chennault's plans for his religious activists. "Chennault did not tell me," Frillmann recalled, that he planned to use missionaries to establish a "combat intelligence formation throughout China," but that was exactly what the general was doing. Frillmann soon discovered that Chennault had also recruited Sven Liljestrand, a missionary son raised in China; Wilfred Smith, another missionary son; and Robert Lynn, a medical missionary. All served under Chennault, working mostly in intelligence. Birch, however, was his star pupil and the first missionary Chennault recruited specifically for intelligence operations. Chennault's secretary remembered Birch's first meeting with the general. "He was a missionary when he entered" Chennault's office, but he "was a second lieutenant when he came out." Chennault later told Birch's parents that he "felt towards him as a father might feel toward a son."[9]

Missionaries back home were proving valuable to the Asia campaign as well. In 1941 Donovan summoned missionary Kenneth Landon to his Washington, DC, office. Roosevelt feared that the Japanese would move against the British in Burma via Thailand. Landon had served in Thailand in the 1930s, and Donovan wanted to pick his brain. But first, he had

President Roosevelt's son James show Landon what they already had in the government's intelligence files on Thailand. Roosevelt pulled the file, which consisted of only four articles, all penned by Landon. The missionary recruit soon became the OSS's top expert on Southeast Asia. Meanwhile, his wife, Margaret Landon, wrote the novel *Anna and the King of Siam* based on her experience in Thailand, which she published in 1944. The book inspired the hit Rogers and Hammerstein musical *The King and I*. While many missionaries such as Landon provided intelligence on Asia for the OSS's Research and Analysis Branch, missionary soldiers like Birch provided a different skill set.[10]

Birch's work for Doolittle and Bissell impressed Chennault. "By the time Birch was rounding up the Doolittle raiders," Chennault later noted, "the Japanese were burning his new mission, so John laid aside his Bible and took up the sword for the duration." He wielded that sword like a crusader trying to retake the Holy Land. The Japanese threatened one hundred years of missionary work in China. Birch believed that God wanted him to stop these enemies of the faith. Serving Chennault was, for Birch, serving the Lord.[11]

Chennault and the CATF leaders had only the most rudimentary intelligence available to them. Most of their information came from their Chinese allies, and they rarely received up-to-date material. They possessed few maps and no photographs for planning missions. The men in the CATF also had difficulty translating the reports they received. They assigned three people to get the operation running smoother: Birch and two other soldiers, one of whom was, Birch recalled, "drunk a lot of the time." And not on the Holy Spirit. The three of them, Birch told an interviewer, "practically had to start from scratch. . . . We were very, very busy." But they got the job done. Chennault called Birch "the pioneer of our field-intelligence net."[12]

As the CATF's contingent of intelligence officers grew, Birch asked to be reassigned. He did not like the tedium of an office job, even if it was near the war zone. He wanted to get back to the front lines, and even beyond them, where he knew he would be happier. Chennault agreed and hatched a plan to embed Birch with a Chinese unit.

During the war, China essentially had two armies fighting the Japanese. The Nationalist Army, or Kuomintang, fought under the central government led by Chiang Kai-shek. In the North, near Japanese-occupied

Birch believed that God wanted him to remain in China for the duration of the war, where he worked to serve both God and country.
Courtesy of National Archives and Records Administration, College Park, Maryland.

territory, a communist force led by Mao Zedong waged an unconventional war against the Japanese. The two groups had united for the war against Japan, but they mostly functioned independently of each other. Chennault worked primarily with the Kuomintang, but as the war progressed the Americans occasionally worked with the communists as well.

Few Americans had traveled with Chinese soldiers—the conditions were too grueling for most "regular" servicemen. The food was poor and the equipment too rudimentary. But missionaries like Birch were used to roughing it and understood the Chinese culture. His work soon reaped dividends for the CATF. He lived and traveled with Kuomintang units, synchronizing US air strikes with Chinese ground operations. Birch was at the center of the war, where he thought he belonged.

The missionary's work earned him the respect of the commanding general of the Chinese forces in the area, which allowed the Americans and the Chinese to coordinate their strategies more directly. According to an ally, Birch's work facilitated a much better "flow of Intelligence." This became a pattern that occurred over and over again. American military leaders dispatched the missionary crusader to whichever Chinese leaders they were seeking to partner with at the time. Because of Birch's background, experience in the region, and cultural sensibilities, he managed to do what few other Americans could: foster better communications and much stronger and mutually beneficial alliances among the Allies. While during downtime he might be praying for his fellow grunts, rolling his eyes at their coarse language, or burying his head in a Bible, when it came time to suit up and head out into the field, he was the person best equipped to sneak past the enemy, orchestrate guerrilla action in the Chinese countryside, and liaise with Chinese generals.[13]

Nevertheless, Birch's missionary duties had not ended. Whether partnering with Americans or Chinese, he constantly tried to win converts to the fundamentalist faith. "Although Birch served as an intelligence officer," Doolittle remarked, "he was still a chaplain at heart. Wherever he was on Sundays, he conducted religious services for Chinese Christians, often at the risk of his life behind Japanese lines." For Birch, the missions overlapped. He had pledged his life to serving God by serving the Chinese people. Whether with a Bible or a gun, that was still what he planned to do.[14]

NINE

"It's Your Souls We Want"

In the months that followed FDR's declaration of war, Stephen Penrose worked to recruit new agents from among missionary organizations, William Eddy courted tribal leaders in North Africa, and John Birch tried to keep his Chinese ministry alive despite Japanese aggression in the region. But none of these religious activists was as close to the enemy as Stewart Herman. The Third Reich was holding the pastor prisoner. The leader of the American Church in Berlin just wanted to get home.

The Germans interned Herman with about one hundred other Americans at the Grand in Bad Nauheim, a once beautiful hotel in a beautiful town. But with the onset of the war a few years earlier, the hotel's staff had packed away all of the dishes and furniture, turned off the utilities, and abandoned the place. The building the Americans found seemed more like a historic ruin than a luxury spa. Nevertheless, Herman assured his family, he was in good health and was getting some much-needed rest. Although he had been "quartered" at the Grand, he was thankful, he joked, that he had not yet been "drawn and quartered."[1]

A few years earlier, while visiting others in internment camps, Herman had almost wished to be with them. He was at the time still somewhat oblivious to the terrors that the Nazi regime was orchestrating. When he learned at one camp that a language teacher was offering classes to internees, he quipped, "I almost feel like getting myself interned too! I might learn some Russian." He was even a little jealous of the internees' free time. "I must say that for a space I envied those men their retreat in that lovely spot. Freedom is a matter of the spirit and I could be free there for a number of months if I had the opportunity to study, walk quietly, rest, and think. I might get some Russian and I might take an inventory of these past years with an eye to the future."[2]

He did not feel quite so enthusiastic about the experience when he actually became an internee in late 1941. He and the other residents tried to make the best of their circumstances. Various members of the group taught classes and Herman offered a regular Bible study. The pastor enrolled in both Russian and Spanish language classes to supplement his excellent French and German, and he likely also took the Russian history course offered by George Kennan, the diplomat who would go on to become one of the key architects of American cold war policy.

Herman fretted that only about half the group attended regular Sunday services, which he jointly led with another interned minister. He grew even more frustrated when attendance began dwindling. What he likely did not know was that the American Catholics interned in the hotel, who were allowed to attend services at the local parish, found that some of their fellow parishioners, the Central Americans interned nearby, had more liquor than they did. Soon more and more Americans were skipping Herman's service for mass in order to swap tobacco for spirits with kneeling Central American worshippers.[3]

While interned, Herman wrote his annual reflection on the previous year. From within the confines of the Grand, the churchman did some serious soul-searching about his life, his work, his future, and the continuing war. He worried that his career to date had been a failure, that he had "done 'nothing' in these 32 years. Ten years ago," he confessed, "I looked forward to 'achievements.' My only consolation is that my nature and my faith won't allow me to give up." But deciding not to give up and knowing what to do with his life were two very different things. "It seems now as though a long apprenticeship is over at last. Or, have I still more years to serve? Will the whole of life seem to be merely an apprenticeship?" The war was discouraging him, as were reports of Nazi abuses of native religious dissenters. He noted that Germany was running out of food and clothes for its citizens and that as winter approached things were bound to get worse. "Yet there is time and energy left to persecute Jews and Christians!" Watching the horror unfolding before his eyes fed his sense of impotence. "These past years have been terribly depressing, largely because I had to observe without being able to help." Whether it was Jews or young members of the Confessing Church who sought his aid during his time in Berlin, he had chosen not to intervene. Perhaps, he hoped, there would be an opportunity to make up for his indifference and inaction.[4]

Herman also had time to ponder his future as a bachelor. His romantic relationships had been about as fleeting as the hot water in the Grand's bathrooms, and he had just about given up on the possibility of finding lasting love. But not for lack of trying. He had dated German women, English women, Australian women, Danish women, and American women. While in Berlin, he came to know Martha Dodd, the US ambassador's daughter. They went on a few dates and at least one went well, Herman noted at the time in his diary, "but diplomacy intervened." Exactly what he meant is a mystery. She was, Herman wrote, "a rather attractive little thing with a good mind which, however, has never been well-disciplined." But "religion," he fretted, "has lost its chance" with her. During the Dodd family's time in Germany, Herman kept tabs on Martha's comings and goings. "Apparently," he told his parents, "her hectic romance with some high Nazi is over." Indeed, Dodd engaged in numerous scandalous relationships with high-ranking German men and then Russians after that, including a leading Soviet spy.[5]

Like Dodd, Herman was not opposed to consorting with the enemy. He met one German woman at a party who entranced him, despite his reservations about her name. "A most attractive girl of very good family but her first name is Lolo so nothing can come of that," he joked. She worked for the German Ministry of War. Although they constantly argued over Nazi policies, they went on many dates over the span of a few years. The two had one final dinner together the day after the Germans declared war on the United States, just as Herman was packing up to leave for internment at the Grand.[6]

Failing to find a partner, Herman sometimes blamed the women he had met. "I am becoming more and more convinced," he confessed to his parents, "that life is only deterred by the average female." But he did not really believe this. He wrote his parents one Valentine's Day lamenting that "I haven't anyone else to whom to write." The real problem for Herman was Herman. And he knew it. Over the years he had dated a few women whom he thought would make excellent wives and who wanted to marry him. But he could never follow through. "The ordinary intimacies which people enjoy seem attractive until they come close to me," he confided to his diary. "Then I back away; why? I don't know." For Herman, opening himself up to others was a never-ending struggle. But to go through life without a family of his own also scared him.[7]

By Herman's second month in the Grand Hotel, boredom and depression had set in. Having so little to do was starting to drive the minister, and everyone else stuck in Bad Nauheim, a bit crazy. Rumors regularly reached the Americans that German and US authorities were negotiating a swap. But nothing happened for almost six months. Finally, the warring powers cut a deal to free Herman and his fellow prisoners. The American internees left Bad Nauheim on May 12 for Lisbon, where they caught a ship back to the United States. On June 1, 1942, Herman arrived on American soil for the first time in years. He was thrilled to be home.

Back in the States permanently for the first time since college, Herman needed a job. His father put him to work helping run the Zion Lutheran Church in Harrisburg. The elder Herman wanted to make his son the large church's permanent associate pastor, but Herman was reluctant. He knew he could not stay home with his overbearing mother for too long. He inquired with friends in Washington about a government position, but he didn't want anything bureaucratic or boring. He told them he wanted a "very special commission of work" if something came available, but that he had no interest in being a "little cog" in the big machine. He also spoke with officers from the navy about a chaplainship.[8]

In addition to helping his father, Herman discovered that he could eke out a living writing and speaking about life in Germany and on the state of the Christian church under the Nazis. He published an article in the *Saturday Evening Post* titled "Hitler Can't Do Business with the Church." He informed readers of the popular magazine that the Nazi regime had created a new set of religious rituals and holidays to mark major life events, which they designed to replace traditional Christian baptisms, confirmations, weddings, and funerals. "The German government today is the new church, and National Socialism is the new religion," he wrote. But the Nazis had not entirely succeeded. "Even in the tightly held land of the Nazis the human soul is a proud and stubborn thing." In *Christianity and Crisis*, a magazine started by Reinhold Niebuhr and Francis Pickens Miller, Herman made the case that although Hitler had erected a false religion, church leaders, both Protestant and Catholic, remained Hitler's staunchest and most dangerous opponents. He sought to convince Americans that not all Germans supported Hitler, and he praised the resistance of many church leaders in the Third Reich.[9]

Herman also did some writing for the government. In an article for the Office of War Information (OWI), Herman discussed the German church as the government's "loyal opposition," which tried to serve Germany without serving Hitler. The article represented Herman's pragmatic position, which grew out of his firsthand experiences. He respected the dissenting Confessing Church, but he also believed that cautious church leaders were wise not to challenge Hitler too directly. Congregations and especially church youth were better off with a pastor who was careful not to antagonize the Third Reich but who simultaneously did not propagandize on its behalf, he argued, rather than with a pastor who took a firm stand against Hitler and in so doing lost his head.[10]

Herman's most important contribution to the Allied propaganda campaign during the first years of the American war was *It's Your Souls We Want*, a book he started writing while interned. Published by Harper, the monograph was part history of the German church struggle, part analysis of the pseudoreligion of Nazism, and part call for the Allies to encourage Germany's Christian dissenters to reconstruct the nation once the war was over. The *New York Times* mostly praised the book, although a reviewer noted that Herman "leans over backward to be fair and sympathetic to the great silent body of Germans who distrust Hitler but go along with him for various reasons of their own. Perhaps he is too sympathetic and too quick to condone the cowardice and apathy of the majority." The reviewer was probably right. Herman occasionally acknowledged that his work in Germany made him more empathetic with the German people than perhaps they deserved.[11]

Herman dedicated the book to the Confessing Church. He told his American and British audiences about Hitler's execution of the weak and disabled, and he warned his readers that the goal of the Nazis' anti-Semitic policies was the total annihilation of Jews. "The German objective," he wrote, "was extermination of the Jews and their method was murder." This was a message that many Americans had not yet heard or understood. He ended his book on a positive note, reiterating the theme that would define his postwar career: "The reconstruction of Europe after this war will not be merely a matter of economic rehabilitation, nor even of re-education in an academic sense, but of spiritual reformation and revival." Yet before that could happen, the Allies needed to stop Hitler.[12]

Over the course of 1942, Herman met occasionally with Henry Smith Leiper, a former missionary and now an executive in the Federal Council of Churches, as well as a leader in the burgeoning World Council of Churches. During his time in Germany, Herman had kept in close touch with the leaders of the FCC. The FCC was the most effective American organization pushing ecumenical Protestantism as a means of securing peace. Leiper was interested in Herman's career and thought Herman should find a position working with a relief agency. Leiper told Herman that he was angling to have a Lutheran stationed in Geneva with the World Council of Churches "for post-war work, linked with other churches." The idea of a WCC position in Geneva stuck with Herman for the next couple of years.[13]

At the end of a restless year that began with internment, the former Berlin minister reflected on what had happened and what he expected the future to hold. The Allies were finally gaining ground, and he felt confident that the Axis powers would eventually lose the fight. But could a permanent peace be achieved? He was not sure. Any lasting peace, he believed, would have to emerge from the Christian faith and the church universal. "The great chance for Christianity," he wrote, "is to get into the private souls of men and give them a sense of the universal communion of saints." Most churches, he feared, were not up to the task. "The usual worship service, conducted in desultory fashion no longer answers the spiritual needs of our time. In most of the services I've attended there is no consciousness of divine presence." He believed that God had called him, working through the global ecumenical movement, to renew the world's churches. He hoped to bring the sense of the divine back into a war-torn world.[14]

In early 1943, the former pastor of the American Church in Berlin accepted an invitation from the British Ministry of Information to go on a preaching tour of England. The British Council of Churches, in collaboration with the Ministry of Information and the United States' Office of War Information, sponsored the trip. Herman was very excited about it as he continued wondering about his future. "I don't know whether I am morally justified in continuing to lecture and write rather than take a parish or go into the chaplaincy," he confessed to his diary. "Some decision will have to be reached after the trip to England which, I think, is important." Although he had been offered a few permanent jobs, none felt right. "Up till now I've refused several offers to become somebody's pastor but I'm still eager to do everything I can to lay a sound basis for world peace." He was still looking for that elusive position that would allow him to serve something greater than himself or a local congregation. He was sure that somehow, somewhere, God had a plan for him to help bring this horrific war to an end.[15]

Herman's UK itinerary was part ministry and part propaganda. He encouraged the British people to remain steadfast as the war dragged on, and he shared insights from his time in Nazi Germany. The trip allowed Herman to see old friends from Berlin and to witness the progress of the war firsthand. It also inspired him to think further about what role he might play in the conflict. He continued to trust that the ecumenical church was the key to global peace, but he did not yet know how best to implement his belief.

Herman returned from London to the United States on April 13, 1943, and rejoined his family in Harrisburg. His book on Nazi religion had sparked a lot of interest, and over the next few months he received many invitations to visit churches and social clubs. That October Herman gave a talk at Cornell University. After the service a few coeds approached him, seeking his counsel regarding a friend of theirs who was apparently a kleptomaniac. One of the Cornell women was Ethelyn "Lyn" Cantrell, an attractive redhead from Georgia. It is not clear if Lyn made an impression on Herman that day, but he certainly made an impression on her. A week after their talk, she wrote him a letter. It was the first and only time she addressed him as "Reverend Herman." She updated him on the kleptomaniac, and then her tone shifted. "I now have a confession to make," she began. She had an "ulterior motive" for writing. "I want very much to know you, sir, for at no other time in my life have I felt such immediate respect and admiration for any person as I felt for you—even before I talked with you." She suggested that they begin a regular correspondence and ended by hoping that he would not find her "unduly forward."[16]

Lyn Cantrell, then only twenty-one years old, was an extraordinary person. She grew up in Georgia in a working-class family that did not have much money in the Depression era. She graduated high school at sixteen and won a fifty-dollar prize for a play she had written for the local radio station. She used the money for a course in stenography at a local business school and then used the skills she learned there to work at various jobs and eventually at the Federal Reserve in Atlanta. She used her salary from that job to pay for classes at the University of Georgia. In 1942 she transferred to the University of Minnesota. Cantrell had barely gotten settled in Minnesota before recruiters convinced her to move to Cornell University to train for a job in aeronautical engineering. In the midst of the war, many businesses were looking to college students to fill the jobs left open by those called up for military service. Cantrell believed that in exchanging her courses in the arts and humanities, at least temporarily, for studying engineering at Cornell, she could contribute to the war effort. At Cornell she met Stewart Herman. And she fell in love.

Over the next few months, the churchman and the coed exchanged a series of letters. In some ways their correspondence reflected their religious heritages. Herman's writing matched that of the stereotypical Lutheran church service. His missives were cautious, conservative, and guarded, with all emotions kept in check. Lyn's letters, in contrast, had all of the passion, enthusiasm, and unbridled excitement of an old-time Methodist revival.

Cantrell was both a romantic and a realist, and she masterfully held these conflicting impulses in balance as she corresponded with Herman. She told him that she had "peace and happiness in my heart because I have worshipped God and because I have walked in the snow and because I have listened to beautiful music." She shared with Herman stories about herself and college life. She had gone to "some of the beer parties" on campus but neither smoked nor drank. She did not want to be judgmental, but at one of these parties many of the students were drunk, and one of the coeds began to perform a striptease. Cantrell bolted from the scene. "Above all things," she wrote her new friend, "I want to live with tolerance and love for everyone. But that desire should prevent no one from the recognition of things as they exist." She concluded by thanking Herman for allowing her to write him so unreservedly. Lyn Cantrell's letters convinced Herman that he needed to see this extraordinary woman again. He asked if she could see him on her way back to Cornell after spending the Christmas holiday in Georgia. But a date with Lyn was not the only thing on Herman's mind.[17]

The increasingly aimless young man continued to struggle to find a clear direction for his life. He received two calls to fill permanent ministerial positions, including one very attractive offer to fill the pulpit at St. Peter's Lutheran Church in New York City. He turned down both jobs. Meanwhile, Dean E. E. Flack of Hamma Divinity School in Ohio, a small Lutheran college and seminary, offered him a one-year lectureship. Flack had spent a few weeks in Berlin in 1937, where he got to know Herman. The minister was not sure how to respond to Flack's offer.

As Herman mulled over his future, he remained active in the global ecumenical peace movement. He participated in a "Roundtable on International Affairs" at Princeton University in 1943. Allen Dulles's brother, John Foster Dulles, organized and led the conference, which grew out of the Federal Council of Churches' "Commission on a Just and Durable Peace." Dulles and his ecumenical allies had been working since 1940 to shape and influence Roosevelt's foreign policy. They drafted blueprints for new, better, and more effective ways to use the international ecumenical movement to prevent another global war from happening ever again. The Roundtable on International Affairs was one of their many efforts. *Life* editors featured Herman and his work with the German church in a story about the Princeton conference.[18]

Perhaps inspired by the work of Dulles and others acting to influence US foreign policy, Herman began feeling out friends in government for a possible job. He wrote Jack Lovell, a fellow internee from Bad Nauheim who was now working in the War Department. He asked Lovell a provocative question: Was the War Department getting "all the information" that it needed "from the Christian underground in Europe"? If not, Herman thought he could help. Perhaps government work was the best way, at least in this extraordinary moment in history, to build the kingdom of God? Perhaps the cross and the flag needed to align more closely, at least for the duration? His letter piqued Lovell's curiosity. Lovell forwarded it to General George Strong, the director of American army intelligence, with a handwritten note observing that rarely did he receive letters "from a parson" that were worthwhile. But this was one exception.[19]

Only a few days after sending off that letter, Herman accepted the teaching job at Hamma Divinity School. He had sat down to write a note rejecting Dean Flack's offer, but ended up changing his mind at the last minute and taking it instead. Although the dean promised the former Berliner one of the best rooms on campus, when he arrived he was not impressed with his accommodations. At Hamma he moved into a "dusty room" with "sternly utilitarian sticks of furniture." His life, he groused, was "primitive," and the meals at the school were "<u>not</u> like Mother's."[20]

Herman's letter to Lovell, along with a recommendation from John Foster Dulles, soon came to the attention of the OSS. At the time Herman was thirty-four years old, six feet tall, and 160 pounds. He described himself as "lanky." He had excellent German-language skills, good French skills, and knew some Italian, Spanish, and Russian. He also had a good temperament for war work. His reserved nature and ability to be emotionally indifferent may not have been ideal characteristics for a pastor, but they were perfect for planning clandestine operations.[21]

OSS investigators checked in with Herman's references, including Ferdinand L. Mayer. Before the United States entered the war, Mayer had served as the chargé d'affaires in the US embassy in Berlin. Mayer had financially supported Herman's church work and once read the preamble to the Declaration of Independence to Herman's congregation at a Fourth of July service. Now a leader in the OSS, Mayer, although not very religious himself, became a steadfast advocate for the use of religion in intelligence work. Mayer vouched for the OSS's newest potential recruit, calling Herman a "fine upstanding priest." On behalf of the OSS, the FBI conducted a full background investigation and interviewed people in Harrisburg about Herman. That the FBI was knocking on neighborhood doors—including the doors of Zion Lutheran Church congregants—worried the churchman's mother. She thought they might get the wrong impression of her son, who had at times seemed to sympathize with the Germans. But soon enough she was bragging about Herman's "secret" wartime work.[22]

Once Wild Bill's men realized what a valuable potential asset they had in Herman, a man who knew the German religious underground and had networked with church leaders all over Europe, they scrambled to enlist him. They brought him in for an interview and immediately offered the minister a job. The work, Herman noted in his diary after his first meeting, seemed "very special and secret in connection with the war effort. It sounds exciting, but that's not a legitimate reason for accepting new jobs." He wrestled over the OSS's offer for a few days while working out his thoughts in his diary. "I'm more interested in the post-war peace effort than in the war effort," he realized, "but by contributing more directly to the latter I may be able to understand the hidden issues and perhaps even prevent certain unwise acts." Herman's thoughts reveal how yet another religious activist could hang up the clerical collar for a spy badge for the duration. His OSS work was always a means to an end. Herman had not changed. The OSS, he decided, was the best route available to him for building the peaceful postwar world for which he had long prayed. His "schooling," he discovered, was "not over yet."[23]

On consecutive days in August 1943, Herman recorded in his diary first that he received an invitation to preach at Cornell University and next that he was interviewing with OSS leaders. The next half century of Stewart Herman's life was defined by decisions he made in that forty-eight-hour period. Routine, mundane, everyday events such as these, seemingly unremarkable to Herman as he recorded them in his diary, would shape the rest of his life.[24]

Convincing the Lutheran to enlist in the OSS was the easy part for the intelligence agency. Freeing him from his other obligations was more difficult. The agency wanted Herman to report to work right away, meaning he would have to quit his new job at Hamma just before the fall semester began. Dean E. E. Flack was having none of it, war crisis or not. The dean refused to release Herman to the government. Flack's intransigence forced Wild Bill himself to intervene with a series of letters, insisting that the OSS, the government, indeed the nation, needed Herman's services. But the dean would not relent. He called Donovan's request "disconcerting." "We beg you," he told the general, "please do not press the situation to take him from us immediately." The dean had announced Herman's courses and advertised various lectures, and to cancel these plans would cause "real embarrassment." If ever a dean was so ensconced in the ivory tower as to be totally oblivious to what was happening in the world around him, it was Dean Flack. He ranked maintaining the integrity of his fall course catalog above the OSS's efforts to penetrate Germany. Ultimately, the dean offered Donovan a compromise—Herman would teach for two months in Ohio and then could leave for Washington.[25]

Herman enjoyed his time at Hamma, limited as it was. "The teaching experience was very pleasant for me," he confessed to his diary, "and, I hope, for the boys who got a rather thorough shaking-up. Too bad that it wasn't possible to stay a full year in order to get some results."[26]

Herman finally arrived at OSS headquarters in November 1943. He had honored his obligation to Hamma Divinity School and was now free to become Donovan's spook. On his first day at headquarters, he had lunch with George Kennan, who, he learned, "still wants to retire to farm and write spiritual history of Russia." OSS supervisors instructed Herman to bring old clothes and plenty of shirts for his two weeks of intensive training in Maryland's Catoctin Mountains. The training took place in the national park that FDR used as a retreat he called Shangri-La, which later became Camp David. There Herman likely went through a brutal regimen of intensive training in combat, weapons, and survival skills. He did not bring his diary with him, noting, "it's too bad that a break must occur in the pedestrian annals contained in these volumes—but, war is war." It was one of the very few times in his life that he did not write daily journal entries. In joining the OSS, he was leaving his past "completely behind" him, he realized, and probably in more ways than one as he transitioned from peacemaker to organizer of violent, clandestine missions.[27]

Once he had graduated from the training class, Herman got to work. Like the other religious activists turned intelligence operatives, he wrestled with the moral ambiguities inherent in the kinds of OSS projects he was now engaged in. "My present work," he confided to his diary, "is far removed from the ministry." His OSS training had "little to do with brotherly love." But he thought the job was necessary, and the experience might provide some benefits. "Few pastors," he reflected, "have had the insights I am getting and perhaps I can act as a medium." Like William Eddy, he knew that his current employment sometimes seemed inconsistent with his Christian calling. But the sacrifices and compromises he was making were necessary for the long-term good of the church.[28]

Herman put in long hours and had little time to socialize. "All I do," he told his parents, "is go back and forth to the office." He wrote sarcastically in his diary that he almost fell asleep in a meeting with some staffers "because these talks aren't as exciting as church council meetings." Other days he felt "dopey" and did his best to "look busy" while he "sat in a stupor" from all the hours he was putting in. Most of the people working alongside him, he noted, "are conscientious at their work and rather conscienceless at their play." He thought the capital was a sad place. "I have seen so much naked loneliness in people's eyes," he observed. "Life revolves around the daily existence at the office, and social amenities are nourished in the bars." He sensed among those around him a deep emptiness that he believed the Christian church could fill. On Sundays he occasionally preached at local churches. For OSS operatives like Stewart Herman and John Birch, intelligence operations did not mean an end to their pastoral work.[29]

While in Washington, Herman was corresponding with Lyn Cantrell as much as possible. They planned to get together for the first time since their initial meeting at Cornell. Lyn was traveling from Georgia through Washington back to school in upstate New York on her return from the Christmas holiday. The churchman asked her to get a lot of sleep and not to get any colds or headaches on the train ride in. "You can't anticipate this reunion with more eagerness than I do," he confessed to Lyn. Because of the rigors of Herman's new job, as well as his desire to maximize his time with Lyn, he asked her to meet him at OSS headquarters once she got off the train. Their meeting must have been one of the only first dates that began with an appointment at Donovan's clandestine lair.[30]

The date went very well. Lyn "is a grand person," Herman recorded in his diary, "with tremendous resources of energy and feeling." For the first time in a long time, he felt "young again" when he was with her. He wished he could see her more frequently. In February he invited her to meet him in Harrisburg, to visit him at his parents' home. He wished, he told her, that she was "a whole lot nearer so that it would be easier to convince myself that it's not too good to be true." Bringing Lyn Cantrell to Harrisburg was a gamble, he knew, certain to set off a "flood of gossipy rumors" among the church people since he was not in the "habit of having young ladies at home for the week-end." He sent his parents a letter telling them that he was coming to visit and was bringing with him a "very attractive southerner" from Georgia. She was "so attractive," he effused, he had decided to "look into the matter further." Herman's vision of a future of monasticism was starting to fade.[31]

Despite Stewart Herman and Lyn Cantrell's mutual attraction, this was not going to be an easy relationship for Lyn. The Herman clan, Stewart acknowledged, was "a very matter-of-fact family without great apparent warmth." Nor was he much different. "I'm afraid," he wrote Lyn, "that you will discover me to be fenced and barricaded behind many years of self-discipline, hard work, and once-spontaneous dreams which have somewhat 'faded in the light of common day.'" He was not sure he could change. "It would be sure magic," he continued, "to regain that paradise in which you live, and if you could lead me there I'd be eternally grateful." She vowed to try.[32]

The next month, she visited Herman in Washington again. The weekend brought at least one romantic kiss, and, sitting by the fire late that Saturday night, Herman spontaneously offered to "chuck the rest of the world" so that he and Lyn could have more time together. In Lyn's first letters after the weekend, she confessed to Herman that she was in love with him. "I love you completely and immeasurably." Her love, she confided, was "pouring forth from me—the floodgate has been lifted. Do not expect that I can stop it now, or channel it into the conventional phrases. It is flooding the field, giving freshness as the water gives life to all it touches. Can you return it, my dear, or will you be drowned by the deluge?"[33]

Herman's response was typically guarded. "I can't answer that of course," he replied, "but I can say I've never felt the same about anyone else and that my capacity for loving—having lain dormant so long—must try its unused wings slowly." He acknowledged that he was replying with what might seem like a "cold letter," and then added that "my writing is like me, even as yours is like you." She encouraged him to "be a complete man," to balance "the precise logic" of "reason" with the "warmth" of "emotions." "I think that some of the deepest roots of the love I have for you," she wrote Herman, "are nourished by my desire to give you all I can of whatever you find beautiful—whenever you want it."[34]

Despite the overwhelming passion she felt for a man she barely knew, Lyn sometimes wondered if she had gone too far in putting so much of herself into her letters. She had made herself quite vulnerable. "I sometimes think it would be wiser for me to refuse expression to some of the things I write and say to you," she confessed, "repeating to myself the rules of the game every girl or woman plays. But it is no use, for I cannot be other than I am." Herman didn't mind. In fact, just the opposite. "You are the finest thing that has ever happened to me," he wrote. Before the two had met, Herman had concluded that he would be alone forever. "And now," he admitted, "I commence to have the feeling that my waiting has not been without its great reward. I hope with all my heart that I am right."[35]

At OSS headquarters in Washington, Donovan placed Herman in charge of the Central European desk overseeing Germany, Austria, Poland, and Czechoslovakia. One of the minister's more substantial jobs was to vet files on Americans of European descent and to conduct interviews to determine if the OSS could use them to infiltrate the countries of their families' origins. Herman also began interviewing German POWs held in the United States to see if they might be useful to the agency. Perhaps interned Germans could provide intelligence or even return to their homelands as OSS agents. However, the plan to flip POWs from the Wehrmacht to the OSS had a fatal flaw. "Some good men were selected" for recruitment, according to an internal OSS history, but agency leaders could not get registered POWs out of their internment camps without provoking unnecessary attention from POWs' families, international aid organizations, and eventually the German government. A registered German POW could not just show up one day back in Germany without arousing suspicion. Eventually, Herman and other leaders realized that they would have to recruit POWs directly from the front lines before the army processed them and sent them to camps. Meanwhile, a few weeks into the new job, Herman's frustration mounted. He didn't feel like the work he was doing was making a difference. "I'd rather resign," he noted in his diary, "than do so little in the <u>active</u> sense."[36]

The parson remained most eager to help with postwar planning for Europe and especially for Germany. While in Washington Herman drafted a pamphlet for the Office of War Information on "freedom of worship." He also found time to travel to New York for a meeting at John Foster Dulles's apartment to discuss ideas about helping rebuild Germany after the war. The meeting included the leaders of the Federal Council of Churches and a who's who of the US ecumenical movement. Herman sat alongside Reinhold Niebuhr, William Ernest Hocking, Henry P. Van Dusen, John C. Bennett, and Fredrick Nolde, who were working on the Just and Durable Peace project. But Herman was not terribly impressed with the discussion. "It was interesting," he recorded in his diary, "but not especially

One of Stewart Herman's saddest days was learning that the American Church in Berlin had been bombed by the Allies and was now rubble. He hoped to exact some revenge on the Nazi Party leaders responsible for the war that had brought such death and destruction to the world.
Courtesy of Stewart Herman III.

Christian." Christian leaders, he concluded, "try too hard to lay policy instead of <u>principle</u>." Rather than begin by establishing a Christian foundation upon which to build policy directives, Herman believed that they were deciding on the policies they wanted and then working backward, seeking a Christian justification for them.[37]

While Herman was working at OSS headquarters, the *New York Times* printed a photo that stunned and saddened him. It was of the American Church in Berlin. In flames. The news made the church's former pastor feel "queer and 'blue.'" The war had destroyed Birch's work in China and threatened Eddy's in Cairo and Penrose's in the wider Middle East. Now Herman felt the war's horrific impact directly on his Christian work as well. He was ready to do everything he could to bring the violence to an end, even if it meant using violence himself.[38]

PART III

TAKING THE FIGHT
TO THE ENEMY
(1943–1944)

TEN

"The Next Jump"

IN JANUARY 1943, ROOSEVELT AND CHURCHILL MET IN CASABLANCA IN North Africa. Their goal was to develop a strategy for the coming year. They wanted to take the war more directly to Hitler in order to relieve some of the pressure on the eastern front, and they agreed to begin major preparations for a cross-Channel invasion of the Continent from England. Stalin wanted the invasion to happen right away, but Churchill believed that the Allies should wait until they had fully prepared. The prime minister convinced FDR that the Americans and British should first drive Italy out of the war. He wanted the Allies to seize the large Italian island of Sicily and use it as a springboard to move onto the Italian mainland. Once again Donovan turned to William Eddy to help produce the results the Americans needed.[1]

The Allied leaders' plans presented Donovan and his fledgling spy organization with another crucial test. North Africa had been neutral territory, where OSS operatives and agents had substantial freedom to move people and equipment as they prepared for the American military invasion. This was not the case in Italy, where Axis forces were ready for battle. The Joint Chiefs of Staff asked the OSS to serve as a support unit for the US Army. Confident that the OSS could make important contributions to the Italian campaign in partnership with the military, Donovan agreed. He put Eddy in charge of all OSS intelligence operations in the Mediterranean. A lot was riding on the missionary's work. "We thought of ourselves as pioneers on a probationary period," one of Eddy's men remembered, "and that it was up to us at any cost to justify by tangible results our belief that an organization like OSS had a specialized and unique function to fulfill in the military intelligence operations in the theater."[2]

Eddy had run small operations in Tangier, which he closely supervised. Overseeing a series of diverse missions and hundreds of agents spread across the Mediterranean and southern France was a much bigger undertaking. As Eddy planned for the Italian campaign, he set up his new headquarters at Villa Magnol, a beautiful estate near the coast in Algiers. The missionary son dispatched agents from there to the nearby French island of Corsica, which the United States hoped to secure as another base of operations. His men established communications networks and stockpiled caches of weapons in hidden locations for future agents sent to the front.

Eddy also sneaked a few people onto Sicily, mostly Sicilian Americans who could blend in among the locals. To make this possible, the Allies had to ensure that the Mafia, with its large presence on Sicily, would help rather than hinder their efforts. Naval intelligence apparently cut a deal with the jailed American crime boss Lucky Luciano. In return for Mafia aid in both Italy and New York, the governor of New York commuted Luciano's sentence.

The OSS men who infiltrated French and Italian territory routinely found refuge among priests and pastors who were often quite willing to work against their Axis occupiers. Sometimes, however, missions went bad. Eddy felt awful about one particular tragedy. He had helped place twenty men behind German lines in Italy, but the enemy captured and tortured them. "I have no regrets for damage to Germans," he confessed, "but I sweat to think what my carelessness may have done to brave friends." Missionary spies routinely held other men's lives in their hands. It was a difficult responsibility to bear.[3]

In Algiers Eddy once again won the respect of most of the men who worked for him. But he scared at least one hapless driver. "I drove the lead jeep with Colonel Eddy sitting on my right," an OSS officer recalled about his time serving with the missionary in the Mediterranean. "He had a habit of dangling his leg outside the jeep." Eddy did this so that his bad hip did not tighten up. It "made me a little nervous," the officer continued, "because I was afraid an accident might sheer it off. As it was not my place to lecture him, I compromised by driving a bit more carefully."

Others felt more relaxed with the colonel. Eddy had lunch with actor and naval officer Douglas Fairbanks Jr. The two likely discussed the upcoming operation, and perhaps Hollywood and religion too. Eddy found Fairbanks "most simpatico."[4]

Although Eddy was again working around the clock, he kept his family up-to-date regarding his mission. A little too up-to-date. He wrote Carmen, his youngest, about how much he was missing her. She had sent him copies of her spelling tests. He loved seeing how she spelled "very hard words perfectly." He reminded her how much fun they had misbehaving when her mother, Mary, was not paying attention. He reminisced about their ghost stories and how he sometimes gave her "a sip" of his cocktail when Mary "wasn't looking." He also loved it, he told her, when she would sit up on his study desk and pretend to smoke her "little pipe" with him. He assured his wife that he had not been at the Casablanca conference with President Roosevelt. "I do not move in political circles," he insisted. "I did before D Day, Nov. 8, when we were inside the territory to be occupied. Now I am doing the same thing for the next jump." His OSS team, he continued, "bound by the 'passion for anonymity,'" worked "ahead of the troops." He finished by assuring her that he was well and needed nothing "except you, and love with you."[5]

Unfortunately for Eddy, he had said too much. His discussion of operations, his talk of the front and the next jump, and his revelation to his family that his apartment in Tangier had served as a headquarters for planning new missions was all information that the army did not want circulating. Censors flagged his letters. The brigadier general to whom the army referred Eddy's case was not pleased. "Colonel Eddy is a capable, efficient officer," he acknowledged, and most of what he wrote could not provide serious aid to enemy troops if they intercepted his letters. But Eddy's reference to the "next jump" was something different. "I view this so seriously," the general concluded, "that despite my high regard for Colonel Eddy, I must recommend that charges be preferred against him with a view to trial by court martial." Luckily, Eddy was not court-martialed. It was not clear that the army had jurisdiction over him, and perhaps Donovan intervened. Eddy apologized and vowed not to make the same mistake again.[6]

Despite the colonel's packed schedule and occasional bureaucratic headaches, or maybe because of them, he continued to dream of reuniting

During William Eddy's time abroad, he often sent letters home to his family. One letter to his wife, Mary (pictured here with the Eddys' youngest daughter, Carmen), revealed secret information and almost earned Eddy a court-martial. *Courtesy of Seeley G. Mudd Manuscript Library, Princeton University.*

with his wife and children. He told them he was imagining that they could all escape to "some spot like Tibet, Shangri-La, Samarkand, or the sultry Sultanate of Muscat." He speculated that his eldest son, Bill, could "command the garrison," Jack could collect revenue, Carmen could "dance the dance of the seven veils," and Marycita, who was now working for the State Department, could direct foreign policy while "vamping the aides-de-camp, managing the bar, and running the dating bureau." He also apologized to Mary for all the work she had to do while he was away. He promised that when he returned to the United States, she would be able to get some rest—except in bed, he joked, where he planned to keep her very busy. He later applauded his daughter's suggestion that he contract a mild form of malaria or leprosy so as to get a short visit home. "The difficulty," he acknowledged, "is to know where the mild form hangs out, and whether or not he is a lethal form in Axis pay." One Saturday night he worked until four thirty. When he awoke, he decided to skip church in order to write his family. His priorities were clear. He ended the letter by telling them, "I was never so well and happy, never so much in love with all my family."[7]

But he was also never so worried about his family. Bill Jr., following in his father's footsteps, graduated from Princeton in 1942 and then enlisted in the marines rather than follow his initial plan of continuing on to seminary to train as a minister. His younger brother, Jack, would soon enlist as well. The marines activated Bill's battalion in 1943, which caused his father substantial consternation. "It will not be so long I suppose," he wrote his son, "before you ship to the South Pacific. You know how much I wish I could see you before you go, and how much I wish I were serving in the same outfit with you." Eddy did not pray for his son to avoid combat duty. Instead, he wished he could be in the fight at his side. Marycita's future was less worrisome, although Bill and Mary had fretted that their oldest daughter had managed to get all the way through four years at Vassar without a husband. That was about to change. Marycita had fallen in love with an OSS man, Bob Costello. Eddy's soon-to-be son-in-law met the colonel for dinner one night in the Mediterranean just days before the invasion of Sicily, where they discussed his plans to propose to Marycita. Costello brought a "fat" letter with him, which he intended to send to Marycita with the proposal. "From the bulk of the letter," Eddy wrote his daughter, "he had apparently taken reams to pop the simple da quesh, but that is the way of youth. I hope he put enough stamps on it. Anyhow, he was grand. We talked over everything, family, politics, religion, Dartmouth, but mostly just you. . . . Your old man was never happier."[8]

Keeping up with changes to his family at home was easy. Keeping a hold of the larger cultural changes under way in the United States proved more difficult. "I feel my two years absence from home when I find I can't understand recent slang," he wrote. "What the hell is a Zoot-suit?" He had likely read that in San Diego and Los Angeles, a series of so-called "Zoot Suit" riots broke out when sailors on leave began picking fights with young Mexican and Mexican American men wearing "zoot" suits, a distinctive fashion. "Pachucos," or zootsuiters, wore long coats with wide lapels, which they paired with pants that were baggy at the top and tapered down to tight cuffs at the ankles. They often sported long, greased hair. The sailors justified their attacks on innocent civilians by claiming that zootsuiters had dodged the draft. In reality, a greater proportion of Mexican Americans and other Latinos served in the military relative to the size of their population than any other group. Eddy, if he survived the war, was going to return to a United States that looked very different from the one he had left.[9]

*

In July 1943, the Allies launched Operation Husky, the invasion of Sicily. In some ways, it was a preview of the invasion of western Europe that was to follow the next summer. The Allies tricked the Germans into believing that they were going to attack elsewhere and then launched an early-morning surprise invasion with thousands of ships and planes and approximately 150,000 troops. The Americans moved in from one direction and the British from the other. After about six weeks, the Allies had secured the island, which opened up more of the Mediterranean to their naval fleets. The Allies' success also sparked a rebellion in Italy, where government leaders removed Mussolini from power. The Allies' actions forced Hitler to reroute forces away from the eastern front and to Italy, which finally relieved a little of the pressure on Stalin's army. As the Eddy family read newspapers back home, Mary and the children wondered "how much Dad has to do with the present invasion of Sicily." A lot, apparently. Carleton Coon believed that Eddy had succeeded again. Eddy directed "extensive intelligence penetration and subversive activities in enemy-occupied countries," he summarized, "notably France and Italy and the Mediterranean islands of Corsica, Sardinia, and Sicily." Eddy's officers provided American leaders with "a constant stream of strategic and tactical intelligence which was indispensable" to the invasion.[10]

Eddy enjoyed his brief time in Sicily. He told a colleague that "the two and a half weeks I had in Sicily made me want never again to return to a bureaucratic life." In fact, bureaucratic life was starting to frustrate Eddy. That year an operative had needed Eddy's approval to transfer to the region, but he had encountered problems with his previous supervisor in Lisbon. The operative wrote a long memo, claiming that his supervisor held a grudge against him because the operative disapproved of his boss's penchant for hiring attractive and underqualified female secretaries and seducing them. Eddy wanted nothing to do with this operative, regardless of who was at fault in the conflict. The colonel wanted to be a missionary, a soldier, or a spy. He did not want to deal with personnel problems. As far as Eddy was concerned, neither this young operative's disgust nor the potential exploitation of the young women who were having sex in the boss's office was any of his business.[11]

*

With Sicily secure, the Allies began organizing for the invasion of mainland Italy. Eddy drafted a memo for the army assistant chief of staff laying out the operations he intended to run in Italy. He had dozens of men in the field, and they were developing plans for assaults behind enemy lines, for political warfare, and for various sabotage and demolition operations. He was also working on recruiting new agents from among Italian prisoners of war. For Eddy, the greatest challenge was coordinating his plans with those of the army and navy.[12]

As military leaders planned for the next stages of the campaign, they decided to leave the OSS somewhat on the sidelines. The British military brass, who were taking the lead on this mission, did not fully trust the OSS, nor did officers from the Secret Intelligence Service, Britain's overseas clandestine agency. Leaders from US naval intelligence in the region thought little better of Donovan's crew. For Eddy and his team, the experience was frustrating. They were doing everything they could to prove themselves, but they still struggled to get respect from older, more established military units. The Joint Chiefs expected the OSS to partner with and work alongside the army as the invasion unfolded. But this was new territory, and no current operations manual outlined how best to divide up and coordinate duties. Add to that the challenges of US-UK relations, OSS-SIS relations, and OSS–military intelligence relations, and the task proved almost impossible. Eddy was accustomed to running a small, tightly knit operation, where he knew all of the people working with him. Now he was dealing with a vastly larger team and command structure as well as responding to orders from Washington from people who could not visualize the actual challenges of the front. Eddy, always the good soldier, prepared to follow his orders. He committed to everything he was asked to do, even when the requests were ill-advised.[13]

In early September 1943, the Allies began their invasion of the Italian mainland. The initial incursion went smoothly, and the Italians quickly surrendered. But the Germans sent substantial numbers of reinforcements into Italy. They occupied many mountainous regions, forcing the Allies to wage a slow, difficult fight over challenging terrain.

As the Italian campaign continued, Eddy's frustration grew. The SIS wanted sole control over intelligence in the region, and British agents were throwing obstacles in Eddy's way. The US Army didn't seem to understand the importance of intelligence or what the OSS had to offer.

Furthermore, the OSS had made some mistakes, such as forwarding a misleading report back to headquarters from a source in the field without giving it careful scrutiny. Eddy dispatched a long memo to Donovan summarizing the progress his team had made and defending its actions. Like Donovan, he wanted to ensure that the OSS stayed in the fight. This was no time to back down. Donovan nevertheless decided to make some changes.[14]

Late that year, Donovan visited the Mediterranean. In part, he hoped to strengthen collaboration between the OSS and the army, which, he decided, necessitated a split in the OSS's regional organizational structure. Wild Bill kept Eddy in charge of intelligence gathering and special operations across the entire Mediterranean, working out of OSS headquarters in Algiers. He separated the missionary son's work from that of the OSS teams partnering directly with and under the command of the army. For the latter job, the spymaster brought in Colonel Ellery Huntington Jr., his squash partner and an OSS leader who had assisted Donovan in Washington. Many of the operatives on the ground, loyal to Eddy, did not want to take orders from Huntington, who seemed to have won the job on the basis of his friendship with the general rather than his skills, experience, or expertise. Furthermore, the split in command led to internecine battles for resources and expert operatives and agents. In trying to bring order to the OSS in the region, Wild Bill made things wilder.

Huntington and Eddy did not get off to a good start. In a whiny memo, Huntington complained to Eddy that "even before I came out from Washington I realized I would not be wanted and that you . . . and everyone involved would consider me a meddler." He was right. "The reception I got in Algiers from you," he told Eddy, "was worse than I expected and that from the Fifth Army officials . . . was little better." He went on to tell the missionary spy that "this mission has been a colossal headache as I well knew it would be when I took the assignment."[15]

Although Huntington did not last long in his position overseeing the OSS's work with the army in Italy, he remained long enough to convince Eddy to take seriously a dispatch the missionary son had just received from headquarters. Donovan and military leaders wanted him back in Washington to discuss a new potential mission under the direction of the "Commander-in-Chief." Unbeknownst to Eddy, FDR's undersecretary of state, Edward Stettinius Jr., had been lobbying the president and Donovan for "a Senior officer expert in the Arabic language and political matters in the Arabic speaking countries of the Levant." Eddy was thrilled to get to return home for Christmas 1943, even if only briefly, to discuss his new orders and, more important, to celebrate the holiday with his family.[16]

ELEVEN

"A Great Hodge-Podge of Conflicting Loyalties"

By the spring of 1943, Americans were growing confident that they could win the war. Thanks to the work of William Eddy, the OSS, and the Anglo-American forces, North Africa and the Mediterranean were securely in Allied hands. On the eastern front, the Soviets and Nazis had fought the bloodiest battle of the war at Stalingrad, and the Germans were now on the defensive. The Axis powers were also facing a serious challenge from the Americans and British in Italy. What the future held for the Middle East, however, with its complicated mix of Arab nationalists, Zionist Jews, Axis spies, and former colonial overlords, remained an open question. One prescient OSS analyst summarized the need for active American engagement in the region. "Stability of the whole area is threatened," he fretted, because nationalist movements, "dissatisfied" religious minorities, "personal politics," and the actions "of foreign imperialistic spheres of influence" were wreaking havoc. "All these make a great hodge-podge of conflicting loyalties and desires." Perhaps missionary executive Stephen Penrose could bring some order?[1]

The major wartime powers were fighting to win the war. Some also saw the conflict as an opportunity to secure and, in some cases, expand their colonial holdings as they searched for new territories with the natural resources they craved. Everyone from the British to the Soviets to the Germans saw the Middle East as ripe for the taking. The British had overseen Palestine since World War I and exercised substantial influence there. They also controlled military bases in Iraq, their former colony. France controlled Syria and Lebanon when the war began. Saudi Arabia remained independent and neutral. The Soviets wanted a greater presence in the region to protect trade routes as well as to provide a defensive buffer. The Americans, though allied with the United Kingdom, did not want to see the old British Empire remade in the Middle East. Many American policy makers supported Arab independence, by which they meant Arab freedom to deal with the United States and American businesses without the meddling of other foreign powers. The one thing that everyone agreed on was that the Middle East mattered. A lot. Its strategic location and valuable oil reserves made it a highly coveted region that the world's most powerful nations sought to control.[2]

In the summer of 1942, Secretary of State Cordell Hull informed the British in a tactless letter that the Americans planned to take the lead in securing the Middle East for the Allies. The sun was setting on the British Empire and rising on the Americans, and Hull felt no reservations about rubbing it in. Implying that the British had lost their hold over the region, he wrote that the United States maintains "a unique position in the Near East," where "American prestige and influence is still high." Local populations, he continued, recognized that the United States "has no territorial or vested political interests there," implicitly suggesting that the British had selfish designs on the area. For more than a century, the people of the region had benefited from "American missionary, educational and philanthropic efforts," and in return, Hull felt confident, the Arabs, Persians, and Jews in the region would rally behind the United States. Hull envisioned the creation of a new, independent diplomatic mission to capitalize on existing "good will." The Americans promised to use the weapons of "political warfare and of propaganda" to safeguard the Middle East for the Allies if only their alliance partners would get out of the way. The alternative, he feared, was that the local populations would side with the Germans against their former colonial overloads.[3]

Donovan, like Hull, wanted to increase the American presence and influence in the Middle East. He even had a man ready for the job of establishing an American foothold in the region: Colonel Harold B. Hoskins. The colonel had grown up in Beirut with his cousin William Eddy, and his parents had taught at the American University with the

Eddys. He spoke Arabic and, like Eddy, knew more about Muslim cultures than all but a small handful of Americans. Donovan dispatched Hoskins in late 1942 to tour the Middle East and ascertain the chances of setting up an OSS outpost in the region. Hoskins visited Egypt, Lebanon, Syria, Palestine, Transjordan, and Iraq. While abroad, he met with American missionaries and leaders of the American missionary schools. He was glad, he explained, to renew "contact with many friends of my father and mother who had served as missionaries in Syria for 50 years." He knew they might be useful for the OSS or the State Department.[4]

Hoskins drafted a lengthy report summarizing his tour and offering recommendations for the American mission. Stephen Penrose, who was helping oversee the Middle East from Donovan's headquarters in Washington, was not impressed with the report. Hoskins had little regard for the work of the British or for the work that others in the OSS (like Penrose) had already begun. "Colonel Hoskins," Penrose fretted, "expects to operate as supreme authority in the area without any regard to the organization which has so far been built up and for which additional extensive plans are in process of development." Hoskins, Penrose concluded, "has a desire to seize the ball and run with it himself without any regard for the rest of the team."[5]

Nor was Penrose the only person troubled by Hoskins's plans. The British wanted American help in the region but expected to take the lead, regardless of Secretary Hull's reservations. They viewed the Americans, and especially the Americans working for Donovan, as amateur interlopers. Cognizant of the OSS's need to remain in the good graces of Britain's Secret Intelligence Service, Donovan put Hoskins's plans on hold.

In the spring of 1943, Donovan assembled a new team for another mission to the Middle East. The Americans were having difficulty communicating from Washington with the small number of agents working in the region, so Donovan decided to open a station in Cairo, which would oversee the Middle East, the Balkans, and Greece. He put Penrose in charge of developing the "Near East" section of the station. His responsibilities included Egypt, Sudan, Turkey, Syria, Lebanon, Palestine, Transjordan, Iraq, Iran, Saudi Arabia, and Afghanistan. The purpose of the section was to "secure secret intelligence on conditions and trends" in this part of the world and to keep the US government up-to-date on political, economic, and sociological developments. Penrose arrived in Cairo in

May 1943. Later that summer, Archie Crawford, a missionary son who had taught at the American University in Beirut, moved to Cairo to assist Penrose. Next came Lewis Leary, another one of Penrose's old friends from the American University. When Leary initially went to work for the OSS in Washington, he moved in with Penrose's family and slept on their couch. Penrose also had the help of Kermit Roosevelt, the grandson of President Theodore Roosevelt. Kermit would later help mastermind the 1953 CIA overthrow of Iran's prime minister, Mohammad Mosaddegh, bolstering the power of Mohammad Reza Shah Pahlavi.[6]

When Penrose arrived in Cairo, he probably wondered what he had gotten himself into. The missionary executive set up shop at the US headquarters located at 14 Ibn Zanki, Zamalek. The look and architecture of the building were the first of many surprises during Penrose's overseas adventure. The headquarters felt like a "bastard version of the Taj Mahal," OSS operative and movie star Sterling Hayden wrote. It had a high wall "pierced by a tall iron gate," "broad verandas of inlaid tile," and trees shading "vast stretches of lawn." Like Hayden, Penrose was impressed by his new home away from home. The OSS billeted him and the other OSS officers in an "immense" house with "a perfectly gorgeous garden." "I can hardly get over the luxury of it," he exclaimed. Although a novice in the world of spy craft, Penrose was not exactly roughing it like John Birch or some of his other counterparts in the field. It would do as the missionary executive's temporary quarters. But this was little compensation for leaving his wife and daughters behind. Penrose, like Eddy, was immediately missing his family, and he mailed a letter to his wife, Peggy, telling her that he had arrived safely and that he longed "terribly" to have her with him.[7]

Penrose's new OSS station had few resources and almost no staff. The missionary executive had a huge, beautiful office, but almost no furniture or equipment in it besides a small desk and two stiff, uncomfortable chairs. He took on multiple duties, serving as reports officer, registry officer, and head of central files. Keeping up with the Research and Analysis Branch's requests for material from the field was a time-consuming job as well. This was especially difficult for someone who never learned how to type properly. During his first few months in Cairo, the missionary executive spent six hours a day "pecking with two fingers on his typewriter." The job

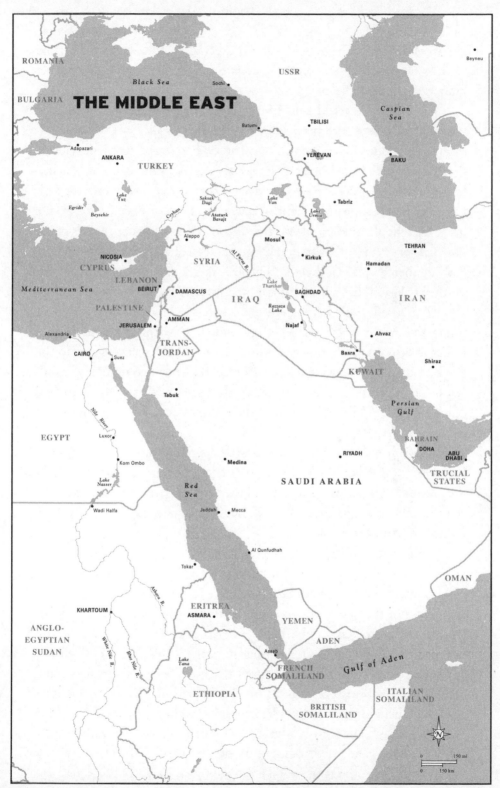

THE MIDDLE EAST. From Stephen Penrose's base in Cairo, he oversaw intelligence activities over much of the Middle East and the surrounding region for the OSS.

overwhelmed him, as it would anyone. According to one report, he had to "beg, borrow, and steal equipment, and shanghai personnel from other branches" simply to keep up.[8]

Before Penrose could launch any serious covert missions, he needed to figure out how to run his operations without provoking his British colleagues. SIS officers, or "cousins" as the OSS referred to them, viewed American work in the Middle East with suspicion. "They came among us," British operative Malcolm Muggeridge recalled about his experience with the OSS, "these aspiring American spy-masters, like innocent girls from a finishing school anxious to learn the seasoned demi-mondaine ways of old practitioners." But rather than defer to the British, they jumped right in, flashing their American dollars. "The finishing school products had learnt all the tricks and devices of the old practitioners in no time at all," Muggeridge groused, "and were operating on their own, sustained by lavish supplies of money whose reckless dispensing sent up the accepted tariff of bribes to astronomical proportions everywhere." The OSS was new to the game, and its leaders made many mistakes. But they had money. According to one operative, "the labor pains" that gave birth to the Cairo field office felt "excruciating," but it nevertheless soon established an important presence in the Middle East.[9]

Donovan sent Penrose to Cairo with a twofold mission: to establish better working relationships between headquarters in the United States and agents in the field and to expand the OSS presence in the region. By the time he arrived in Egypt, Penrose had at least nine operatives working for him, and four more were en route.

Iran became an early focus of Penrose's work. The State Department wanted a stable, independent Iran to serve as a "buffer" to protect American oil interests in Saudi Arabia, which left Penrose and his operatives at the center of the action in a country teeming with foreign agents. They tracked the movements and actions of Nazis in the region, and they also watched the Soviets. They feared that Russians active in Persia might try to claim the territory as their own after the war. Penrose sometimes cooperated with his British cousins on intelligence operations, and sometimes he worked behind their backs as he kept tabs on the many spooks working the Middle East. The British, who had colonized Iraq decades earlier, knew they had to avoid any appearance of trying to expand their empire, or they would surely drive the Arabs and Persians into the hands of the Axis.[10]

One of Penrose's best agents in Iran was Harold Lamb, an accomplished and successful writer who had published several highly regarded books on Asia and the Middle East. Lamb had also worked on film projects with Cecil DeMille. Lamb's fame gave him entrée into the highest levels of Persian society, and the shah of Iran became one of his close friends. Penrose was excited that he had a covert agent on his team whose prewar career provided "exceptional" cover for clandestine work. That Lamb worked for the OSS was a closely guarded secret.[11]

Missionary Thomas B. W. Allen was also working for Penrose in Iran. Allen had spent some time in the Middle East before the war, and he knew the region and its languages. Once Penrose joined the OSS, he schemed to send Allen to northern Iran. To make this happen, he called on his Presbyterian missionary executive contact to help establish a cover for Allen. The Presbyterians proved willing to help. The missionary board sponsored Allen's trip, placing him in one of its mission orphanages. His true purpose for returning to the Middle East was not to share the Christian gospel with children, but to keep tabs on the Russians. When US military leaders in the area learned that Allen was not just a missionary but an OSS operative, they balked. They did not want to anger their Russian allies, and they were not sure Allen could keep his true employer a secret. They shouldn't have worried. He maintained his cover throughout the war and proved to be an effective source for Penrose and the OSS.[12]

Penrose also worked with Edwin M. Wright. Born in Iran to missionary parents, Wright grew up speaking Persian, Turkish, and Armenian. He returned to Iran from 1921 to 1937, where he worked as an educator and missionary. When the war began, the OSS reached out to Wright. Few people in the United States at the time were fluent in Persian—Wright thought he was one of only six Americans. Donovan sent him to Iran in 1942, where, unlike Thomas Allen, he quickly ran into trouble. "The Russians protested my being there," Wright recalled. "They reported that I was an American spy and a dangerous character, and that I would be shot immediately because I was so hated by the Russians—a bluff which had its effect." The Soviet attention forced the OSS to move Wright out of Iran and over to Cairo, where he continued to work for Penrose on various projects in the Middle East.[13]

Wright was wise to worry about the Soviets. The USSR boasted one the most extensive and effective intelligence organizations in the world.

Because the Soviets had been aiming for world revolution since 1917, they had been recruiting, training, and placing spies around the globe well before anyone realized another major war was going to begin. In addition, the job of the Soviet intelligence services was made easier because in almost every country, agents could identify and attract native-born citizens who dreamed of communist revolution. They were relatively easy to recruit and often asked for little in return. During the war, only the Soviets managed to infiltrate all of the major wartime capitals, including London, Paris, Berlin, Tokyo, and Washington, DC. The Soviets also used the priesthood as cover, planting agents in Russian Orthodox churches in German-controlled areas. At one point, Donovan hoped to partner with Soviet intelligence services, but his plans were shot down in Washington.[14]

In the midst of this wrangling among the major intelligence agencies in the Middle East, Roosevelt, Churchill, and Stalin held a summit in Iran. The Tehran Conference in late 1943 marked the first time that the American president and the Soviet premier met face-to-face. The most important issue on their agenda was working out plans for the invasion of France. FDR and Churchill promised Stalin that they would launch the attack no later than May 1944, and Stalin pledged to join the war against Japan shortly after the defeat of the Nazis. The big three also agreed to support Iranian sovereignty and territorial integrity during the war and after.

Palestine, like Iran, was another heavily contested territory. Penrose's top agent in the Holy Land was American rabbi Nelson Glueck, one of the world's leading archaeologists. A friend described the desert-tanned scholar as young, tall, handsome, and erudite. His students credited him with breathing "fresh air into the lungs of Judaism" through his ability to stay committed to the faith while keeping it relevant to the modern world.[15]

Glueck was born in 1900 in Cincinnati, Ohio. He went to the University of Cincinnati and then to Hebrew Union College, where he was ordained a rabbi. After college he traveled to Germany, where he earned a PhD at the University of Jena. In the 1920s, he taught at Hebrew Union College and ran numerous archaeological expeditions in the Middle East. His work brought him into close association with famed American archaeologist William F. Albright, who had spent his career tracking and writing about archaeological sites described in the Hebrew Bible. For much of the 1930s, the rabbi ran the American School for Oriental Research in Jerusalem, following in Albright's footsteps. The school was sponsored by numerous American universities and societies to help facilitate archaeological expeditions. Through his work, Glueck came to know the Middle East better than almost any other American of his generation.

Just before FDR declared war on Japan, leaders of the new American foreign intelligence agency tried to recruit the archaeologist. They liked him, they said, because he was a "non-Zionist Jew" who was "highly thought of and has wide connections in Palestine and Arabia." Zionists, they believed, would always put their commitment to a Jewish homeland in Palestine above American interests. Glueck, they assumed, would not.[16]

Rabbi Glueck was not initially interested in joining the OSS. But the attack on Pearl Harbor changed his mind. "I want to offer my services to the Government," he wrote to his contact at the government agency just days after the United States entered the war, "and am prepared to go anywhere, at any time, under any conditions." He assured OSS leaders that he "never shunned danger." The operative who interviewed Glueck described the rabbi as "a very enthusiastic and highly patriotic citizen—I might say, a noble soul. He is willing to do anything that is required of him and is capable of being a most valuable agent." Donovan offered Glueck a position with the OSS and then sent him back to Palestine. Glueck resumed his old job, directing the American School for Oriental Research, which served as an ideal cover.[17]

Glueck mostly worked on his own, collecting as much information as he could. He also masterminded a handful of potential operations. While Eddy was preparing for Operation Torch, the archaeologist was formulating plans in case the action in North Africa spilled into the Middle East. One of Glueck's early responsibilities was to identify an escape route through Palestine if the Germans managed to push the Allies back during their fight for El Alamein in the Egyptian desert. The battle coincided with the larger Allied invasion of North Africa. The British won the fight, so Glueck did not have to enact his plans. "Should the Germans have broken through into Palestine and Transjordan," he was prepared, he reported, "to organize a guerrilla band of picked Arabs whom I have known for many years" to fight the Germans. He felt confident that "we would have found sufficient Arabs to have carried on such warfare for a very long time indeed." For the entire duration of the war, he stood at the ready "to participate in guerrilla activities" if necessary.[18]

The OSS guarded Glueck's identity carefully. Officers referred to the rabbi using the pseudonym "William Hicks" in all documents and correspondence, which is how Glueck signed his name on all OSS reports. That Hicks was in fact the famed archaeologist was a secret that very few people in the OSS knew. At one point, Glueck's handler lamented that he could not include in internal intelligence reports some of the excellent material Glueck wrote for his American School for Oriental Research newsletters. He feared that if he did, OSS staff in Washington might realize that Hicks and Glueck were the same person. The OSS also feared that the British might recruit the rabbi, hoping to use him to support their colonial aspirations. The OSS did not want him to take on, as one operative put it, "a role parallel to that played by Colonel Lawrence in the last war." Glueck may have been secretly working with SIS, but he did everything the OSS asked of him.[19]

Penrose did not initially know what to make of this rabbi-archaeologist–secret agent. In the summer of 1943, just as Penrose was

Rabbi and pathbreaking archaeologist Nelson Glueck served as the director of the American School for Oriental Research in Jerusalem. That he was also an intelligence operative was one of the OSS's most closely guarded secrets. Glueck kept a close eye on changes occurring in the Middle East.
Courtesy of the Jacob Rader Marcus Center of the American Jewish Archives, Cincinnati, at americanjewisharchives.org.

getting the OSS's Middle East operations rolling, Glueck asked the Cairo office to arrange transportation for him to return to the United States. He said the matter was urgent. Penrose vetoed the request. Glueck, in turn, threatened to quit. Soon thereafter, Penrose learned from another colleague who happened to be traveling through Jerusalem that behind Glueck's request to return home was "much more than meets the eye."[20]

Many American Jews in the Reform tradition viewed Rabbi Glueck as a respected leader. Reform Judaism traces its origins to the mid-nineteenth century. At that time, a group of Jews seeking to blend in better in Europe and the United States developed a new, liberal form of the faith. They started worshipping on Sundays instead of on the traditional Saturday Sabbath, they let men and women sit together at worship, they denounced circumcision, they turned bar mitzvahs into confirmations, and they flaunted traditional purity laws. They aimed to bring the faith up-to-date with the realities of the modern world. Their focus on integrating into their local communities led most Reform Jews to reject Zionism.

During the war, however, some Reform rabbis in the United States began rethinking their relationship to the Zionist movement, viewing it as perhaps worth their support. But not Glueck. His allies sent frantic letters pleading with him to come home in order to help quash the Zionists' efforts. Once Penrose understood why Glueck needed to get back to the United States, he wholeheartedly supported the rabbi's mission. "He is about the only man" who can quell the Zionist uprising, Penrose told his counterpart in Washington, "for he has the respect of both sides and tremendous influence with the reformed group." Penrose was probably exaggerating Glueck's power, but there is no doubt that the rabbi had a good deal of influence among Reform Jews. "In view of all of this," Penrose concluded, "and with my own experience of what is going on at home, I feel very strongly that Hicks should go."[21]

In August 1943, while on his way back to the United States, Glueck traveled through Cairo, where he met Penrose for the first time. Glueck brought with him forty pounds of maps and documents, which Penrose called "exceedingly useful." Penrose sent the intelligence materials to Washington and told Gordon Loud at OSS headquarters that he had been "favorably impressed" with Glueck's work. He hoped "that it may be possible for him to return after he has done the job he needs to do in the States."[22]

*

That Penrose supported Glueck's efforts to rein in the enthusiasm of Zionists was no surprise to those who knew the OSS leader. Penrose believed that ongoing Jewish efforts to establish a homeland in Palestine would inevitably lead to instability and violence in the region. Penrose's prewar work as a teacher at the American University in Beirut, the author of a history of the university, and a leader of the Near East College Association had fostered in him a deep empathy for Arabs, as well as a deep skepticism of Zionism. He claimed that his opposition to Zionism had nothing to do with what he defined as real Judaism. "Those people," he insisted, "who have real sympathy for the Jews will not give their support to political Zionism."[23]

Leading the Zionist charge during the war was the Palestine-based Jewish Agency, which was working to raise its own military force. The agency hoped that its army would fight under its own flag—a Star of David—alongside the other Allied militaries. Churchill was reluctant to support the Jewish army idea. So was Roosevelt. No major Western power, then or now, wants an independent, stateless army roaming around Europe or the Middle East.

David Ben-Gurion, a leader of the Jewish Agency and future Israeli prime minister, met with Donovan in 1942 to outline his vision for the army. Wild Bill, however, along with other leaders of the OSS and the State Department, feared that to support the Jewish army would be to alienate potential Muslim allies in North Africa and the Middle East. Furthermore, in keeping with the ideal of political self-determination that FDR had laid out in the Atlantic Charter, OSS leaders believed that Muslims in Palestine deserved a hand in shaping the postwar Middle East. "The numerical preponderance of Arabs," a secret memo concluded, "would then make impossible American support of an all-out Jewish state in Palestine."[24]

There was perhaps another reason American leaders opposed the idea of a Jewish army. Anti-Semitism was rife in the State Department and other government agencies at the time. Few high-ranking officials had any interest in supporting Jewish aspirations. Some American Jews and many American fundamentalists supported a Jewish state in Palestine—few other Americans cared about the resurrection of a new Israel. Penrose's anti-Zionist views were very consistent with those of many leaders in the US government.

With both American and British leaders hesitant to recognize a Jewish army, the Jewish Agency launched a full-scale propaganda campaign aimed at persuading the public. On December 7, 1942, coinciding with the anniversary of Pearl Harbor, a group called the Committee for a Jewish Army of Stateless and Palestinian Jews, which had close ties to the Jewish Agency, took out an ad in the *New York Times* issuing a proclamation. They wanted the American people and especially the American government to support the creation of an independent Jewish army that would join the Allied coalition. Thousands of prominent Americans, including 41 senators and 123 congressmen, endorsed the proclamation. "We proclaim our belief in the moral right of the disinherited, stateless Jews of Palestine to fight—as they ask to fight—as fellow-soldiers in this war," the committee declared, "standing forth in their own name and under their own banner, fighting as the Jewish Army."[25]

As innocuous as a call for a Jewish army to battle Hitler might seem, Penrose thought that more was behind the proposed army than signatories and *Times* readers realized. He believed that the leaders who signed the document had inadvertently cast a vote in support of an autonomous, independent Jewish state in Palestine. He wrote to eight of the signatories that he knew well, including Washington State University's president, Ernest O. Holland. Not mincing words, he told his father's old friend that he "was unhappily surprised to see" Holland's name under the proclamation. Penrose believed that recognition of the Jewish army and Jewish flag would "constitute de facto recognition of a Jewish statehood" in Palestine. "The movement for a Jewish army, fighting under its own flag," he continued, "is thus intended as a political wedge." "There would be as much point to demanding a Catholic army, or perhaps a Baptist navy, as there would be to setting up a separate Jewish army."[26]

The missionary executive told his family that "the Zionists don't really give a damn about the army—they want their flag recognized on the same status as the government-in-exile, so that after the war they can present the allies with a fait accompli which will entitle them, in their view, to national sovereignty in Palestine." Penrose wrote these words just months after the Nazi regime started implementation of the "Final Solution"—its campaign to murder all Jews in Europe. Penrose, probably not fully aware at the time of how desperate the situation was becoming for Jews in Europe, was correct that raising a Zionist army would likely help facilitate the rise of a Zionist state. Nevertheless, the Zionists certainly did give a damn about doing everything in their power to stop Hitler.[27]

The Jewish Agency's methods "distressed" Penrose, who called Zionists "the greatest single obstacle to the attainment of the cooperation of the Arab world for the Allied cause." He fretted that the mobilizing of an American-backed Jewish army would arouse Muslim anger around the globe, threatening the United States' chances to use the Middle East as a launchpad for missions into the European theater. The United States needed to maintain good relations with Muslims, especially in North Africa, Palestine, and Saudi Arabia, since the armed forces needed access to their "lands as bases for future operations." He even went so far as to request that the OSS pressure the State Department for an official statement denouncing Zionism. Many American leaders shared Penrose's conviction that the United States needed to avoid driving the world's Muslims, and particularly Arabs, into the hands of the Axis. Hitler's persecution of Jews had hardly any impact on their priorities. Like Stewart Herman in Berlin, Penrose appeared immune to the pain and suffering of Europe's Jews and never considered how the United States might help.[28]

During Penrose's first year in Cairo, the missionary executive expanded the US intelligence network in the Middle East, Greece, Bulgaria, and Romania. Most of his operatives ran their own networks of subsources, many of whom did not know that their contacts were actually working for the US government. To reward subsources for information, Penrose's office provided cigarettes, lighters, and other hard-to-get items. At one point, Penrose even procured a "sex stimulant" for an agent to deliver to a "potent but failing monarch" in exchange for valuable intelligence.[29]

As Penrose built the OSS in his corner of the globe, he grew increasingly creative in his recruitment efforts. He schemed to enlist more Muslims for the agency and floated a plan for how best to do this. He recommended that the British let Muslims in regions under their control participate in the annual hajj to Mecca. "Among the Indians and Indonesians going there would be a pile of potential agents," he speculated to an OSS colleague. These Muslims "could then return to carry out our nefarious purposes. We could be prepared to train them in Jiddah or even Mecca if necessary."[30]

While eager to recruit Muslims, Penrose fretted over the extent to which he should use the Christian missionary institutions in the Middle East, including the American University in Cairo and the American University in Beirut, for OSS recruitment and covers. OSS leader Allen Dulles had already been tapping professors at AUB for information. He suggested to Penrose that they "help" the schools fill open positions by providing them with OSS men. Initially Penrose agreed, but he later had second thoughts. "We should in no way," he warned his OSS bosses, "jeopardize the operations of these institutions by tying them in with our activities." Meanwhile, his team sought to keep a step ahead of Axis spies, some of whom the Germans recruited from the same American missionary institutions that the OSS had trolled for new agents. Donovan told Roosevelt confidentially that the Nazis had enlisted two men from Robert College in Turkey, one of the schools that Penrose helped oversee before the war.[31]

As Penrose dreamed of new indigenous spies, he worked to fix the problems caused by those already working under him. He could not get one operative sent by the Washington office out of his jurisdiction fast enough. "If he doesn't get his throat cut first," Penrose reported, "he can't possibly be useful." The operative had never previously been to the region and had no understanding of local cultures or languages. To use a person for espionage "who has never been in the Near East is like using a ditch-digger to repair watches," Penrose complained to his fellow officers. Another agent stumbled unannounced into Penrose's office for help. The OSS leader hadn't even known the spy was in Cairo. "If super-secret sleuths are to be sent through here without our knowing it, they had better be instructed to handle their own affairs and stay away from the office. . . . Sometimes I can understand why the British think we are a bunch of enthusiastic amateurs who don't really know the score."[32]

Other visits were more pleasant. Despite sometimes disagreeing with William Eddy's cousin Harold Hoskins over Middle East policy, Penrose considered Hoskins an ally and, increasingly, a friend. When Hoskins came to Cairo, Penrose pledged to "have him up to the flat soon for a more thorough catharsis." Glueck had seen Hoskins in Jerusalem that year as well. The rabbi described the missionary son as "one of the nicest and most intelligent men I have met out here." They may not have realized that they were both working for the OSS, given how closely they each guarded the secret of their affiliations with the nascent spy agency.[33]

One of Penrose's top agents, a medical doctor and foreign national living in Iraq, just about had his identity blown by mistakes made in Washington. While secretly employed by the OSS, the doctor was working under the cover of the US Surgeon General's Office. Someone at OSS headquarters sent the doctor-spy four boxes of medical supplies addressed to the doctor, "OSS." Penrose aide Archie Crawford acknowledged this was "a blow, and a very discouraging one. We are a bunch of amateurs trying to do a professional job, and tho we can laugh at some slips our allied cousins make, we permit ruinous howlers to take place." On another occasion Penrose had to inform his bosses in Washington that a special intelligence operative had run out on a huge liquor bill in Beirut and that the operative and a friend, on a trip to Damascus, "went on a wild toot" during which "they hit every bar on the route and created considerable stir."[34]

From Penrose's earliest days at the Cairo headquarters, he wanted to get out of the office to meet with agents. But his lack of staff help at the station initially tied him to his desk. Penrose's counterpart in Washington, Gordon Loud, called Penrose's delay in meeting agents under his supervision "detrimental" to the agents' "morale." Penrose had little choice but to wait until Archie Crawford arrived to manage the station. Once Crawford was ready to take the reins in late summer of 1943, Penrose embarked on a field trip that lasted for almost two months. Just before he left, he wrote Loud that he was looking forward to "a little more activity than that to which I have become accustomed."[35]

Activity is what he got. He traveled from Cairo to Iraq, Iran, Bahrain, Saudi Arabia, Damascus, and Beirut. The OSS depended on the cooperation of the State Department and its offices in the region to secure communications, and things had not been going smoothly. Penrose met with his British counterparts in an effort to ease tensions over turf. He sought to "re-indoctrinate" "old field men" and to meet with OSS agents and contacts to get a sense of their potential. Finally, he wanted to identify new agents and to put into place a better system for recruiting and retaining subagents. But most of all, he labored to establish good working habits among his people, a means of ensuring that communications remained secure, and protection for his sources. He had hoped also to visit Palestine but came down with pneumonia at the end of the trip and had to cut it a little short. Through it all, he sweltered in the desert heat.[36]

The longer Penrose was away from home, the more he missed his family and worried about how his wife, Peggy, was faring without his help. But his job was a necessary one. He told Peggy that he was engaged in the war for her sake and especially for the children's sake. "My interests here," he wrote her, "are solely devoted to cutting short the situations which have arisen to keep us apart. . . . The love of my wife and family is perhaps the most powerful motivating factor in taking me away from them, if that isn't too paradoxical to believe." Penrose believed that he could help create a better world for his children than the one he had inherited. But building that better world required sacrifice.[37]

Shortly after Penrose returned from the field to the Cairo office, Donovan summoned him back to Washington for a series of meetings. Penrose had a little time off to see his family, which he was thrilled about. That the time was not wasted was evident nine months later, when Peggy Penrose gave birth to a new son.

Donovan had brought Penrose back to the States to offer him a more challenging assignment and a new title. No longer was he overseeing the Near East desk; Wild Bill promoted Penrose to head of Secret Intelligence for all of the jurisdictions under the Cairo office, a job that would draw Penrose closer than ever to the front lines.

TWELVE

"The Angry Saint Who Kept a Soldier's Faith"

JOHN BIRCH BEGAN HIS TOUR OF DUTY AS A SOMEWHAT RELUCTANT soldier. He had joined the army in 1942 primarily because he needed money in his pocket and food in his stomach. Serving in the military was just about the only way he could survive in wartime China once the conflict had cut him off from his missionary agency. But as Birch's service evolved, he became increasingly committed to his work. One of Birch's fellow soldiers called him "the angry saint who kept a soldier's faith." He had come to save the Chinese from the fires of hell, and now he intended to save them instead from Japanese tyranny. Then, and only then, could the Christian gospel reach its fullest potential in China. For Birch, the war was a means to an end. His ultimate plan was to return to evangelism.[1]

In the fight against Japan, the United States had many weapons in its arsenal. One of the Americans' most closely guarded secrets was that they had cracked Japanese communication codes. Army and navy intelligence analysts, working in Arlington Hall in northern Virginia, decoded radio traffic between Tokyo and Japanese generals and diplomats around the world. They used the code name "Magic" to refer to the intelligence that derived from their efforts. The Magic intercepts allowed US admirals to prepare for Japanese naval assaults. When the Japanese moved to attack Midway Island in the summer of 1942, believing that capturing Midway would provide them with an important base from which to finish the job they had started in Hawaii, they found three US aircraft carriers waiting for them. Over the course of the battle, the Americans destroyed four of the six Japanese carriers that had attacked Pearl Harbor. For the first time, the United States had the advantage in the Pacific. Its navy was bigger than Japan's, and the difference in size of fleets would grow during the rest of the war. The Japanese never made code breaking a priority and quickly fell behind their adversaries in the intelligence game.

While American sailors were battling the imperial navy in the Pacific, the US Army Air Force's soldiers and pilots were fighting the enemy in China. Birch was right in there with them. Most of the missionary's assignments took advantage of his seemingly unmatched ability to go out into the field undetected, acquire important information, and communicate it back to his commanding officers. Birch was smart, he thought on his feet, and he was willing to perform any mission, no matter the risk. He told his parents that Christians "stand up better and longer under dangerous and uncomfortable conditions" than those with more secular backgrounds. That might have been true. Men like Birch had little fear of death since they believed a heavenly paradise awaited them on the other side.[2]

Birch's work varied according to what General Claire Chennault most needed at the time and in response to changing conditions in the war. When the Fourteenth Air Force was not getting reliable intelligence

Missionaries like Birch (*second from left*) were used to living among foreign peoples, and many had mastered multiple languages and cultures. US leaders embedded Birch with the Chinese army, where he coordinated military operations with the US Army Air Force.
Courtesy of Arlington Baptist College Heritage Collection.

from the Chinese Nationalist army despite their military alliance, Chennault dispatched Birch and fellow missionary Paul Frillmann to embed with the Chinese. While in the field, Birch surveyed and photographed damage done by the Japanese and scouted Chinese airfields to ensure that Chennault had accurate estimates of how much fuel was available for his pilots. For months, Frillmann recalled, "we lived on a shoestring of hope and doubt" while surrounded by the enemy.[3]

One of Birch's most dangerous and exhausting jobs, which he undertook in the summer of 1943, was sneaking across hundreds of miles of territory and past the Japanese lines in order to rendezvous with Chinese guerrillas. For this mission, he dressed as a Chinese peasant in order to blend better into his surroundings. He covered three hundred miles by foot. According to one report, he walked between twenty and thirty miles a day, climbing six- to eight-thousand-foot mountains in tremendous heat. During the trip he learned that the Japanese were securing much-needed resources from nearby iron mines. Birch provided the intelligence necessary for Chennault's pilots to destroy the mines. According to a report from the field, the missionary had the "satisfaction of watching" the first B-25 bombers hit their targets before he scrambled away.[4]

Mines were not all Birch found. While operating behind enemy lines, the missionary discovered a large Japanese munitions dump and garrison that the Americans did not previously know existed. The Japanese had stationed between ten and twenty thousand men there. From a nearby hillside Birch studied the village through a pair of binoculars. He identified the officers' quarters and the hidden locations of the munitions. He returned to his base with this information. American aviators proved unable to find the secret camp, so Birch joined the crew of a B-25 bomber and rode in the nose of the lead plan. From the sky he was able to pinpoint the target. American bombs rained down on the village, lighting up the munitions dump. "The seemingly deserted town erupted," Chennault recalled, "into a volcano of smoke and fire." The Chinese allies on the ground who coordinated with Birch reported that they had counted "30 Jap trucks piled high with bodies, leaving the village." In a major understatement, Birch reported that this was "about the only direct contribution I ever made to the war effort." Nor did he seem to ever feel any guilt over his actions. Taking human life did not run counter to this missionary's understanding of the Christian faith.[5]

Birch also served sometimes as a human homing beacon for American pilots in search of targets in Japanese-controlled territory. He routinely went into the field to scout enemy positions and communicate precise information on their locations, providing what one of his fellow soldiers described as "faster and more accurate intelligence than any other American outfit was getting in China." Once Birch came within visual range of a target, he relayed descriptions of the target via portable radio to pilots already in the air. If bombers missed their mark, Birch got back onto the radio to coach them further, instructing them to aim higher, or lower, a little to the left, or a little to right. The American pilots dubbed him the "eyes of the 14th air force."[6]

Chennault relied on Birch to bolster the air force's communications network as well. In the fall of 1943, the missionary worked with the Chinese to set up a line of secret radio stations in main ports on the Yangtze, China's longest and one of its most important rivers, which ran from Shanghai past the wartime Chinese provisional capital of Chongqing. The Allies used the broadcasting stations to track Japanese ship movements. Birch carried and operated his own radio transmitter during the project. He was supposed to have help, but the soldier Chennault assigned to assist the missionary had allegedly seen "a pretty American nurse and fell sick the next day." This meant Birch, as usual, had to do the jobs of multiple people. The experience made him a first-class radioman. Not only could Birch operate the devices, but he also renewed his childhood proficiency at taking them apart and putting them back together again, fixing any problems. He also went to work training locals to operate the transmitters as quickly as he could set them up.[7]

The project required Birch to work as near as possible to the Japanese troops supervising commerce and shipping on the river. At one point he came under enemy fire. Although he dismissed the danger, claiming that the Japanese "were pretty poor shots," he did not waste any time taking cover. These particular soldiers may have been poor shots, but more often than not, American soldiers traded in racial stereotypes, convinced that the shape of Japanese soldiers' eyes gave them inferior vision, which led to poor aim. They were mistaken. Birch told his parents that he "came rather close to death a few weeks ago" but did not elaborate, which must have worried them. The stations that Birch established remained hidden from the Japanese for an entire year, providing Chennault with valuable information.[8]

As much as Birch was doing to help the air force, he believed he could be doing more. He informed Chennault that he wanted to become a pilot. He told his parents that learning to fly would enhance his postwar missionary work—a missionary pilot was a rare and valuable thing. According to one of his fellow soldiers, Birch "did not feel that he was doing enough walking around behind enemy lines, but wanted to be in there shooting." Chennault decided that Birch was too important to lose to flight school. John, he wrote, was "more valuable than any pilot I had in my entire force." As a result, Birch's request went nowhere. A few months later, he wrote home that the "importance" of his current work in China was "increasing." He would not be returning to the United States for pilot training.[9]

As Birch's responsibilities as an intelligence officer grew, he did not forget the original work that he believed God had called him to. Birch always tried to follow the Apostle Paul's directive to "work out" his "salvation" with "fear and trembling." While dodging Japanese bullets, establishing new radio networks, and helping bombers hit their targets, he continued to preach the gospel. He believed, he confessed, that a Christian should "work as earnestly to win the lost today as though Christ were sure to return tonight." This was truer than ever living in a war zone. In just about every village that Birch visited, he preached and distributed New Testaments to local residents. His commanding officers approved of his actions. They decided that letting Birch continue with his evangelism while on duty made him a better and more valuable soldier. "John," one officer recalled, was best suited to integrating both roles at once, to serve as "a soldier missionary." In the same way that FDR blended God and war at the ideological level, Birch embodied the codependence of the two in the field. Birch never separated his faith from his work for Chennault.[10]

The stoic and steadfast Christian warrior continued to impress almost everyone who encountered him. In the fall of 1943, Birch's parents received a letter from Lieutenant Colonel Fred P. Manget, sent from "Somewhere, Indian Ocean." Before the war, Manget had been a China-based medical missionary. He had just met Birch, and John asked him to get a letter off to his family. Manget's missive expressed the paradox that was John Birch. In a short letter Manget revealed that Birch's secret work was of "the highest importance to our armed forces." Then, shifting gears, he explained that he had attended numerous "devotional services" led by Birch, and "it would have done your heart good" to hear John preach. Birch, he added, "seems thoroughly happy tho his task is an arduous one."[11]

Yet the fundamentalism that so animated Birch during college and seminary was difficult to translate onto both the missions field and the battlefield. Sure, Birch believed that demons really had existed in the first century and that to treat demon possession as mental illness was wrong. But did that really matter in a region where people were struggling to survive? Where they had a rudimentary education? Where native-language Bibles were scarce? Did the theological nuances that shaped American fundamentalism and made it distinct in the US context matter to peasants in wartime China? Were Darwin's theories really a threat to people who had never heard of them? For Birch, just as for William Eddy, Stephen Penrose, and Stewart Herman, what truly mattered was bringing more people into the kingdom of God. This realization allowed Birch to worry less about the doctrinal details that had obsessed him in college. Making Christians, not defending particular theological precepts, was now his mission.

The softening of Birch's fundamentalism did not, however, indicate that he was doubting fundamentalism's apocalyptic understanding of time. Just the opposite. The war reaffirmed fundamentalists' faith that the end of the world was coming. Birch sought to understand the significance of global events and their position in the grand scheme of divine history. He believed that the battle of Armageddon and the Second Coming of Christ were approaching. In letters to friends and family, Birch often referred to events that would continue "until Jesus comes," an allusion to the millennial theology that imagined the world's end as a looming reality. He felt confident that the Allies would win the war, but he was equally confident that peace would not last. "Ours is and will be a spiritual warfare against 'principalities and powers,'" he wrote home, "evil in high places even after the 'peace' of Franklin [Roosevelt] and Winston [Churchill]." For Birch, the coming of a diabolical anti-Christ was imminent, and the war was setting the stage for his rise. This did not mean, however, that the soldiers of God should retreat or bury their heads in the sand and wait for Armageddon. Instead, Jesus had called them to "occupy" until he came. They interpreted this as a call to battle without fear to the very end.[12]

Stewart Herman understood time very differently. His reading of the Bible convinced him that God called Christians to work toward establishing a universal church that could bring global peace. Herman, and other Protestant liberals like Stephen Penrose and William Eddy, labored to build the kingdom of God on earth. For them, as for Birch, the war was significant—but for entirely different reasons. They believed that the conflict might serve as a refining fire, purging evil from the world in order to set up the millennial paradise. Despite these differences, the role of these men in the conflict was the same—fight to win.

Birch's apocalyptic theology shaped his view of the enemy as well, which surprised Paul Frillmann. The Lutheran missionary and intelligence officer could not square Birch's evangelistic impulses with his hatred of the Japanese. Frillmann recalled that Birch was a "very religious man" who "daily invoked the help of God to help him kill the Japanese." This made no sense to Frillmann. "Birch," he summarized, "thought it was God's war and our side was all good, the Japanese all bad. It was God's will for Americans to kill Japanese." For Birch, hostility if not outright hatred for the Japanese made total sense. He confided to his religious mentor, Texas fundamentalist J. Frank Norris, that the Japanese were committing atrocities, including the beheading of native Chinese Christian ministers. He wanted to avenge them. Birch, Frillmann noted, had witnessed enough Japanese outrages "to become implacably anti-Japanese." Another soldier who served with John told Birch's parents that the missionary likened the "godless forces" motivating the Japanese to "the Philistines in the Bible." Birch apparently styled himself a modern David, slinging stones at the giant until the Second Coming of Christ.[13]

Birch, like many young fundamentalists, faced numerous challenges as he worked to apply his faith in a complicated world, one that was far less black-and-white than what he and his classmates imagined from their classrooms at Fundamental Bible Baptist Institute. In late 1943, Birch experienced a spiritual crisis. He started to wonder if he was fulfilling his commitment to God. Was he really following God's will? Was this what God had planned for his life? Herman had wondered the same thing as the Axis powers threatened his ministry. Despite Birch's doubts, he agreed to deliver a Christmas sermon to a group of American soldiers, missionaries, and Chinese Christians. Although he had been somewhat reluctant to preach, he confessed that "it helped" him "lots," and he trusted that it helped "the others too." A few months later, he was still in turmoil. "I have grown colder spiritually," he wrote his aunt, "since serving in the Air Force (despite my conducting of some services) but my trust is still in Jesus. . . . I constantly pray that He will forgive my failures and yet use me mightily in China."[14]

Although Birch's military work was dampening his spiritual life, he did not want to give it up until the job was done and the war was over. One of the army chaplains at the Christmas service recalled Birch's "powers as a gifted, intelligent, evangelistic young preacher." The chaplain claimed that he repeatedly tried to recruit Birch for the chaplaincy, but Birch turned him down every time. Things had certainly changed since early in the war, when Birch would have jumped at such an opportunity. "He was convinced," the chaplain wrote, that he could better serve his country in intelligence work rather than in the chaplaincy. Although "his great ambition" was still to serve as a missionary, Birch, according to this minister, believed that first he needed to help win the war. One of Birch's colleagues in the Fourteenth Air Force intelligence division summarized Birch's thinking. "John knew more lucidly what we were fighting for in China," he wrote, "than any other American soldier in the theater."[15]

Fueling Birch's self-doubt and spiritual crisis, at least in part, was growing loneliness. He did not have close friends in China, and he had never experienced a serious romantic relationship. Upon receiving the news that a friend back home had become engaged to a "Christian girl," he lamented to his mother, "Sometimes I wish I had one but when I look at the messed up world am glad I don't." He didn't think he had time for love with the globe enveloped in war. For the moment, satisfaction had to come not from friends but instead from the chocolates his mother mailed to him, which he compared to "manna from Heaven."[16]

Birch came into contact with numerous women in China—missionaries, nurses, educators, and humanitarian workers. Initially, he didn't think about starting a relationship with any of them. Yet as the challenges of living at the front deepened, he began to spend some of his free time with various civilian workers. One was Audrey Mair.

In 1942 the British Red Cross took over a small fundamentalist school that the Bible Institute of Los Angeles had abandoned during the war. Mair, a Scottish nurse, moved into the compound along with a team of humanitarian workers. Like Birch, she was a missionary kid. She was born in China to parents working for the China Inland Mission, one of the oldest and most established missionary groups in Asia. Although she was no fundamentalist, she felt curious about the stern American missionary soldier who would come by in the evenings.

Despite Birch's seemingly laser-sharp focus on his work, Mair had captured his attention. By the end of 1943, they were in a serious relationship. The fundamentalist had a romantic side, which he expressed in letters to the attractive aid worker. "For many hours in the night," he wrote, "I cannot fall asleep, and when dreams finally come, bringing you with them, I no sooner recall your lips with mine that I awake trembling, to find you gone, and I am left with a lost and lonely feeling." His heart, he told her, was in her hands.[17]

Fundamentalism creates in its adherents a rigorous need for total control, or those with an overriding need for control are sometimes drawn to fundamentalism, or both. God, in their minds, is always judging, and the believer must always prove himself worthy. Birch, like all devout fundamentalists, labored to control both his emotions and his actions. He always knew what he was doing. Except, apparently, when he was around the woman he loved. He admitted to his sister that he lost "what little sense God gave" him when he was near Mair.[18]

As the relationship blossomed, Birch began to worry. He wondered if Audrey wanted to follow the path that he had chosen for his life. He described his goals and plans for the future to her in a letter, making sure that she knew exactly what she was getting into with him. "I am something of a farmer, something of a minister, something of a roving soldier," he wrote. He knew that he would always be poor, and, after the war, he expected to be a "pioneer missionary."[19]

Indeed, Birch had big dreams for his postwar missionary activity. "If God leads," he wrote to Frank Norris, "I should like to push westward, possibly in an effort to storm the mountainous Buddhist citadel of Tibet, or else to move through Lanchow to little-reached Chinese Turkistan

(Sinkiang) and some day to load with the Word of God and itinerant native preachers the camel caravans and eventual airships of Central Asia!" He asked Norris for his prayers in reaching "this strange part of the empire of Islam." Birch was enamored with the history of the region, especially its ancient religious history. He told Norris that "winds sweeping the desert sands of this Mohammidan wilderness sometimes uncover cities buried for centuries" that have Christian inscriptions written onto ancient Nestorian tombs. These were signs to Birch that Christianity had once thrived in the region and that he could help it do so again.[20]

Despite the challenges of the war, Birch remained optimistic. "I believe most profoundly," he confessed to Norris, "that the Far East will play a rising part in the affairs of the post-war world,—a world that should be more ripe for the gospel than ever before." And he vowed to help. Birch believed that his work in the army was giving him access not just to local men and women, but also to regional leaders and politicians. "My present activities are giving me excellent opportunities to make friendships" with Chinese military and civilian officials "in high places." He hoped to use such relationships to build the fundamentalist movement in China. Norris believed that when the war ended, Birch would supervise his organization's ongoing work in Asia. Norris, exaggerating Birch's influence, told his followers that the missionary was essentially Chennault's right-hand man and a hero to both Doolittle and Madame Chiang Kai-shek.[21]

The challenge for Birch, however, was integrating Audrey Mair into these ambitious plans. He wrote to his father about his relationship with the Scotswoman, vowing that if she could not follow him wherever he believed God was leading, he would go it alone. He made this pledge to his dad, "even tho," he admitted, "I love her so much that all other women (except Mother) no longer exist for me." Luckily for John, Audrey seemed up to the challenge. She had been raised by missionaries and risked her life by volunteering to serve near the front lines with the Red Cross. She understood what a relationship with Birch meant. The next time Audrey traveled through Kunming, where the Fourteenth Air Force was based, she and John met again. Birch proposed to Audrey, and she accepted. "I'd rather be poor with you," she told him, "than to have a million dollars with anyone else in the world."[22]

Just a few weeks later, the warrior-missionary backed out. Birch had doubts almost immediately after the engagement about whether Mair was really cut out for the hard life of a missionary. He worried too that she was not as dedicated to the fundamentalist faith as he was. He was disappointed in himself for having let things progress so far. He assured his father that despite how serious things had become with Audrey, he remained a virgin. Birch even hinted that Audrey may not have been a virgin, which might have been part of the problem. Audrey never married, and she dedicated the rest of her life to using her medical skills to help the poor. Birch, never one to express much emotion, dealt with the breakup by focusing on his work. He was eager to get back into the field and to put Audrey behind him as quickly as possible.

THIRTEEN

"The Thorough Beating They So Richly Deserve"

It did not take long for Stewart Herman to impress the staff at OSS headquarters in Washington. Just a few months after joining the agency in late 1943, Donovan promoted Herman and dispatched the minister to London. At the time, William Eddy was contemplating new orders from the State Department, John Birch was deep in enemy territory in China, and Stephen Penrose was on his way back to Cairo to take charge of Secret Intelligence for the OSS across the Middle East, Greece, the Balkans, and beyond.

Donovan directed Herman to report to the Western European Special Operations desk at the London Branch. The voyage by ship over to the United Kingdom in March 1944 went smoothly. Herman did not tell his bunkmates, all soldiers, about his ministerial past. He described the GIs as "very masculine and profane. Strange how men together feel they must be 'he-men.'" The soldiers eventually saw the picture of Herman at Princeton in an old issue of *Life*, where he had attended the Federal Council of Churches' Roundtable on International Affairs, and realized that he was a clergyman. They toned down their profanity. Herman had not wanted to "lose a good opportunity to see how the uninhibited army acts." There were also a few members of the Women's Army Corps onboard the ship. Herman noted in his diary that they had little freedom, "which seemed rather pointless because the vast majority were selected (apparently) for their homeliness."[1]

Shortly after arriving in London, Herman lost his OSS identification card. Not an auspicious start for a secret operative. He moved into a good flat on the eighth floor of the Mayfair Hotel overlooking Hyde Park. During the little free time he had, he wandered the park. He watched British soldiers struggle to understand the rules of the softball games that the American GIs were playing, and he enjoyed listening to the orators who had made the park famous.

The UK station was playing an ever-growing role in the OSS and in the wider war as the military began planning in earnest for the invasion of France. During the first years of the war, OSS leaders working in Europe had focused primarily on infiltrating neutral countries and, to a lesser extent, occupied nations where they knew they might find sympathetic allies on the ground. American and British intelligence services could drop agents into occupied France or the Netherlands, for example, and count on local sympathizers to assist them. Not so in Germany. Without substantial planning and perfectly executed plans, a foreign agent dropped into the Third Reich was certain to end up dead.

The United States mostly had to rely on code breaking, or signals intelligence rather than human intelligence, to anticipate Germany's next

OSS officers including Stewart Herman were issued army uniforms and ID cards, which facilitated smoother foreign travel and ensured that they would have some protections if captured by an enemy.
Courtesy of Seminary Archives, A. R. Wentz Memorial Library, United Lutheran Seminary.

moves. The Germans had created a very complex machine called the Enigma for encoding secret messages. The British, led by mathematician Alan Turing, eventually broke the code after they built their own duplicate machine with the help of Polish agents. They shared the information they received with the OSS. The success of this project, which the Nazis never discovered and which the United States kept secret for decades after the war, played an important role in helping defeat the Third Reich.

Donovan appreciated the work that mathematicians in classrooms and scientists in labs had done in cracking the Enigma. But the general was also eager to use old-fashioned human intelligence to analyze conditions in Central Europe. He wanted to place agents in Germany, and so did the president. The United States and the United Kingdom had spent the first years of the war in Europe on the defensive. Pivoting to offense with any hope of success took time, ingenuity, and a good deal of luck. OSS agent Kermit Roosevelt noted that the OSS's late start in the intelligence business "was a considerable handicap." Nevertheless, Wild Bill hoped that Stewart Herman could draw up the plans and recruit the agents needed to infiltrate Nazi Germany.[2]

The churchman's first job in London was to assist western European operations with identifying and interviewing soldiers for possible covert work in Germany. Problems quickly arose. Various OSS outposts, including Bern and Cairo, were developing their own plans for inserting agents into the Third Reich. In Cairo Stephen Penrose had a smart proposal for a German operation in the works. But which stations was Herman finding agents for? Were the various branches going to end up stepping on each other's toes? How would the agency divvy up false papers and stolen German uniforms? What of their British cousins and their plans for German infiltration?

If the OSS was going to launch successful missions into Germany, the agency had to coordinate the work of its disparate branches. OSS leaders determined that they needed a single office to oversee the plans being hatched around the agency and to coordinate with the British; otherwise, they would have agents tripping all over each other and duplicating efforts. To meet this need, they created a London-based Central European Operations desk in April 1944. Donovan tasked the CEO with overseeing the "penetration" of Germany, Austria, Czechoslovakia, and Hungary. OSS leaders hoped they could do this by way of existing operations and networks running out of Algiers, London, Istanbul, Stockholm, and Bern.[3]

Donovan, following the recommendation of one of his best aides, put Herman in charge of the new CEO desk. It is difficult to know how to interpret this move. What does it say about the OSS that its top brass put a pastor, relatively new to the OSS, with no military experience, in charge of masterminding operations aimed at infiltrating the Third Reich? Is this a testament to Herman's extraordinary skills and smarts? Or an example of the haphazard and sometimes amateurish nature of the OSS? Or perhaps a little of both?

For Herman and his bare-bones staff to get the CEO desk up and running took time. Like just about every other new OSS project, funding and resources lagged well behind vision and initiative. Nevertheless, Herman was pleased with the progress he was making. He reported back to his family that he had finally gotten his "teeth into a couple projects which make me feel as though I am earning my keep." He told his girlfriend, Lyn Cantrell, that "little by little, I'm carving a place for myself in this vast mountain of war-effort which, we hope, will bring forth something larger than a mouse." But he also described sometimes feeling "like a squirrel in a cage," doomed to running in circles. He told his parents he expected soon to have "a fairly large staff" working for him. This turned out to be wishful thinking.[4]

Herman fell into a busy routine in London. On Sundays he either preached guest sermons in churches around the region or visited local congregations. As much as possible, he met with British and exiled religious leaders from all over Europe to discuss problems of reconstruction. During the week he often had lunch with coworkers, saw old friends for dinner, and at night went to the theater or the movies to relax. One of his more colorful new acquaintances was Moe Berg, the former New York Yankees catcher, who worked for the OSS tailing famous German scientists in Switzerland and reporting on the progress of Nazi weapons technology. Berg had, Herman recorded in his diary in what was likely a serious understatement, "some interesting stories to tell. He is having quite a time."[5]

While Herman learned the ins and outs of his new job, he and Lyn Cantrell kept up a lively correspondence. They had agreed to date other people, although both also knew that they were really interested only in each other. "My longing for you," she confessed, "is often almost unbearable. . . . Only the knowledge that you are pursuing a good greater than either of us sustains me." Herman believed that he was indeed pursuing a greater good, but through a circuitous route. To build the global ecumenical church that he envisioned as the solution to the world's ills, he had to come to the defense of Germany's Christians. To save the German church, he had to stop Hitler.[6]

Cantrell sent a framed photograph of herself to Herman in London. It was pretty badly beaten in the mail, but Herman repaired the valuable treasure, which he was thrilled to have. "It means a great deal to me," he told Lyn, "because it brings you closer than I had dared to hope and eases that loneliness which has been a part of me for so many years." He took the picture into work with him. "My officer friends," he wrote, "keep asking me who you are, where you are from, and why I haven't 'done something about you.' I couldn't give any adequate answer" to that last question "and was reminded that 'pin-up' girls like you don't 'run around loose' very long." She took a few more photographs but changed her mind about sending one that apparently was a bit sexier. "It was taken," she teased Herman, "to keep your mind off the English girls—and came out a little too well." "Pin-ups" of popular Hollywood stars were popular among servicemen. To keep their beaus focused on them and not on the Rita Hayworths and Betty Grables of the world, many young women like Lyn took their own pin-up-type photos to send to their boyfriends.[7]

While living an ocean apart, Herman and Cantrell explored each other's religious heritages. Lyn started visiting Lutheran churches and asked Herman to explain the distinctive theology of his ecclesiastical tradition. Herman, meanwhile, was seeking to commune with the ghosts of Methodism. One damp Sunday he walked to John Wesley's old church. Wesley, an Anglican, had famously felt his heart "strangely warmed" at a revival meeting, which eventually inspired him to launch the Methodist movement. But Herman did not go into the church. "A glance told me that it was occupied by only a handful of reedy-voiced oldsters intoning the Anglican order and so I went elsewhere." The following week he attended the service but was disappointed that the sermon lacked the "fire" that during Wesley's day had "once ignited indifferent Anglican hearts."[8]

*

As spring turned to summer in England, Herman and his small staff began interviewing potential agents and working on German-incursion plans. He partnered with Lieutenant Colonel George Brewer in Stockholm, who before the war had been a successful playwright, on a scheme to move agents into Germany from Sweden. They discussed various potential recruits and the strengths and weaknesses of each. Herman also brought his British counterparts on board with the emerging plan. Meanwhile, he worked with others in the OSS to identify possible men from the United States who could enter Germany through France.[9]

While Herman was working out new operations, he knew the invasion of western Europe was imminent. In 1944 the tides of war were shifting, and the former pastor and the rest of the officers in the OSS were growing even more confident that an American victory was on the horizon. General Dwight D. Eisenhower, whom Roosevelt put in charge of Operation Overlord, the code name for the invasion of western Europe, was planning a joint US-UK multifaceted attack by land, sea, and air. The general needed hundreds of thousands of troops, about five thousand ships, and more than ten thousand planes for the operation, along with tremendous amounts of supplies. Furthermore, Eisenhower needed to ensure that Hitler did not know when or where the incursion would begin. In one of the great intelligence coups of the war, the Allies managed to trick the führer into believing that the offensive would begin at the Pas de Calais, the closest point in France to England, rather than at Normandy, the actual site of the invasion.

In the London office, Herman worked parallel to another leading American Christian ecumenist, Francis Pickens Miller, to prepare for the invasion. Miller had served with the Young Men's Christian Association and then the army during World War I. After the war, he went to Oxford as a Rhodes Scholar. In Europe he plunged into the global ecumenical student missionary movement and joined the World's Student Christian Federation (WSCF), a major interwar organization founded by American evangelist John R. Mott. During this time, Miller developed a close friendship with Willem Visser 't Hooft, Herman's longtime friend. When Mott retired from the WSCF in the 1920s, Miller moved to Geneva to help run the federation. He was free, he reminisced, "to work toward my dream of a World Christian Student Movement. The one human reality that had begun to possess me was the reality of the Church Universal." In the 1930s he partnered with Reinhold Niebuhr and helped Niebuhr launch *Christianity and Crisis*, which published one of Herman's articles on religion and the Nazis. Shortly after Pearl Harbor, Miller went to work for the Office of War Information and then the OSS. During World War I, he had earned the rank of colonel in the army, which made partnering with the military on OSS operations much easier for him than for the civilian Herman.[10]

By 1944 Miller, like Herman, was working for Donovan in the London Branch. The two ecumenical missionaries did similar work for the American intelligence agency. One was charged with running secret operations into France, the other into Germany. They used their knowledge of cultures, languages, and people, honed through their missionary experiences, to help wage war. Yet despite having overlapping prewar careers, mutual friends, and similar OSS assignments at the same station, they somehow inexplicably did not meet, which may have been for the best. Herman could be arrogant, and Miller was even more so. The latter had thought he could run the international Christian student movement better than John Mott, and he believed he could run the OSS better than Donovan.

As D-Day approached, Herman continued fine-tuning possible operations for Germany, but he had not yet been able to get anything past the planning stages. The OSS was at the time putting a lot more resources into Miller's work, which was more essential in the short term. In late May 1944, Miller helped orchestrate Operation Sussex, in which the OSS dropped dozens of two-man teams of mostly French agents into occupied France within about one hundred miles of the coast. Miller directed them to collect intelligence to prepare for the invasion and then to serve as support units once the invasion began. These agents carried with them another OSS invention—an "L" pill, or suicide tablet, which they were supposed to take if captured by the enemy. The mission was a success. The Sussex teams communicated important information back to London as Eisenhower readied his plans.

The Allies needed a near-perfect combination of the right tides (not too high, not too low) and calm weather to initiate Operation Overlord. As the date approached, Herman's excitement grew. London, he wrote his family, "resembles a college campus just before the big football game of the season, when all graduates have returned for informal reunion."[11]

In early June, conditions seemed right. Eisenhower hoped to launch the operation on the fifth, but a storm came into the English Channel, forcing him to delay the invasion. He took advantage of a brief break in the weather on June 6 to launch the attack. The Allies caught the Wehrmacht leaders by surprise, who had thought the weather would further delay the invasion.

D-Day began before dawn with paratroop drops behind German lines. A one-hundred-mile-wide flotilla of ships then crept into view just off the five Normandy beaches chosen for the incursion. The Germans had fortified the coast and mined the beaches, but most of their army was trying to stop the Soviet invasion in the East, and by this point the Allies had destroyed much of the German Luftwaffe. Some landing parties encountered a staunch line of German defenses, while others faced only minimal resistance. The Americans landing at Omaha Beach and Utah Beach engaged in bloody battles with German troops. For those first waves of soldiers who crawled over the bodies of their fallen comrades on the beaches of Normandy while taking fire, D-Day was a horrific experience. While the number of casualties was substantial, far fewer people died in the invasion than US military planners had expected. By the end of the first day, more than one hundred thousand Allied troops were on French soil. That afternoon, Herman went to Westminster Abbey to pray for the success of the mission and the soldiers who were risking their lives.

Donovan had wanted to be part of the invading force. Once word got out that the spymaster planned to join the fight, Generals George Marshall and Dwight Eisenhower, as well as the secretary of the navy, all forbade it. They were not going to be responsible for the death of the director of the nation's new foreign intelligence agency. Yet Wild Bill had no intention of sitting this out. From London, Donovan took a train to Plymouth, boarded a destroyer as it was casting off for Belfast, and then hitched a ride on a launch that transported him to the USS *Tuscaloosa*, a cruiser that was slated to anchor off Utah beach during the invasion. The vice admiral in charge of the *Tuscaloosa* had struck up a friendship with Donovan a few years back. He was willing to let Donovan come along as long as the general stayed on the ship.

Donovan was aboard the *Tuscaloosa* as the ship's guns shelled the beaches of Normandy on the morning of D-Day. Donovan, and everyone else on the ship, felt the vibrations of the artillery and tried not to inhale too much of the smoke generated by the ship's cannons. The Germans occasionally returned fire. On the second day, Donovan begged the vice admiral to let him off the *Tuscaloosa*. The naval officer finally relented. He told the spymaster that he could not let the general take one of his boats, but that if Donovan managed to hitch a ride with someone else, he would not stand in the way. That was all the permission Wild Bill needed. He and an aide climbed down a rope ladder and jumped into a launch that was passing by carrying rescued airmen. They delivered Donovan to a destroyer escort, where he claimed that he needed to get ashore on urgent OSS business. Nobody he talked to knew what to make of this general with the Medal of Honor around his chest, traveling with a single aide and barking orders demanding that he get to the front as quickly as possible. From the escort ship he hailed a landing craft vehicle and then, rather than swim through the surf to the shore, managed to get the attention of the driver of an amphibious "DUKW" vehicle, which picked him up. He rolled onto the hood of the "duck" landing craft and made it onto the beach, at long last. He was soon under fire from both German planes and nearby machine guns, but he got off the beach and into the countryside without getting himself killed. He checked on the Allies' progress and after a few days near the frontline action returned to the job he was supposed to be doing. He also mailed off a report of his experience to Roosevelt, ensuring that the president knew of his heroics, despite how reckless they were.[12]

Herman's experience of the invasion was far less dramatic. He reported that little seemed to have changed in London as a result of D-Day. He chastised his parents for not writing him promptly while he was keeping up with his letters home. "Of course I haven't been busy," he groused, "that is, aside from the small matter of being on the sidelines for the grand invasion. I wish I could say of myself that I were even a water-boy, but not even that modest honor can be claimed." Still, he was thrilled with the progress the Allies made that summer. In a letter to Lyn Cantrell, he reflected on what was happening. "I remember," he wrote, "the sickening sensations which I felt as the Nazi war machine swept over country after country and now it is not without a grim satisfaction that I watch our armies giving the German forces the thorough beating they so richly deserve. I never believed that they were 'supermen.'"[13]

*

The Germans put up a strong initial fight, pinning down the Allies for the first few weeks after D-Day. Soon, however, the Allies began gaining ground, which forced Herman to accelerate his work. Although he was missing home and wanted to get back to his family and girlfriend, he knew this was not likely to happen anytime soon. "Just now," he wrote to his parents shortly after D-Day, "I have begun things which cannot be abandoned" without destroying months of planning. A few weeks later, he admitted that his life had "been somewhat enlivened since the military campaigns on all fronts have gone into high gear." Lyn worried about how hard he was working. "Every night," she told him, "I take your weariness in my two hands and with my hands caress it into rest. Did you know? Can you feel my kisses close your eyes in sleep?" Perhaps he could. The young woman was often on the officer's mind. His itinerary one afternoon, as recorded in his diary, made this clear. He "shopped at the PX," where US servicemen bought supplies, "visited bank, had lunch, . . . got theater tickets, thought about buying a diamond ring. Back to office to keep pot boiling."[14]

Herman wanted to do in Germany what William Eddy had done in Italy—to stay ahead of the troops in order to soften the ground for the incoming army. If he could get the right operatives into Germany, they could provide intelligence for the Allied forces, commit sabotage, and incite chaos. The OSS's goal was to hasten the collapse of the German empire and pave the way for Allied military forces. Herman's plan was to build a small guerrilla army to operate in the shadows, which meant that he needed dozens of German-speaking agents, whether from the United States or captured from the German army on the front lines.

Herman experimented with various plans. He sent a Swedish agent into Germany seeking information on an attempted assassination of Hitler. He tried to send a team to occupied Denmark to liaise with the underground and to enter Germany from there. He hoped to place an agent on a ship that frequented German ports in Scandinavia in order to eventually smuggle supplies to resistance fighters. He schemed to get OSS men into Austria where he thought they could seek refuge among four sympathetic Catholic priests. He also had a "young aviator" come to him with a plan. The pilot wanted to get shot down purposely over Germany, get captured, and then "induce the high officers to surrender to him." Herman kindly set the overeager American pilot straight.[15]

With multiple plans in the offing, the parson and his team shopped POW camps, looking for German soldiers they could turn into effective intelligence agents. Collaborating with and borrowing tactics from the British, they identified a few for OSS missions. They put their new recruits through a rigorous training course. The soldiers needed jump training to get into Germany and paramilitary training to launch operations once on the ground. Herman envisioned using more than one hundred men organized into small five- or ten-person teams for field missions of sabotage or guerrilla warfare against the Axis. He also recruited a handful of individual operatives who could parachute into Germany and wreak havoc on their own. One, he noted, "will work best as a lone wolf. A man of strong determination; does not fear danger. Forceful, resourceful, and sure of himself. Does not work too well in a group." However, the OSS had not developed an effective means of connecting with agents once they landed in Germany. What was the good of ordering agents to risk their lives collecting intelligence if the agents could not get that intelligence back to headquarters?[16]

The logistics proved just as complicated as the sabotage. To make penetration of the Third Reich a realistic possibility, Herman's agents needed numerous supplies. The pastor had to secure enemy uniforms and other materials from occupied territories to use with cover stories for operatives dispatched behind enemy lines. He partnered with his British counterparts on this, which allowed the Americans to draw on their cousins' knowledge as well as their expertise when it came to forging papers, railroad tickets, and other documents that agents might need on the ground in occupied territories. Yet the British remained somewhat reluctant partners. They were already providing forged documents to their operatives who planned to sneak into Germany. They did not want to put their own people at risk if American operatives got caught with similar counterfeit papers. Nevertheless, to facilitate better collaboration, the British provided Herman with his own desk at their spy agency.

The relationship with the British Secret Intelligence Service was important for Herman and for the Americans in general. As historian Max Hastings summarized, the British SIS's reputation was "unmatched by that of any other." British leaders had used secret agents for centuries. Rudyard Kipling's early twentieth-century novel *Kim* romanticized spy craft and demonstrated the value of good intelligence for empire building. SIS had been very effective during World War I, having among other things decoded the infamous Zimmermann Telegram that helped drive the United States into the conflict. During World War II, SIS again proved its worth, bringing together both human intelligence and signals intelligence to aid the Allies in the fight.[17]

Like Stephen Penrose, Herman partnered with Allen Dulles on some of his projects. Dulles had left the United States in late 1942 for Switzerland, where he became the OSS's most important asset in Europe. Dulles set up his headquarters in an apartment on the ground floor of a beautiful building with views of the Aare River at 23 Herrengasse, in Bern's old city, near the historic cathedral. It was an ideal location in a busy section of the town. People could come and go from the flat relatively unnoticed using either the front door or a concealed back door. Working near the German border, he had the opportunity to meet with dissidents and spies who were moving in and out of the Third Reich. In those rooms Dulles vacillated from sleeping with beautiful women to planning Hitler's overthrow to assessing the religious needs of postwar Germany with fellow OSS men like Stewart Herman.

Herman's most ambitious operation, which he worked out with Dulles, involved Virginia Hall, a woman who had just come to work for the OSS. She was one of the most experienced and successful field operatives ever to join Wild Bill's organization. Before the war, Hall had attended Radcliffe and Barnard and then took additional courses in Paris and Vienna, where she mastered multiple languages, including French, Italian, and German. Wanting to stay abroad, she took a job in the US embassy in Warsaw. For the next few years, she moved around Europe, working in various American outposts. Then tragedy struck. During a hunting trip in Turkey, the rifle she was carrying slipped. When she grabbed it, she hit the trigger, shooting herself. Doctors had to amputate her left leg from the knee down. She named the wooden prosthetic that replaced her leg "Cuthbert."

Hall hoped to have a career in the US foreign service, but her handicap disqualified her. State Department leaders refused to hire people with disabilities, even if those disabilities did not interfere with the jobs they wanted to do. When the war began, she volunteered for service in

France, helping the resistance. When France fell to the Nazis, she made her way to the United Kingdom, where she landed a job with British intelligence. The British trained her in covert operations, sabotage, and spy craft. Then they sent her back to France, where she collected intelligence for the Allies and developed a secret network of local spies. As the war unfolded and the British started dropping agents into occupied France, she offered support in many ways—she provided money, safehouses, radios, and basically whatever Allied agents needed. She also rescued those who were injured, creating an underground transport network to get them back to safety. When the Nazis began closing in on her, she fled France yet again for the United Kingdom, where she joined the OSS.[18]

Herman wanted to get Hall, code-named "Diane," and a male officer into Austria in order to liaise with resistance groups and to secure intelligence useful for the approaching Allied forces. The OSS called the mission "Crocus." Dulles, from his location in Bern, had the best, most reliable information on resistance groups in Austria. He worked with Herman to devise a list of potential contacts for Hall. Herman and his team also developed an elaborate cover story. Hall would pretend to be a "Volksdeutscher," a German of Austrian-Swedish descent, who had been living in Paris since 1938. Meanwhile, her partner, who was really a second lieutenant in the US Army, was supposed to be a Frenchman who had worked at a Parisian club frequented by German officers. If they were captured by the Nazis, they would claim that they had gone into hiding in fear of the Allied advance.

Herman planned to pay Hall well above what the OSS paid most operatives. Apparently, her background, skills, and potential justified giving her more money than her male counterparts, a rarity in the OSS or any other government agency at the time. Herman also planned to provide the couple with cash as well as items they could easily trade or sell should the need arise, including a gold- and silver-plated cigarette case, a gold- and silver-plated vanity case, a silver watch chain, and one-carat diamond earrings. But the operation never got off the ground. Despite Herman's protestations, OSS officers sent Hall back into France on a different mission rather than into Austria. Once again, the young clergyman's hard work and planning had been in vain.[19]

Even worse than missions that did not get off the ground were some that did. One person the OSS tried to send back to occupied France proved to be a dismal failure. Agents signed up the former vicar from Bitche, a town in northeastern France, whom Vichy leaders had expelled during the early years of the war. "With his shaven head, long brown robe, and dirty tassels," he was, according to OSS officer Stewart Alsop, "an obvious choice" for the OSS to recruit and use to jump enemy lines. The Americans dispatched him to his hometown, where he was supposed to help procure information for the OSS. The first time he arrived at a German checkpoint, guards asked him if American officers had spoken with him. "I cannot lie," he told the Nazis, admitting that he was on an American mission. They sent him to Dachau, where the Germans sentenced him to death.[20]

On some missions Herman collaborated with the OSS's Labor Branch. Donovan created the Labor Branch to work with the many underground labor union and socialist trade groups scattered across Europe. While every other OSS branch focused on a particular geographic region, the Labor desk worked with all of the stations around the globe. Sometimes Labor operatives ran their own missions, and sometimes they partnered with other OSS units.

Herman had lunch with Arthur Goldberg, the head of the Labor Branch, many times in London, where they debated and planned numerous operations together. They plotted to return exiled German socialists to their native land, and they collaborated together with the British on an operation code-named "Downend" in which the OSS successfully dropped an agent into Sögel, Germany. They also tried to get agents into Austria via Yugoslavia, but the OSS's relationship with the Yugoslavian rebel leader, Tito, was complicated. The OSS needed to find people who were politically acceptable to Tito and qualified to do the work that was needed, which was no easy task. Despite Herman's indifference to the plight of Jews in Berlin, he had no trouble befriending the OSS's American Jews. The churchman developed comfortable friendships with both Moe Berg and Arthur Goldberg.[21]

A few months after D-Day, Colonel Joseph Haskell, Herman's boss, told Donovan that getting spies on the ground in Germany was unrealistic, if not foolhardy. The OSS simply didn't have the staff or the resources. "Nevertheless," Haskell pledged to Wild Bill, "you may be assured that the matter will be pursued with the greatest energy." OSS leaders determined that they had put the cart before the horse. They could not run operations into Germany until they had better intelligence coming out of the region. They needed to do more "spade work," leaders in London decided, before they could realistically think about launching the kinds of guerrilla operations Herman had proposed. Donovan, in turn, assured President Roosevelt that although the OSS was still drawing up plans for Germany, the job was a difficult one. "We must place behind enemy lines," he wrote, "men of coolness, daring and resourcefulness, who fully understand that they must depend upon their own enterprise rather than on support of the inhabitants." Wild Bill was still counting on Herman to find such men.[22]

Feeling increasingly marginalized on the special operations front, the minister tried to go in a new direction. Rather than continue brainstorming plans to drop agents into the Third Reich, perhaps the Central European Operations desk could focus instead on postwar planning for Germany? This was where Herman's heart had always been. But just as quickly as he proposed the idea, his London bosses nixed it.[23]

Like all of the other religious activists turned spies, Herman was also wrestling with the morality of the work that Donovan had called on him to do. He had not expected to use his education, experience, and training for spy craft. But Lyn Cantrell understood what her boyfriend was doing and why. "Allow me to remind you, sir," she wrote, "of a man I know who is now doing things he finds—to put it mildly—disagreeable in order that later he may be of fuller, greater service." Herman was putting Reinhold Niebuhr's ideas into practice. He was supporting the government's use of coercive violence so that peace might prevail. Herman understood that the only hope for the German people was defeat, which would, he trusted, allow the churches to take the lead in reconstructing Europe. To make that possible, the former pastor of the American Church in Berlin had to get his hands dirty, just like William Eddy and John Birch.[24]

In the end, Herman's schemes for OSS action in Germany came mostly to naught. Donovan had given him an almost impossible task. His team consisted of five people, including two secretaries, to plan complicated operations behind an evolving front. He worked relentlessly, trying to convince his bosses that he needed more staff and resources, but with the army driving toward Germany, staffing and funding the Central European Operations desk never became a priority for the OSS.

*

Despite the Berlin pastor's inability to get his operational plans off the ground, Herman contributed to the OSS's ongoing propaganda efforts. The OSS's Western European Operations leaders decided that "one of the best activities" that Herman's small team could engage in was helping the Morale Operations (MO) desk craft "subversive propaganda" for Central Europe. The pastor took seriously their requests for his team to develop and provide text of "rumors" that the Allies could use to undermine German morale. Herman shaped misinformation about financial crises, the German army's poor treatment of its own wounded soldiers, dissension among military leaders, and even the health of Hitler. His team also drafted a letter purportedly from SS leader Heinrich Himmler, with false instructions that made it look like the brutal Nazi was now working against Hitler. The MO branch printed three hundred copies for distribution to German soldiers in Norway—on paper stamped "British Manufacture." Not exactly a foolproof propaganda letter. More successfully, Herman also helped design fake ration coupons for food—the OSS printed and distributed 1.4 million of them.[25]

One of Herman's goals was convincing German soldiers to leave their posts. He always believed that most Germans did not really want to serve Hitler. He proposed that the OSS drop forged papers that deserting soldiers could use if captured by their own army to claim that they were on leave or had been exempted from service. These papers would serve as the means for those wanting to go AWOL to actually do so. Furthermore, the propaganda pamphlet Herman wanted to drop with the forged papers promised that any German soldiers who used the false papers would receive special treatment from the Americans. The churchman hoped that this plan would expedite the collapse of the German military.[26]

Religion played an important role in OSS propaganda as well. Father Felix Morlion, the Belgian Dominican working on building a Catholic intelligence network for Donovan, put together a lengthy rationale for the OSS to broadcast religious propaganda into German-occupied territories with the hope of inciting a religious revolution. "All peaceful means to obtain freedom of religion in German occupied countries have failed," Morlion explained. It was time for religious believers to act. He and his allies suggested that the United States craft a series of radio addresses calling for "a real Christian crusade against the evil masters of Germany." They compared the potential German resisters against Hitler to those in the early church who challenged the government of Rome. "The time of the catacombs has come again," they opined in a sample broadcast. "It is the time for Christian heroism." Herman agreed.[27]

At the center of any Christian crusade to defeat and then rebuild Germany, Herman believed, was the nation's churches. Despite OSS leaders' reluctance to put Herman's desk in charge of reconstruction, the minister was eager to do everything he could to help shape the direction of postwar Germany. He regularly consulted with American and British planners responsible for reestablishing some form of civil society in Germany. In his free time, he attended a series of meetings in London with religious and humanitarian activists. "Whenever I see such a gathering at work on postwar plans," he wrote, "and become conscious of their innate generosity of spirit, my confidence in the united nations gets a big boost." He believed that the German churches represented the key to rebuilding Germany, and he made his views known to leaders in both US and British intelligence. A few church leaders openly defied Hitler, and many fought to maintain as much independence from the government as possible. He called the churches "the marrow of whatever admittedly spineless resistance there has been" to Hitler and his regime. During his time in the OSS, he maintained contact with German exiles in England, especially those from the Confessing Church, including Franz Hildebrandt, a refugee, a pastor, and a good friend of ministers Dietrich Bonhoeffer and Martin Niemöller, both of whom had been jailed by the Nazis. Hildebrandt, whose mother was Jewish, was a persistent critic of the Nazi regime, its anti-Semitism, and its religious policies.[28]

American leaders trusted Herman's judgment as they drew up plans for postwar Germany. Herman's long experience in Berlin's religious circles meant that he knew whom the Allies could trust and whom they could not. Various OSS officers sought out Herman to vouch for the reliability of particular German religious leaders. Had they collaborated with the Nazis? Could they be useful to the Allies? As the United States began planning shortly after D-Day to prosecute Germans for war crimes, Herman sent a long letter defending the German churches to the new War Crimes Commission. He suggested that the commission treat the churches separately from other civil institutions. He described the churches as "the corner-stones upon which a responsible new government may gradually be established." That OSS and commission leaders seemed to be listening pleased Herman. He reported that one conversation, in which Allied leaders "pumped" him "dry," might have made his entire mission to London worthwhile. He told his parents exactly what he was trying to accomplish through his work. "I still believe," he wrote home, "that the only eventual way to establish an international order is by setting up an ecumenical brotherhood among Christians." This was the goal to which he had worked his entire career, first as a student, then as a pastor in the Third Reich, and now as an officer in the United States' first foreign intelligence agency. He believed that linking Europe's churches, including Germany's, with those around the rest of the world was the key to a future peace.[29]

Herman's faith in German Christians was partially rewarded in July 1944. He received word of a nearly successful attempted assassination of Hitler. If he knew that some members of the Confessing Church had long schemed to help kill Hitler, he did not acknowledge this in writing. But he did tell his parents that it was a "relief to have such a practical demonstration of internal opposition. Too many people assume that the country is 100% Nazi."[30]

That fall, Herman visited recently liberated Paris. He regretted that he reached the City of Lights "too late to profit by the generous kissing which the first arrivals received." He also went to Brussels and to Eindhoven and Nijmegen in the Netherlands to assess the work of field units. Herman, along with many others working out of the London office, was trailing behind the army as it made its way toward Berlin.[31]

The Allies' success was not making Herman's job any easier. Directions coming out of Washington were often vague, confusing, and contradictory. He and some colleagues agreed that "the best work was done while big bosses were off on junkets to gather souvenirs." Herman made clear that as soon as the OSS could replace him, he wanted out. He believed he could better help reconstruct the postwar world from outside the government agency than from within it. Early that November, he told his boss that he planned to resign in one month. "When I begin to become short-tempered, irritable and nervous, the danger signals are commencing to blink," he told Lyn Cantrell. "If conditions were more favorable, it might be possible to have a short leave over here fobbed off on me. However I am rather beyond that point already."[32]

Herman was missing home more than ever. His father had been sick and his family had conspired to keep the news from him, but a friend let the news slip. Herman felt awful that he was not in Harrisburg to help. His father, he told Lyn, "may not be a great man but to me he is the most unselfish and noblest spirit I have known." Then Herman provided some insight into his family and into himself. "I wish that I could tell him so but we are not a very demonstrative family and no doubt we have lost a great deal for want of that." Herman had a hard time letting down his guard to show compassion and empathy, whether to Jews who needed his help in Berlin or to members of his own family.[33]

Where Herman's blossoming relationship with Lyn was going remained unclear as well, further driving the churchman's desire to get home. As reasons mounted for a trip back to the United States, only the pastor's sense of duty had kept him from resigning immediately. "I am still in the midst of jobs," he wrote Lyn, "that appear to stretch into infinity unless the Nazis would conveniently collapse." He admitted that he had a "selfish desire" to see her "in order to discover, as you said, whether or not our mutual magnetism is something transitory or permanent." Yet his eagerness to see the Georgian redhead was perhaps making him a better OSS man. He told Lyn that his wish to return to her "must be one of Eisenhower's greatest aids in pushing forward." Lyn, who was keeping Herman well stocked with chocolate and cookies from home, was looking into taking a job with the Office of War Information in London to get nearer to Herman. Even if he was "walking with Dante in the Inferno," she told him, "I'd find a way to be there too."[34]

While Herman was wrestling over his future with Lyn, he had not given up on his spy agency work. He continued to lobby his bosses for a larger staff, and he provided revised and updated plans for recruiting German POWs. He wanted captured soldiers "chosen primarily for their alleged contact with small groups of dissident Germans who would protect them under cover and be amenable to organization as resistance groups." To identify such potential recruits, he needed German-speaking OSS operatives traveling with the US Army in order to identify them from among the newly captured POWs. But the OSS simply did not have the resources to implement Herman's plans.[35]

Just before Christmas 1944, Herman returned to the United States on leave. His bosses at the OSS gave him thirty days off and hoped he would be back, but he knew that was unlikely. The OSS wanted to send him next to France to help run operations from there. Herman felt that he was fighting both the Nazis and the OSS bureaucracy. The OSS, he complained to a fellow officer, "made rather a mess of the German angle from beginning to end." He was also suffering from what he called the "heebie-jeebies." Indeed, he had been near the front lines for much of the war, dodging bombs first in Berlin and then in London, and more recently the Germans' V-1 and V-2 rockets. He told his closest colleagues at the OSS before he left London that he didn't think he would return.[36]

Safely back home, Herman realized that the war was not over yet. A German counteroffensive that began that December had revealed that "very rough sledding is ahead." "I still believe," Herman confided in his diary, "that the only permanent pacification will emerge from a gradual spiritual revival connected with a world Christian movement." While the OSS had frustrated the churchman, the global ecumenical movement, led by the nascent World Council of Churches, offered the best chance for salvation. Herman wanted to play a role in fostering the spiritual revival that he believed was so essential for the future of the world.[37]

Herman's days with the OSS, at least as an official member, were numbered. Just over three months after D-Day, he had received a tantalizing offer from a different kind of agency, which he had been mulling over in London that fall. At the end of 1944, he decided to make another major change, one that allowed him to merge his faith in country with his global ecumenical aspirations and his hope for playing a role in the reconstruction of Europe. But he was not going to be as free of the OSS or covert operations as he might have thought.

PART IV

OCCUPYING HOLY LANDS (1944–1945)

FOURTEEN

"America's One Priority
in the Arab World"

MISSIONARIES LIKE WILLIAM EDDY HAD LONG SOUGHT, MOSTLY IN VAIN, to convince American policy makers of the significance of the kingdom of Saudi Arabia. Known primarily for its holy cities of Mecca and Medina and as the setting for popular fairy tales about lamps and genies, the region had long seemed to American government officials to be of little value. But as the war expanded, their views started changing. Both the OSS and the State Department came to understand that the Middle East had both short- and long-term importance for the United States. Its strategic location and the oil that lay beneath its scorching deserts and adjoining cool waters guaranteed that the Arabian Peninsula would be an emerging force on the global stage.

American military leaders believed that the Saudi peninsula, located between Asia and the Mediterranean and away from the German peril, might be an excellent place to build new military bases. The Americans knew, however, that the question of Palestine, and whether Jews would carve out a territory for themselves from it, was a diplomatic minefield that endangered US-Saudi relations. Arab leaders around the Persian Gulf saw the Zionist movement as a direct threat. As the Americans began to court Saudi leaders, they had two goals in mind: to get Arab leaders on board with the Allies, and to ensure that Jewish Zionists did not wreak too much havoc for them as they debated the future of Palestine. The

Americans dispatched Eddy for the first job, courting the Saudis; Stephen Penrose took charge of the second, working to keep a lid on Zionism. Both came to their work with a great deal of experience and strong convictions about the future of the Middle East. They both were as interested in laying the foundations for a postwar world compatible with their sense of global Christian mission as in defeating the Nazis.

King Abdul Aziz ibn Saud, referred to by Westerners at the time simply as "Ibn Saud," meaning "son of Saud" (but now more often referred to by his given name, Abdul Aziz), had conquered and unified the tribes of the Arabian desert and declared the birth of the new nation-state of Saudi Arabia in 1932. In 1939 Standard Oil began extracting oil from the country with the king's blessing. Over the course of the war, Roosevelt felt confident that reaching out to and partnering with Abdul Aziz was a smart move for the United States. He also knew that if he did not do so soon, the British would. This was an opportunity he did not want to lose.

Eddy's prewar work as an attaché had convinced him that a US-Saudi alliance was in the best interests of the United States. Saudi Arabia was "very strategic to the Allied cause," the missionary advised the director of naval intelligence in 1941. Abdul Aziz, he argued, had held back the Axis powers and helped restrain "extremists on his borders." Perhaps most important, he had tremendous influence over Muslims the world over. "As he goes," Eddy insisted, "so will go the Arab people and Islam." The colonel believed that the Saudi king was key to the United States' long-term success. "The development of the resources of his country, begun so largely by Americans, lies ahead in the future. The only question is who will furnish him with the technical and financial assistance." He believed the United States had "at present, an unparalleled opportunity" to make Saudi Arabia "America's one priority in the Arab world." He could not have known when he penned those words in the months before Pearl Harbor that he would be central to making this priority a reality.[1]

Donovan, like Eddy, saw a lot of potential in a Saudi alliance, and early in the war he had hoped to send an officer to the kingdom. An aide, drawing on racial stereotypes common in that era, warned the general that they needed to think carefully about whom to dispatch because "any westerner in Saudi Arabia is as conspicuous as the negro in a New England village." One person they considered was Nelson Glueck, Stephen

Penrose's rabbi archaeologist. The rabbi, Donovan's aide reasoned, might be able to pull off this job despite his ethnicity. He was not a Zionist, and "his Jewishness is not a factor in any sense." He added that Glueck "has no visible characteristics" of a Jew, although what he meant by this he did not say. "In the second place," the aide continued, "he is one of the few thoroughly balanced Jews who have survived residence in Palestine through the troubled times." Glueck had managed to win the respect of Arabs and Jews alike in the Middle East. Perhaps he could help the agency in Saudi Arabia. But Donovan decided Glueck was more important in Palestine, where he could continue his work as the director for the American School of Oriental Research while moonlighting for the OSS. Without a good candidate available to establish a post in Saudi Arabia, Donovan temporarily halted plans for sending an operative to the kingdom.[2]

In 1942 the State Department established its first diplomatic legation at the Saudi port of Jeddah. At about the same time, FDR dispatched Eddy's cousin Harold Hoskins to Saudi Arabia to discuss the issue of Palestine with the king. Apparently, leaders of the Jewish Agency, the leading wartime Zionist organization, sought a meeting with Abdul Aziz to see if they could find a compromise that would allow Jews to settle permanently in Palestine. Abdul Aziz refused even to meet with Zionist leaders. The king had already written FDR with his views. He was relentless in insisting that no more Jews should leave Europe for permanent residence in Palestine, and he pledged to forever oppose any attempts to create a Jewish territory in the region. "The establishment of a Jewish State in Palestine," Hoskins warned FDR after his meeting, "can only be imposed by force and can only be maintained by force." He advised the president that the United States should stay clear of such plans.[3]

The State Department wanted to get more people on the ground in Saudi Arabia and to better engage with the region's power brokers. Leaders from State knew that Eddy was a perfect candidate for a diplomatic post in the Arab world, and they began lobbying Donovan to release him from the spy agency. Eddy was, at the time, struggling to manage the growing scope of operations in the Mediterranean. Wild Bill, eager to get one of his most trusted operatives into Saudi Arabia, recalled Eddy from Algiers. The two men discussed their options and agreed that transferring Eddy to State could benefit both the OSS and the nation. Eddy's life was about to take yet another unpredictable turn.

*

Eddy arrived in Jeddah, the bustling seaport city on the Red Sea, on March 15, 1944. His job was to serve as "special assistant" to the American minister to Saudi Arabia. Although his new employer was the State Department, he remained in uniform as a Marine Corps officer under the Department of the Navy and maintained his position in the OSS, which had simply put him "on loan" to the State Department. Everyone wanted to claim this successful missionary spy as their own.

Eddy's orders were clear. "It is desired," an assistant to the secretary of state wrote to the OSS officer, "that you visit other parts of Arabia, including Bahrain and Kuwait, also Iraq, Syria, Lebanon, Palestine, Transjordan, and Egypt." He instructed Eddy to "establish contact with both official and nonofficial persons for the purpose of acquainting yourself with local personalities, problems, currents of thought, wants, needs and aspirations, both political and nonpolitical, with particular reference to American interests." Essentially, the colonel had carte blanche to go where he wanted, when he wanted, to do what he wanted as the United States began to establish a larger presence in the region.[4]

As soon as Eddy landed in Jeddah, he wrote his family. "This town is so Arab," he observed, "camels, goats, cows roam and often block the streets. They are the only transport excepting the few official automobiles." The city was hot and humid with few modern conveniences. Eddy did not initially have running water in his apartment, which required him to get water delivered each morning in a pail by a local boy. He didn't bother to boil it, and he did not get sick, which, he thought, was proof that he was ready for naturalization papers. He decided that building up his immune system was "the only way" to survive. For the first time in his life, Eddy did not have a church to go to. "Christian priests and ministers are forbidden to enter this country at all," he reported. He attributed this to the Saudis' desire to present Islam as a faith without competitors.[5]

Despite these challenges, the job was important and the location ideal. "Jidda is the port for Mecca, which is its chief business," he explained. Hundreds of thousands of pilgrims passed through the area each year. Communicating with the pilgrims, and with the locals, was no problem for Eddy. "I am glad to find no trouble in understanding the local Arabic," he told his wife, Mary, "and I guess the natives of Jidda have gotten used to pilgrim Arabic of every variety so they understand me too." But he was never satisfied. He brought with him a handful of Arabic readers and grammar books and planned to study a bit every day.[6]

The colonel pestered everyone he encountered for information. When he met a Dutch banker who had traveled widely and lived much of his life in the Middle East, Eddy had "much pleasure and profit from pumping him about his experiences." He called his new friend "a very useful schoolmaster." He also wanted to keep up with events at home. He asked Mary for a copy of *Rebel Without a Cause*, "the crazy book on psycho-analysis." Eddy never stopped learning.[7]

The missionary son soon began to explore the surrounding area, despite advice that no good reason existed for leaving Jeddah. "I am told the trip will be very monotonous," he wrote Mary, "that when I have seen an hour of the countryside I shall have seen it all, but I don't believe it. You know my gypsy blood, there isn't a trail I wouldn't take anywhere." He packed only the most essential items: family pictures, an Arabic dictionary and grammar book, a mystery novel, and a prayer book. This was the first of his many trips into the desert.[8]

Within about a month of Eddy's arrival, he met King Abdul Aziz in Riyadh. He wore Arab garb for the series of meetings, which became a habit throughout his time in Saudi Arabia. During that first encounter, the State Department did not allow him to present a gift to the king— only the most senior official brought a gift—but Abdul Aziz nonetheless gave Eddy a gold watch, new robes for summer and winter, and a gold dagger. The trip marked the start of an important friendship between Eddy and the king. While in the capital, he also visited the crown prince's estate, which he described as "out of a Hollywood set." One of his guides gave him a "vivid description of frolics that take place in the villa." Eddy later traveled with the king on multiple occasions to visit the region's various tribal groups. On these grueling desert excursions, the two men and their small entourage lived like the nomads they were visiting, camping in the vast desert. Like missionary to China John Birch, Eddy knew how to adapt to the cultures around him in a way that was both smart and authentic.[9]

Eddy's new mission put Stephen Penrose on the defensive, at least initially. Their various directives in some ways overlapped. Donovan received a memo from Penrose's Cairo office just days after Eddy's arrival warning him that Eddy had been traveling in the Middle East with what

In Jeddah William Eddy immersed himself in the local culture and quickly struck up a friendship with King Abdul Aziz ibn Saud. This photograph was taken in 1945 at the king's palace in Riyadh.
Courtesy of Seeley G. Mudd Manuscript Library, Princeton University.

Penrose's team interpreted as the goal of establishing a permanent intelligence organization in the region. This was exactly what Penrose thought he had gone to Cairo to do. "We are speculating," OSS officers in the Cairo station asked, "whether our activities should be coordinated with those of Col. Eddy and whether there is any risk of crossing wires if this is not done." They had no reason to fear. The nature of Eddy's work was changing.[10]

Late in the spring of 1944, FDR nominated Eddy for the job of envoy extraordinary and minister plenipotentiary to Saudi Arabia, the top diplomatic post in the region, and the Senate confirmed him in August. The rationale for promoting the missionary son was clear enough. Secretary of State Cordell Hull wrote a memo to FDR, linking Eddy's new job to "the increasing importance of our relations with Saudi Arabia arising from its interest in its petroleum resources." In other words, Eddy was in Saudi Arabia for oil. After his confirmation, the State Department issued a press release summarizing the new minister's career: he had been a marine, a missionary, a professor, and an attaché. The memo did not mention that he had also been an officer with the OSS.[11]

The Saudis, along with the Egyptians, were pleased with Eddy's appointment. The Egyptian prime minister heaped praise on the United States' decision to establish a larger presence in the Middle East and thought Eddy was the perfect person for the job. In a secret memo intercepted by the OSS, the Egyptians called Eddy "the expert on Arab Affairs in the White House." They viewed him, based on his wartime work in North Africa, as an important ally who would support a Pan-Arab unity movement and who would stand against Great Britain's colonial aspirations. They also believed that his appointment indicated that Roosevelt understood the growing influence that Saudi Arabia had and would have in the future on the direction of the Middle East.[12]

On August 12, 1944, Eddy began his new job, at which point he severed all official connections with the OSS. The position of minister to Saudi Arabia was more permanent and far different from that of secret spy and fomenter of uprisings. Rather than move from location to location while trying to remain somewhat in the shadows, holding a diplomatic post required Eddy to maintain a public presence. He bought a house and the furniture to fill it and made plans for Mary to join him. "You will simply love our new house, precious," he wrote his wife. "There is a wonderful terrace just off our bedroom where we can sun-bathe together and where we can sleep if you find it better to sleep in the open air. It looks over the sea, and has complete privacy. . . . I would write more were it not for the prudish censor, but soon we won't have to write at all."[13]

Shortly after moving into the new house, Eddy hosted a party for the local Americans in the area, most of whom worked for Standard Oil. "We had a buffet supper with coffee," he reported back to Mary, "liqueurs and cigars on the porch." This was not the kind of party John Birch would have enjoyed or that the king would have endorsed. But everything went well. "Even I was conscious of good cooking, tasty food, quiet efficient service." But he was missing Mary. "This is really going to be a great adventure together darling." Eddy even promised his wife that he had been practicing his tennis and would not let her down. "You will find me a better partner, darling. Let's become the mixed-doubles champions of Arabia." As the day of Mary's arrival approached, Bill's excitement grew. "I want to cherish you," he wrote, "and love you passionately very often. You will accuse me of a one-track mind, but it is you who are on my mind."[14]

That fall Mary traveled with Carmen, the only Eddy child still living at home, to Beirut, where she enrolled Carmen in a boarding school.

Then Mary traveled on to join her husband in Jeddah. Entertaining became Mary's primary obligation. She told the older children that a "continual stream of guests" regularly dropped "out of planes" essentially onto their doorstep. One typical evening, the Eddys had a son of the Saudi king along with other dignitaries over. Mary fretted that "with Prince Feisal on my right tonight at dinner I will certainly have to do the best by my Arabic!" Not everything that occurred that evening was translatable. An American general asked her to warn the prince, who was preparing to depart for the United Nations conference in San Francisco, that the "bucket" seats on modern planes would imprint "a waffle seat on his fanny." She refused to translate that remark to the prince. Eddy and the prince had developed a good relationship, and Mary noted that the two men took turns telling jokes to the delight of the guests. The Eddys respected Muslim convictions and did not serve alcohol at their dinners with Arab guests. But once the Arabs left, the Westerners typically stuck around for drinks on the Eddys' roof.[15]

Despite the parties, life was hard for Mary in Saudi Arabia. She preferred hiking the woods of New England or skiing down Vermont's hillsides to serving as desert diplomat. In Jeddah she had little to do other than play hostess for her husband's events. Only a few other foreign women lived in the city, she was often the only woman at parties, and no public entertainments existed for women. Plus, the heat was overwhelming. "I am getting used to feeling damp all the time," Mary wrote her daughter Marycita. "It is useless to try to be glamorous as a shiny nose is inevitable in Arabia." Nor was swimming a respite. The swells off the local beach were often infested with sharks.[16]

Nevertheless, it was not all bad. She and Bill sailed for recreation, and they showed movies every week on the roof of their house. Eddy convinced the king to let them ship Mary's piano over from the States, a major concession in a kingdom where musical instruments were forbidden. They also brought over their Pontiac, which Mary drove around the city to the surprise of the locals.

Carmen's visits to Jeddah during school breaks were some of the Eddys' favorite times. Bill was not a typical father of his generation. While many men were reserved with their children and sometimes left the child rearing to their wives, the colonel never hesitated to get down on the floor and play. He and Carmen competed at Parcheesi and tennis, boated and swam, and did schoolwork together. Eddy threatened to crack her on the "bean" with his cane whenever she made a math mistake, but in reality the plotter of assassinations was putty in his daughter's hands. Carmen helped her parents with entertaining, and at a Christmas party she made drinks for the guests. She "helps me dispense spirituous comfort as a very personable barmaid," the colonel bragged to his eldest son.[17]

By the fall of 1944, Americans in the European theater sensed that the tide had turned. Stephen Penrose, Stewart Herman, and Bill Eddy all recognized that German defenses were weakening and the Allies were going to prevail. "The events are moving so fast in the war that it makes me dizzy," Eddy wrote. "It is hard to realize that we really have the Blitz in reverse and that the liberation of Europe is actually happening, by leaps and bounds today. One can only hear the news breathlessly." The Allies had just liberated Paris and were making rapid progress toward Germany. On the eastern front, the Soviets were also driving the Germans back. The war in the Pacific was turning as well. The marines liberated Guam, and the strategically important Mariana Islands were now under Allied control.[18]

Meanwhile, Eddy's work with the OSS was clearly not finished, despite all appearances to the contrary. An internal memo noted that Eddy's appointment to Saudi Arabia "opened certain possibilities for further field men" to work in the region and that Eddy "has expressed his willingness to help in placing men." Once Penrose realized that Eddy was not his competition, the two men corresponded regularly, sharing information. Penrose promised to get Eddy "the dope which you requested" and at one point suggested that Eddy bring in David Dodge from the Cairo office as a military attaché and undercover operative. Dodge, he reported, had "done a surprisingly good job for us in Damascus. . . . He might prove to be quite useful." Dodge, as Eddy surely knew, was another missionary son born in Beirut. His great-grandfather had founded the American University in Beirut, and he would later serve as its president. He gained international fame when in 1981 kidnappers snatched him in Beirut and then held him in Iran.[19]

Eddy had to turn down Penrose's suggestion. Dodge was a second lieutenant in the army, and the War Department had insisted that the United

States have no military presence in Saudi Arabia for the time being. Eddy did, however, offer some suggestions to Penrose about getting nonmilitary OSS agents into the Gulf region, but he wanted the US mission there "entirely free from the taint of any super-rogatory intelligence function." What he meant was not entirely clear. He probably just didn't want anyone to undermine the goodwill he was building with the king.[20]

As Eddy and Penrose were debating who best to place in the region, a far more important asset was planning a trip to the Middle East. Eddy's evolution from missionary to secret spy to American diplomat was not yet complete. He was soon going to be working at the side of the president of the United States.

FIFTEEN

"Top-Notch and Absolutely Fearless"

THE WAR WAS ABOUT TO GET MUCH MORE PERSONAL FOR STEPHEN Penrose. Donovan had promoted the missionary executive to chief of intelligence for all jurisdictions under the Cairo station, which meant that he oversaw intelligence operations across the Middle East, Greece, and the Balkans—and the OSS was running a lot of them. Donovan believed that this region was the "soft underbelly" of the Axis and the "most vulnerable point of attack." He slated Penrose to help rip it open. As the US Army drove toward the heart of the Third Reich from the west, Penrose managed multiple missions over a wide territory to the south and east of Germany, each with its own possibilities and challenges. At least one ended in tragedy, which would haunt him to the end of his life.[1]

Since joining the OSS, Penrose had built an excellent reputation among the agency's leaders back in Washington and among most of his coworkers in the field. One of Penrose's aides in Cairo, Jane Smiley Hart, was awestruck by her boss's ability to handle dozens of difficult and complex jobs. "Steve was an almost mystical figure to me," she told an interviewer years later. "He resided in an upper room, and people went up and saw him and came out solemn and walked off." Penrose seemed more like a Mafia don than a missionary executive, setting up operations, dispensing advice, and dismissing poorly conceived plans. Hart viewed him as "a man of enormous analytical capability." She noted that Penrose's Cairo staff "felt of Steve as rather an emperor, he was so calm, and so always present, and so carefully analytical, and so discreet." Nor, she noted, was he flappable.[2]

Penrose's temperament was ideal for the difficult work Donovan had asked him to do, which was constantly evolving as conditions on the ground and orders from Washington changed. Penrose took it all in stride. "I have been around long enough," he told his wife, Peggy, "to know that the best laid plans of mice and men gang aft agley." A person, he concluded, "has to become philosophical in wartime or go nuts."[3]

In the months after D-Day, Penrose and the staff in Cairo were working around the clock. On four consecutive nights, Stephen reported to Peggy, he had managed to fall into bed at three, two, four, and one in the morning. He was at headquarters seven days a week, almost never taking a day off, and he felt "as busy as a boy killing snakes." He was "beginning," he acknowledged, "to get a little tired." His secretary noticed the burden Penrose carried. "I think often of the strain that must have been placed on the men who were chiefs of station," Hart explained, "which would really be Steve. Steve really headed the wildly diverse office in Cairo over a very active period." Every time Penrose's secretary came into the office, she noted, "no matter what time I came to work, Steve seemed to be there." Not only that, but Wild Bill would occasionally show up in Cairo. Donovan "would sweep in, almost without notice, and make rather severe demands." The small staff did what it could to support Penrose, but this was his show to run.[4]

One of Penrose's most important jobs was overseeing American incursions into Greece. The Germans had invaded Greece in the spring of 1941, driving King George II into exile. Some Greeks, rather than submit to Nazi domination, organized secret resistance movements. The Greek Communist Party launched the largest one, the broadly inclusive Ethnikón Apeleftherotikón Métopon (EAM), or National Liberation Front, which in turn established a guerrilla force, the Ethnikós Laïkós Apeleftherotikós Strátos (ELAS), or Greek People's Liberation Army, to wage war against their nation's occupiers. ELAS put up a consistent and relentless fight against the German invaders.

American and British leaders believed that the future of Greece was important to their geopolitical interests, and they determined that securing a pro-Allied Greek government would help them maintain influence in the Mediterranean. At the 1943 Tehran Conference, the Soviets mostly conceded control of Greece to the Western powers, which gave the OSS a somewhat free hand to act. But US and British policy makers did not entirely agree on who should govern Greece once they had expelled the Germans. The British were committed to restoring the monarchy, while the Americans believed that the EAM better lived up to the democratic ideals for which the Americans claimed to be fighting.

Penrose and others in the OSS launched multiple missions into Greece in their effort to support the resistance. One of the most import- ant was "Pericles," which Penrose ran in conjunction with the OSS's Labor section. The purpose of the mission was to make contact and ally with the EAM. Penrose, along with Arthur Goldberg's labor group, sent in teams that mixed renegade Greek nationals, many of whom were communists, with OSS-trained Greek Americans. The OSS's partnership with the Na- tional Liberation Front proved very successful. Penrose's teams produced a "veritable torrent" of information, which they regularly transmitted to Cairo for processing. The reports included information on enemy troop movements, ship sailings, and important inside information on the politi- cal wrangling of the various factions in Greece.[5]

One of Jane Hart's jobs was to receive and analyze some of the in- coming reports from the Greek teams. Each night, after she received and decoded their reports, she wrote her own summary. She then placed it on Penrose's desk by seven the next morning, where it joined the reports of a handful of other secretaries who were maintaining contact with other teams in Greece, as well as in Hungary and Yugoslavia. Hart had no idea how broad the scope of Penrose's work was at the time, but she knew it was substantial. "Mine was such a tiny little corner of what Steve must have done," she recalled, "because they observed the same rules that they always do in intelligence services, that each little corner did not know what the other corner was doing."[6]

Despite the long hours, Penrose kept in touch with his family. One evening he found a few minutes to start a letter, but writing with a house full of fellow officers was never easy. His "apartment mates," he told Peggy, "are sitting out on the balcony with highballs in their hands making snide remarks about my ability to write a decent letter on the typewriter, about my unsociability, and in general casting aspersions on my character, my devotion to you and anything else they can think of." No doubt, once

Penrose had his own highball in hand, he returned the insults. He loved his family, and he loved engaging in sharp banter with his friends in the hypermasculine world of the OSS.[7]

In late 1944, Allied and Greek rebel forces drove the Germans out of Greece. Penrose was happy to report to Peggy that although she might "imagine that the Greek situation has caused me some woe," none of "my boys have been lost yet but several have had miraculous escapes." The thought of losing one of his "boys" was the part of the work Penrose struggled with the most. The OSS quickly moved in to establish a new field station in Athens. The OSS's "customers," as officers referred to the US military and the British, were eager for help from the intelligence agency. They were "practically screaming for intelligence such as we can give them," Penrose told his boss, "for their own facilities are either exceedingly limited or completely undeveloped." The OSS, thanks to its wartime contacts and missions, "is the only source of information upon which they feel that they can rely." Penrose flew to the Greek capital to help set up the new station, which the Allies housed on the top floors of the German Archeological Institute. The missionary executive was very busy, but he did steal some time for a quick excursion to the Acropolis. Yet neither the ancient Greek gods Penrose visited nor his incisive analytical skills could stop the quarreling over control of the nation among internal factions and external power brokers.[8]

Running OSS operations in the Balkans proved to be as complicated as those in Greece, if not more so. Penrose and his team drew up multiple missions, which the OSS and the military executed. He sent teams of covert agents into Yugoslavia, Romania, and Bulgaria, most of whom arrived in enemy territory via parachute. At the same time that Stewart Herman was struggling in the London office to get any of his missions off the ground, Penrose had his hands full working with dozens of agents deep in enemy territory.

Late in the summer of 1944, Penrose launched two missions—one into Bulgaria and another into Romania, two nations that had allied with the Axis powers. The OSS dubbed the Romanian mission "Hammerhead." Penrose dropped a team of American soldiers, two of whom spoke Romanian, near Bucharest from a Romanian plane that a defector had stolen and flown to Cairo. Penrose sent the pilot of the stolen plane with his team as "jump-master" and instructed him to push the agents "out of the plane at the proper moment." They wore stolen enemy uniforms and carried forged papers as well as a radio for communicating back to the OSS. The danger inherent in the mission worried the missionary. "In spite of the rather facetious way in which I have described the mission," Penrose confessed to Whitney Shepardson, the head of Secret Intelligence for the entire OSS, "I am perfectly well aware that it is the most hazardous undertaking we have yet entertained." The team, he continued, "is top-notch" and "absolutely fearless." Their primary job was to do intelligence work and also to help downed Allied airmen stranded in Romania escape. Penrose took this operation, like all of the missions he orchestrated, very seriously. "I am deeply concerned over the welfare of these men," he wrote. "They are all exceedingly good boys."[9]

The US and British armies used the intelligence they received from the OSS teams dropped into Romania to track enemy movements, partner with local resistance groups, and identify potential targets. Helping run the mission for the OSS from on the ground in Romania was Frank Wisner. The officer secured valuable intelligence from around the region, and, over the course of many months, he and his teams rescued more than two thousand Allied airmen. Near the end of the war, Wisner also kept close tabs on the Soviet agents in the region. The Americans worried that the Russians had designs on Romania. When the Germans started retreating, Wisner stayed behind, and from Bucharest he established a broad network of anticommunist agents aimed at undermining the growing communist movement. Historian Hugh Wilford notes that American leaders back in Washington later saw Wisner as "a prophet of postwar Soviet intentions."[10]

Other missions yielded fewer positive results. A team Penrose dropped into Bulgaria went silent. Failing to hear from his men, Penrose reported that he was "exceedingly worried." The possibility "of their being wiped out in a fight with the Germans or of being taken over by the Russians are too good to be overlooked entirely." Luckily, they survived and made it to Sofia, where they reestablished contact with the OSS. Penrose attributed the good news to "telepathy" because he had been "mentally ordering" the team to head for Sofia for days. Penrose understood that his agents were risking their lives based on his orders, which he never took for granted.[11]

Penrose also sent a team into Czechoslovakia, where members of a resistance movement were waging a heroic fight against the Germans. They captured and took control of some territory that included a POW camp where the Germans were holding captured American fliers. Once Penrose got word of liberated Americans stranded in the region, he helped coordinate a plan to drop multiple teams of agents to try to rescue them. After extracting the pilots, he ordered his teams to remain behind to conduct additional intelligence work. He wanted them to connect with the Slovak underground and help organize more resistance groups to drive the Germans out. For the OSS agents and operatives to do their job, they had to navigate a politically challenging terrain still occupied by the Germans in which Americans, Soviet agents, and the various ethnic groups living in the region were all suspicious of one other.

One of the men working for Penrose on this mission was Tibor Keszthelyi, an American Jew born in Croatia. For two months, he worked on the ground in enemy-occupied Czechoslovakia and Hungary. He helped rescue downed American fliers, liaised with the local underground, established a link between guerrilla groups and the OSS, and ushered additional agents into Hungary. Keszthelyi also fell in love with a Romanian schoolteacher and rebel, who was helping the OSS operatives in their work. He was eventually captured along with some of the other Americans on his team. German troops took him to the concentration camp at Mauthausen in Austria. There the Americans faced brutal interrogations from special agents from the SS and the Gestapo who had traveled from Berlin to extract as much information from them as possible.[12]

Exactly what happened at the camp is not entirely clear. The best eyewitness to the Americans' interrogation was a translator, but since Keszthelyi spoke German, the translator was not present for his interrogations. Some of Tibor's group were hung from chains, some were whipped, and some were beaten with sticks. Gestapo agents also administered a torture called the "Tibetan prayer mill," in which they used small pieces of wood to crush the Americans' fingers. Once the Gestapo agents had extracted all the information they could get, they took Keszthelyi and the other Americans into a courtyard and executed them.[13]

The Americans eventually recovered Keszthelyi's body and held a military funeral for him. Penrose wrote his wife afterward, commenting on how much the service had affected him. "It was the first time I had ever witnessed such a spectacle in person," he told Peggy. "I hope I don't have to do it again for any of my men. I can't view it with sufficient detachment. This isn't the first of them who has died, but this hit me harder than any of the others because of the circumstances." Years later, Penrose's wife told a friend that Keszthelyi "was the agent" that Steve for "so many years mourned, because he had been killed in one of the missions that Steve had organized." Unlike William Eddy, Penrose never reflected after the war on how his actions and decisions impacted him. But it is clear from his family that for the rest of his life, he mourned the loss of men like Keszthelyi. Penrose had thought that God had called him to be a missionary or an educator; he never expected that in serving God, he would become an intelligence operative sending young men to their deaths at the hands of the Gestapo.[14]

Like William Eddy, Penrose also worried about how his family was coping with his absence. Penrose wrote a letter to his seven-year-old daughter, Dale, to wish her a happy birthday. It was another milestone he was sorry to miss. The letter was packed with warm thoughts and advice. He especially wanted Dale to be sure to help her mother, Peggy, who was pregnant, with the household chores and with her little sister, whom they called "Skipper." "You must try to keep Mother from getting tired," he

Like many of those who served in the war, Stephen Penrose hated being away from his family. But he believed that his work was helping to establish a better world for his children than the one he had inherited.
Courtesy of Dale Penrose Harrell.

wrote, "and the easiest way for her to get tired is to have to tell you and Skipper over and over again to do something." He reminded Dale to write him a lot of letters and asked Peggy to make sure that she did. A letter from Dale, he confessed, "would make me very happy indeed." At the end of July 1944, Peggy gave birth to a son, whom she named Stephen, after his father. Penrose was sorry he could not be there.[15]

Despite Penrose's absence, he very much missed his wife and worked to assure her that he still cared deeply for her. "You are far more often in my thoughts than you will believe," he wrote her. "And I love you more than I would ever have believed possible before I was married." In fact, the longer they were together, he realized, the more he loved her. He dreamed of taking Peggy on a vacation where they could "dine and dance every night." He also begged her to send him a photograph of herself. "I need one very badly," he admitted. For Penrose, the sacrifice he was making was about establishing a new world in which babies would not have to grow up fearing for the future, wives would not have to raise children without their husbands at their sides, and seven-year-olds would not have to miss out on time with their fathers as a result of wars.[16]

Penrose continued to count on Rabbi Glueck to ensure that OSS operations in and around Palestine ran smoothly. After the archaeologist's trip to Cincinnati in late 1943 to put down the rabbinical Zionist rebellion, Glueck had traveled to Washington, DC, where the OSS put him through a quick training regimen. The secret operative impressed his instructors at headquarters, and one suggested that the OSS recruit "more men like this." Glueck, he reported, "contributed to every discussion, to every mealtime discussion, suggested improvements in the curriculum and stimulated the better students. He was a splendid influence and a credit to the organization."[17]

The rabbi was at the time getting a lot more attention than a spy normally would or should. In February 1944, *National Geographic* ran a long feature by Glueck about one of his major archaeological expeditions, illustrated with many beautiful photographs, titled "On the Trail of King Solomon's Mines." Glueck argued that the Hebrew Bible "continues to prove a rich geography and guide to exploration of the Holy Land." Scholars had long debated how King Solomon could have filled his temple with gold and bronze objects as described in the first book of Kings without having a serious mining operation. Glueck believed that he had solved the mystery and located Solomon's mines.[18]

When Glueck returned to Jerusalem in early 1944, he requested additional funds for his work. He had the full support of Penrose and the rest of the Cairo staff. His bosses rated his performance in the field as "excellent," and his request won easy approval. The OSS also provided the rabbi with a gun. Extant correspondence does not say why, but clearly Glueck believed that he might be in danger. Perhaps the nature of his intelligence job worried him, or, more likely, the growing tension in Palestine over the migration of Jews and the increasing Arab resistance to that migration convinced him that carrying a weapon might not be a bad idea. He also wanted a car. Securing such a luxury, especially in the Middle East, was a challenge, but the OSS Cairo office came through for the secret agent. Unfortunately, not long after the rabbi took delivery of the car, burglars broke into his garage and stole three of its wheels. Replacing the missing parts when wartime supplies were so scarce was about as difficult as replacing the entire vehicle.[19]

Helping Penrose oversee the Middle East was his longtime friend Lewis Leary, who knew they had something special in Glueck. "I wish I could really tell you," he wrote the rabbi, "how good it makes Steve and me feel to know that you are there on the spot ready to give us the advantage of your observations and experience." Others in the Cairo office were also impressed with Glueck, but perhaps for a different reason. The tan archaeologist made famous by *National Geographic* garnered plenty of attention from the OSS secretaries when he visited. Or at least that is what his jealous male colleagues believed. "It was awfully good to see you here," Leary wrote, "in spite of the devastation you have left behind in the hearts and minds of each secretary with whom we were unwise enough to allow you to come in contact." His "prettier lady friends," Leary continued, were eager for Glueck's next visit.[20]

Glueck's instructions from the Cairo office remained clear. "Keep your nose clean," Leary advised him, "your eye on the ball, and your energy directed toward helping us discover what there is that you can most effectively do for us and the cause we represent." Glueck traveled the region and most of the time returned with valuable intel. However, one letter he sent to Leary carried a different tone. "This whole goddam trip is strictly

SNAFU." Glueck had contracted bronchitis and was not happy about it, as it forced him to cancel meetings. The Cairo office staff eagerly digested most of his missives and then forwarded them to Washington. By mid-1944 Glueck had written thirty-three intelligence reports, ten of which his bosses rated as "extremely valuable."[21]

Impressed with Glueck's abilities, OSS leaders discussed bringing him in from the field and making him the Cairo station's lead analyst on the Middle East. Historian William Langer, the director of the OSS's Research and Analysis Branch in Washington, DC, liked Glueck but thought the rabbi was a "queer duck." Glueck, the Harvard professor determined, seemed "a 'tortured soul' and the sort of intellectual autocrat who would not get along with people working under him." Perhaps Langer's time as chairman of a history department had made him an expert on identifying both tortured souls and intellectual autocrats.[22]

Despite Glueck's obvious skill, anti-Semitism within the OSS dampened his career in espionage. Leary noted that Glueck "feels very strongly that whatever he reports on the situation as it exists in Palestine would be interpreted by the anti-Semites in our organization as an example of an essential Jewish bias in him." He did not identify those OSS anti-Semites by name, and whether Glueck (or Leary) considered Penrose an anti-Semite is not clear. But it is clear that despite how substantially the work of Glueck and Penrose overlapped, the two men never seemed close. At one point, Penrose even confided to Gordon Loud back in Washington that perhaps Glueck could do some good, but "I continue to maintain the skeptical attitude which long experience with this bird has engendered in my soul!" What he meant he did not say.[23]

On multiple occasions Glueck threatened to resign. It was physically and emotionally taxing to try to navigate between Zionist Jews and anti-Zionist Arabs in Palestine on behalf of the OSS while doing his full-time job for the American School of Oriental Research. Fighting an intelligence war against Nazism on behalf of an agency that seemed not to care about the plight of Jews wore on him, too. The more he learned about the Holocaust, the more troubled and distraught he became. His bosses showed little interest in using their networks and resources to try to save European Jews from Hitler's clutches.

Glueck's Jewish identity shaped how almost everyone in the Protestant-dominated OSS viewed him. Leary secretly noted that "though it was none of my business, I considered it a serious mistake to place one of his religion" in a position to help shape policy in the Middle East. Then, in a confidential performance review, Leary described Glueck as a "lone wolf" agent, who did not work well with others. With friends like these, it is no wonder that Glueck occasionally felt inspired to resign, despite his patriotic love for country and desire to help the United States win the war. In the end, OSS leaders decided to keep him exactly where he was. They asked the rabbi to serve as a "listening post" in Palestine, to keep the United States up-to-date on everything happening in his corner of the world.[24]

Despite Glueck's frustrations, he continued to do the work the OSS assigned him and even proposed continuing his clandestine activities after the war. When the National Geographic Society agreed to fund a new expedition for Glueck, he urged Leary and Penrose to consider how such an expedition might provide him with an excellent cover, an opportunity to again "combine interests." He also drafted a memo for the OSS, advising leaders on how they could make better use of archaeologists for intelligence work, and he recommended that they raise up a generation of archaeologist spies for assignments in the Middle East.[25]

Because Penrose and others in the Cairo station were deeply concerned about the future of the Middle East and especially Palestine, they had regular contact with the Jerusalem-based Jewish Agency, which had its own intelligence service that oversaw the work of agents placed all over Europe. The agency worked to defeat the Axis, support Jews in Europe, and lay the foundations for a Jewish homeland in Palestine. As head of Secret Intelligence for the Cairo station, Penrose had to decide to what extent to partner with the Jewish Agency and to determine what the long-term results might be of any OSS–Jewish Agency relationship.

Throughout the war, leaders of the Jewish Agency sought to collaborate with the Americans. Its leaders wanted to place a few of their people with OSS teams that were preparing to parachute behind enemy lines. The agency had plenty of potential recruits from which to choose. It had at its disposal thousands of Jews who had fled Europe as Hitler's blitzkrieg thundered over their homelands and who wanted nothing more than to get in on the action and to exact some revenge. "There is a sizeable number of people," one agency operative assured OSS leaders, "ready to volunteer for operations behind the lines in order to participate in the war effort against Hitler, and to get contact with the remainder of the Jews still alive there." Agency leaders felt confident that offering agents from their organization to the OSS was mutually beneficial. "In every place where Jews exist," an agency operative explained, "there exists also a Jewish underground" that would help with whatever projects the OSS launched.[26]

To sweeten the offer, the Jewish Agency promised to defer to the OSS in developing potential missions. An agency intelligence officer guaranteed Penrose full "use of his facilities and personnel" and granted the OSS "full control of the operations of any agents he may supply and yet providing sufficient freedom so that the objectives of the Jewish Agency may be accomplished within the limits" of OSS oversight. Agency officers asked only one thing in exchange for the service of their members. They wanted their agents to be able to transmit over OSS lines information to the Jewish Agency, including the "number of Jews alive, their presence in forced labor camps, their movements and propositions for the means of their rescue." Not a big ask, yet it proved too much for the anti-Zionist Penrose.[27]

The missionary executive and some other OSS leaders remained skeptical about partnering with the agency. "If occasions arise where the interest of the Jewish Agency and the United States conflict," one analyst observed, "we can expect that subject, as an agent, will work against our interests." This was true not only of Jewish Agency spies but also of British SIS partners, and of just about every other foreign national that the United States recruited, of which there were many. Others in the OSS thought the benefits of working with the agency significantly outweighed the costs.[28]

Penrose continued to disagree. Past experience, he claimed, demonstrated that "the effort which had been put into placing" agency men in the field with the OSS "had been very largely wasted." While he acknowledged that the leader of the Jewish Agency was "exceedingly capable and straightforward," his "single-minded concern is directed toward the rescue of Jews from Europe and the establishment of Zionist policies among those who remain." Penrose was not particularly interested in the former, and he was staunchly opposed to the latter. His overriding fear was that the Jewish Agency would view a partnership with the OSS as de facto American support of Zionist aims. "At a later date," he insisted, Zionists might make much "of the fact that the Jewish Agency received the assistance of the American Government in putting agents into the field and thus securing an increase in the population of Palestine." He believed that they would claim that by saving Jews and allowing them to relocate to Palestine, the United States had contributed to the establishment of a Jewish state. Like Stewart Herman when he was in Berlin, Penrose never expressed much concern about helping recue Jews from the Germans, and when he had a chance to do something proactive, he squandered it.[29]

Penrose was not naive, and he recognized what his refusal to partner with the Jewish Agency implied. "You will probably think from the above that I am an anti-Semite as well as a cynic," he wrote to an OSS colleague. "I am not the first, although my experiences during the past three or four years may have made me the second." He fretted that "Americans will have to become more suspicious if they are to avoid having the wool pulled entirely over their eyes as has been the case in the past." He did his best to convince others in the OSS to adopt his position. "If you knew my own sentiments," he confided to Frank Wisner, "as I think you do, you could be sure that I would never recruit a representative from the Jewish Agency to go on any intelligence mission for us. I have fought that line of activity from the time of my earliest arrival here."[30]

This was a problem. The OSS had tasked Penrose with organizing the American clandestine network in the Middle East, Greece, and the Balkans, yet he refused to partner with the leading Jewish intelligence agency in the region. Without the Jewish Agency on his team, with its extensive contacts and fresh recruits, the Cairo office faced a serious handicap. Penrose was focusing more on what a wartime relationship with the Jewish Agency might mean for political developments in the Middle East in the postwar years rather than on how such a relationship could help the United States speed the war to its end.

Although Penrose had little interest in partnering with the Jewish Agency, he was not its only potential source for collaboration. Jewish Agency leaders also turned to Arthur Goldberg's Labor Branch. The Jewish Agency saw Goldberg as a potential ally for multiple reasons. First, Goldberg was one of the few Jews in the OSS, and he was a Zionist, although he was cautious about making his opinions known in the Waspy American spy agency. And second, the Labor desk worked across Europe and the Middle East and had already established relationships with various

Jewish leaders, especially those who before the war had been involved in labor organizing. Goldberg and his team were eager to cooperate with the Jewish Agency.

Carl Devoe, a representative from Goldberg's Labor section, was impressed by the Jewish Agency work he witnessed firsthand in Palestine. Agency leaders, he reported back to Penrose, "made every effort to be cooperative in all respects," and they opened their files to him. He thought a partnership was wise. He reassured Penrose that collaboration between the Labor section and the Jewish Agency was simply about intelligence sharing and had no significance or relationship to American foreign policy or official American views toward Palestine. "The Jewish Agency," he tried to assure a skeptical Penrose, "definitely understands that no quid pro quo is involved in this relationship."[31]

The Labor Branch was moving in one direction with the Jewish Agency, and Penrose was moving the Cairo Branch in another. Eventually, they arrived at a workable middle ground. Penrose agreed that the OSS could accept "without any commitments in return, materials which the Jewish Agency may send to us of its own accord or in response to special requests from us." In other words, this relationship ran on a one-way street. Penrose was not going to turn down anything the agency sent his way, but he promised nothing in return. This was not exactly what the Jewish Agency wanted, and perhaps as a result the OSS received little usable intelligence from the Zionist organization. "In spite of considerable prodding from us," wrote an operative with the Labor Branch, "the material received from the Agency has decreased to a mere trickle." An agency representative blamed their limited output on being shorthanded—they did not have a large-enough staff to keep up with translating materials into English. He suggested that if the OSS could provide an operative who read Hebrew or Arabic or both, he or she could work out of the agency's Jerusalem office. OSS leaders again refused.[32]

The Labor desk believed that the Jewish Agency was a good partner, despite the obstacles that Penrose constantly threw in its way. "Although the liaison has existed for only a short time," one of Goldberg's operatives summarized, "the good faith of the Jewish Agency in abiding by the agreement has already been demonstrated." In addition, various reports mentioned valuable intelligence coming to the OSS field offices from the agency. Yet according to an internal Labor Branch history, the partnership never lived up to its full potential. No doubt, Stephen Penrose was partly to blame.[33]

In late 1944, Lieutenant Colonel John E. Toulmin, who had supervised Penrose in Cairo, nominated the missionary executive for a Bronze Star for his work "organizing, planning and operating secret intelligence in the Middle East, and in supervising similar activities in Greece, Bulgaria and Romania." Toulmin highlighted Penrose's many contributions in justifying the nomination. Penrose's "knowledge of the area," Toulmin wrote, "was of inestimable value to OSS in recruiting future representatives who were to operate in countries where strong religious, political and racial differences existed." He noted that Penrose had been "most successful" in placing agents in Iran, recruiting people who could collect intelligence on both the Germans and the Soviets active in the region. "In addition, Mr. Penrose's undercover agents were placed in Afghanistan, Iraq, Arabia, and Transjordan." Penrose's missionary background, and his knowledge of religion and cultures and the intersection of the two, made him successful in a particularly volatile part of the world.[34]

While Penrose's nomination was under consideration by army leaders, Donovan summoned him back to the capital for a meeting. Penrose was overjoyed to be heading home. He was finally going to meet his new son and see his wife and daughters again. He hoped to make it in time for Christmas, but before he could leave he needed Lewis Leary, who was back in New York, to relieve him in the Cairo office. As Christmas approached, he told Peggy that if Leary was purposely delaying his departure to celebrate the holidays in the United States, he would "gladly gut him with a carving knife—and dull too." When he learned that, indeed, Leary was still in New York, he wrote Peggy: "GDSOB!!!" (probably an acronym for "God Damn Son of a Bitch!!!")[35]

Penrose eventually made it home, but not before Christmas. Back in Washington, DC, he met with Donovan. The general had his most ambitious plans yet for the operative from Walla Walla.

SIXTEEN

"The Beginning of the End of Japan's Ungodly Power"

WHEN JOHN BIRCH WENT TO WORK FOR CLAIRE CHENNAULT AND THE American army air force, he had no idea what the OSS was, nor had any OSS leader heard the name John Birch. That was about to change. Birch was a reluctant soldier, and he became an even more reluctant OSS man, but his contributions to the Allies' campaign in China proved significant nonetheless. His actions and work eventually made him one of the war's best-known soldier spies.[1]

The US Army and Navy leaders responsible for running the Pacific war mostly disliked and distrusted William Donovan and his nascent spy agency. General Joseph "Vinegar Joe" Stilwell, who oversaw the American military mission on Japan's western flank in the China-Burma-India theater, was not interested in partnering with the OSS. Nor was General Douglas MacArthur, who had substantial influence over the trajectory of the US war in the Pacific. The man famous for his corncob pipes and defiance of civilian authority couldn't stand Wild Bill.

But they did like missionaries. The Department of the Navy put marine Sherwood Moran to work as an interrogator. Moran had served as a missionary in Japan and knew the language and the culture. His ecumenical Protestant sensibilities led him to the firm conviction that all men were "brothers," regardless of race and ethnicity. Rather than try to beat or force information out of Japanese prisoners of war, his interrogation techniques were cautious and humane. He spoke to captives as if they were close friends and tried to show them how their nation would benefit by their cooperation with the United States. His techniques proved so successful that the navy put him in charge of training new interrogators. He also drafted a manual on interrogation for the military. As historian David Hollinger notes, Moran's legacy endures to this day. In 2003 some US Marines rediscovered his work and posted it online. In the context of the CIA's sometimes brutal "enhanced interrogation techniques" of suspected terrorists and their allies in the years immediately following 9/11, a debate ensued across numerous media platforms. How best should the United States seek information from prisoners of war? The sympathetic, compassionate, and effective wartime work of missionary turned marine Sherwood Moran served as a powerful critique of the use of torture practiced by some in the George W. Bush administration. John Birch would have a different kind of legacy.[2]

Despite Pacific theater military leaders' skepticism of the OSS, Wild Bill managed to convince them to let him run a few operations in Asia. The Americans were desperate to secure an overland route for moving war materials coming into India to units on the front lines in China. Their best option was to go through Tibet, but the Americans needed the permission of the seven-year-old Dalai Lama. FDR assigned the task to Donovan, who in late 1942 dispatched two of his men to Tibet. The mission was a success: the Americans got their transportation route, and Donovan's team sent the president some rare Tibetan postage stamps to add to his impressive collection. Birch later benefited from the supplies that made their way along this route.[3]

The OSS also launched operations against the Japanese in Burma. There Donovan's men once again discovered the value of missionaries. In the northern part of the country, operatives worked to organize a group of local natives whom Americans called Kachins. They created a unit that blended American soldiers, local resistance fighters, and a third group that bridged the two cultures—"fighting priests." The priests were missionaries who had been working with the Kachins for many years. Journalist and OSS operative Stewart Alsop quipped that they obviously believed "in the Church Militant." They were happy to seek revenge against the

Japanese on behalf of the people they had dedicated their lives to serving. "They proved invaluable," Alsop summarized, "as interpreters, not only of the language but of the Kachin customs, and as guides, philosophers, and friends to the woefully inexperienced Americans." They were good soldiers as well.[4]

Despite these and other small-scale operations, the OSS initially failed to establish a real presence in Asia. But Donovan kept battling. Eventually, he turned to General Claire Chennault, the leader of the American air force in Asia. Unlike General Joseph Stilwell, Chennault was eager to partner with the OSS. Finally, Wild Bill had an opening into the war in China. In the spring of 1944, Chennault and Donovan merged their intelligence units into a new, combined group called the 5329th Air and Ground Forces Resources Technical Staff, which they gave the unfortunate acronym AGFRTS ("ag-farts") for short.

Once the OSS got the green light to expand in China, a mad scramble to identify and recruit capable agents was on. Many of the most qualified people were already working in army or navy intelligence. One operative reported to Donovan that the OSS had no choice but to partner with existing military leaders, since they "control the source of suitable recruits." They had "a virtual monopoly of the best qualified personnel" for intelligence work in the China theater, he wrote, including "young, vigorous officers and enlisted men with area background and language qualifications, such as missionary sons." Working with the army, the OSS managed to identify and recruit numerous missionaries for operations in Asia.[5]

The most talented missionary son the OSS landed was John Birch. On May 25, 1944, Chennault transferred his intelligence officers from the Fourteenth Air Force to the OSS. Donovan's outfit was headquartered in the wartime provisional Chinese capital of Chongqing, where Chiang Kai-shek and the leaders of the Kuomintang had fled as the war with the Japanese escalated. The fundamentalist did not learn of his new status for months. When Birch received word that the new spy agency had taken over intelligence operations in the region, he sent Chennault a telegram, asking the general to take him back into the army. Birch was furious that the army had relinquished control of intelligence to Donovan's upstart agency. Birch did not believe that anyone but Chennault could do the job properly. "Right now," he told an army air force interviewer, "it makes me sick to see liaison in the field given over to the OSS, they will mess up the whole situation as sure as shooting because these men are working on an entirely different basis." He feared that the OSS newcomers simply did not understand the local culture. "They think you can buy every man and every Chinese has his price, and all they are going to buy is the contempt of the Chinese." The OSS, he claimed, talked a lot and accomplished little. Birch even sent a radiogram to his superior officer, stating that he would rather be a "buck private" in the Fourteenth Air Force than a major in Donovan's spy agency. The radiogram "was seen by everybody," according to fellow operative and missionary son Wilfred Smith, further aggravating the tense relationship between the OSS and the army as their new partnership was developing.[6]

At the time that Donovan and Chennault were launching AGFRTS, Birch was very busy in the field, putting in as many as twenty hours a day. Chennault had dispatched him to liaise between the Fourteenth Air Force and the Chinese army in Shandong Province. Military leaders needed better intelligence from the guerrillas working in the North and more information on railways used by the Japanese. While en route, Birch and his team received word that the Japanese were moving south toward them. Chennault directed them to return to the base. Birch stalled. The missionary soldier believed that he and his team could sneak through a gap in the Japanese lines and complete their mission. Reluctantly, Chennault gave in, and the group continued north "by truck, foot and horseback." One night they even bunked with some German priests at a Catholic mission. In early June they reached the Chinese army unit they were seeking.[7]

Together Birch and his Chinese allies built a series of new landing strips that allowed American planes to get into and out of the region safely. One was especially important. "Our fighters," Chennault recalled, "used this Japanese-surrounded field for many months, making surprise penetrations to areas the enemy never suspected were vulnerable to fighter strikes and hitting the Japanese as far north as the Great Wall." Birch radioed back reports on Japanese reinforcements as well as the size and scope of the enemy military presence in the area. The missionary spy also set up a rudimentary communications system for tracking Japanese aircraft. He had peasant farmers keep an eye out for Japanese planes. When they spotted one, they used hand-cranked telephones to call into a central receiving station. Based on the location of the callers, the American and Chinese armies could track the location and direction of incoming enemy planes.[8]

While in the field, Birch had little time to write his family. "I do have an excuse," though, he later told them, "in that I have been very busy and moving around quite a bit in my business." The specifics of what that business was, he did not say, although he gave some hints. "My work is becoming more interesting and even promises a little danger and excitement in the near future." But he had no fear. "If my hour to depart should strike," he acknowledged, "I am ready to go, thanks to the grace and merit of our Saviour, the Lord Jesus." He hoped, however, that his time was not yet up, because he had so much still to do. He warned his family that he would be out of contact again and not able to write, but he instructed them not to worry. He also told them that although he was feeling "pretty low and unfit to help others spiritually," he had nevertheless accepted an invitation to give a sermon at a local mission. He preached in Chinese to a group of young people. The service was a success, and he felt it had "renewed" his faith.[9]

Over the summer, Birch and his team kept the intelligence flowing to Chennault. While soldiers and sailors on the western front were storming the beaches of Normandy, Birch's team, according to one report, helped the Fourteenth Air Force "destroy approximately 100 vehicles and 300 soldiers," and they identified numerous additional "bombing objectives" for pilots. Birch asked for materials necessary to "carry out some sabotage and demolition projects," and one of his partners wrote headquarters that the missionary needed "as much railway demolition supplies as possible" to blow up the engines transporting Japanese materials.[10]

Like William Eddy and Stewart Herman, Birch grew frustrated when his bosses did not follow his advice. At one point, he sent an urgent message that the United States needed to intervene with strategic bombing in a developing battle between Chinese and Japanese forces. He was overruled, and the Chinese were slaughtered. "I was never so mad at vested authority in my life," he recalled. "Definitely good training for anarchistic feeling."[11]

By late that summer, Birch was working as the commanding officer at a small AGFRTS base near the Yangtze River. His team ran various exploratory and reconnaissance missions and collaborated with guerrilla groups in the region. They also built and repaired airstrips for air force use, he recalled, "almost under the Japs' noses." He described himself to an interviewer at the time as an "ex-Baptist missionary." Why "ex" was not clear. Perhaps he was still experiencing a spiritual crisis, or maybe he felt uncomfortable telling an air force staffer that he was still a missionary while discussing the violent operations he was orchestrating and the casualties he was inflicting. While at the base, Birch caught up on his writing. He reported to his parents that he had spent so much time on horseback that he soon expected to have "an iron bottom." Birch thanked his mother for the chocolate sent from home as well as for letters from family and friends. The letters "brot tears to my eyes," he confessed, "and I don't cry easily these days."[12]

Birch traveled using all means at his disposal. When the army asked for the identification codes on his vehicles, he replied that his vehicles consisted of "four black mules and they didn't have serial numbers." Sometimes he also traveled by watercraft. He wrote a letter to his sister with a captivating description of the local scenery he viewed from a sampan boat and confessed that he had found "plenty" of time for "swimming and sunbathing." But he wished he "had someone besides these Chinese boatmen to share it" with. He was also thrilled to have an air mattress on which to sleep on the boat's deck—"a luxury unknown when I used to make trips like this as a missionary."[13]

John Birch traveled the Chinese countryside using every kind of transportation imaginable. In this photograph he is posing with one of his mules. As he told his bosses in the OSS, the mule did not have a serial number.
Courtesy of Arlington Baptist College Heritage Collection.

The trip was one of his most memorable during the war. "For three days we have been gliding eastward," he told a friend, "through a fairyland: a swift, clear little river winding through towering green mountains, some of which still have snow on the peaks; sheer sandstone cliffs hanging over us, with little flocks of goats (all white) looking as though they'd topple over and come crashing down into the water any minute." He also saw "mountaineers' huts; all of stone and very squat, perched on the hillsides; great rocks that look like elephants out in the river, splitting the stream into numerous roaring channels" and "foaming rapids" that "give us thrills a-plenty, as the boatmen fight to keep the sampan under control and off the rocks!" He thought the downriver trip was "lots of fun if you don't mind a few fleas and the enforced intimacies and quaint curiosity of three or four boatmen." He reveled "in the feel of the wind and sun, the sight of the ever-changing shore, and the sound of the creaking oars. It's almost paradise!" he concluded, despite its location in the middle of a war.[14]

Reconnaissance was not the only thing on Birch's mind that year. For Easter Sunday the missionary agreed to deliver a sermon for troops and other Allied workers in the city of Changsha, an important transportation hub and also the location of intermittent battles between Chinese and Japanese forces. During the service an American nurse working with the nearby Yale-in-China missionary organization's hospital played the organ. This was the first time Marjorie Tooker laid eyes on John Birch. "The clergyman for the service was not a missionary, as usual," she recalled of the meeting, "but a young lieutenant in the U. S. Air Force, very handsome in his uniform, tall, dark, with a square forehead. He stood very straight and strong." When they met, Tooker recalled, "shock waves of recognition passed between us, as though we had known each other forever, or in a previous existence." Birch later described the meeting similarly in a letter to Marjorie. "I just felt the keen awareness of your presence, distinct from the group as a whole, together with a feeling that the gates were open in the mental walls that separate us all the time, that if the others had not been there, you would have understood any thoughts I addressed to you, and vice versa, with the exchange of very few spoken words."[15]

Birch began seeing Tooker regularly whenever he was in town. Only a few months had passed since he had ended his relationship with Audrey

Mair. On Tooker's evenings away from the hospital, she cooked "home-style food" and offered "good company" to the small team of lonely American intelligence officers. She and Birch grew closer, according to the nurse, as they "sat by the fire in winter, or strolled under the trees in the tropical summer."[16]

Birch, she realized, was not a typical soldier. She described him as "not only a southerner but a true 'Bible Baptist' from Georgia." He "didn't drink, smoke, dance or play cards." Marjorie did all of these things. She believed that he "had charm and a good measure of southern courtesy," and she called him "the finest man I have ever known: kind, idealistic, determined." His dedication to his work impressed her. "He loved the Chinese," she observed. He aimed to "help free the people from the enemy and then convert them to Christ." He was also willing to court Tooker with cigarettes, "a priceless" (and for John surprising) gift during the war.[17]

They were not immediately in love. At least Tooker was not. Birch, she wrote, "talked about going back to preaching after the war, perhaps to Tibet where missionaries were unknown. I had no desire to live in Tibet and was glad I wasn't in love with him."[18]

Birch eventually returned to air force headquarters in Kunming for new orders, and Tooker focused on her hospital duties. Her job was getting more and more difficult, as the Japanese moved ever closer. When supplies ran short, she grew desperate. Then she thought of Birch. She knew that he was a problem solver, and so she wrote him, telling him what drugs the hospital needed. He found the medicine and delivered it on his next trip to Changsha. Together once again, the two walked the now-abandoned Yale-in-China grounds. "The campus," Marjorie recalled, "was deserted and the bombed school buildings stood out starkly in the moonlight. But the perfume of tropical flowers, the songs of the night birds and a full moon made an intoxicating combination. At the last bend in the walk, John turned and kissed me good-bye. That moment, that spot and that kiss haunted many of John's letters to me and had to last us both through the rest of the war."[19]

Once the Japanese captured Changsha and with it the Yale-in-China compound in the summer of 1944, Marjorie found a new employer. She joined the Army Nurse Corps. She feared that Birch would disapprove. Because of nurses' close work with servicemen, and the personal intimacy that came with medical care, soldiers sometimes stereotyped nurses as sex objects or as promiscuous. But Birch was not worried. He knew she would never be "tainted by any atmosphere or scene, however foul. You see," he assured her, "you still haven't convinced me that you are 'human as the rest.'"[20]

Over the course of their separation, Marjorie realized she loved Birch. "As I followed his written descriptions of his travels, long days on the river, or slogging through paddy fields with a few companions, or climbing mountains to avoid the enemy, I found that I was becoming more and more attached to this dreamer." Birch hoped that letters would allow the young couple to get further acquainted. In one he provided Marjorie with a list of his likes. They began with the abstract and absolute: sharing the love of Jesus, spending time in nature, thinking about eternity with Christ, and much more. Then, on to the mundane. "I also enjoy movies, cocacolas (4 years ago), double thick malts, streamlined, air-conditioned trains, some banquets, any football game." He shared what he didn't like as well. "I have never found joy," he confessed to her, "in my brief nibbles at smoking, drinking or dancing; this might be due to prejudice built by strict discipline back home, or maybe these pleasures really aren't good for me—I don't know." Perhaps Marjorie Tooker could change that.[21]

As Birch got to know Tooker better, he fell hard for the American nurse. Tooker too was excited about their relationship. The arrival of one of his letters would leave her feeling elated for days. Noticing a full moon, he wrote Marjorie that he "couldn't help wanting" her. Their night alone together on the deserted Yale-in-China campus was always on his mind. "Perhaps before too long I can go back to the Long Sands for a moonlight rendezvous with a beautiful ghost on a mission pathway." Unfortunately for John, he would have to be content with ghosts, at least for the moment.[22]

While Birch was running missions near Changsha where the Chinese and Japanese continued to battle, Tooker returned to the United States for a brief furlough. The Birch family invited the nurse to Macon for a visit. John warned his long-distance girlfriend that his mother "will be slightly dismayed by your cigarettes and your excellent dancing." Although Marjorie was reluctant to go, she cared enough for John to make the trip. While in Georgia, she went with the Birches to their "little Baptist church. The panorama on the wall," Marjorie wrote, "depicting the tortures of hell, made me uncomfortable."[23]

John's relationship with Marjorie challenged him in all kinds of ways. The two spent some time corresponding about the problems of race in the United States and abroad. "Yes, Marjorie," John admitted, "you're right; I have a lot of race prejudice in me, especially toward Negroes. I believe this to be a wrong and unfair attitude, and I have always tried to repress it, but I know it's still there." A few months later, he read Lillian Smith's *Strange Fruit*, a best-selling 1944 progressive novel about an interracial couple, set in Birch's home state. He told Marjorie that he was not convinced that it fairly represented "the white-negro relation."[24]

The longer the two were apart, the more their love seemed to grow. And so did the obstacles between them. "Ever since that night I discovered my goddess was of warm flesh and blood instead of cold marble," John wrote Marjorie, "I have increasingly hungered for your companionship, and have been increasingly convinced of my unworthiness to have it." He fretted that even if he could transform into a "Prince Charming," he would still have to deal with his commitments as a missionary to "far western China after the war—a life too hard and insecure for a princess, even one so strong as yourself." He felt conflicting emotions welling up inside him. "Fool that I am, I am torn between two desires: a hunger for your nearness, and a conviction that the only right thing is to stay out of your life entirely."[25]

As the correspondence continued, the differences that separated them—their beliefs and their future plans—became increasingly apparent. John began to wonder if the relationship was doomed to fail. Marjorie was a religious moderate who represented the new wave of liberal Protestant American workers in China. "You also speak," Birch wrote her, "of wanting to make people well and happy rather than to change their faith." Birch aimed for just the opposite. As a fundamentalist, he believed that faith was all that mattered. Fixing the body without attending to the soul was a fool's errand. Her statement of her goals, John realized, "blasts some hopes I had just realized I had." But he was not done with her yet. "I intend to find you once more this side of Heaven and have one more talk before abandoning finally the dream that was born on that path at Changsha."[26]

*

That fall Birch returned to Fourteenth Air Force headquarters in Kunming. While Stewart Herman was walking the streets of the newly liberated Paris, Birch learned that Chennault had traded him and the rest of the air force's intelligence officers to the OSS. Because Birch had been fighting the transfer all summer, Chennault had delayed moving him over to Donovan's outfit. But eventually, Birch had to accept his new assignment. Although he was less than enthused about leaving the army air force, the OSS was thrilled to have him. An intelligence report from regional headquarters summed up the missionary's accomplishments: "Pioneering work in this area has been initiated by Captain John Birch . . . and all indications point to their successful accomplishment in laying a solid foundation for immediate development of a profitable intelligence organization in an area whose strategic significance cannot be underestimated." OSS leaders planned to have the missionary begin "systematic gathering of enemy publications, collection of passes of all types used in enemy territory and inauguration of demolition work against enemy installations."[27]

On September 21, 1944, the army honored the fundamentalist with a Legion of Merit medal. In Birch's official award letter, General Stilwell laid out the reasons for the honor. Birch had established contacts with local Chinese forces that "resulted in the speedy relay of vital information." His facilitation of "close cooperation" between Chinese ground troops and US flyers helped the Allies "destroy important targets in a changing tactical situation," and he "firmly cemented friendly relations and increased the effectiveness of future liaison work." The missionary responded with characteristic humility. "I don't deserve this decoration," Birch wrote his parents, "but since they were foolish enough to give it to me, I want you to have the pleasure of knowing I have it." Just days earlier, he had received a different kind of gift. This one was from his family, and it included a new book by popular fundamentalist H. A. Ironside, the leader of the Moody Memorial Church in Chicago. As Birch was growing as an intelligence officer, he was also keeping abreast of the fundamentalist movement back home.[28]

Birch once again asked his parents to forgive the "scarcity" of letters from him. He had "been in a spot where mail was out of the question." Birch did reveal, however, that he had been intermittently suffering from malaria. The missionary had nearly worked himself to death. Chennault tried to get Birch to take a break. "For three years," the general later

John Birch performed many extraordinary acts of service and heroism, which grew out of the skills and knowledge he had developed as a missionary. Here General Claire Chennault recognizes Birch's accomplishments with a Legion of Merit.
Courtesy of National Archives and Records Administration, College Park, Maryland.

recalled, "he worked steadily in the field with only brief respites for medical treatment. He refused all leave or temporary duty in the United States with the comment, 'I'll leave China when the last Jap is gone.'"[29]

As Birch prepared for his latest OSS missions, he filed a supply request. He wanted cash and radio equipment, certainly invaluable items for any field operative. He also needed weapons. He requested six carbines with fifty rounds each, six .38 pistols with fifty rounds each, two knives, and miscellaneous demolitions supplies. Then the list took a curious turn. The fundamentalist also required three lipsticks, three watches, three fountain pens, two cartons of cigarettes (preferably Camels), and three lighters. Strange items for a soldier that a colleague once described as a kind of "ascetic." But Birch didn't want these things for himself. He rejected the few American "luxuries" that soldiers enjoyed but instead aimed to live on the bare minimum, like his Chinese allies. However, he did acquire supplies to share generously with the men under him and with his Chinese contacts.[30]

One of the OSS's priorities in China, as in so many other jurisdictions, was to help rescue downed airmen. Finding Doolittle's raiders had brought Birch into the war, and a few years later he was still at it. He'd locate missing Americans, identify places to hide them until he could move them to safety, and then arrange for them to get picked up from rudimentary airstrips. In some cases, he even worked with local Chinese to carve new emergency airstrips out of the land. Birch became so skilled at partnering with native groups that Chennault began sending the missionary into the field alone to arrange the rescues of missing American crews.[31]

In late 1944, Birch came to the rescue of Ernie Johnson, a member of Chennault's Fourteenth Air Force, and the rest of his B-25 team. During Johnson's very first wartime mission, his plane took a bullet from the enemy to one of its engines. The pilot flew the damaged bomber as far as he could and then made an emergency landing. There Johnson and his crew sought refuge in a missionary hospital run by a young Norwegian family. Birch happened to be at the compound at the same time. Johnson struck up a quick friendship with Birch. "There was a charisma about him," Johnson wrote, "and a twinkle in his eye that made me like him at once." The two spent the next few days together. It did not take long, Johnson recalled, to realize that "Birch was first and foremost a Christian missionary, and only incidentally a soldier and a spy." While killing time in the village, Johnson and his crew bought wine from the other missionaries in town—a couple of French Catholic priests. He noted that "while John Birch did not drink, smoke, or sleep with women, he also did not self-righteously criticize those who did."[32]

Others who worked with Birch made similar observations. His headquarters were always well run, though with a sterner discipline than perhaps was necessary. "It was the only non-drinking American outpost I ever visited in China," one of his colleagues noted. "I never heard he had banned drink, but his men respected him and knew he didn't approve, so they either did their drinking in town or very much on the Q.T."[33]

Johnson soon discovered that Birch did not limit his rescue missions to pilots and their crews. He also looked after stranded missionaries. When they needed a way out, Birch would organize military flights that could serve the dual purpose of transferring important intelligence resources, while also transporting missionaries out of harm's way. One of Birch's superior officers noted that no one would ever know how many missionaries Birch saved.[34]

Birch's skill at rescuing Americans—missionaries and flyers—was put to the test in late 1944. While on an assignment liaising with a lost flight

crew, Birch came into contact with stranded members of the China Inland Mission. The group included some elderly missionaries who were not
fit for rigorous travel. Birch arranged to have the missionaries picked up by
plane along with the latest group of marooned flyers. But this was easier
said than done. "The missionaries," one of Birch's fellow operatives noted,
"never realized what a favor this was that John took upon himself—it was
difficult to accomplish." In all, the group consisted of nine missionaries
(the oldest arrived by wheelbarrow), three flyers, and one of Birch's men.
They all hid out in a house during a very cold December, waiting for their
rescue flight. Getting enough food and water for the large group was a
challenge. Then the snow came. Realizing that there was no way a plane
was going to arrive during the storm, Birch led the group to the nearby
town of Linchuan for a Christmas celebration. They feasted on goat and
celebrated with a Chinese man dressed up as Saint Nicholas. A few weeks
later, back at the house, the snow had stopped falling but was not melting.
Desperate to get the missionaries and airmen to safety, Birch convinced
seven hundred "coolies" to go to the airstrip with small shovels to remove
the snow. Finally, the plane made it in. After weeks of waiting, the air
force crew and the missionaries were saved.[35]

Just days before Christmas 1944, Donovan wrote FDR a memo, outlining the success the OSS was having in China now that his operatives
were in the game. Essentially, every point he raised reflected the work and
innovations Birch and his men had spearheaded. Wild Bill highlighted
OSS teams' embedding with the Chinese army, the work of operatives on
the front lines, their successful guiding of allied planes "in dive-bombing
and strafing attacks which have killed many thousands of Japs and destroyed much valuable equipment," and their collection of valuable intelligence. He also emphasized the OSS's work retrieving missing airmen,
another job at which Birch excelled. The actions of his agency, Donovan summarized, made the "enemy's territorial gains much costlier" and
shifted the preponderance of power in China to the Allies.[36]

Birch's success as an OSS operative did not bring him peace, however.
He continued to worry that he was unworthy to preach, and he sometimes
fretted over minor sins. Fundamentalists have a hard time forgiving others
for mistakes, and the more faithful ones often have a hard time forgiving themselves. "I sometimes find myself," he lamented in a letter to his
parents, "dropping into 'Hardshell Baptist' frame of mind regarding the

spiritual condition and destiny of men." But he was grateful, he wrote, that "the Lord has cared for me far, far more faithfully than I have served Him this past year; sometimes I become so disgusted with my own attitudes and those of the men around me, that I wonder the Lord even tolerates us." But God, he believed, had not given up on him or on those around him.[37]

Despite Birch's spiritual travails, he felt excited that the tide of the war was turning. The world, he noted, was witnessing "the beginning of the end of Japan's ungodly power." The fundamentalist did not expect a permanent peace to follow. "I believe that this war and the ensuing federations," Birch confessed in a letter to his aunt, "will set the world stage, as never before, for the rise of Anti-Christ! What a privilege it will be to stand as a witness for the King of Kings in that day, provided Christ does not return and take us out first." For Birch, the war meant something very different than it did to mainstream liberal Protestants like Herman, Eddy, and Penrose. Birch embodied the deep apocalypticism at the heart of the growing fundamentalist movement. He believed that he was waging not just a material war against the Axis, but also a spiritual war against the forces of the Antichrist. This meant he would take no breaks from the battle, and he would not hesitate to kill his enemies. He would stomach no negotiated peace and no armistices. Jesus was preparing to return soon, and with him judgment was coming. As difficult as the year had been, Birch vowed to be ready. He saw himself first and foremost as a foot soldier in the army of the Lord.[38]

SEVENTEEN

"Pilgrim's Progress"

In January 1945, Franklin Roosevelt took the oath of office, marking the start of an unprecedented fourth term as president. The American people had yet to win the war, and FDR believed they needed him to stay on as their commander in chief. In the Pacific, the marines and the navy were hopping from island to island, battling the Japanese and driving ever closer to their enemy's homeland. General Douglas MacArthur launched an invasion of the Philippines, which provoked a counterattack by the Imperial Japanese Navy. The fighting was fierce and evolved into what became the largest naval offensive in history in the Leyte Gulf, with more than 280 ships and two hundred thousand airmen and sailors participating. The Americans decimated the Japanese fleet. Near the end of the battle, Japanese pilots began launching "kamikaze" attacks—suicide missions in which pilots flew their planes into enemy ships.

On the island of Saipan, American marines watched in horror and disbelief as hundreds of local Japanese women and children jumped off towering cliffs to their deaths. They preferred suicide to capture by the Americans. Although the United States maintained the upper hand in the war, the fight to end the conflict was far from over.

Meanwhile, in Europe, the Germans launched a major counteroffensive of their own, in the mountainous Ardennes Forest in Belgium. It turned out to be their last. They captured a small American contingent and forced other units to retreat, creating a "bulge," or semicircle, in the Allied line. The Americans regrouped, brought in additional troops, and

263

then went back on the attack. This "Battle of the Bulge" resulted in ninety thousand American casualties and near one hundred thousand German casualties. It was the largest land battle Americans had ever fought and one of the most brutal in the war. In the end, the Allies proved victorious.

With the Americans gaining momentum, OSS leaders, including Stephen Penrose, continued to find new ways for the spy agency to help speed the end of the conflict. On February 1, 1945, William Donovan promoted Penrose to European divisional deputy for special intelligence, a top position in the OSS. The job came with a hefty raise and a lot of responsibility. It was a big undertaking, but more bureaucratic than operational. The missionary executive spent less time liaising with spies and planning daring missions and more time wrestling with budgets and personnel issues. From his new perch back in Washington, DC, he played an important role in helping the OSS wrap up the war in the Middle East and Europe.

One of Penrose's most important projects, which had been under way long before he took over the special intelligence post, focused on the Vatican. Donovan, after his D-Day shenanigans that culminated in his storming the beach at Normandy, had proceeded to Cairo, where he met with Penrose, and to Italy, where he checked in with William Eddy. Then he visited the Vatican, where he had an audience with the pope. Pius XII asked Wild Bill to convey to FDR his support for the president's fourth electoral victory and "all" his "heart's affection." What the pope did not know at the time was that Donovan was scheming to place OSS agents right under the pontiff's nose in the Vatican.[1]

The Vatican served as an important intermediary among the cobelligerents during the war. American policy makers' interest in the heart of global Catholicism revealed a new sensitivity to the ways that international religious organizations could contribute to the attainment of American goals. FDR surmised that making the case for religious freedom could foster alliances all over the world, and there was no religious alliance he coveted more than with the pope. His first step in building a Catholic partnership had been to dispatch Myron Taylor in 1940 as his "personal envoy" to the Holy See. This was a controversial move back home. American Protestants had a long tradition of anti-Catholicism, and they believed that sending a political representative to the Vatican was tacit acknowledgment of the political nature of the Catholic Church, which US Protestants saw as a violation of the Constitution's separation of church and state. Roosevelt was not dissuaded. Always the pragmatist, he believed that if sending a delegate to Rome could help the United States achieve its foreign policy objectives, he was going to do it.

Donovan was also thinking about how to ally with the Catholic Church. He feared that Vatican City was teeming with enemy spies, some of whom might be using the priesthood for cover. Before the Allies captured Rome in June 1944, the ostensibly neutral city was a safe space for Allied agents to roam, an island deep within Axis-controlled territory. After the defeat of the Axis in Italy, the Eternal City became safe territory for Axis agents, and the OSS wanted to keep tabs on them. Wild Bill was working behind the scenes, quietly using various moles in Vatican City to watch his nation's enemies and to try to harness and potentially manipulate the power of the global Catholic Church on behalf of the United States.

Donovan had good reasons to worry about potential enemy agents posing as clergy. Some Nazi leaders believed that the Vatican could provide important intelligence on the state of their enemies if only they could secure the cooperation of well-placed sources. This proved harder than expected. Hitler had been so brutal in his repression of church freedoms in Germany that even though the pope professed official neutrality, he was not about to cooperate with the German leadership. Nor were those under him. Failing to recruit any sources within the Vatican, one of SS leader Heinrich Himmler's subordinates developed a plan to enlist bright and ardent young Nazis, have them conceal their political beliefs, and send them to seminary to train for the priesthood. Then, ideally, the church would recruit them, providing the Nazi regime with its own undercover operatives within the church hierarchy. But Hitler never implemented the project.[2]

As both Hitler and Donovan sought information from Rome, neither knew that the pope had secretly pledged his support to an anti-Nazi espionage ring operating between Berlin and the Vatican. Recognizing that the Nazi regime represented a substantial threat to European Catholicism, the pope indirectly encouraged those close to him in the German government to scheme against Hitler. He provided moral justification for the assassination of a tyrant and agreed to recognize the new government that the anti-Hitler conspirators planned to put into place if they could kill the führer. Both of these moves by the pope were essential to propelling the plotters' work forward.

A small group of German Catholic officers almost succeeded in assassinating the Nazi leader. They came closest to killing Hitler in July 1944 when devoted Catholic and army colonel Claus Schenk von Stauffenberg placed a bomb under a table near where Hitler was examining a map. The bomb exploded, but to the surprise of the conspirators, Hitler managed to walk away with only minor burns and bruises. Allen Dulles had been keeping tabs from Switzerland on many of the plotters, but he did not seem to have realized how high up in the church the efforts to overthrow Hitler had reached.[3]

The Americans lacked consistent, reliable sources inside the Vatican, which forced them to be creative in their efforts to build Catholic support as they sought to tap into the power of the church. Stanley Lovell, Donovan's evil genius inventor, could usually be counted on to pitch the more harebrained ideas. When he and Donovan received word early in the war about a planned meeting between Hitler and Mussolini, Lovell proposed that they send an OSS agent into the meeting room ahead of time with a capsule containing liquid nitrogen–mustard gas. The agent was supposed to drop the tablet into a vase with water and flowers on his way out of the room. The men at the meeting, including the fascist leaders, would be rendered blind by the odorless, clear gas. To maximize the effect of the leaders' sudden blindness, Lovell wanted Donovan to secure the help of the pope. He suggested that Donovan ask the Holy Father to issue a decree reading, "My Children, God in His infinite wisdom has stricken your leaders blind. His sixth Commandment is Thou Shalt Not Kill. This blindness of your leaders is a warning that you should lay down your arms and return to the ways of peace." Donovan was not so sure the pope would agree to this, but he promised to take it up with his contacts in the church. The larger problem of how the OSS would get an agent into the meeting room ahead of Hitler and Mussolini was apparently not as much of a worry, at least in Lovell's version of the story.[4]

Rather than dropping poison pills and persuading the pope to issue disingenuous declarations, covert operations became the OSS's primary means of assessing the church, its role in the war, and its potential for alliances. Agency leaders hoped to recruit men from the Roman Catholic Church who could serve the interests of the spy agency from within Vatican City walls. But they needed someone on the ground to make the connections and to secure the information they desired. The OSS ran two important operations within the Vatican, code-named "Pilgrim's Progress" and "Vessel." Father Felix Morlion, the Belgian priest who for years provided the OSS with a steady stream of valuable intelligence reports while G-men kept him under close watch in New York, ran the first. OSS leaders dubbed his operation Pilgrim's Progress, after the classic Christian book by Puritan John Bunyan, which traces the journey of its protagonist through many challenges and hardships on the road to eternal salvation. It apparently escaped OSS leaders that this was a very Protestant name to give to a very Catholic operation. Nor was this the only problem with identifying the operation. Early on, some operatives referred to the mission with the code name "John Calvin," after the anti-Catholic Protestant reformer, which caused even more confusion.[5]

OSS leaders knew that Morlion was perhaps their best option for infiltrating the Vatican. They praised the work he was already doing and the information he was providing them through his secret network of informants located all over Europe. But they thought he was capable of much more. "My interest," operative Hugh Wilson summarized as they started developing their plans for Morlion, "has been in the future rather than the present." Wilson suspected that if their Pilgrim's Progress operation "works out as we believe it should," the Flemish priest "will be one of the most valuable of our sources. One could put no limits" on his "potentialities." Wilson had worked closely with Stewart Herman in prewar Berlin and with Penrose on recruiting missionary agents, and, once again, he was witnessing firsthand how closely foreign policy and religion overlapped.[6]

The purpose of Pilgrim's Progress was, according to one of its architects, to develop "more complete and accurate information concerning Vatican policy, practice and current knowledge." OSS memos describe Morlion as "a certain Dominican father whose vocation—an aggressive evangelism—appeared to make him not only sympathetic with the expressed moral and political aims of the American Government but also appeared to make him anxious to collaborate with the American Government in any effort to understand and work with the Vatican." The Dominican, OSS leaders decided, was the ideal man for a mission to Rome.[7]

The OSS began developing plans to send Morlion to the Vatican in the fall of 1943, but the project took more time than expected to get under way. Operatives could not get Morlion safe transportation to Vatican City until the US Army drove the Axis out of Rome. In the meantime, American Dominicans did not know what to make of the Belgian's continuing presence in the United States. Morlion did not tell them that he was moonlighting for the spy agency, but they recognized that something was afoot. Morlion had to repeatedly assure his church superiors that he was being faithful to his vows and his religious order, despite the mysteries surrounding his work and movements.[8]

Shortly after D-Day, Donovan's men finally launched the Pilgrim's Progress operation and sent Morlion to Rome. "At the end of this month," Donovan aide John Hughes wrote to the Belgian ambassador, Morlion "is undertaking a work of special importance for which it would be impossible to find another person of his experience and qualities." Indeed, the OSS had an innovative, ambitious mission for Morlion.[9]

At about the same time that Morlion was getting settled in Vatican City, another important OSS agent, Hungarian-born Catholic journalist Zsolt Aradi, submitted a memo to OSS headquarters summarizing the costs and benefits of an alliance with the Vatican and potential strategies for the OSS to consider. The main priority of the Vatican, Aradi explained, was "guaranteeing religious freedom and freedom of conscience." The church, he continued, tried to stay above nationalist politics. "But its impartiality ends where someone tries to touch religious freedom or freedom of conscience." He suggested that the OSS penetrate the Vatican, to stay abreast of news regarding both allies and enemies. He also believed that the agency could send spies out under Vatican cover. Aradi ended his memo by offering to meet with Pius XII as well as the Vatican secretary of state to begin to facilitate a closer alliance between the church and the OSS. A few weeks later, he submitted an even more ambitious proposal. He offered to serve as the OSS's mole in the Vatican. His position as a journalist could easily provide the necessary cover, plus he had spent years developing sources in Rome for his reporting. Little did he realize that Donovan had dispatched Morlion for exactly this job.[10]

The OSS did not begin receiving reports from Morlion until the fall of 1944. Most of Morlion's dispatches ran through Ferdinand L. Mayer, Stewart Herman's old friend from the Berlin embassy and the operative who vouched for Herman when the OSS was investigating him as a potential employee. The few operatives entrusted with the original drafts of this supersecret material ran into some of the less exciting problems of spy craft. "Black's handwriting"—Black was one of the code names for Morlion—"presents many problems," one analyst complained. "We have furnished him a typewriter and he has agreed to learn to use it." But deciphering the reports proved worth the trouble. An OSS leader sent Allen Dulles in Bern copies of Morlion's reports. "The outstanding quality of this material," he assured Dulles, "is its reliability: Black has reached unimpeachably authoritative sources." Donovan forwarded the most significant documents directly to President Roosevelt.[11]

The Pilgrim's Progress series of reports ran into the hundreds of pages. Morlion's sources included influential Catholic leaders positioned all over the Vatican, as well as priests and delegates who were visiting Rome from both Allied and Axis nations. Pope Pius supported Morlion's prodemocracy journalistic work and personally met with the American operative multiple times. Agency leaders took great care not to blow Morlion's cover or that of his sources. His handlers routinely removed the names of the priest's secret contacts from his reports in order to protect their identities. OSS leaders hoped that their partnership with Morlion would last. They sought his immediate analysis as the war wound down, but they also wanted him positioned in the Vatican for whatever the postwar era might bring.[12]

Morlion's reports covered many different topics and issues, including the Christian Left in Italy, the influence of the Soviets on the Vatican, German Catholic resistance against the Nazis, conditions among the Arabs in Algiers, political splits among the French, the state of monarchism in Portugal, and much more. They were so extensive that mission leaders got word that "possibly we are giving to General Donovan more material than he really wants." At the same time, they felt that "it is very difficult to determine just what subjects the General is interested in."[13]

Ferdinand Mayer rated Morlion's early reports "extraordinarily interesting and valuable." He drew up plans to distribute them widely once he felt confident that they had expunged all traces of Morlion's identity. OSS leaders wanted to share the reports with the British, the State Department, and all OSS stations. Over time, however, their enthusiasm for the project and the value of the intel diminished. Another OSS leader fretted that the reports were slanted and distorted facts, even though he felt the information they provided tended to prove accurate in the long run. In the final weeks of the war, another analyst offered a mixed review of the value of Morlion's work. He called the Pilgrim's Progress reports "dangerously on the borderline between useless and useful intelligence."[14]

In 1945 the War Department tasked Penrose, who was now overseeing all OSS intelligence efforts in Europe, with assessing the Pilgrim's Progress operation. Military officials wanted to determine if the OSS should maintain its relationship with Morlion in Rome after the war. The missionary executive's detailed criticism of the reports demonstrated his broad knowledge of even the smallest facts on the ground in every theater of the war. Overall, he wrote, his opinion of the reports was "not high," and he called the operation "a very disappointing showing," but he remained hopeful that Morlion's material might improve. Penrose did not want to sever this relationship with the Vatican mole yet.[15]

The OSS's decision to send Morlion to Italy was a carefully planned, well-thought-out operation. A second project, code-named "Vessel," was just the opposite. It proved to be one of the OSS's greatest intelligence debacles. At the same time that Morlion was building his Pilgrim's Progress network around the Vatican, a mysterious stranger approached a member of the OSS's Rome office with an offer to sell valuable documents stolen from the Vatican. The documents provided a window into the top-secret diplomacy that the pope and his aides were conducting with all of the major powers in the war. They also included reports out of Japan about conditions within the empire, information that the Americans desperately wanted.

The OSS eagerly bought report after report from the mysterious seller. Donovan, convinced of their authenticity, sent the most important documents directly to President Roosevelt. They detailed secret efforts by the pope to negotiate an end to the war, turmoil in Latin America, the agendas of Nazis posted in the Vatican, conditions in Japan and occupied China, negotiations with the Kremlin, and many other topics. Some reports even included word-for-word transcripts of discussions held in the pope's private office. A top Donovan aide thought the OSS had found an invaluable source of intelligence, but he knew some caution was necessary.

"This series offers great promise," he wrote to the Rome Branch. "For its full usefulness a careful evaluation of the source or sources is essential."[16]

The source, the man providing the material to the OSS, was Virgilio Scattolini. A journalist and publisher of pornographic literature during the 1920s, Scattolini found a new outlet for his creative talents during the war. He claimed to have secret access to the Vatican's notes, detailing confidential papal meetings with foreign leaders. The OSS later learned that the materials they so eagerly bought and circulated were probably the product of little more than Scattolini's imagination. Scattolini used published reports of the pope's schedule and his knowledge of who was coming and going around the Vatican to fashion elaborate tales to sell to intelligence agencies from all over the world.

As reports continued to arrive in Washington, DC, in the first months of 1945, OSS analysts grew suspicious. One operative, after crosschecking Vessel materials against other sources, noted, "Whereas some unimportant items of Vessel material may be based on factual knowledge of the source, the more important items are believed to be manufactured by the source out of whole cloth or are plants." But Donovan refused to believe that the source was a fake. Even after some members of the OSS began raising doubts about the legitimacy of the material, Wild Bill inexplicably continued to pass Vessel material on to FDR. He even forwarded a report detailing secret negotiations between Myron Taylor, FDR's representative to the pope, and a Japanese diplomat. When State Department officials learned of Taylor's actions, they were incensed. They had not authorized Taylor to negotiate with a representative of the Japanese government.[17]

He hadn't. Scattolini made up the meeting. OSS operatives finally knew for sure that much of the Vessel material regarding Europe was worthless. Nevertheless, they refused to lose faith totally. The Americans were so desperate for information on conditions in Japan that they continued to pay Scattolini for reports, hoping that they would shed light on their enemy. They did not.[18]

Shortly after the war ended, Donovan received the Order of Saint Sylvester on behalf of Pius XII from Francis Spellman, the famed archbishop of New York. The award recognized how much Wild Bill had done for the church through his role as director of the OSS. He had lobbied the president and military leaders on its behalf, secured important positions in the US government for prominent churchmen and their relatives, and worked to convince Americans inside and outside of the OSS that the Catholic Church was an ally. The OSS's efforts to work with the Vatican had not been perfect. But the pope knew he had a true friend in Donovan and in the United States. As the specter of communism spread in the immediate postwar world, and religious liberty around the globe seemed once again in jeopardy, the foundation that Roosevelt and Donovan laid together at the Vatican proved invaluable. With a cold war in the offing, the Catholic Church would be neutral no longer.

PART V

WINNING THE WAR
(1945)

EIGHTEEN

"God Help Us!"

WHEN STEPHEN PENROSE WENT TO WORK FOR THE OSS SHORTLY AFTER Pearl Harbor, he hoped to influence the United States' actions in the Middle East. Now, with his promotion to European divisional deputy for special intelligence, he supervised far more territory and dealt with far more pressing problems than ever before. Nevertheless, rather than leave ongoing projects in the Middle East to his subordinates, he used his power to continue to guide policy in Palestine and to manage the relationship between the OSS and the Jewish Agency. At the start of the war, Penrose had been a missionary executive and civilian with little real power to shape the United States' relationship with Zionism. By the end of the war, he was a leader in the OSS with access to the top policy makers in the nation. He and a significant contingent of so-called Arabists serving in the State Department wanted to do everything they could to win Roosevelt and then Harry Truman over to their position. Penrose was fighting two wars through his role in the OSS: he wanted to defeat the Axis, and he battled to keep Zionists from creating a Jewish state in the Middle East.[1]

Shortly after Penrose's promotion, he groused to his old friend from Beirut Lewis Leary about how busy he was overseeing intelligence across Europe. He had to learn a new field and deal with a new staff and a new series of operations ranging from those launched by Stewart Herman's colleagues in the London office to Father Morlion's Pilgrim's Progress. Leary was not thrilled by his old friend's advancement. "I never have really congratulated you on your new job," he wrote Penrose, "mainly because I don't approve of it at all." He believed that many people could do the job in Europe, learning the ropes just as well as Penrose could, but few people in the OSS had Penrose's experience and qualifications for work in the Middle East. This, Leary concluded, "is certainly a back-handed, dirty, Irish way of congratulating a guy who has just gotten a good job." Leary didn't have to worry. Penrose was far from done with the Middle East.[2]

Controversies over postwar Palestine continued to preoccupy the missionary executive and his OSS agents, including Rabbi Nelson Glueck. The archaeologist believed that finding a reasonable solution to the Zionist debate required "the wisdom of Solomon, the patience of Job, and the love of humanity of Jesus. God help us!" He knew that what happened in Palestine as the war wrapped up would have substantial ramifications for the postwar world.[3]

For Glueck, the establishment of a Jewish homeland in Palestine was not a realistic possibility and therefore not worth debating, which is why he could simultaneously do everything in his power to support his fellow Jews while also trying to clamp down on American Zionism. "I am," he wrote in early 1945, "coming to the conclusion that far fewer Jews are still alive in Europe today than I had reason to believe was the case 6 months ago." Palestinian Arabs, he felt confident, should have no fear of becoming a minority since there were not enough Jews left in Europe to establish a state in Palestine. "Both the Zionists and Arabs," he fretted, "are shouting their heads off about something which has no point to it."[4]

For Penrose, the larger question of a Jewish homeland related directly to a more immediate issue for the OSS. The spy agency's leaders continued to debate the extent to which they should collaborate with the Palestine-based, Zionist-focused Jewish Agency. Shortly after assuming his new position, the missionary executive wrote Allen Dulles a long note, primarily about the Jewish Agency, and he also invited Dulles to collaborate more closely with him. Penrose felt optimistic at the time. He had met with Jewish Agency leaders again, and they convinced him that they could perform a real function checking the rise of an underground Nazi movement after the war. They also detailed their plans for channeling the energy and anger of younger Jews who might be bent on revenge into more positive directions. Penrose told Dulles, perhaps disingenuously, that he maintained good relations with the agency in Cairo and viewed agency operatives as useful collaborators.[5]

Dulles, from his position in Bern, Switzerland, also needed to decide how far to go with the agency. Irving Sherman, an officer in the OSS's New York office, tried to convince him that collaboration served the interests of the OSS. Before the war began Sherman had worked with Stewart Herman in Berlin, where he had secretly conspired to rescue German Jews. Having seen firsthand what life was like under the Nazi regime, he wanted to enlist the OSS in any legitimate efforts to rescue Jews. "The Intelligence Section of the Jewish Agency has been very effective," Sherman told Dulles. Furthermore, the OSS could partner strategically with the agency on mutually reinforcing intelligence work and rescue activities. Jews delivered from Europe represented a fresh crop of potential agents with excellent, up-to-date firsthand knowledge.

Sherman believed that the Jewish Agency could also help the OSS prepare Jews in occupied regions for the Allied invasion. He forwarded a memo to Dulles outlining a rationale for collaborating with the agency. The United States, the memo stated, had worked to support "underground organizations for sabotage, escape, and revolt" among POWs and others held in German labor camps but had done little work among Jews. The Jews must be "organized by us, in order to take in their share when the signal is given for the final uprising." On the other hand, if the OSS squandered this opportunity, the consequences would be dire. "If left unarmed and unorganized, without contacts and instructions," the memo continued, "we shall lose the last remnants of the European Jewry in the turmoil of a collapsing Germany. The Jews have proven their ability to make a firm stand and fight even in the most desperate situations, if organized for resistance. We must, therefore," the author of the memo insisted, "act immediately, in cooperation with the Allies."[6]

Sherman's appeal fell mostly on deaf ears. Dulles, like Penrose, continued to question the logic of partnering with the agency. "Doubt if at this stage," he cabled Sherman, "we want too close a tie in with Kantars," using the code name for the Jewish Agency. "But could express better judgement if exact nature latest proposition were known to me. Kantars main aim is probably to further their refugee plans through using us." Penrose and Dulles believed that if rescuing Jews from Europe and relocating them to Palestine might exacerbate the controversy about a future Jewish state, perhaps it was better to let them fend for themselves in enemy territory. No one knows how many Jews perished at the hands of the Nazis because

OSS leaders dismissed the Jewish Agency's "refugee" efforts as unimportant. Hardened by the horrors of the war, most OSS leaders focused on one goal and one goal only. They intended to serve the explicit interests of the United States and its people and no one else.[7]

While bureaucrats in Washington and New York mulled over potential OSS–Jewish Agency collaboration, officers in both organizations were apparently trying to infiltrate each other's groups. At one point, OSS leaders proposed getting agents inside the Jewish Agency, suggesting that "penetration of the organization might be wise." The Jewish Agency was thinking along the same lines, but in reverse. Allied forces, searching a Jewish Agency spy at a border-control station, discovered evidence that the agency hoped to burrow inside the OSS and other Allied intelligence agencies. Penrose claimed that he had sniffed out and blocked their plans. This agent's mistake gave Penrose the perfect excuse for raising even higher boundaries between the intelligence organizations.[8]

Despite Penrose's misgivings, Lewis Leary, who since Penrose's promotion was running Middle East intelligence operations from Cairo, believed that partnering with the Jewish Agency was worthwhile. "I am becoming convinced," he conceded to Penrose, "which is perhaps in your eyes enough for my immediate removal—that there is a good deal to be gained by us in at least a token cooperation with them." He was only partly joking about getting fired for his thoughts. To ease the tension over his disagreement with his old friend and boss, he threw in an anti-Semitic joke, claiming that he was becoming Jewish—"Bergson Leary, that's what they call me." He reminded Penrose that his views were based on the simple fact that he thought a partnership would produce good results. He subtly warned Penrose that their job was not to craft foreign policy. Instead, Donovan had tasked them with collaborating with Allied groups based on their usefulness to the OSS. And the Jewish Agency could be very useful.[9]

Leary identified numerous ways that the OSS could benefit from the Jewish Agency and suggested covertly placing an officer within the agency. He had already identified an ideal "cut out" to go between the infiltrator and the OSS—an American army private and undercover OSS man named Herbert Katzki, then working officially for the War Refugee Board. Roosevelt established the WRB in early 1944 to help rescue various groups, especially Jews, in danger in Europe. Leary won over Penrose to the plan. The missionary executive brought Dulles on board too, since Katzki was operating in and around Switzerland. He advised Dulles to get to know Katzki, whom he thought might prove useful to the spymaster in any number of ways.[10]

In working with the Jewish Agency, Leary promised to be cautious. In a report to Whitney Shepardson, one of Donovan's top lieutenants, copied to Penrose, Leary suggested that they "maintain the strict control" of information, which guaranteed that "little possibility" existed "that we can become involved to our detriment in any matters of Zionist policy or propaganda." But he acknowledged that "Mr. Penrose, I am sure, will view the matter with dark suspicion." He was right. OSS brass soon shut down Leary's plans, although Penrose claimed that others had made the decision. He worried that "the Agency is much interested in putting into Central and Southeastern Europe men who will do a concentrated propaganda job to secure increased immigration into Palestine."[11]

Of course, it was doing just that. Agency leaders wanted to save their fellow Jews from the gas chambers. Penrose, apparently, would rather Jews still under or near Nazi occupation take their chances in Europe than flee to Palestine, where they might intentionally or inadvertently bolster the Zionist cause. The missionary executive made one concession, however. He allowed Leary to collect intelligence from the Jewish Agency. "The only condition under which we may play with them at all," he insisted, "is that of passive receptivity to a one-way flow of information" from them to the OSS.[12]

Whatever chance Leary had of winning OSS leaders over to his position with regards to the Jewish Agency vanished when the OSS discovered that yet again Jewish Agency leaders were secretly aiming to place a mole in the OSS. The agency was playing the same clandestine games that the OSS played. For Penrose, this was all the excuse he needed to quash any deals, including Leary's plan to accept freely offered intelligence. The Secret Intelligence Branch, Penrose instructed, "will have nothing to do with the Kantars, even on the level of passive acceptance of their intelligence materials." He instructed operatives that "definitely . . . all cooperation with the Jewish Agency, including even the acceptance of its intelligence material, should cease." He told Dulles sarcastically that "the noble experiment I had anticipated will have to be suspended before it is tried. This causes me a certain amount of regret but the volume is very small."[13]

Penrose's decision, Leary noted to a colleague, "seems effectively to close our period of flirting with this organization." Leary undersold the relationship. This was more than flirting—it was a long on-and-off cycle of mistrust, missed opportunities, and confusion. Yet Leary was definitely not done flirting. He felt confident, he told another colleague, that OSS and army leaders would not approve of his dissolving "a contact without receiving from us full particulars as to how this contact is maintained and what value it can be to our intelligence probing in the Middle East."[14]

Leary believed the real problem was the OSS and not the Jewish Agency. "I am happy that we had decided to drop our Kantar relations forthwith," he told Penrose in a biting memo, "though if we had matured more professionally, they could have been of value to us. I do not believe that we are yet in condition to play in their league."[15]

Leary also wrote archaeologist Nelson Glueck. Due to some failures on the part of the Jewish Agency to deliver what it promised, he explained, "we have received today very definite word from Washington that we are not to have any more official contacts with that group for any purpose. This is very ridiculous and I know will soon be rescinded." Until then, however, Leary told Glueck, "I am going to have to count on you more than ever to be my ears and eyes and nose in your territory." He wanted Glueck to continue to report back to him on the plans and aims of the agency and offered to visit the rabbi in Jerusalem. He promised Glueck that he would "squeeze your bulging udders dry in providing us the rich and foaming cream of your intelligence."[16]

Leary was not the only one in the OSS who disagreed with Penrose's actions. William Langer, the director of the Research and Analysis Branch, received a memo from one of his men in the field who wanted to sustain the flow of material coming from the Jewish Agency. "We know that the Agency has an active political department which gathers a lot of information on Palestine and the Middle East, and on Jews in Europe," the operative summarized. "If we can obtain some of their information simply by asking for it rather than by other devious means, and if the information is valuable, I submit that we stand to gain by continuing to have relationships with the Agency." As the United States began assembling materials for war-crimes prosecutions, American leaders realized that they could not afford to cut off the Jewish Agency. The agency had boxes and boxes of evidence about Nazi atrocities, and the US government needed that material to ensure that justice was served.[17]

Despite Penrose's suspicion of all things Zionist, the internal OSS history of the Cairo station treats the OSS–Jewish Agency relationship as a positive one. The Jewish Agency acted "in good faith," the report summarized, provided numerous reports, and sought new ways to help the OSS with its work.[18]

Over the course of the conflict, Penrose used his knowledge of religion and background as a missionary executive to supervise important operations into the centers of global religious power. He had become, by the end of the war, one of Donovan's most effective leaders. Acting OSS director John Magruder recommended the missionary in 1945 for a Bronze Star, despite his civilian status. In justifying the recommendation, Magruder noted that Penrose had been in charge of "recruiting, briefing and actual infiltration of units" into the Balkans and the Middle East. The War Department agreed to make the award, although the citation, which simply offered some generic praise for vague contributions, was classified top secret.[19]

As the war neared its end, Penrose understood that the question of Palestine was far from settled. He had every intention of doing what he could to convince the president that Zionism was a danger to the United States. This was a battle he was destined to lose.

NINETEEN

"An Unusual Opportunity"

JUST A COUPLE OF DAYS AFTER FDR's FOURTH INAUGURATION IN January 1945, the president boarded a ship and sailed across the Atlantic to Malta, in the Mediterranean Sea. He rendezvoused with Churchill, and then the two leaders flew to Yalta, a resort town on the Soviet Union's Crimean Peninsula, where they joined Stalin. The Allied leaders' goal was to set the terms of the potential German and Japanese surrenders and to work on postwar plans. Churchill's physician, who attended the conference, was worried about the American president. Roosevelt, he noted, did not look well.

It was clearer than ever during the meetings that the Soviets, who now controlled much of eastern Europe, expected to have wide latitude over the reconstruction of the territory they had conquered. FDR did not put up much of a fight. The big three also agreed on a plan for dealing with postwar Germany. Initially, at least, they decided to divide Germany into four occupational zones, controlled by the British, the French, the Americans, and the Soviets. Stalin pledged to FDR that the Soviets would enter the Pacific war against Japan once the Allies had wrapped up the German fight in exchange for territory that they had lost to Japan decades earlier and for a variety of other concessions in Asia. After experiencing so much death on the eastern front, the Soviet people needed a worthwhile reason for entering the Pacific war. The leaders also agreed to form a new United Nations, with the hope that it could help maintain the postwar peace. The terms of the Yalta Conference were less than ideal for the Americans but matched the reality of the way the war was fought. The United States and Great Britain had needed Stalin to help defeat Hitler, and he demanded some of the spoils of war in return.

While FDR, Churchill, and Stalin were debating how to govern Germany after the war, Allen Dulles and other OSS leaders including Stephen Penrose were discussing how to rebuild German civil society. The international ecumenical movement played a significant role in their plans. Dulles believed that religion was key, and he sought out church leaders from Europe and North America for their advice. "My main objective," he reported to Donovan, "is to develop the church connections to Germany, both Catholic and Protestant." As the Allies gained more and more territory in Europe, Dulles summoned various religious leaders to his headquarters in Bern, where he could begin preparing them to help with German reconstruction. One minister he hoped to consult was Stewart Herman.[1]

By the fall of 1944, Herman's frustration with the OSS had just about reached its limit. No matter how hard he tried, he could not get his Central European desk operations off the ground. At about that time, he received an intriguing letter from former missionary Henry Smith Leiper. The American Protestant leader offered the OSS operative a position in the Federal Council of Churches' New York office working with the nascent, Geneva-based World Council of Churches on relief and rehabilitation programs in Europe. The WCC is a global Protestant ecumenical organization aimed at fostering unity among the world's churches and serving as a witness for the faith. The WCC's founders had hoped to launch the organization in the 1930s, but the war delayed their plans. By the mid-1940s, they were ready to try again.[2]

Herman was excited by Leiper's offer and promised to pray about it. He was hoping to return as soon as possible to the United States, where his girlfriend, Lyn Cantrell, was waiting for him, and he had been debating whether he could better serve the postwar world through a position with the United Lutheran Church or as a leader in the global ecumenical movement. He also wondered whether he should perhaps look for a job as a pastor serving a local congregation. Despite his doubts, Herman's response to Leiper was enthusiastic. "Nothing is closer to my heart," he revealed, "than the rapid progress of the ecumenical movement which, I believe, can make an enormous contribution to the pacification of nations." The question for the preacher was what role he might play in that work.[3]

Meanwhile, Dulles reached out to Herman to get his impression of various German religious leaders. The spymaster was looking for native partners to join him in his postwar rebuilding project. Herman offered Dulles a frank assessment of the strengths and weaknesses of each German clergyman Dulles had identified and what role the clergyman might play in reconstruction. Herman spoke of the Confessing Church in nothing but the most laudatory of terms, and he agreed that religious leaders should be central to rebuilding civil society within Germany. They could serve as a bridge reconnecting Germans to the outside world. "These considerations," he told Dulles, "lead me to observe that a German Church provides the strongest organized basis for stabilizing post-war Germany." He also followed up on Dulles's request that he ask WCC leaders to get a representative to Dulles in Switzerland as soon as possible to prepare for work in Germany. What additional role Herman might play in Dulles's plans was still unclear. In the meantime, from his Central European Operations desk the former Berlin pastor remained busy drafting OSS missions for operations into the Third Reich.[4]

Herman met with Dulles that October in London, where the two spent hours discussing German reconstruction and Herman's job offer from the Federal Council of Churches. Then Dulles sprung a new idea on Herman. Why choose between church work and intelligence work? Perhaps the churchman might serve both the global ecumenical movement and the OSS at the same time? Dulles suggested that Herman sever his official connection with the OSS and seek a position with the World Council of Churches, reaching out to the German churches in an "'unofficial' mission" separate from the work of the American occupying forces. Herman joked that if Dulles's scheme came to fruition, for once the Protestants would have the jump on the Catholics in getting into the field. The imminent Allied victory reinforced the convictions of leaders of various US government agencies that American strategic interests and the expansion of Christendom were interconnected.[5]

Despite Herman's levity, he was initially a little uncomfortable with what Dulles was asking of him. "I protested," he confided in his diary, "against any connection which might eventually cause church to be considered a 'quisling.'" But the next day, he wrote Henry Smith Leiper, outlining the scheme he and Dulles had cooked up. Instead of the job Leiper had offered him working with the WCC in New York, perhaps he could work out of the WCC's headquarters in Geneva, as Leiper had suggested years earlier. He wanted to be ready to get to the German churches "shortly after the collapse of Hitler's armies." Maintaining close ties with Dulles could make that possible.[6]

As Herman mulled over his conversation with the OSS leader and waited for a response from the WCC, Dulles continued looking for other possible recruits willing to help him with German reconstruction. One was A. Livingston Warnshuis, a longtime missionary to China turned missionary executive. Warnshuis led the International Missionary Council and worked on wartime relief and refugee issues, along with postwar planning, for both the Federal Council of Churches and the World Council of Churches. Dulles wrote Donovan, asking the OSS to work with the State Department to get Warnshuis to Bern as quickly as possible. Dulles told the London office that he was very interested in the missionary leader, "since it appears to me that the organized religions offer a great opportunity for the occupying authorities after the collapse of Germany since, from present indications, they may be the only already organized groups ready to collaborate with us." Warnshuis, he believed, was perhaps his means of penetrating those groups.[7]

Warnshuis traveled from New York to London in November 1944, his first stop en route to Dulles. He carried with him a letter of introduction from President Roosevelt as well as letters from OSS leaders in the states. The White House had intervened with the State Department and the War Department on behalf of the OSS to expedite the trip. Warnshuis earned "Class I" priority travel orders, ranking him above most generals and top diplomats. He shared the cabin of a Pan Am Clipper with Admiral Richard Byrd, the famous explorer and naval officer, who was only a Class II priority. Throughout the trip, the missionary seemingly failed to grasp who he was really working for and why doors kept opening for him. "I'll be one of the very first American civilians—not on a government mission—to get into France," he wrote a friend. He seemed not to understand that he was indeed on a government mission—one orchestrated by Dulles and Donovan and approved by Roosevelt.[8]

In London Warnshuis met with Herman. "I had long talks with him," Herman recorded, "about the reopening of connections with Europe." Warnshuis, for his part, continued to be willfully naive, or perhaps he just didn't want his wife and colleagues to know that he was serving two masters. In a letter home, he identified Herman simply as a friend "connected with the embassy." Whether Warnshuis understood that Herman was at that time organizing daring operations behind German lines as the two men were working together on postwar ideas for the WCC is unclear.[9]

Warnshuis then flew to Bern to see Dulles. After meeting with the missionary at his home, Dulles decided that perhaps Warnshuis was not the best candidate for the kind of mission the spymaster had in mind. Warnshuis showed little interest in remaining in Europe to study the situation on the ground, and Dulles thought that the missionary's command of French and German was poor. But the trip had a silver lining—Dulles learned from Warnshuis that the WCC was still hoping to recruit Herman. Realizing that Herman might be in play, Warnshuis's trip, Dulles reported to OSS leader John Hughes, "has done good." Dulles thought Herman "would be an excellent choice" to serve as his main contact in the WCC and his intermediary with German religious leaders. Hughes agreed with Dulles that Herman was a perfect candidate, capable of fulfilling Dulles's plans for securing an operative within the Geneva-based religious organization in order to guide the resurrection of a network of German churches linked with the global ecumenical movement.[10]

As Dulles floated Herman's name as a possible candidate for infiltrating the WCC, some confusion arose at the London Branch. A debate began among OSS leaders in the United Kingdom as to whether there might be two Stewart Hermans, since they could not fathom that the preacher Dulles wanted was the spook who was planning dangerous incursions into Germany. John Wilson, a leader of OSS operations in the European theater, felt sure that the "Herman" that Dulles intended to recruit for work in the WCC could not be the same Stewart Herman who ran the Central European Operations desk. But he was indeed the same man. The war had turned a religious leader into a master of espionage and propaganda, at least for the duration. Herman joked that he "heartily" wished there had been two different Stewart Hermans, one serving the churches and the other the OSS. It was the evolution of this kind of dual identity that made the war so interesting and challenging for people like John Birch,

William Eddy, Stephen Penrose, Nelson Glueck, Felix Morlion, and Stewart Herman—religious leaders who pivoted from spiritual to clandestine work and back again.[11]

In the midst of Herman's high-stakes negotiations with Dulles and ecumenical leaders, the churchman traveled back to the United States for a thirty-day leave. He had threatened to quit the OSS in anger over his bosses' failure to support the Central European Operations desk with the staff and resources Herman thought it deserved. OSS leaders in London offered him a break, hoping that perhaps he would be ready for additional OSS work after a little rest. Taking over control of the desk for Herman was a young naval officer, William Casey, whom the churchman had brought up to speed on plans for missions into German before he left. Casey would later serve as a director of the CIA. Not long after Herman reached the United States, the OSS ordered him to Paris. He refused to go. He told the agency that he needed to get things settled with his girlfriend, Lyn Cantrell, first, as well as with the World Council of Churches. The OSS backed down. Herman was a valuable-enough operative that agency leaders were eager to lure him back, and so they let him set the terms of his return.

Herman met with Leiper and Warnshuis in New York to discuss the WCC's plans and how the former Berliner might fit within them. Herman and Warnshuis later met in Washington, DC, with representatives from both the State Department and the OSS to discuss Herman's and Dulles's developing ideas for German reconstruction. "Everywhere," Warnshuis wrote of his work with Herman, "I find enthusiastic support for what we have in mind." Herman finally made his decision. The WCC was willing to give him a job in Geneva, which, the pastor decided, would allow him "an unusual opportunity to serve both the war—and the peace—effort."[12]

While in Washington, Herman introduced OSS leaders to his long-time friend from the ecumenical movement Willem Visser 't Hooft. The energetic Dutchman would soon become the first general secretary of the WCC. During the war the Dutch ecumenist had routinely met with Allen Dulles in Switzerland to keep him abreast of his work with the Dutch resistance and provide the superspy with information on various topics. He was also a friend of John Foster Dulles, who was very interested in

Visser 't Hooft's postwar plans for establishing the WCC as one of the world's leading peace organizations.[13]

Visser 't Hooft, like Birch, Eddy, Herman, and Penrose, lived a double life during the war. While holed up in Geneva during the Nazi occupation of his native Netherlands, Visser 't Hooft fell into clandestine work. The Dutchman's apartment served as the meeting place for the leaders of various European resistance movements, where they coordinated plans aimed at Hitler's defeat. "It began in a most innocent way," Visser 't Hooft acknowledged, but it did not remain that way for long. His connections with Dutch churchmen gave him access to the Dutch underground. Its leaders managed to transmit material to the cleric, who then forwarded their information to the Dutch government in exile in the United Kingdom. Visser 't Hooft established a relatively efficient intelligence service that agents called "the Swiss Road." "During these two years, from the summer of 1942 to the summer of 1944," he recalled, "I was therefore in the strange position of having a substantial spare-time activity about which my colleagues in the office of the World Council knew nothing and should know nothing."[14]

The material he transmitted occasionally helped the Allies kill their enemies. For Visser 't Hooft, the calculus was worthwhile. He would help facilitate the taking of some lives to ensure the saving of others. Like William Eddy, he expressed few regrets. "As I looked back on the adventure which had taken me into regions which I had never expected to enter," Visser 't Hooft wrote years later, "I had much reason to feel that it had been truly worthwhile. I had had an opportunity to do something for my country and to become involved in its life." He had embraced Niebuhr's Christian realist philosophy, recognizing that states must sometimes use force to secure peace. The experience helped prepare him for his WCC position in that it taught him "a great deal about the realities of politics and government." "It was difficult to know," he concluded, "whether these years had been the worst or the best years of our lives."[15]

Herman's furlough did not provide the time for rest and relaxation that he had hoped for. Over the Christmas holiday, he assisted at his father's church in Pennsylvania, preaching, meeting with congregants, offering communion, and leading various services. He also helped his sister with her new baby while his brother-in-law was fighting abroad. Then, finally, in January 1945, he made it to Georgia to see Lyn Cantrell for only the fourth time since their first meeting at Cornell. She was working for the Bell Aircraft Corporation as the only female engineer in a factory that employed twenty-four thousand people assembling the new B-29 Superfortress bombers.

A couple of days into Stewart Herman's visit to Georgia, he and Lyn went for a walk with the Cantrells' mangy mutt named Old Faithful and Lyn's precocious four-year-old brother. While Stewart and Lyn sat on an old fallen log in the forest near the Cantrell family home, Stewart proposed. Lyn told the churchman that she needed to think about his offer. A few days later, Herman recorded in his diary, she "finally and emphatically" said yes. Although Herman had a difficult time expressing his emotions, he told Lyn she was everything he wanted and needed: "wife, mistress, playmate, secretary, chief executive, glamour girl, nurse, hostess—my Juliet, Wife of Bath, Emily Dickinson, Florence Nightingale, Cleopatra, Eleanor Roosevelt."[16]

Despite the daunting comparison with some of the world's most accomplished women, Lyn was up to the challenge of marriage to Herman. But she also felt a bit nervous, especially when she thought about how little she actually knew about her fiancé with the cautious and conservative temperament. Just weeks before the wedding, she told him he was "in so many ways . . . a stranger. You are a very charming stranger," she confided, "but a stranger. Why is it that I've never felt that I've reached inside you? You are so self-sufficient; must I remain always on the periphery? And I'm a little frightened too." She always knew, she told him, that it was going to be difficult for him to learn "to love." She vowed to try to teach him nevertheless.[17]

Herman officially quit the OSS on February 19, 1945. OSS leaders in Paris had again called and pleaded with the parson to come to the Continent and work for them until the end of the war, when he could then transition to the WCC. But he refused. He wanted to stay in the United States at least long enough to get married. Resigning from the agency, he decided, was the only way to ensure that OSS Paris got the message. He was not coming back. Aware that Herman was leaving, one of his allies in the London office asked Donovan to sign a letter of commendation. Herman's "recent knowledge of Germany made him an extremely valuable man in London," the commendation read. "With little or no aid and with very meager additions to his staff, he set up plans for operations inside Germany. He was extremely conscientious and hard working, and this Branch regrets his decision to resign but respects his judgement in that he considers his new position more important." Herman's "intelligent efforts toward penetration of the Reich is presently showing results," the memo concluded.[18]

Although Herman's relationship with the OSS changed substantially, it did not end. Over the next couple of months, Herman planned a wedding with Lyn and continued to travel back and forth from his parents' home in Harrisburg to Washington for meetings at OSS headquarters. The churchman intended to move to Geneva with his new wife as soon as possible after the wedding, and when he did, he promised to get in touch with Allen Dulles. An internal OSS memo summarizing Herman's separation from the organization noted that "110," the code name for Dulles, "thinks that this position will be of value to this organization."[19]

Stewart Herman and Lyn Cantrell married on April 5, 1945. Lyn, Herman wrote in his diary, "in a cloud of loveliness, came up the aisle and

Stewart Herman could be cold and in-different, but the one person who was able to (sometimes) break through the OSS leader's hard shell was Lyn Cantrell. Herman took leave from the OSS in late 1944 to marry Lyn.
Courtesy of Stewart Herman III.

the ceremony was perfect." Meanwhile, the Allies were closing in on Berlin. The first American troops reached the Elbe River on April 11. There they waited for the Soviet army, which was driving toward Berlin from the east. They did not have to wait for long. On May 8, Germany surrendered, and the war in Europe ended. Two days later, Herman saw Reinhold Niebuhr in Harrisburg. He continued to admire the theologian and described his latest book as "some sound political thinking." Niebuhr's practical, pragmatic theology had shaped Herman's early work in Berlin, and it provided a justification for maintaining his ties with the OSS while returning to full-time ministry.[20]

Although the war in Europe had ended, Herman's work was far from done. That July he and Lyn moved to Geneva for his new job working on refugee issues for the World Council of Churches. It was exactly what he and Dulles had planned months earlier. Dulles and other OSS leaders wanted to get people on the ground in Germany as soon as possible in order to assess the options for rebuilding a civil society. Although Herman was now officially working for the WCC, the OSS secretly placed him back on "temporary duty" in August. His job was to travel across Germany, stopping in various cities to meet with religious leaders. The death and destruction he encountered upon his return were awful. He visited his old Berlin church, now a ruin, and referred to the experience in his diary as a "strange and horrible nightmare."[21]

During the trip, Herman interviewed numerous prominent German religious leaders and drafted reports for various US government agencies detailing what he learned. He also preached and gave communion. In Berlin he finally met Francis Pickens Miller, his fellow ecumenist and counterpart in the London Branch who had dropped rebels into occupied France before D-Day. Miller was now with army intelligence, tracking the Russians' clandestine actions in Germany.[22]

Throughout the mission, Herman worked closely with Allen Dulles. They met more than ten times in the months following Germany's surrender. One night they even shared a hotel room, although Herman was definitely a downgrade from Dulles's preferred nighttime companions. The minister also met with Donovan on various occasions. Wild Bill was in Germany helping prepare for the Nuremberg war-crimes trials. Herman advised him on what information he could get from Germany's religious leaders. The clergyman spy also met with General Dwight Eisenhower to discuss the role of the churches in postwar Germany.[23]

Nobody expected the German reconstruction effort to be easy. Leaders of the German Protestant churches were divided on many issues, and one of Herman's main priorities was to reconcile them to each other and to the global ecumenical movement. It was a tough job that required him to bring the members of the many wartime factions back into fellowship. Some had compromised with the Nazi regime, while others had gone to jail in protest of Hitler's policies. Some thought the churches had nothing to apologize for, and others saw German Christian leaders as complicit in the war. Herman had to convince his theological allies that "squabbles and splits" with ministers such as influential Swiss German theologian Karl Barth, whose theology Herman had never liked, "would be disastrous." Even more difficult was his work keeping Martin Niemöller out of trouble. The Confessing Church leader and dissident who had been incarcerated by the Nazis publicly criticized some of the actions of the US occupational forces, and Herman had to smooth things over with American leaders.[24]

In October 1945, a handful of the leaders of Germany's Protestant churches, led by those who had defied Hitler, met in Stuttgart. They wanted to discuss the war and determine what role the churches had played in it and how they might move forward. Leaders from the WCC wanted to attend the conference—they believed that it was crucial to restore relations with German church leaders and to bring them back into the ecumenical fold. When WCC leaders asked US occupational authorities for permission to travel to Stuttgart for the conference, the latter initially balked. Then Herman intervened. His actions made possible a historic meeting that brought together old and new, German and non-German, leaders of the ecumenical movement.

The foreign churchmen believed that German Christians needed to take some responsibility for not doing more to stop Hitler. The German church leaders at the meeting agreed. They issued a declaration acknowledging that although they had spoken out against the Nazi regime, they should have witnessed more courageously, prayed more faithfully, and loved more ardently. Additionally, Niemöller added a controversial sentence to the declaration. All Germans, he insisted, bore some blame for the actions of their government. Yet the very presence of Herman and other foreign leaders made the Stuttgart declaration contentious. For some German religious leaders, the declaration looked like an admission of guilt forced upon Germany by foreigners, exactly the same thing that had happened in Versailles after World War I.[25]

In Stuttgart Herman, American ecumenical leader Samuel McCrea Cavert, WCC leader Willem Visser t' Hooft, Confessing Church leader Martin Niemöller, theologian Karl Barth, and others laid out a plan for the future. They all hoped to make a thriving ecumenical church movement the foundation for a peaceful postwar world. The Americans and British also learned from their German colleagues that religious freedom was under siege in Soviet-occupied eastern Germany, something that would increasingly occupy the attention of groups like the WCC.

Herman wrote a report summarizing the proceedings for the World Council. He also sent a copy of the report to John Foster Dulles, at the behest of Allen, who wanted to make sure that his more pious brother was apprised of the latest developments in the ecumenical movement's efforts in Germany. He hoped the elder Dulles might convince people in the State Department to take more seriously the church work of the occupation forces. "Briefly," Herman summarized, "the World Council wants to give the German Church in its weakened state as much support as is needed to make the German Church a bulwark of Christian principles and democratic procedure in the ex-Nazi state." Herman had also sent a long report to Allen Dulles, outlining all that the German ministers had accomplished at the recent Tresya conference, which Herman had also helped facilitate. He assured the spymaster that he was working behind the scenes to oust any former Nazi collaborators.[26]

Herman's relentless schedule meant that he did not have as much time for his new bride as he had hoped. In his annual reflection on the events of the year, he expressed real joy in finding Lyn, a partner with whom to share his life. "She is a young woman of rare spirit and loveliness, for whom and to whom I am profoundly thankful," he wrote. "It has hurt us to be separated so much in this first year, especially as she is so young and away from home for the first time & thrown into a wholly new world of foreign associations." Yet this was the cost of marrying Herman. "During our brief courtship," he confessed, "I tried to warn her of the sort of husband she would have, but things like that cannot be depicted effectively. I'm sure that we have lived and loved our way into each other, inescapably,—but I wish heartily that I possessed more adequate ways of showing and saying it."[27]

Over the next year, under the auspices of the WCC, Herman continued to use his secret connections with the OSS to get permission to travel around Europe to meet with religious leaders, and he communicated what he saw and learned to American intelligence agencies. He had matured since his younger days or at least had developed more empathy for people with fewer resources than he had. The cities he visited had been reduced to rubble, hotel rooms were dirty, and fresh food was hard to come by. Herman didn't complain. During his travels he continued to work closely with Niemöller. The Confessing Church leader thanked Herman for acting "so often as an interpreter and lawyer for me," and he would later baptize two of Herman's sons.[28]

As Herman delved deeper into projects for the World Council of Churches, his direct work for the US government diminished. But his wartime experiences, along with those of Visser 't Hooft, ensured that with a cold war developing, the WCC was going to be on the front lines in defense of global ecumenical Protestantism and against "godless" communism. With Allen Dulles at the helm of the CIA in the 1950s, and Herman's Central European Operations desk substitute William Casey running the CIA in the 1980s, there could be no doubt that churchmen like Herman were going to be spies once again.

TWENTY

"The High Point of Muslim Alliance"

ROOSEVELT BELIEVED THAT THE FEBRUARY 1945 YALTA CONFERENCE WITH Churchill and Stalin had been a success. They had settled many of the key questions regarding the reconstruction of Europe and outlined a vision for maintaining the postwar peace. As the American president looked to the future, he was also eager to bolster the United States' alliances in the Middle East. Rather than return straight home after negotiating with his British and Soviet counterparts, the president decided to make a slight detour in order to meet King Abdul Aziz of Saudi Arabia. To ensure Roosevelt's safety, his staff kept his itinerary a secret. The State Department gave William Eddy, the US minister to Saudi Arabia and former OSS man, only one week's advance notice of the meeting. In Saudi Arabia only the king, the Saudi foreign minister, a coding clerk in the American legation, and Eddy's wife, Mary, knew that the historic summit was imminent.

The State Department instructed Eddy to make the necessary preparations for the meeting. He served as translator of both language and culture and needed to ensure that the king and the US Navy agreed on the basic terms for the conference. Problems arose immediately. Eddy had to determine how best to get the king and his entourage on board a relatively small and crowded destroyer that would ferry the Arabs to Roosevelt's cruiser. Eddy told his Saudi counterpart that the Americans could accommodate only twelve people, including the king. Eddy feared that the king would try to bring a harem. He told Abdul Aziz that as much as the king might want his wives to travel with him, the ship was no place for Muslim women. Having them climbing up and down narrow companionways and walking tight hallways with American sailors was not a good idea. Luckily for Eddy, the women stayed behind.

As Eddy was arranging the final details, Mary, on the balcony of the Eddy home in Jeddah, saw the USS *Murphy* steam into the harbor. She got to work. While the crew prepared the ship for the Saudi royalty, the Eddys entertained some of the officers at their home. Then they toured the vessel and enjoyed an American meal onboard, which delighted Mary. Once everything was set on the ship, Mary disembarked, leaving her husband behind. Bill, she wrote, "looked very nice in his Marine Corps uniform, but he had a certain harassed look about him."[1]

On the morning of embarkation, the king's entourage of forty-eight men, rather than the twelve Eddy had negotiated to ferry, showed up for the trip, along with one hundred live sheep, rice, grain, and vegetables. The king insisted that they have fresh meat available and refused to believe that meat preserved by refrigeration was safe to consume. Eddy brokered a deal—the Arabs could bring seven sheep on board, one for each day. As soon as the Arabs boarded the *Murphy*, they slaughtered the first one on the fantail of the ship to the amusement of the American sailors. Abdul Aziz refused to move into the cabin that the navy provided for him—the space was too confining. So his men spread fine rugs over the deck of the ship and erected a canvas cover, the most rudimentary of tents over the most modern of ships. Mary noted the irony of the situation. She described seeing high-powered cannons "sticking through the canvas" and poking out from "underneath all this royal splendor." When the ship steamed out of port, the local citizens of Jeddah were left wondering what had happened to their king, where the Americans were taking him, and whether he would return.[2]

According to Eddy, the sailors and the Arabs got along fabulously, communicating with gestures and acting. The Arabs were a little confused, however, when they encountered an African American sailor. They were sure that he must be an Arab and a Muslim, and they insisted on talking to him in Arabic.

For Eddy, the trip was a lot of work. "I said that a good time was had by all on the voyage," he reported, "but a good time was had by all except me." For the colonel, walking the diplomatic tightrope inherent in the mission was stressful. He dealt with everything from food to religious practices. He convinced the king's servants not to boil coffee on top of ammunition and American sailors not to walk in front of Muslims during their prayers. Movies also generated problems for Eddy. The sailors regularly watched popular Hollywood films belowdecks in the evenings. The king strongly disapproved of modern movies and the values they ostensibly represented. However, Abdul Aziz's sons had gotten wind of the film screenings, and one approached Eddy. The prince quietly asked the colonel if he preferred "to be destroyed all at once or to be chopped up in small pieces bit by bit" for neglecting to invite him and his brother. In the end, the princes won out—they saw a film starring Lucille Ball, which included a scene of her running half naked through a college men's dormitory. Eddy was relieved the king never learned that he had ushered the princes to the doors of Hades.[3]

On February 14, 1945, the USS *Murphy* came alongside the USS *Quincy* in the Great Bitter Lake in the Suez Canal. The king, Eddy, and a few aides crossed the gangplank from the *Murphy* to FDR's ship. The president and Abdul Aziz talked for about an hour on the deck, with Eddy serving as the sole translator for both men. Then they retreated to lunch. Eddy and the king took one elevator down; FDR and the president's top military adviser, Admiral William Leahy, took another. FDR was slow to catch up to Eddy and the king. Eddy later learned from Leahy that the president pulled the emergency-stop lever on the elevator on its descent and quickly smoked two cigarettes. He hadn't wanted to offend the king by smoking in front of him, and he certainly couldn't go another hour without a smoke. The conversation continued over lunch and well into the afternoon, with Eddy again serving as the sole translator for both men.

The exchange of gifts was another area where Eddy's knowledge and experience proved invaluable. After significant debate at the State Department, and with substantial input from the missionary, FDR gave Abdul Aziz a DC-3 airplane. He also spontaneously gave the king his spare

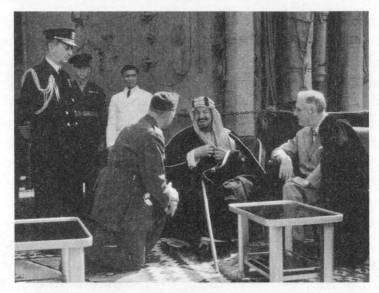

In early 1945, President Roosevelt and King Abdul Aziz ibn Saud held a historic conference on a naval cruiser, laying the foundations for an enduring US-Saudi partnership. The sole translator for the meeting was William Eddy. His wife and children thought it was funny that in the official pictures documenting the event, only the back of Eddy's head is visible. *Courtesy of Franklin D. Roosevelt Presidential Library.*

wheelchair after the two men discussed the downsides of aging. As the king grew older, the effects of life as a desert warrior were catching up with him. Although the gift was more symbolic than practical, it touched the king deeply. The king gave FDR a diamond-encrusted sword. Eddy viewed the meeting as a tremendous success. The colonel described FDR as "in top form as a charming host, witty conversationalist, with the spark and light in his eyes and that gracious smile, which always won people over to him whenever he talked with them as a friend."[4]

After the long day of meetings, Eddy drew up a summary in both English and Arabic, and the king and FDR both signed it. At the heart of the leaders' discussion was a debate about what to do about displaced Jews. "The President asked His Majesty," Eddy summarized, "for his advice regarding the problem of Jewish refugees driven from their homes in Europe. His Majesty replied that in his opinion the Jews should return to live in the lands from which they were driven." Abdul Aziz was clear. "The Jews," the king asserted, "whose homes were completely destroyed and who have no chance of livelihood in their homelands should be given living space in the Axis countries which oppressed them." FDR was hoping that the king would encourage Muslims in the Middle East to show their heralded Arab hospitality to Jews. Abdul Aziz, in turn, insisted that since the Germans were soon to be vanquished, the Allies should use German land and treasure to resettle Jews in Germany. "Make the enemy and the oppressor pay," he told FDR. "That is how we Arabs wage war. Amends should be made by the criminal," not by the Palestinian Arabs, "the innocent bystander. What injury have Arabs done to the Jews of Europe? It is the 'Christian' Germans who stole their homes and lives. Let the Germans pay."[5]

FDR told Abdul Aziz that he understood. "The President," Eddy continued, promised the king "that he would do nothing to assist the Jews against the Arabs and would make no move hostile to the Arab people." Eddy believed that FDR's "reassurance concerned his own future policy as Chief Executive of the United States Government." The king wanted FDR to recommit to what he had long promised Abdul Aziz in letters— that the Arabs in Palestine would have the right to govern themselves. Abdul Aziz did not want European powers trying to control the Middle East any longer. According to Eddy, FDR pledged to not make any moves in Palestine without consulting both Jewish and Arab leaders.[6]

Eddy believed the president, and he hoped the meeting would bring the world's millions of Muslims into an alliance with the United States based on mutual trust and respect. "The guardian of the Holy Places of Islam," Eddy wrote of the king, "the nearest we have to a successor to the Caliphs, the Defender of the Muslim Faith and of the Holy Cities of three hundred million people," on that day "cemented a friendship with the head of a great Western and Christian nation. The meeting," he insisted, "marks the high point of Muslim alliance with the West. This moral alliance, this willingness of the leader of Islam to face West and bind his fortunes to ours, symbolizes a consummation devoutly to be wished in the world today." What Eddy may not have known was that the president was talking out of both sides of his mouth. At about the same time, Roosevelt gave American Zionists the impression that he supported their cause. Perhaps he believed a compromise could be reached.[7]

Eddy was glad when the meetings concluded. "It was a relief to know that my responsibilities were over," he confessed, "without any potentate being assassinated or any miscarriage of the confidential arrangements." He told his daughter Marycita that he did not enjoy his time as a "'Hey-you' man" for the king. Additionally, he grew desperate for a few puffs of tobacco from his pipe, but could not manage to get away long enough to get it lit. "I am against the Wahhabi and all Puritan cults," he conceded, "and when I become a chronic valet I want to valet someone who likes the fleshpots more than my present boss." He also groused to his son Jack. "Believe me, mine was a twenty-four hour job, mediating between the royal party and the U.S. Navy en route, and doing all the interpreting and fixing of minor arrangements from A to Z. I do not covet a job as court flunky permanently." Nevertheless, he noted with pride that the creation of a "Bedouin royal camp" on a modern destroyer was "a fantastic, incredible scene" that he had helped stage.[8]

After meeting with FDR, Abdul Aziz joined Winston Churchill at a resort outside of Cairo. The king was not nearly as impressed with the British leader as with the American president. Churchill gave Abdul Aziz a Rolls-Royce with the customary steering wheel on the right, which would require the king to sit to the driver's left. To sit to the left of a person, thought the king, was a sign of inferior status. He had no intention of ever sitting in the Rolls. Nor did Churchill follow FDR's example of refraining from drinking and smoking in front of the king. "If it was the religion of His Majesty to deprive himself of smoking and alcohol," the prime minister later wrote, "I must point out that my rule of life prescribed as an absolutely sacred rite smoking cigars and also the drinking of alcohol before, after, and if need be during all meals and in the intervals between them."[9]

But the gift and the cigar smoke were not the real problems. Abdul Aziz did not like Britain's colonial policies in the Middle East or its history of support for Zionism. Shortly after the meeting, the king summoned Eddy and gave him a report on his conversation with the British prime minister. Churchill tried to convince the king that the United States was only a temporary partner of the Saudis and that the Americans would return to their prewar isolationism after the conflict. Churchill claimed that the British, in contrast, were looking for long-term alliances.

Churchill also tried to bully the king into making a compromise on Zionism. This did not go over well either. "I told him," Abdul Aziz reported to Eddy, "that what he proposes is not help to Britain or the Allies, but an act of treachery to the Prophet and all believing Muslims which would wipe out my honor and destroy my soul. I could not acquiesce in a compromise with Zionism much less take any initiative." Promotion of Zionism, he continued, "from any quarter must indubitably bring bloodshed, wide-spread disorder in the Arab lands, with certainly no benefit to Britain or anyone else." He claimed that Churchill, who had opened the conversation by metaphorically trying to wield a big stick over the king, now chastised, "laid the big stick down."[10]

For FDR, and for Eddy, the real key to the American relationship with Abdul Aziz was not finding a home for displaced Jews but getting access to Arabian oil and land for the US military. Eddy succeeded on both counts. Abdul Aziz knew that the Saudis needed Western equipment and technology to drill, and the Americans in turn wanted a cut of the black gold. According to Eddy, the king described the relationship this way: "We Muslims have the one, true faith, but Allah gave you the iron which is inanimate, amoral, neither prohibited nor mentioned in the Qur'an. We will use your iron, but leave our faith alone." Eddy knew, however, that a people could not adopt modern technology without seeing their beliefs and values impacted.[11]

Eddy's work shaped US policy in the Middle East in substantial ways for decades to come. In addition to helping FDR forge a partnership with Abdul Aziz, he helped the War Department negotiate the rights to build an air base near Dhahran. That base would prove essential to the US Air Force during the Cold War.[12]

During Eddy's meetings with Saudi and Allied leaders, the missionary had more on his mind than just diplomacy. American naval leaders at the summit reported that the marines were experiencing "heavy fighting" in the Pacific, and he knew that his oldest son, Bill Jr., was among them, engaged in the battle for Iwo Jima. Bill Jr. had earlier seen heavy action in Saipan and Tinian, but this was his first combat mission as captain and as a company commander. "We can think of little else," Eddy wrote his younger son, Jack, just after the presidential conference. The senior Eddy later learned that Bill Jr. had performed admirably, which did not surprise him. On multiple occasions on Iwo Jima, with his unit pinned down by heavy fire, Bill Jr. took the lead, rallying his men and encouraging them not to back down. When he was hit in the arm by enemy fire, he refused treatment and instead continued to lead his company. The younger Eddy, like his father, proved to be an excellent marine and would earn a Navy Cross and a Bronze Star for his actions.[13]

In the spring of 1945, Bill Eddy Jr. received a promotion to aide-de-camp to Major General Clifton B. Cates, who after the war served as commandant of the US Marines. Eddy quipped that at least Bill won't have to "buy dancing pumps," as other military aides in his position sometimes needed to do, since "dancing is not on the program of the Marines in wartime." He also sent Bill some memo pads as a symbolic gift. He told Bill to use them "to jot down future dates, expenditures, telephone numbers of the Hula-who-who gals, etc." Eddy's younger son, Jack, also performed well in the marines. As both boys moved up the ranks, Eddy joked that he expected to retire and live off their "charity." "Then I get my false teeth and a rocking chair and chewing tobacco and begin to reminisce."[14]

Eddy's professional and personal optimism about the war's outcome was momentarily shaken when word reached him that President Roosevelt had died, just a few months after his meeting with Abdul Aziz. The night before they heard the news in Jeddah, the Eddys had screened a newsreel of the FDR–Abdul Aziz meeting to "fifty prominent Arabs" on their rooftop. They did not know at the time that the president was already gone. "Let us hope," Mary wrote upon hearing the news, "that Truman will carry out Roosevelt's foreign policy and surround himself with wise leaders." Bill worried about the future of the OSS. Donovan, he knew, maintained what the colonel called "a private pipeline to the White Father which got him most of the things he wanted. Will the patronage continue, I ask myself, and I get no reply." Eddy sensed correctly that the loss of Roosevelt represented a loss to the OSS.[15]

Mary and twelve-year-old Carmen, the youngest Eddy child, returned to the United States in the summer of 1945. Jeddah was no place to be during the hottest time of the year, if you could avoid it. The two Eddy women had met the Saudi king months earlier. "To put it mildly," Bill wrote to Bill Jr., "it was certainly the first time the fierce old battle-scarred but essentially kind monarch had ever received a small American girl." That the king met Eddy's family indicated the diplomat's growing stature among the Saudi leaders. The king later sent gifts to the two women. He gave Carmen "a multiple stranded pearl necklace," and he gave Mary what Eddy described as "a ring with a circle of diamonds around the biggest diamond I have ever seen outside of the Crown Jewels in the Tower of London." He joked that he might pawn the diamonds so he could afford to quit his job. But the gift, he feared, indicated that Mary might have been "making altogether too much of a hit with the King, and I did well by myself to take her afar off."[16]

Colonel Eddy continued to wonder what changes the new president might make and how those would impact the Middle East. Truman, three months into his presidency, met Stalin and Churchill in Potsdam, Germany. In the midst of the July conference, Britain's Labour Party won a landslide victory and replaced Prime Minister Churchill with Clement Attlee. The Allied leaders decided that they would accept only an unconditional surrender from Japan, and Stalin reaffirmed his pledge to join the Pacific war on August 15. While at the conference, Truman received word that scientists in New Mexico had staged the first successful test of an atomic bomb. The president hinted to Stalin that the United States had a powerful new weapon in the works. Stalin was not surprised. Although Truman had only recently learned of the Manhattan Project, Stalin's spies in the United States had been reporting on it to Moscow for years.

With negotiations among the Allied leaders ongoing, Eddy wrote Mary about his feelings on the Soviet Union. He believed that an enduring US-USSR alliance could "keep the peace in Europe and Asia." Whether working with Arab resistance fighters or Spanish communists, Eddy lobbied for a realistic foreign policy. "Russia is going to be very strong in her part of the world and for my part I don't see anything to be done but make her a strong friend instead of a strong enemy." Eddy's views were very different from those of fundamentalist missionaries like Birch. Before the war fundamentalists had identified communism as a serious threat to the Christian gospel, and the war did little to change their minds. Ecumenists like Eddy, in contrast, were more pragmatically minded and recognized why communism might be attractive to some people, especially to those who had suffered under Western colonial rule. The differences between Birch's and Eddy's perspectives reflected the growing divide between evangelical and ecumenical missionaries in the postwar period. As the fundamentalism of people like John Birch morphed into the postwar evangelicalism of people like Billy Graham, evangelicals became ardent cold warriors, while ecumenists were more open to evaluating both the strengths and the weaknesses of capitalism and communism side by side. Nevertheless, it did not take long for Eddy to see Stalin for what he was—a threat to the United States, to freedom of religion, and to global peace.[17]

During the last weeks of the war, Eddy fretted about the ends to which the belligerent nations were putting science. "What can be done about this capacity of mankind to invent shortcuts to wholesale murder?" he asked. "The truth is we had better destroy science if it is not to have any moral obligations."[18]

Despite his worries about science untethered from morals, Eddy's letter to his family on August 9 was full of joy. He had just learned of the detonation of the atomic bomb over Hiroshima on August 6 and hoped this meant the war might be over by Christmas. It was actually over just a few days later. He thanked God that Bill and Jack would not have to "take Japan rock by rock." He was especially eager to celebrate with his wife, who was coming back to their home in Saudi Arabia at the end of summer. "You know, darling, it is funny, but all the world shaking consequences of the peace omit Jeddah. I wonder if there is any place in the world where there will be so little direct effect? Life will go on." He hoped that Mary would agree that they should spend a "two-week honeymoon" in Cyprus, high in the mountains, where they would not encounter anyone they knew to "mortgage any of our time." Mary cut out the last paragraph of the letter with scissors. We can only guess at what it said, but Mary often scribbled over, cut out, or otherwise omitted the more sexually explicit paragraphs her husband sent before sharing the letters with family and friends. And those usually came at the end—exactly where this paragraph is missing.[19]

Eddy was not sure what work was to come his way after the war. He heard that West Point might be interested in bringing him on as an English professor, but he feared he was not cut out for that. "I doubt also whether West Point would suit my advanced stage of inertia and laziness." Eddy also considered taking the presidency of the American University in Beirut, but he worried that the school had "too much ingrowing and inter-marrying," which he compared to the Ptolemaic dynasty. "A few families' children have intermarried all over the place and live on the prestige they think should be theirs because their grandparents used to run the place." In the end, he realized he could still be of service to the US government, helping recover the best pieces of the OSS from the postwar rubble. Or at least he would try.[20]

TWENTY-ONE

"Between a Strife-Torn Earth and Wrath-Darkened Heavens"

As THE END OF THE WAR SEEMED WITHIN REACH, JOHN BIRCH CONTINUED living a double life. He was working as both a spy and a missionary, equally accountable to Wild Bill Donovan and to God. His commanding officer in the OSS, like those who worked with Birch in the army, recognized why the Baptist was in the fight. "He was a very fervent Christian," OSS leader Wilfred Smith observed. "He was also a very fine soldier, he reconciled the work he was doing in the army with his burning missionary zeal and a strong feeling that China would have to be freed from Jap menace before missionary work could be started again." Smith was a China-born missionary son himself, with a PhD in "Oriental" history. He understood Birch's passion for his adopted homeland and that the missionary crusader would not back down until the Allies drove the Japanese out.[1]

Birch submitted a report to his OSS supervisors in early 1945 that provides a glimpse into his work at the time. He and his team had collected and analyzed information for the air force on Japanese movements, the impact of American bombing runs, and the local political situation among the Chinese in some of the northern providences. He listed the downed airmen that his team had recently rescued and summarized his plans for securing the safe return of a few others who had recently bailed out over enemy territory. In order for the good work to continue, Birch insisted, he needed more supplies. He requested additional radios to establish more communications stations behind enemy lines and competent native radiomen to run them. He also asked for a "demo expert who can bring in his own plastic and devices," although he did not say why. Finally, he identified a Chinese American soldier who impressed him—he recommended that the OSS scoop the man up from army intelligence. Despite the positive contributions he was making with the OSS, he again asked to be reassigned to the Fourteenth Air Force. He remained convinced that working with his old mentor General Claire Chennault was far better for him—and for China—than "all Donovan's equipment and slush funds." The OSS denied his request.[2]

In the last year of the war, American military authorities began showing more interest in Korea. OSS leaders recognized that some of the tens of thousands of Koreans, conscripted into the Imperial Japanese Army, might be willing to work against their Japanese overlords. Numerous deserters had made their way past the Japanese lines and to the Americans and Chinese. OSS leaders, partnering with Korean exiles, wanted to make the most of this opportunity. Birch was at the time running operations in the North, somewhat near where Korean rebel groups had established a base of operations. The OSS dispatched the missionary to meet with leaders of one of the exile groups, the Third Detachment of the Korean Restoration Army. The meeting went well, and OSS officers tasked Birch and two of his colleagues with crafting a plan to train and supply a group of forty-five Korean exiles, who would return to Korea to collect intelligence, engage in sabotage, and, ideally, spark revolution. The OSS mission, called "Project Eagle," laid the foundation for the first wartime military alliance between Koreans and the United States.[3]

As Birch labored at the front, his concern over the communist menace grew. Tensions had long been rising in China between Chiang Kai-shek's Kuomintang forces and the communist insurgency led by Mao Zedong. American policy makers held mixed views of the two leaders. They were uncomfortable with Mao's communism, but they also recognized that Chiang was corrupt and had mismanaged his country for years. Many State Department, military, and intelligence officials had come to recognize that partnering with communists was becoming inevitable. Some even sought to apply the lessons they had learned in Europe to the situation in Asia. When Stephen Penrose took over as head of special intelligence for Europe, he drew on what he had discovered working with communists in Greece and the Balkans as he advised those overseeing US intelligence operations in China. Many Americans leaders understood that they could not ignore Chiang Kai-shek's unpopularity or the growing appeal of Mao Zedong's communist movement. For Birch, however, the issues remained clear. Despite working with Chinese communists on various temporary projects, he felt confident that if the communists governed China, they would likely restrict missionary work. They were never, therefore, to be trusted.

In the summer of 1945, OSS leaders put Birch in charge of a new operation code-named "Crow." Birch's partner in the mission was Xue Yuhua (Hsueh Yu Hwa). Under the leadership of these two men—the OSS operative and his native recruit—a team of Chinese guerrillas set up two radio stations for broadcasting intelligence back to the regional OSS headquarters. They established one near Jinan, the capital of the Yellow Sea province of Shandong, and the other near the port city of Tianjin. According to an internal memo, Xue's job was to recruit agents who could cover "extensive territories" and obtain the "desired information" to transmit from the clandestine stations. If the project proved as effective as OSS leaders expected, they planned to have Birch set up additional teams and radio transmitters.[4]

Birch and his agents sought intelligence of various kinds for the Crow mission. The OSS was keen to learn the number, identification, and movement of Japanese troops; the locations of Japanese military supplies and storage dumps; the nature of Japanese shipping activities and transportation on the interior railway and highway systems; the extent of Japanese supplies of coal, iron, and steel; and, finally, how political and economic conditions in occupied territories were changing. Once agents had information relating to these items, their job was to convey it to their leaders by means of the new radio stations that Birch had helped to set up.

Birch and the OSS also worked to root out "puppet" collaborators, those Chinese who worked with the Japanese. The missionary reported that a Chinese general was carrying on a secret and illegal trade with the enemy that allegedly made the general $10 million per year. The Chinese general traded oil and lumber for cloth, money, ammunition, and other goods. Birch believed that local Chinese leaders were intentionally ignoring the underground trade since the supplies they received were so important. The Japanese, he claimed, drove American intelligence officers out of the region when the deals occurred, and they also had their own special contingent of intelligence officers dressed as beggars.[5]

While putting his life on the line with these dangerous missions, Birch still grappled with plans for the future. He had fallen briefly for a local Chinese woman whom he had rescued from a burning building. In the literal heat of the moment, they kissed. But John was not as interested in the local woman as she was in him. They agreed to separate for a few months, and John hoped that she would get "over it." Meanwhile, Birch told Marjorie Tooker, the nurse he had kissed a few months earlier, that he felt as if they were still "measuring" themselves "as prospective wedding candidates." "I know that I admire and like you," he assured her, "I think that I am in love with you," but he worried about her feelings toward him. "Upon closer acquaintance, you will find me disappointing, perhaps disgusting." John warned her that "there are still too many things about which I am not sure."[6]

Religion was probably one of those things, although over the course of the war Birch seemed to grow less rigid, less fundamentalist. He once told a colleague that he had learned to respect local Catholics and to assess people on the basis of their hearts and not their denominations. He shared his excitement with his family that a new intelligence officer recently assigned to his group was a Christian—a Presbyterian. Birch joked that he hoped the soldier was baptized by immersion soon. Unlike Baptists, Presbyterians usually performed baptisms by a light sprinkling of water. John wanted to get his new friend fully dunked.[7]

Around the time that the war in Europe was ending, Birch had another opportunity to take a temporary leave from the front. He refused. He continued to feel baffled by those who chose to step away from the fight. "I don't see why so few officers and soldiers share my feeling that for 3½ years we in China have been waiting and preparing to give the Jap Army the licking it deserves," he wrote Marjorie. "Now the real game is starting," which was "not the time to go home!"[8]

In the months after John disclosed to Marjorie his relationship with the Chinese woman, the distance between the missionary and the nurse grew. "Marjorie," he wrote, "I'm sorry my few letters are so cheerless and empty; I'll try to do better next time, unless you are so bored you send me a note to stop writing." The letter was signed just "John" rather than the usual "Love, John."[9]

Although Birch's love life was a mess, he had not lost his sense of purpose in the war. "In these dark days," he wrote his sister, "I see all human or part-human institutions so unreliable, even churches." It was up to individuals like him to make the difference. "Somehow, I want to stand alone, between a strife-torn earth and wrath-darkened heavens, and thunder out, late in time, a call to repentance and belated trust in Christ, during the lust-ridden years which will follow this war." He doubted that the world's leaders would find any lasting peace. As they laid the groundwork for the new United Nations organization, John expressed skepticism. "I shall count it victory if our generation is free for the next twenty or thirty years to live our own lives without the regimentation of tyrants or totalitarian bureaucrats," he wrote. "I regard Liberty as more precious than Peace."[10]

Birch believed that the war was serving as a kind of apprenticeship for him, preparing him for his postwar missionary work. He had learned independence and self-reliance and planned to venture out on his own to spread the gospel. At one point, he thought perhaps he might run a ranch in a remote part of China and use the profits to fund his evangelical work. He told his friends back home that his work as an intelligence officer was "not much different from being a missionary." A few weeks later, he preached a compelling sermon to six hundred Chinese men and women, proving his point. Birch continued to believe that while engaged in the war, he was still first and foremost an evangelist.[11]

On August 6, 1945, a B-29 Superfortress, the *Enola Gay*, dropped an atomic bomb that detonated over Hiroshima, Japan. Forty thousand people died instantly. In the following weeks one hundred thousand more died from radiation poisoning or burns. On August 8, the USSR declared war on Japan and raced to get into the Pacific fight while there was still time to reap some of the spoils. The next day the United States dropped another atomic bomb, this time over Nagasaki. Neither Hiroshima nor Nagasaki had sustained much damage up until that point. Military leaders chose these targets to maximize the impact of the bombs. For Birch, as for just about all other Americans in the war, the detonation of atomic bombs over Hiroshima and Nagasaki was a relief. When the missionary heard radio reports that the Japanese were hoping to keep the emperor on the throne, he suggested that "two or three more" atomic bombs would cure them of the idea. That Sunday he delivered a sermon "thanking God for bringing us to the eve of victory."[12]

On August 15, the Japanese surrendered. They feared the opening of a second front by the Soviets as well as the detonation of a third atomic bomb, not knowing that the United States did not yet have one. Birch was in the midst of penning an impassioned letter to a friend back home when he heard that the war was over. He was reporting and justifying his actions in the OSS and his willingness to suspend partially his missionary work for the duration. Apparently, his fundamentalist friend believed that as the world rapidly moved toward the battle of Armageddon and the final apocalypse, Christians had no business serving earthly leaders. Birch disagreed. His response perfectly articulated how and why missionaries like him were so committed to the war effort: "To me, it is of the utmost importance to gain the temporary opportunity to preach Christ's Gospel! Have you ever seen a humble Chinese brother, who was beheaded because he preached Christ rather than the Emperor of Japan? I have. . . . Have you ever seen Chinese girls after the Japanese machine-gunned them? I have. I want peace, but not that purchased by tolerance of such evils as I saw Japan spreading across this part of the world!" Since the day he had enlisted, Birch continued, "I have tried as whole-heartedly as I could, to serve the flag that had protected my life so far." Word of Japan's surrender reinforced his views. "No, brother of mine, we did not vainly beat our heads against a wall; we cut our hands smashing the teeth of a monstrous mouth that was devouring, and that rapidly the lives, land, liberty, and happiness of poor helpless human beings in many parts of the world. And now that mouth, even tho it be temporarily, is <u>closed</u>! Yes, George, liberty is worth its price!"[13]

The end of the war and the thought of returning to civilian life renewed Birch's feelings for Marjorie Tooker, whom he had just seen in a dream. When he awoke, he felt overwhelmed with grief. "The sense of loss, even of just your ghost, was a painful and disturbing experience," he told her. "Thoughts of you and wishes for your happiness run back and forth thru my mind almost incessantly and yet these thoughts seem never to tire. God guard you, Marjorie, and grant me an early meeting with you."[14]

Birch continued to reflect on the significance of the war as well as his role in it. "I still am quite convinced," he wrote Marjorie, "of the <u>right</u> that has been ours in fighting Germany and Japan, but I feel that a tremendous load of guilt lies on the heads of our own and other major governments." He thought they had permitted "the development of those circumstances which made such a world-staggering sacrifice necessary." He believed that the Allied leaders had not done enough in the 1930s to stop fascism.[15]

Birch, like William Eddy, Stewart Herman, and Stephen Penrose, had the opportunity to continue working in American intelligence. But the missionary was not proud of some of his actions during the conflict, and, with the war won, he wanted to separate as quickly as possible from spy craft. "Some people want me to enter the post-war intelligence service," he told Marjorie, "but they are barking up an empty tree." He wanted to return to full-time missionary work, but that was not his only reason for leaving the OSS. "I could never stick [to] the game of spying on those for whom I profess friendship. This sounds pompous and self-righteous, but this secret police business, necessary as it may be, has always seemed to me a slimy sort of job. No, ma'am, I'd rather be a poor preacher." Birch believed that his wartime work was necessary, but it was always a means to an end, protecting and expanding the opportunity for missionaries to work in Asia.[16]

Despite Birch's reservations about the "spying game," he did not immediately quit the OSS. Shortly after Japan's surrender, agency officers ordered Birch to proceed to the Shandong Peninsula via Suzhou "for the purpose of collecting Japanese documents before the Japanese could destroy them." They also wanted him to "make a full report on the condition of roads and railroads so that American and Chinese forces could be dispatched to these areas without delay" and to "check on all airfields."[17]

Birch was exhausted. He confessed to Marjorie that he realized for the first time how "utterly weary, even heartsick, this war has made me feel." The missionary was finally ready for a break, and he looked forward to a visit home. Some scholars have speculated that he was probably suffering from post-traumatic stress disorder. Nevertheless, the OSS needed Birch for the operation, and he agreed to go. "He was sent on this mission," an internal OSS report noted, "because he was the only officer in that area who had a sound knowledge of that section of China." He may have also been seeking the release of American prisoners of war—Chennault believed that this was the real reason the missionary went back into the field.[18]

For this mission, Birch's team included fourteen men: four Americans, two Koreans, and eight Chinese. The missionary took three books with him on the trip: a copy of Gruden's Bible concordance, the complete works of Shakespeare, and a copy of the classic apologetics book *The Analogy of Religion Natural and Revealed*. Birch was a well-read fundamentalist. The men initially planned to go by plane, but their orders changed. They departed on August 20 and for the first few days traveled by foot and by boat. Then they caught a train for Shandong. They had to abandon the train in Dangshan because Chinese communists had sabotaged the rail lines. Birch and his team acquired a handcart to proceed as best they could on the damaged rails. Along the line they encountered a few groups of communist guerrillas without incident. At one stop, Birch even shared watermelon with the rebels. However, Birch's primary Chinese aide, Dong Qinsheng, reported that as they traveled farther, Birch's attitude grew increasingly hostile toward the communists. Dong later told OSS operatives that he had warned Birch that his tone might provoke a confrontation. "Never mind," Birch told him. "I want to see how the Communists treat Americans. I don't mind if they kill me for America will then stop the Communist movement with Atomic bombs."[19]

Birch's staunch, relentless, unapologetic anticommunism was typical of fundamentalists. A more ecumenically minded, less dogmatic missionary might have had fewer problems in the field. William Eddy, for example, had worked with Spanish communists and then lamented their mistreatment by the Allies. Disagreements over the dangers of communism that separated fundamentalists and liberals rippled into the postwar era. The more theologically liberal missionaries in China who claimed that the communists were perhaps better at serving the people than the current governing authorities made them prime targets of McCarthyism in the 1950s.

Birch's anticommunist suspicions seemed confirmed when he and his team arrived near Huangkou, west of Shanghai, late on the afternoon of August 25. There another communist rebel group met them. Per the team's prior arrangements, Dong and not the Americans did the initial talking. Unlike the previous groups they had encountered, these men were more confrontational. Dong heard them whispering that Birch's unit might be spies, and they might have to kill them. Dong reported this back to Birch. Birch then turned to the sixty or seventy armed communist soldiers and scolded them in their native tongue. "Well, you want to disarm us!" The Americans, he continued, "have liberated the whole world, and you want to stop us and disarm us! Are you bandits? Are you responsible men? Do we have to give our guns to you?" In calling the guerrillas "bandits," Birch was leveling a major insult. This was a term the Chinese Nationalist forces used to describe and delegitimize the Chinese communists. In Birch's choice of terms, he was playing into and exacerbating tensions between rival Chinese factions.[20]

Birch demanded to see the person in charge. He had no intention of giving an inch, not after the United States had just defeated Japan and helped to liberate China. One of the communist officers offered to take Birch and Dong to the local commander. At that point, they separated from the rest of their party, and Dong was the only witness on the American side to what happened next. The communist officer led the two OSS operatives in circles, literally giving them the run-around. Nobody ever came forward or identified as the commanding officer. Birch grew increasingly frustrated as his team fell further behind schedule. He grabbed his escort by the collar and again asked if they were bandits—and perhaps "worse than bandits." At that point one of the communist officers ordered his men to disarm Birch. Dong offered to take the missionary's gun rather than risk an even more heated confrontation. The officer then ordered his men to shoot Dong and Birch. They shot Dong above the knee and Birch in the upper right thigh.[21]

Although Birch was defenseless and wounded, the Chinese rebels were not done with him. After the guerrillas shot the American, they stripped him and likely tied him to a pole. To conceal his identity, the communists mutilated his face, cutting the flesh to the bone, probably with a bayonet or a knife. They also knocked out his front teeth, hit him hard in the head, and slit his throat "from ear to ear." They also cut off his nose and stabbed him in his chest. The communist soldiers later tossed the two OSS men into an open pit. Birch was likely dead by the time they moved him to the pit, and the communists probably thought Dong was dead as well. A couple of local farmers approached the hole a few hours later, intending to bury the bodies. Dong called out for help. The farmers warned him that communists were still in the area, but they came back later and helped him to safety.[22]

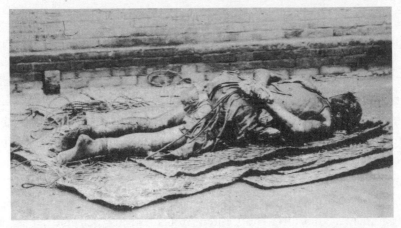

About a week after the war ended, John Birch, while on an OSS mission, encountered a group of hostile Chinese communists. They tortured and killed him and then mutilated his body to remove any identifying marks. The US government initially covered up the details surrounding his death.
Courtesy of National Archives and Records Administration, College Park, Maryland.

When the OSS learned of Birch's death, agency leaders dispatched William T. Miller, the operative closest to the area not on Birch's mission, to investigate and to recover Birch's body. Miller knew Birch and wanted to get to the bottom of what happened. The two men had discussed the threat posed by Chinese communism many times. Miller believed that Birch understood the risk of proceeding through communist-occupied territory. "Capt Birch felt that the Communist movement was menacing China's only hope and chance of ever becoming a real Democratic Nation," Miller recalled. "He was very strongly against Communism in China. Because of his unique position . . . Capt Birch knew perhaps better than any other man about Communistic activities in that region."[23]

Miller exhumed Birch's body, made his investigation, and then brought the dead operative to Xuzhou. He organized a funeral on September 2, the same day that the Japanese officially surrendered on the deck of the USS *Missouri* in Tokyo Bay. Most of the missionaries and Chinese Christians in the region, Catholic and Protestant, attended the service. The missionary received full military honors from both Nationalist Chinese and Japanese troops. They wrapped Birch's body in white silk, placed him in a coffin, and buried him on a hill outside the city under the inscription, "He died for Righteousness." The OSS told Birch's family that John's death "was instantaneous and without pain." This is highly doubtful, given the eyewitness testimony. The service card in his OSS personnel file contains another dubious claim. It recorded the cause of Birch's death as "killed result of stray bullets."[24]

Meanwhile, the American brass wanted answers. US ambassador to China Patrick Hurley had a previously scheduled meeting with the leader of the communist forces in China, Mao Zedong, on August 30. General Albert Wedemeyer, the commander of the US forces in China, had just learned of Birch's death that day and asked to be at the meeting. He wanted to confront Mao directly about what had happened.

Mao initially evaded responsibility and claimed to know nothing of the incident. "We can not say the Communist troops killed him or not," he told the Americans. "If this is true that the Communist troops shot this American officer, I extend my deepest apology." Mao believed that if communists killed Birch, Wedemeyer needed to understand the incident from Mao's perspective. "The shooting must have been done by the local guerrillas who were fighting the Japanese and during the fighting some misunderstanding very probably could have happened." Wedemeyer in turn asked for Mao's assurance that this would not happen again. "I am directed by the President of the United States," he warned Mao, "to use whatever force I require to protect American lives in China." He also assured Mao that if the American people learned of this incident and others where communists had mistreated American troops, any possible support they might have for Mao—or even their willingness to simply stay out of China's internal politics—would evaporate. "When the American people learn about Captain Birch's death it will have a very disturbing effect," he warned. The general then asked the communist leader to investigate the matter and to provide him with a full report, which he promised to turn over to President Truman. Wedemeyer then reiterated his message: "I cannot have American soldiers killed by Chinese Communists or by Chinese Kuomintang troops. I cannot tolerate it."[25]

A summary investigation and report by Deputy Theater Judge Advocate Jeremiah J. O'Connor offered little additional information. However, the report concluded that Birch's actions prior to his death "indicated a lack of good judgment and failure to take proper precautions in a dangerous situation." Nevertheless, "it is abundantly evident that the shooting was done maliciously and that the killing was completely without justification." The report also noted, "Officers who knew Birch state that he was a man of strong opinions and habitually talked of the Communists as bandits and obstructers of Chinese unity." Mao's military leaders claimed that their guerrillas did not know Birch was an American and that their men had acted in self-defense. This was ridiculous and they knew it. Birch was in uniform, identified himself, and carried one gun, which he voluntarily gave up.[26]

In recognition of Birch's service and sacrifice, the army awarded the missionary a posthumous Legion of Merit award "for exceptionally meritorious service during the period 18 January to 25 August 1945." Chennault did not think that the army had done enough. "If I had still been in China," he wrote, "there would have been a squadron of B-25s blasting the Communist position with no further questions asked."[27]

For years the US government covered up the killing of John Birch. Wedemeyer had been right. American officials did not want the public to know that Chinese communists killed an American soldier after the secession of hostilities. When the communists took over China in 1949, critics believed that US government leaders were partially to blame. Had the government publicized the 1945 death of Birch at the hands of Mao's soldiers, they argued, perhaps the United States would have recognized the communist threat sooner. Instead, they claimed, procommunist forces within the State Department, the old "China hands," some of whom were Protestant ecumenical missionary sons, helped cover-up Birch's death rather than imperil Mao's work.

There is a second reason the OSS might have covered up the details of Birch's death. That missionaries were serving in the spy agency was still a carefully guarded secret. Lutheran missionary Paul Frillmann, Birch's ally in China, kept in touch with General Claire Chennault for decades after the conflict. Chennault was disappointed that the role of missionaries in American wartime intelligence had never been told. He encouraged Frillmann to write about his experiences in the field and his partnership with Birch. Frillmann hesitated. "I tried to explain to Chennault," he told an interviewer, "that it would be very difficult for me to write this story of John Birch and of myself and the others who operated as Combat Intelligence officers for the General, first of all, because John Birch was a missionary, and I was a missionary." He worried that if OSS missionary operatives told their stories, they would endanger all American foreign missionaries. If Americans and foreign governments learned that the OSS used missionaries as spies, who was to say that the CIA was not still doing the same thing? It is for this reason that the stories of men like John Birch, Stephen Penrose, William Eddy, and Stewart Herman have remained hidden for so long. A grateful military and a grateful intelligence agency did not want to jeopardize the religious work of those who sometimes served their god and the gods of war at the same time.[28]

PART VI

LEGACIES
(1945–Present)

TWENTY-TWO

"The CIA Holds Nothing Sacred Including the Sacred"

Near the end of the war, Donovan received an important memo from Ferdinand L. Mayer, Stewart Herman's old friend from Berlin who later oversaw the Pilgrim's Progress operation. Mayer laid out a plan for postwar intelligence based on what the OSS had accomplished so far. A centerpiece of the plan was substantial use of religion. "It remains my view," Mayer wrote to the chief, "that the religious approach . . . is one of the super-secret activities that the Central Agency could best manipulate." He suggested the OSS find new ways to build relationships with the Orthodox Church in eastern Europe, Mormons across the European continent, "and whatever development we can work out in the Moslem and Hindu worlds." He also proposed that the agency choose a single director to oversee "all of these religious approaches." He wanted the nation's clandestine services to establish a superspy for all things God. As the Cold War developed, his recommendations proved prescient.[1]

Nevertheless, in the short term, Mayer's plans to manipulate religion for spy-agency ends seemed dead on arrival, at least as far as Donovan and the OSS were concerned. Donovan had been lobbying President Roosevelt to make the OSS a permanent agency. In the fall of 1944, Roosevelt finally asked Wild Bill to draw up a secret memorandum laying out his proposal for a permanent, peacetime American clandestine service. The president, however, was not sure that this was what he actually wanted.

He knew that when the war ended, he needed to shutter as many agencies as possible in order to bring the budget back into line.

Donovan sent FDR his proposal in November 1944. "Once our enemies are defeated," the spymaster wrote, "the demand will be equally pressing for information that will aid us in solving the problems of peace." An intelligence agency, he argued, was as important in peacetime as it was in war. Donovan told the president that a permanent and successful intelligence agency required two things. First, it needed direct control by the president. Wild Bill didn't like reporting to the Joint Chiefs of Staff. Second, he wanted the agency to do intelligence analysis, to have the freedom to "frame intelligence objectives and to collect and coordinate the intelligence material required by the Executive Branch in planning and carrying out national policy and strategy." While FDR was thinking over Wild Bill's proposal, editors at the staunchly conservative *Chicago Tribune* managed to secure a copy of it. They printed the proposal and ran a series of stories warning the American people that Donovan was championing the creation of an American Gestapo that would threaten their liberties. Donovan was sure that FBI director J. Edgar Hoover, who jealously guarded his own terrain and had never been happy about the creation of the OSS, had leaked the memo to the *Tribune*. He was probably right.[2]

Wild Bill's plan generated a good deal of controversy. Rather than acting on it, Roosevelt sat back and let the debate rage among his advisers, Congress, and journalists. He did not reach a decision before he died, leaving it to Harry Truman to determine if the United States needed a permanent intelligence agency. The new president wanted nothing to do with Donovan or his ragtag group of secret operatives and agents. On September 20, 1945, just weeks after the defeat of Japan, Truman issued an executive order disbanding the OSS. He moved the two operational branches of the OSS—Secret Intelligence and Special Operations—to the War Department and renamed them the Strategic Services Unit. Stephen Penrose took charge of operations for the Strategic Services Unit. Truman moved the Research and Analysis Branch over to the State Department, where Secretary of State James Byrnes placed it under the supervision of William Eddy. The missionary son had returned from Saudi Arabia and was now serving as special assistant to the secretary of state for research and intelligence.

Congress worried that the remaining members of OSS's Research and Analysis Branch, now housed under Eddy within the State Department, included dangerous communists, socialists, and other radicals. To reduce OSS veterans' influence, Congress cut their research funding. The State Department responded by assigning Eddy the task of breaking up the research division and assigning its specialists to the department's various geographic divisions. The *New York Times* criticized the move, arguing that integrating intelligence and diplomacy, analysis and policy, would undermine the importance and objectivity of intelligence analysts' work. But there was one glimmer of hope. "If anything constructive can be done in this quarter," the *Times* surmised, "Colonel Eddy is the man to do it."[3]

Dispersing the research and analysis division into separate geographical regions was a bad idea, and Eddy knew it. When Truman appointed General George Marshall as secretary of state in January 1947 and named Dean Acheson undersecretary of state for political affairs, Eddy sensed an opportunity. He proposed that the State Department pull its intelligence analysts back into a single unit. Together he and Acheson established what is now the State Department's Bureau of Intelligence and Research. Eddy chaired State's Advisory Committee on Intelligence, helping to coordinate the work of various departments and branches while fighting across agencies to make his department the center of US intelligence.[4]

Although Truman was happy to be rid of Donovan, whom he never trusted, it did not take the president long to realize that perhaps he had acted too hastily. No modern nation, and certainly not one as powerful as the United States then gearing up for a cold war, could survive without a serious, independent foreign intelligence agency. In January 1946, just a few months after he shut down the OSS, the new president created the National Intelligence Authority to work in conjunction with the army, navy, and State Department. Under the NIA, Truman established a Central Intelligence Group led by a director of central intelligence. Truman marked the birth of the new intelligence agency with a secret and playful White House ceremony in which he presented its new leaders, Admirals William Leahy and Sidney Souers, with black hats, black cloaks, and wooden daggers.[5]

Truman's creation of the NIA and Eddy's launch of the Bureau of Intelligence and Research was a start, but leaders in the US government knew they needed a more comprehensive intelligence agency to maintain the postwar peace, especially as they eyed the growing Soviet threat. In 1947 the leaders of the NIA began working on new legislation to bring before Congress. They wanted to streamline their work and to make their fledging agency permanent. After a lot of wrangling over proposals, Congress passed the National Security Act, which President Truman signed into law on July 26, 1947. It reshaped the government's ability to implement foreign policy plans as well as to wage the Cold War. The act established the cabinet-level civilian position of Secretary of Defense to oversee the army, navy, marines, and the newly independent air force and housed them all in the new Department of Defense. The "War" Department was no more. The act also made the Joint Chiefs of Staff a permanent institution, established the National Security Council to assist the president in crafting policy, and created the Central Intelligence Agency. The rules governing the CIA were murky, an ambiguity that leaders of the new agency would exploit to build an incredibly powerful organization.

Over the past seventy-five years, critics have found plenty of reasons to disparage the work of the CIA. Many of their concerns center on a couple of core issues. First, the CIA is not just an intelligence agency, but has become at times a paramilitary organization that runs its own clandestine operations all over the world without waiting for a declaration of war. Second, it functions with little supervision or oversight outside of the executive branch. For much of the CIA's history, Congress has had little idea what the agency was up to, while officers were running controversial missions in places ranging from Iran to Guatemala to Cuba to Iraq. Essentially, the CIA became the president's own secret, private military unit. Since the creation of the Senate Select Committee on Intelligence in 1976, Congress has tried to assert some control over the CIA, but legislators' only real power over the CIA is their control of the budget.

The CIA's freedom to act independently was not an unanticipated consequence of the 1947 National Security Act. At the time Congress passed the act, the CIA's advocates ensured that Congress did not prohibit it from engaging in covert action, and they were careful to also ensure that the agency remained free from serious oversight. Its charter was purposefully ambiguous, placing few restrictions on the agency. This was how some of its founders wanted it.

This was how William Eddy and Stephen Penrose wanted it. Eddy served as the point man representing the State Department on National

Intelligence Agency discussions that led to the proposed National Security Act of 1947, and he helped craft some of the core tenets that went before the legislature. One of his key contributions was insisting that operatives working for the new intelligence agency remain totally separate from the US military. He wanted a civilian director without "allegiance to any single department." The CIA, he argued, should have a military function, but it had to remain independent of the Joint Chiefs of Staff and the armed services. Eddy feared that if the CIA director was too close to one of the branches of the military, the agency would lack true independence. He did not want a repeat of what had happened to him in 1943 as the Allies prepared for the Italian invasion and OSS operatives came under the army's supervision. He wanted the CIA to have the kind of operational freedom that he had enjoyed in Tangier prior to the invasion of North Africa during Operation Torch.[6]

But that was not Eddy's only reason for fighting to establish the CIA on an independent footing. He wanted the CIA to be separate from the military so that American leaders could deny responsibility for or knowledge of the extralegal and sometimes illegal actions of secret operatives. "Under-cover intelligence and espionage abroad," he argued, "should not compromise the official representatives of the United States of America. Espionage, which is certainly needed, and which involves the employment of unofficial agents, both American and foreign, should be operated by an agency outside the Departments and with funds not subject to departmental accounting." If agents and operatives got into trouble or were captured, American leaders needed to be able to disavow them.[7]

That the CIA during the first decades of its history could act as a rogue, covert force independent of the armed forces or the military chain of command, and that it did much more than gather intelligence, was in part Eddy's legacy. He and his allies set it up to do just that. When Dean Acheson prepared to go before Congress in 1947 to defend and explain these proposals, Eddy briefed him and wrote up a series of talking points for the secretary's use. Then Eddy sat at Acheson's side as this key architect of the Cold War testified before Congress.

Secretary of the Navy James Forrestal, like Acheson and Eddy, was eager to restore the United States' foreign intelligence apparatus. He appointed missionary executive Stephen Penrose to help Central Intelligence Group leaders shape the new intelligence agency. After running operations for the Strategic Services Unit, Penrose had taken the position of "special assistant" to Forrestal. Like Eddy, Penrose wanted the new CIA to be independent. The missionary executive criticized plans to establish a congressional committee charged with overseeing the intelligence agency. "In so far as possible," Penrose argued, "the Director of CIA should avoid becoming a figure of public interest in order to devote his entire energies to directing the operations of his agency. He should be protected from the constant strain of external, amateur inquiry, and he should certainly protect his subordinates from such inquiry." In other words, Penrose wanted to ensure that Congress left the spy business to the spies.[8]

The making of the CIA was a long and complicated process, and its charter resulted from input and ideas from many different people in many different branches of government with many different agendas. Yet like the OSS before it, it was to some extent the creation of amateurs, of the missionaries who had become wartime spies. Eddy and Penrose had proved themselves in the field, becoming some of the nation's best intelligence operatives. But that did not necessarily qualify them to help shape the CIA. In retrospect, perhaps the nation would have been better off with less idealistic policy makers. Eddy and Penrose were men of great faith. Perhaps the nation would have been better served by men of great doubt. Perhaps a fundamentalist like John Birch, with his dark view of the future and his sense that humans were inherently depraved, would have insisted on more checks and balances on the nation's new intelligence agency. Birch always feared humans' capacity for evil and worried about concentrations of power. Eddy and Penrose did not. Nor did enough of the other architects of the CIA.

Independence from the military and civilian leadership, freedom from congressional oversight, budgets without accountability, and the autonomy to run rogue covert operations all came to define the CIA's early history. OSS veterans including Eddy and Penrose were pleased that in many ways they had convinced Truman to re-create the OSS somewhat as Wild Bill had envisioned it. Over time, however, it was exactly these features that made the CIA one of the most controversial agencies in the US government and around the world. Who could have imagined that when Truman and Congress were debating the contours of the new CIA, two missionaries with the best of intentions were key to establishing and defending some of the policies that paved the way for the CIA, working under orders from American presidents, to orchestrate some of the greatest abuses, misuses of power, and tragedies in modern American foreign policy? This is part of a pattern that had repeated itself over and over in American history. From purging witches from Salem, Massachusetts, to seeking to "Christianize" Native Americans by eradicating their cultures, to lobbying for the full prohibition of alcohol, people of faith in exercising political power in the United States have made many mistakes. In trying to expand the kingdom of God, Christians have too often wreaked havoc on the kingdoms of man.

Eddy quit his job with the State Department in October 1947. He had many reasons for leaving government work, but none weighed on him more heavily than changes in the Middle East. That year frustrated British leaders turned control of Palestine over to the new United Nations. The UN, in turn, proposed partitioning Palestine into Jewish and Arab states. Eddy, and probably Penrose, helped draft a secret government document titled "The Consequences of the Partition of Palestine," which advised Truman that violence would result if the United Nations went forward with its plans. The paper did not identify its authors but credited it to the coordinated efforts of the State Department (where Eddy worked at the time), the navy (where Penrose served), the army, and the air force. The authors feared that if Truman supported a Jewish state in Palestine, he would risk destroying the goodwill the United States had generated with Arab leaders. Truman refused to follow their advice. "I am sorry, gentlemen," he apparently told Eddy and a few others during an Oval Office meeting, "but I have to answer to hundreds of thousands who are anxious for the success of Zionism; I do not have hundreds of thousands of Arabs among my constituents."[9]

Eddy left government work at the right time. Congress cut his State Department budget, and he feared that all his efforts at fostering positive US-Arab relations evaporated with Truman's May 14, 1948, recognition of the Jewish state of Israel. Eddy seemed to loathe the new president, or at least the choices the president was making regarding American policy in the Middle East. When a communist magazine in the Soviet Union, in a story on Eddy's work in Saudi Arabia, identified Eddy as an agent of the "Truman doctrine," the missionary son was quick to clarify: "Support of anything labelled 'Truman' denied by Eddy."[10]

After leaving the State Department, Eddy took a job working for the Arabian-American Oil Company, or ARAMCO, as a senior adviser. He no longer had to fear that he might not be able to support his family financially. But for most of the rest of his life, he continued to consult with the CIA, keeping the agency abreast of Middle Eastern affairs. Nor did he think his work for God was done. Perhaps a little disingenuously, the oil-man saw himself as a missionary still. "I am involved," he told his children, "as were my father and grandfather in programs of education, health, imparting skills for vocations, and extending goodwill for the U.S.A., which is the legacy of our pioneer missionaries." It is a bit ironic that the man who had spent his career defending Arabs in the Middle East went to work for a company that played a leading role in fomenting some of the crises that have made that region of the world so unstable. But he would not have seen it this way. Like many of the other liberal Protestants of his generation, he believed that exporting American values, the Christian faith, and modern technology would secure peace abroad. God and black gold, he convinced himself, did not have to be pitted against each other.[11]

On May 3, 1962, Eddy complained to his wife, Mary, over breakfast that he was not feeling well. He returned to his bedroom in their Beirut home and laid down. A few hours later, the sixty-eight-year-old was dead. Per Eddy's wishes, his family buried him in Sidon, in the graveyard near the American University. They laid him to rest near his parents, and the family later buried Mary there, too. They are the only Americans in the small cemetery. All around them are Arabs, the people the missionary dedicated his life to serving.

Like Eddy, Penrose helped create the CIA, and then he too left full-time government work. As the old members of the Central Intelligence Group worked to launch the new Central Intelligence Agency, Penrose's frustration mounted. In 1948 the missionary executive, who was still deeply immersed in the evolving world of US intelligence, decided it was time for him to move on. He was troubled by the CIA's lukewarm efforts to bring experienced operatives into leadership positions and by the rate at which the agency was hemorrhaging OSS veterans. He was particularly frustrated by CIA director Roscoe H. Hillenkoetter's decision to put Colonel Donald H. Galloway in charge of special operations, the job Penrose previously held under the Special Services Unit. "Special Operations," he wrote in an angry memo, "is headed by an officer known among his Army friends as 'Wrong-Way' Galloway. Their doubtful esteem of him is more than matched by that of his associates and subordinates within his office and by that of the heads of other branches within CIA."

Penrose offered a laundry list of criticisms of Galloway. "Colonel Galloway has little comprehension," he wrote, "of the real nature of secret operations, and is so irascible and dogmatic that he discourages any efforts to discuss technical details with him." This was not the right way to build a new spy agency. "The disturbing situation which has been described is the more alarming," Penrose's screed continued, "because it occurs at a time when, as almost never before, the government needs an effective, expanding, professional intelligence service. On the contrary, CIA is losing its professionals, and is not acquiring competent new personnel who might gain experience in the only rapid way possible, namely by close association with those professionals." He loathed the career military men whom he believed misunderstood the nature of clandestine work. The CIA, he continued, "is dependent in most working branches for imaginative and energetic direction upon career military men of a type which is not apt to be either imaginative or energetic as regards non-military intelligence or procedures." He worried that the CIA had already lost the confidence of the military and the State Department "and is rapidly losing what confidence they had had in its predecessor organizations. Yet effective cooperation with these departments is a sine qua non of CIA success." The project, he feared, was on the verge of failure. A couple of weeks later, Penrose wrote to Allen Dulles. He implored his old friend to intervene. They could not let the experience and knowledge gained by OSS operatives be lost.[12]

Penrose knew that in putting his concerns about the new CIA onto paper, he would not have a job in American intelligence much longer. In 1948 Penrose took the position that was once offered to Eddy. He became the president of the American University of Beirut. The board of trustees, led by Harold Hoskins, Eddy's cousin and one of the OSS's top men in the Middle East, made the arrangements. Penrose took over for acting president Archie Crawford, his old partner in the OSS's Cairo office. James

Forrestal, who was now the secretary of defense, was sorry to see the missionary executive leave government service. But he was grateful, he told Penrose, "for your assurance that you will be available to assist us in the future."[13]

Penrose was shocked upon his return to Beirut to see how the school's current leaders had let its Christian mission fade. Always the missionary, Penrose reinstituted daily prayer, ensured that chapel services included scripture readings, and regularly preached. He also continued to see old friends, including Eddy's right-hand man during Torch, Carleton Coon. Peggy, Penrose's wife, described Coon as "a large man, never still, almost like a bull in a China shop." Eddy's sister also stopped by on her way through the region.[14]

Penrose had big plans for expanding Christianity in the Middle East, but they were cut short. On December 9, 1954, just six years after his return to Beirut, Penrose died of a heart attack at the age of forty-six. Bill and Mary Eddy, who were living nearby, stepped in to help Peggy Penrose and the three children with the funeral arrangements and then in securing travel back to the United States.

Herman, too, continued reporting to the US government after the war. Officially employed by the World Council of Churches, he labored to shape not only the council's global missions work but also the ways in which Protestant ecumenism aligned with the strategic interests of the United States. He submitted an August 1946 report to the WCC that documented his experiences in Poland. But Herman's account was not just for the benefit of the church agency. He also sent a copy to Penrose's Strategic Services Unit. An SSU cover sheet filed with the report instructed analysts to guard the documents carefully, especially their origins. They wanted to be sure not to "compromise" the WCC as they circulated Herman's findings.[15]

Meanwhile, the former pastor turned planner of covert operations was finally doing what he always wanted—working to establish peace by uniting the world's Protestants. He returned to the United States in the fall of 1947 to raise additional support for the WCC's reconstruction projects, and he spoke about his work in various churches. One Sunday he preached at Manhattan's famed Riverside Church, where he used the recently announced European Recovery Program, better known as the "Marshall Plan," to call for a "spiritual" recovery plan for Europe. Speaking with Herman that day was his old colleague Allen Dulles. The spy master and soon-to-be CIA director, with Herman at his side, called on American churches to set up a "Marshall Plan of the spirit."[16]

Herman worked for the WCC until 1948 and then became the director of refugee services for the World Lutheran Federation. For more than a decade he remained involved in global ecumenical Lutheran ministries. In 1964 he became president of the Lutheran School of Theology in Chicago. The next year he did something that he had been unwilling to do as a young man in Nazi Germany: he put his neck on the line for a racial group suffering under state-sanctioned discrimination and abuse.

Herman was home on Sunday, March 7, 1965, a date later dubbed "Bloody Sunday." That night he was watching *Judgment at Nuremberg* on TV, which focused on Nazis' war crimes. Breaking news interrupted the show. Viewers expecting to see analysis of German atrocities instead saw brutal footage of state troopers beating peaceful black protesters on a civil rights march as they tried to cross Edmund Pettus Bridge over the Alabama River in Selma on a march to the state capital. It was not difficult for the television audience to make a connection between what happened in Germany and what was happening in the United States. Herman, of all people, knew the significance of what he was watching unfold in the state of Alabama. He had also been reading *The Deputy* at the time, a play that condemned the pope and Christian leaders in Germany and throughout Europe for not doing more to stop the Holocaust. The play had affected him deeply. Herman believed that Bloody Sunday was his chance, as he later wrote, to "stand up and be counted." He had chosen to remain on the sidelines in Berlin. Not this time. He left late the next night for Alabama with a group of church leaders from Chicago, including historian Martin Marty. Two days later, they marched with Martin Luther King Jr. in Selma to the scene of the violence as a statement that civil rights activists were not going to back down.[17]

Herman spent the rest of his life doing what he cared about most—working to bolster the ecumenical church. He retired in 1971 and lived part-time on Shelter Island, in New York. There he helped revive a small, historic ecumenical chapel where a different pastor took the pulpit each Sunday to preach to summer vacationers. He also taught at Gettysburg, the Lutheran seminary that had shaped him. His students remembered a good teacher whose office was filled with odd relics from Germany. He died in February 2006, leaving behind his wife, Lyn, and their four children.

Birch had a different kind of legacy, which grew out of some Americans' fears that the United States was losing the Cold War. Throughout the 1930s and into World War II, the missionary had witnessed the growing split in China between those who supported the ruling government led by Chiang Kai-shek and those who wanted to install a communist regime led by Mao Zedong. The end of the war and the withdrawal of Japanese forces allowed the brewing tensions between these groups to turn into a bloody civil war. Truman chose to let the internecine conflict run its course rather than intervene. He feared that the cost to the United States of intervention was too great and the potential benefits too few. In 1949 Mao's communists took control of the Chinese mainland and established the People's Republic of China. Chiang and his allies fled to the nearby island of Taiwan, where they established a government in exile.

Many American businessmen, missionaries, and cold warriors blamed the president for "losing" China. Among the Americans furious at Truman was candy maker Robert Welch, famous for his Sugar Babies and Junior Mints. He dubbed Birch the first casualty of the Cold War and insisted that if Truman had told the American people in 1945 that Mao's men had executed Birch, they would have rallied against communism and prevented the Cold War. He used the life and death of John Birch to launch a virulent anticommunist crusade, and in 1958 he founded the secretive, conspiratorial John Birch Society, with the goal of waging a relentless crusade against communism.

The JBS became an influential, far-right organization. Its members, whose identities the organization closely guarded, worked to drive the Republican Party to the political right, and they traded in various conspiracy theories. Robert Welch claimed that communists had infiltrated the government and that President Eisenhower, General George Marshall, and Allen and John Foster Dulles were all communists. As the society grew and garnered more media attention, conservative leaders felt compelled to address its influence on the broader conservative movement. They did not want to alienate the JBS's tens of thousands of members, but they also knew that Welch's theories were so outlandish that they were giving conservatism a bad name. Eventually, conservative intellectual William F. Buckley condemned the group, establishing a boundary between mainstream conservatives and fringe organizations like the JBS. But others were less threatened by the group. At the 1964 Republican Convention, presidential candidate Barry Goldwater famously came to the defense of the society's members, insisting that "extremism in the defense of liberty is no vice. And . . . moderation in the pursuit of justice is no virtue." In the debate over the relationship among conservatism, the GOP, and the JBS, the actual John Birch became little more than a symbol for battles that had almost nothing to do with him. The JBS is still active today and has been experiencing a bit of a revival.[18]

Donovan, knocked out of the intelligence game by Truman, returned to Germany in early October 1945 to help the US government run the Nuremberg war-crimes prosecutions. However, he almost immediately clashed with his boss, Robert Jackson, the US chief counsel. Unable to work out his differences with Jackson, by the end of November Wild Bill was on his way back home to resume his law career in New York City. He campaigned for Dwight Eisenhower in 1952 and hoped that the new president would appoint him director of the CIA, but Ike went instead with one of Donovan's star OSS pupils—Allen Dulles. In 1953 Eisenhower appointed Donovan ambassador to Thailand. He had offered Donovan the prestigious ambassadorship to France, but Donovan thought that in Europe he would be too much under the thumb of Secretary of State John Foster Dulles. In Thailand he would have more freedom to monitor the growing communist threat and help shape American policy in Asia. Donovan worked until his death in 1959 to ensure that Americans understood the many contributions of the OSS to winning the war. But he remained mostly silent on the roles played by his missionaries, priests, and rabbi.[19]

Although the OSS's religious activists did not get much public attention, they had a substantial impact on the United States' global relations. In many ways, the work they did in the OSS laid the foundations for Truman's Cold War crusade against "godless" communism. Stalin had long cracked down on religious freedom in the Soviet Union. Communism, in the minds of many Americans, came to mean not just anticapitalism but also atheism. To counter the threat of atheistic communism, Truman worked to assemble a coalition of religious leaders the world over. He reached out to the Orthodox churches of Greece and Eastern Europe, to the Vatican and its huge global network of Catholics, and to Jewish and Muslim leaders. Religious faith, or the lack thereof, became a tool of Cold War diplomacy.

Historians have generally treated Truman's efforts to organize the world's religious power brokers into a unified force against communism as a new way to craft foreign policy. But the president was actually building on the legacy of Franklin Roosevelt and the wartime religious activists in the OSS. Eddy, Penrose, Birch, Herman, Glueck, Morlion, and Allen Dulles had already reached out to those in the centers of global religious power, inviting them to join the American crusade to defend religious freedom against its many threats. Truman simply continued their work, redirecting global religious leaders' focus from Nazi and imperial Japanese dangers to the communist menace.[20]

World War II served as an unparalleled moment for the United States to redefine its role in the world. Americans reclaimed the old Puritan notion that their nation was a city upon a hill, chosen by God to bring his salvation to humankind. The nation's old isolationist tendencies vanished, giving way to a powerful sense of divine destiny that demanded global intervention. American leaders—political and religious—embarked on a crusade to remake the rest of the world in their image. God, they believed, expected no less from his chosen people and his chosen land. The integration of ecumenical Christian ideas of religious freedom with advocacy of an aggressive, interventionist American foreign policy, forged in the embers of the war, echoed throughout the speeches and policies of just about every president since FDR. Victory over Japan and Germany seemingly demonstrated that God had anointed the United States to use its military and economic might to establish peace, security, and religious freedom for all.

Truman and his successors followed in FDR's footsteps in another way. Unbeknownst to the American people, at the end of the war, leaders of the OSS, then the Strategic Services Unit, then the CIA, recommended that American intelligence agencies hire missionaries and other religious activists for clandestine work. The CIA also created fake religious groups.[21]

One of the agency's most ingenious moves in the 1950s was to create a fictitious "Organization of the Militant Godless" in Guatemala. American operatives fabricated a series of letters that claimed to be from the OMG, promoting a communist revolution in Guatemala for the sake of advancing atheism. The letters accused the Catholic Church of working on behalf of the United States and the Vatican. "We are determined," one letter explained, "to take a more active hand in cutting down the nefarious influence of the Catholic Church in Guatemala." CIA officers sent the letters to those Guatemalans whom they thought "might be likely prospects for an atheist organization, such as intellectuals, students, officials of the various communist front organizations, and others." The agency then "leaked" the letters to journalists, church leaders, and politicians, hoping to frame Guatemalan leftists as participants in a conspiracy against the Catholic Church.[22]

The CIA's use of missionaries and religious institutions, real and phony, remained secret until 1966, when the *New York Times* ran an exposé. Among the revelations was that deep-cover CIA officers routinely masqueraded "as businessmen, tourists, scholars, students, missionaries or charity workers." A few liberal Protestant magazines took note of the *Times* piece. "There are hints," a writer in Reinhold Niebuhr's *Christianity and Crisis* acknowledged, "that CIA agents have appeared in the guise of missionaries and that Christian groups have been used by the CIA." The author doubted, however, that "even the most politically parochial and patriotic American working abroad for the Church would jeopardize the integrity of his commitment by serving the CIA directly." He was wrong to doubt it.[23]

A few writers, whistleblowers, and ex-agents were also investigating and disclosing some of the CIA's more controversial actions. Former CIA officer Victor Marchetti and former State Department foreign service officer John D. Marks published *The CIA and the Cult of Intelligence* in 1974. It contained one brief sentence on religion, most likely lifted from the 1966 *New York Times* report. "In addition to official cover," the authors wrote, "the CIA sometimes puts officers under 'deep cover' as businessmen, students, newsmen, or missionaries." The line piqued the curiosity of the religious press. In an interview about the book, Marks told a reporter that the CIA "has been heavily involved in church activities, religious activities. They've infiltrated the church and used the church or church groups as funding mechanisms. They solicit information from missionaries, try to hire missionaries."[24]

As the story gained steam, Marks claimed that in an informal survey of missionaries, 30 to 40 percent of those he contacted "either had a CIA-church connection story to tell or knew someone who did." Marks then listed some examples of what he learned: that a Catholic bishop was working for the CIA in Vietnam; a missionary in India had been collecting information for the agency; a Protestant missionary in Bolivia sent the CIA regular reports about the communist party, labor unions, and farmers' cooperatives; and another missionary in Bolivia regularly supplied the CIA with the names of suspected communists. Marks offered no evidence to support his allegations, and nobody ever investigated his claims. While his observations were almost certainly founded in some fact, they were so vague and unsubstantiated as to be almost worthless. Nevertheless, various religious news agencies publicized his allegations. The *Washington Post*, the *New York Times*, and other papers began examining the CIA's missionary tactics. A late 1974 *New York Times* investigation by Seymour Hersh uncovered even more evidence that the agency might be doing more harm than good.[25]

Congress was also taking note. In the aftermath of Watergate, senators and representatives grew more aggressive in their oversight of various federal agencies. No longer willing or able to turn a blind eye, in 1975 the US Senate created an eleven-member special committee to investigate the CIA. The Senate Select Committee to Study Governmental Operations with Respect to Intelligence Activities (aptly known as the "Church Committee" for its chair, Senator Frank Church of Idaho) interviewed eight hundred people and held 250 executive and 21 public hearings.

The CIA informed the Church Committee that the number of missionaries and clergy working for the agency at the time was small—"a total of 14 covert arrangements which involved direct operational use of 21 individuals." The CIA paid most of these American missionaries to collect and provide intelligence. One person, however, helped preserve the "cover" of other agents or officers. Most of the religious activists' work, according to the CIA, was "directed at 'competing' with communism in the Third World." In addition, the CIA, the report noted, funded the ministries of various groups deemed valuable for American intelligence purposes or for promoting the United States' global anticommunist agenda. In other words, collaboration was a two-way street in which both sides benefited. This paralleled the wartime partnerships orchestrated by Stephen Penrose in which missionary agencies traded intelligence for government resources.[26]

Church Committee members denounced the CIA's recruitment of American missionaries, but they expressed fewer reservations about the agency's use of religion in general as a tool of warfare. Religion, the Church Committee solemnly assured the public, was "inherently supranational. Making operational use of U.S. religious groups for national purposes both violates their nature and undermines their bonds with kindred groups around the world." The committee, however, made no inquiry into or criticism of the CIA's use of non-American religious organizations or the agency's manipulation of religion itself. How much the senators actually knew about CIA operations is not clear. But if they were aware that the CIA had created fake atheist societies in Guatemala, or had fabricated horoscopes in Vietnam to suit the agency's purposes, or brainstormed about using religious holidays to mask military operations in Cuba, senators seemed to have no objections.[27]

Although the CIA-religion revelation garnered only three pages in the Church Committee's hundreds of pages of reports, the investigation fueled a growing controversy. At the height of the Cold War, many Americans seemed willing to turn a blind eye to the actions of the CIA. By the 1970s, their complacency had evaporated. The Senate findings struck a powerful chord, revealing how torn many Protestants and Catholics were about how closely entwined their work in foreign fields was with the state.

Religious leaders all understood the significance of this issue. Missionaries working abroad were always vulnerable, and the increasing controversy did not help. In 1964 a rebel group in the Congo had killed missionary Paul Carlson after accusing him of spying for the United States. By the early 1970s, missionaries were regularly suspected of working for the US government.

Upon learning in 1975 that the CIA used American religious activists for intelligence gathering and covert operations, Oregon senator Mark

Hatfield, an outspoken evangelical and Baptist, wrote then CIA director William Colby, an old OSS veteran, to express his concerns. Colby, however, had no intention of restricting the agency's use of missionaries. He may well have understood and remembered how effective they had been working for the OSS during the war. In many countries, clergy, both indigenous and American, the director told the senator, "play a significant role and can be of assistance to the United States through CIA with no reflection upon their integrity nor their mission." He blamed the controversy on "sensational publicity" rather than the facts on the ground.[28]

Unsatisfied with Colby's response, Hatfield then turned to President Gerald Ford. He argued that CIA involvement with clergy, members of religious orders, and missionaries "tarnishes the image of the United States in foreign countries and prostitutes the church." In allowing the CIA to use missionaries, he continued, "we pervert the church's mission and create the view that the United States will resort to any means in pursuit of its particular interests." He ended by asking the president to take executive action to stop the CIA from using religious activists for American espionage. Once again, the senator did not get the response he was hoping for. Not only did Ford refuse to take action, but one of his aides exacerbated the situation by telling Hatfield that "many" clergymen were engaged in regular communication with the agency.[29]

The senator recognized that the missionaries that the CIA was most likely recruiting were evangelicals, men and women from his own tradition. Evangelicals had mostly taken over the missions project after World War II. They continued to focus on making converts to Christianity, while their mainline counterparts focused increasingly on humanitarian outreach. Evangelicals ran most of the postwar missionary societies while ecumenists worked through nongovernmental organizations. Evangelicals were relentless cold warriors, which made them attractive to the CIA. They also tended to be far more nationalistic than their ecumenical counterparts and staunch critics of communism and left-leaning governments. Hatfield was desperate to protect evangelical missionaries' autonomy and effectiveness abroad. He wanted to ensure that the CIA did not compromise their work.[30]

Hatfield took to the floor of the US Senate in late 1975 to denounce the CIA's practices and the president's refusal to intervene. He claimed that the CIA's actions violated church-state separation, adding, "In this country . . . the church is not an arm of the state, nor is the state the tool of the church. The first amendment and all our history . . . make that abundantly clear." Having failed to convince the CIA director and the president of the importance of classifying clergy as out-of-bounds for clandestine work, Hatfield introduced a bill to outlaw federal intelligence agency engagement with religious activists "for the purpose of manipulating political events or collecting intelligence." The legislation would have prohibited the National Security Agency, the Central Intelligence Agency, and the Defense Intelligence Agency from paying "any member of the clergy or any employees or affiliate of a religious organization, association, or society for intelligence gathering or for any other participation in agency operations." The bill also would have prohibited intelligence operatives from "soliciting or accepting the services" of religious activists. For the next few months, missionaries, journalists, and legislators debated the bill.[31]

In the wake of the Church Committee findings and other revelations about the CIA, few Christian leaders thought that it was a good idea for religious activists to work with the agency. For decades many Christians—though certainly not all—saw partnering with US intelligence services as a worthwhile and patriotic duty. The United States protected their freedom to work abroad and intelligence work for the CIA sometimes provided material benefits. But as Americans learned about the agency's actions in Latin America and Vietnam—undermining democratically elected leaders, working to rig elections, and bolstering the regimes of right-wing dictators—the CIA no longer looked like the right hand of a godly Uncle Sam, but sometimes like an exploitative, manipulative, hypocritical tool of the devil. Missionaries risked undermining their hard work through association with the agency.

Missionaries during the Cold War faced the same moral dilemmas that their World War II era peers wrestled with. They aimed to serve their nation and understood that their ability to conduct much of their work abroad depended on a strong United States. But as had been the case with Herman, Birch, Eddy, and Penrose, they still wondered and debated how far to go. Those missionaries who opposed CIA collaborations spoke out. Those who might have been willing to partner with the agency did not go public with their views, which would have compromised the secret nature of their work, but journalists made the moral arguments for them. "The CIA holds nothing sacred including the sacred," opined historian and columnist Garry Wills. "What we need, right now, is not so much a wall of separation between church and state but a wall between us and the CIA, to protect us from its imperial meddling." Conservative Catholic journalist Michael Novak disagreed. "I prefer a war fought through intelligence services to a war fought with atomic weapons." He advised journalists and agency critics to back off and let the CIA do its business, even if that business included using missionaries and priests as officers or agents.[32]

The protests of leading missionaries and church leaders, along with Hatfield's threat of legislation aimed at curtailing the power and independence of the CIA, had an impact. When George Herbert Walker Bush took over as director of the Central Intelligence Agency in early 1976, his first act addressed the missionary controversy. Bush vowed that the "CIA shall establish no secret, paid or unpaid contractual relationship with any American clergyman or missionary." Bush's policy directive was pure genius. It had all the appearance of providing much of what Hatfield and the major American denominations and missionary organizations wanted, without actually doing much at all. "In addition," Bush promised, "American church groups will not be funded nor used as funding cutouts for CIA purposes. The CIA will, however, continue to welcome information volunteered by American clergymen or missionaries." Nevertheless, the CIA maintained the right to "initiate contact" with missionaries in the United States if senior agency officials believed that religious workers returning from abroad "might possess important foreign intelligence information." Hatfield was satisfied with Bush's promises. He returned to the Senate floor to laud the policy shift, share a series of warm letters that he and Bush had exchanged, and withdraw his bill from consideration. The CIA was off the hook, allowed to continue its long practice of crafting and implementing its own policies with religious groups without serious congressional oversight.[33]

Although many religious leaders continued to lobby Bush for a more explicit change of policy, the director well knew that with Hatfield pacified, the churches had no chance of undermining the power of the Central Intelligence Agency. Soon the controversy died down. Without congressional support, American church and missions leaders returned to business as usual. As CIA abuses receded from the headlines, church leaders had less and less incentive for bringing continued attention to the many ways that their missionaries and activists had helped support some of the

United States' most controversial global ambitions. But agency leaders were certainly not completely done with missionaries. In 1977 Stansfield Turner, Bush's successor at the CIA, privately clarified that Bush's policy directive did not "prohibit overt relationships with missionaries or members of the clergy on matters which are unrelated to their religious status, such as the providing of unclassified translation services." Apparently, the CIA believed that it could still draw clear lines between what was religious and what was not. The agency, the memo implied, could keep missionaries on the payroll.[34]

Over the next few decades, journalists, activists, and members of Congress occasionally revived the controversy, but it never again received such sustained attention. Few church leaders or missionary organizations waged a persistent battle against the government's recruitment of their people or of fellow believers abroad. The less they publicized the history of the OSS's and the CIA's employment of religious activists, the better. What nobody outside of the CIA realized, however, was that not only did Bush's policy directive do far less than Hatfield had demanded, but it was not even binding. In 1996 CIA director John Deutch testified before the Senate Select Committee on Intelligence that although the 1976 ban on paid relationships with clergy was technically still in effect, he maintained the authority to waive the ban in cases of unique and special threats to national security. He revealed that since 1976, he and his predecessors had agreed "that the Agency should not be prohibited from considering the use of American . . . clergy in exceptional circumstances." What qualified as "exceptional," he did not say.[35]

Mark Hatfield was incensed to learn that the CIA had secretly maintained the right to recruit missionaries for intelligence operations. CIA leaders had not told him or anyone else in Congress that the agency could waive the policy established in 1976 by George H. W. Bush. "Allowing a waiver of this policy," Hatfield argued, "is tantamount to declaring no policy at all." The senator noted that the "suspicion" created by the CIA's use of just a single missionary overseas "puts the welfare of all missionaries in jeopardy." He again pleaded with CIA leaders to put an end to their recruitment of missionaries once and for all. And once again, he failed to secure the commitment from the CIA that he wanted.[36]

Indeed, CIA leaders masterfully built into its own policies a series of gaping loopholes. Publicly, the agency promised not to use American missionaries for covert operations or intelligence gathering. But privately, the agency maintained the right to do just that if its leaders believed that the circumstances warranted it or if the missionaries were on American soil. The agency also felt free to distinguish between activists' explicit "religious work" and their nonreligious work and believed that it had the right to hire them for the latter. Meanwhile, the agency never stopped or even denied using foreign clergy and missionaries to further its goals, nor did officers have any reservations about creating fictitious religious organizations to disseminate propaganda. Across the second half of the twentieth century, the CIA found in God a useful, consistent, and powerful ally. OSS leader Ferdinand Mayer was right. The religious approach, as he had assured Wild Bill Donovan at the end of World War II, was indeed "one of the super-secret activities that the Central Agency could best manipulate." Missionaries, diplomats, intelligence operatives, and the military marched together in the name of freedom of religion, the expansion of American power, and the furtherance of the Christian faith across much of the twentieth century, just as they had in the nineteenth in China, Hawaii, the Philippines, and many other places.

Contemporary CIA leaders, we hope, understand what the Church Committee and Mark Hatfield tried to tell the agency in the 1970s, and what Hatfield reiterated in 1996. Using missionaries for undercover jobs is almost always a bad idea. But the CIA still has not completely closed the door to this possibility. According to an internal CIA policy dating from 2013 and declassified in 2015, CIA officers may never use a "clergy or missionary, whether or not ordained, who is sent out by a mission or church organization to preach, teach, heal, or proselytize" for a job without disclosing to that missionary their CIA affiliation. The CIA also promises never to use "missionary" as a cover for its agents or activities. The CIA can, however, establish "open" relationships with missionaries or clergy. By "open," the agency means that it acknowledges "the fact and nature of the relationship to senior management officials of the organizations involved," presumably the agency and the missionaries' supervisors. In other words, the CIA will not recruit American missionaries or priests behind the backs of church officials. The CIA also maintains the right to recruit independent missionaries. It is then up to the missionaries and their agencies, just as it was up to their World War II–era counterparts, to wrestle with the moral dilemmas involved in mixing their religious ministry with intelligence work. That the agency can still employ missionaries seems to be a far cry from the kinds of prohibitions that Mark Hatfield wanted and that missionary agencies thought they were getting in 1976 from George H. W. Bush.[37]

Nevertheless, much has changed since John Birch, Stephen Penrose, Stewart Herman, and William Eddy went to work for the Office of Strategic Services during World War II. Government agencies are now more willing to honor the separation of church and state, and they do not want to endanger missionaries around the globe. This suits religious activists. They understand that close affiliation with their government can sometimes undermine rather than bolster their missionary efforts. Modern missionaries generally work hard to separate the religion they preach from the specific American cultural values that inadvertently shape some of their attitudes and ideas. They depend on gaining the trust of the people they serve and never want those to whom they are ministering to fear that they are not who they say that they are or that they are secretly working for a clandestine government agency.

In the 1940s, the United States had few people with the skills and experience necessary to do effective intelligence work. American leaders needed missionaries and other religious activists to partner with the OSS to help defeat their Axis enemies. Today, in contrast, the United States boasts an expansive, professional, modern Central Intelligence Agency. It does not need missionaries to achieve its goals.

We can be grateful that during World War II, American missionaries carried dung bombs and poison pills with their Bibles, and some even hatched assassination plots. We can also be grateful that today, they shouldn't have to.

ACKNOWLEDGMENTS

Plunging into the world of spies and scoundrels, missionaries and martyrs, has been a lot of fun. So has talking through my ideas about them with colleagues and friends. My longtime mentors Jane Sherron De Hart and Grant Wacker both offered excellent advice and recommendations from the start. I had the benefit of superb suggestions and criticism on the entire manuscript from Rebecca Davis, David Hollinger, Michael McVicar, G. Kurt Piehler, Andrew Preston, Stephen Slick, Hugh Wilford, and Daniel K. Williams. John Amstutz, Christopher Cantwell, Darren Dochuk, Joseph Fronczak, Timothy Gloege, Michael Graziano, Paul Harvey, Derek Hastings, Kevin Kruse, Brendan Pietsch, Jeffrey Sanders, Kevin Schultz, James Seckington, and Daniel Silliman offered valuable feedback on partial drafts. Terry Lautz generously shared ideas about John Birch and some of the photographs that he had tracked down. I also benefited from the insights offered by the children of some of the book's major characters. Stewart Herman III and Christopher Herman graciously shared their thoughts and memories of their father and made his private diaries and letters available to me. Dale Penrose Harrell helped me think about her father's life and contributions to the American war effort, and she and Herb Harrell shared letters and photographs.

I had a top-tier team of professionals helping me along every step of the way. I am grateful to my agent, Sandra Dijkstra, for her excellent advice as I launched this project. At Basic Books, Dan Gerstle helped me shape the raw material I found in the archives into a compelling story, and Lara Heimert helped carry the book across the finish line. Roger Labrie pushed me to clarify my ideas, and Annette Wenda cleaned up my grammar. Randal Powell helped me double-check footnotes, and Liz Miller helped with the index.

Acknowledgments

Many librarians and archivists across the country have been essential to this project. I am particularly grateful to Eric S. Van Slander at the National Archives for helping me navigate the labyrinth that is the OSS papers. I also had support from numerous institutions. At Washington State University, Senior Associate Dean Paul Whitney, and Deans Darryl DeWald and Matthew Jockers, provided critical support in various ways. I am also grateful for a WSU Center for the Arts and Humanities Fellowship and to hold an Edward R. Meyer Distinguished Professorship, which helped cover research expenses. I received a National Endowment for the Humanities Public Scholars Fellowship and a John Simon Guggenheim Foundation Fellowship, which freed me from some of my teaching in order to focus on writing this book.

Most of all, I am grateful to my family for their everlasting support of my work, including John and Kathleen Sutton, Daniel and Roxanne Coke, Sarah Nielsen, Christopher Sutton, Julia Lampe, and their families. I am dedicating this book to my wife, Kristen, and our boys, Jackson and Nathan. I love the three of them so much, and love every minute that we spend together.

NOTES

ABBREVIATIONS

Brady Papers   Anne M. Brady Papers, Lauinger Library, Georgetown University, Washington, DC

CREST   CIA Records Search Tool, Central Intelligence Agency (online)

Dale Penrose Papers   Stephen B. L. Penrose Jr. Papers in the possession of Dale Penrose Harrell, Chesapeake, VA

Eddy Papers   William Alfred Eddy Papers, Public Policy Papers, Department of Rare Books and Special Collections, Mudd Manuscript Library, Princeton University, Princeton, NJ

FDR Library   Franklin D. Roosevelt Presidential Library, Hyde Park, NY

Fierman Papers   Floyd Fierman Papers, American Jewish Archives, Cincinnati, OH

FRUS   Foreign Relations of the United States

Heresy trial   Proceedings of Investigation Conducted by Executive Committee, Board of Trustees of Mercer University, in Connection with Heresy Charges Alleged Against Five Professors (March 30, 1939), Special Collections, Tarver Library, Mercer University, Macon, GA

Herman diary   Herman diaries in the possession of Stewart Herman III, Minneapolis, MN

Herman letters   Herman-Cantrell letters in the possession of Christopher Herman, Washington, DC

Herman Papers   Stewart W. Herman Jr. Papers, A. R. Wentz Library, Lutheran Theological Seminary, Gettysburg, PA

Knowland Papers   William F. Knowland Papers, Bancroft Library, University of California, Berkeley

Morlion FBI file   "Father Felix Morlion," FBI file 100-HQ-93828, National Archives and Records Administration, College Park, MD (Freedom of Information Act request)

NARA   National Archives and Records Administration, College Park, MD

NARA-STL   National Personnel Records Center, National Archives and Records Administration, St. Louis, MO

Norris Papers	J. Frank Norris Papers, Southern Baptist Historical Library and Archives, Nashville, TN
Penrose Papers	Stephen B. L. Penrose Jr. Papers, Whitman College and Northwest Archives, Walla Walla, WA
Warnshuis Papers	Abbe Livingston Warnshuis Papers, Burke Library, Columbia University, New York, NY
Wedemeyer Papers	Albert C. Wedemeyer Papers, Hoover Institution Archives, Stanford University, Stanford, CA
Whittlesey Papers	Marjorie Tooker Whittlesey Papers, Yale Divinity School Library, New Haven, CT
WJD Papers	William J. Donovan Papers, US Army War College Library and Archives, Carlisle, PA

INTRODUCTION

1. A. D. Gascoigne to J. Rives Childs, April 17, 1942, "Tangier," box 2, entry UD 2978, RG 84, NARA.

2. William Eddy to William Donovan, August 26, 1942, frame 208, roll 34, M1642, RG 226, NARA.

3. Eddy to Donovan, August 26, 1942, frame 208; Donovan to Admiral William Leahy, August 30, 1942, frame 363, roll 34, M1642, RG 226, NARA.

4. Eddy to Marycita Eddy, March 27, 1942, folder 10, box 5; Eddy to Mary Eddy, March 13, 1942, folder 8, box 10, Eddy Papers.

5. William J. Donovan, "Intelligence: Key to Defense," *Life*, September 30, 1946, 114.

6. William Eddy, "Manuscripts: 'Adventures in Arab Lands,'" folder 18, box 14, Eddy Papers; Malcolm Muggeridge, *Chronicles of Wasted Time: An Autobiography* (Vancouver, BC: Regent College, 1972), 431; Stalin quoted in Max Hastings, *The Secret War: Spies, Ciphers, and Guerillas, 1939–1945* (New York: HarperCollins, 2016), xviii.

7. Muggeridge, *Chronicles of Wasted Time*, 397.

8. Eddy to Mary Eddy, June 9, 1941, folder 11, box 5, Eddy Papers.

9. Stephen B. L. Penrose Jr. to mother and father, December 9 and 23, 1941, folder 3, box 1, Penrose Papers.

10. William Alfred Eddy, "Arms and the Man," *Outlook*, November 5, 1924, 374.

11. In their otherwise excellent histories of World War II, Max Hastings and David M. Kennedy, for example, say little about religion. Max Hastings, *Inferno: The World at War, 1939–1945* (New York: Alfred A. Knopf, 2011); David M. Kennedy, *Freedom from Fear: The American People in Depression and War* (New York: Oxford University Press, 2005).

12. Henry Luce, "The American Century," *Life*, February 17, 1941, 61–65.

13. On the rise of the CIA, see Rhodri Jeffreys-Jones, *Cloak and Dollar: A History of American Secret Intelligence* (New Haven, CT: Yale University Press, 2003) and *In Spies We Trust: The Story of Western Intelligence* (New York: Oxford University Press, 2013); Tim Weiner, *Legacy of Ashes: The History of the CIA* (New York: Penguin, 2007); and Hugh Wilford, *The Mighty Wurlitzer: How the CIA Played America* (Cambridge, MA: Harvard University Press, 2008). The historian who has best captured how religious ideals played out in American foreign policy is Andrew Preston. See his *Sword of the Spirit,*

Shield of Faith: Religion in American War and Diplomacy (New York: Alfred A. Knopf, 2012). William Inboden's *Religion and American Foreign Policy, 1945–1960: The Soul of Containment* (Cambridge: Cambridge University Press, 2008) brilliantly analyzes the religious foundations for the Cold War. David Hollinger traces the ways in which missionaries sparked domestic change in his pathbreaking *Protestants Abroad: How Missionaries Tried to Change the World but Changed America* (Princeton, NJ: Princeton University Press, 2017).

Religion has served as a popular tool for American spies for good reason. Policy makers have demonstrated by their actions that they believe that religion substantially influences individuals' lives, impacts their decisions, and shapes their loyalties. Scholars should treat it equally seriously. In recent years, historians such as Emily Conroy-Krutz, Melani McAlister, and others have demonstrated that religion did (and does) play an important, even if underacknowledged, role in foreign policy. Michael Graziano has shown how religion has been central to the work of the OSS and CIA. Emily Conroy-Krutz, *Christian Imperialism: Converting the World in the Early American Republic* (Ithaca, NY: Cornell University Press, 2015); Melani McAlister, *Epic Encounters: Culture, Media, and U.S. Interests in the Middle East Since 1945*, 2nd ed. (Berkeley: University of California Press, 2005); Michael Graziano, *Errand into the Wilderness of Mirrors: Religion, American Intelligence, and National Security* (Chicago: University of Chicago Press, forthcoming).

CHAPTER 1. "THE MORAL AND SPIRITUAL DEFENSES OF A NATION"

1. William J. Donovan, "Memorandum of Establishment of Service of Strategic Information," June 10, 1941, CREST, CIA-RDP13X00001R000100240004-4.

2. William J. Donovan, "Memorandum of Establishment of Service of Strategic Information," June 10, 1941, President's Secretary's File, box 128, FDR Library.

3. "Executive Order Designating a Coordinator of Information," July 11, 1941, box 80A, WJD Papers.

4. Donovan to General Wavell, July 6, 1942, box 119B, WJD Papers. On the history of the OSS, see R. Harris Smith, *OSS: The Secret History of America's First Central Intelligence Agency* (Berkeley: University of California Press, 1972); Bradley F. Smith, *The Shadow Warriors: O.S.S. and the Origins of the C.I.A.* (New York: Basic Books, 1983); and Joseph E. Persico, *Roosevelt's Secret War: FDR and World War II Espionage* (New York: Random House, 2001). See also Hastings, *Secret War.*

5. On Donovan's early life, see Douglas Waller, *Wild Bill Donovan: The Spymaster Who Created the OSS and Modern American Espionage* (New York: Free Press, 2011). See also Anthony Cave Brown, *The Last Hero: Wild Bill Donovan* (New York: Times Books, 1982).

6. Woodrow Wilson, "Address to a Joint Session of Congress Requesting a Declaration of War Against Germany," online by Gerhard Peters and John T. Woolley, the American Presidency Project, https://www.presidency.ucsb.edu/node/207620.

7. Francis P. Duffy to Pere Vincent, n.d., box 135, WJD Papers.

8. Donovan to Ruth Donovan, August 7, 1918, box 135, WJD Papers.

9. Donovan to Ruth Donovan, August 7, 1918.

10. Donovan diary, "Mediterranean Cruise, 1923," January 26, February 4, and February 6–7, 1923, box 132B, WJD Papers.

11. "Watertown Rally," *New York Times*, October 20, 1932.

12. Donovan, "Address to Women's Republican Club," July 23, 1935, box 2A, WJD Papers.

13. Stanley P. Lovell, *Of Spies and Stratagems* (New York: Pocket Books, 1963), 36–37.

14. Arthur M. Schlesinger Jr., *A Life in the Twentieth Century: Innocent Beginnings, 1917–1950* (Boston: Houghton Mifflin, 2000), 305.

15. Jane Smiley Hart, interview by Frances Stickles, October 1, 1990, folder 9, box 3, Penrose Papers. Women made important contributions to OSS morale operations. See Ann Todd, *OSS Operation Black Mail: One Woman's Covert War Against the Imperial Japanese Army* (Annapolis: Naval Institute Press, 2017). On Child, see Jennet Conant, *A Covert Affair: Julia Child and Paul Child in the OSS* (New York: Simon & Schuster, 2011). Donovan also recruited numerous academics, especially for the Research and Analysis Branch. See Robin W. Winks, *Cloak and Gown: Scholars in the Secret War, 1939–1961*, 2nd ed. (New Haven, CT: Yale University Press, 1996).

16. On Dulles, see Stephen Kinzer, *The Brothers: John Foster Dulles, Allen Dulles, and Their Secret World War* (New York: Times Books, 2013).

17. Lovell, *Of Spies and Stratagems*, 92, 93.

18. Lovell, *Of Spies and Stratagems*, vii.

19. Lovell, *Of Spies and Stratagems*, 27, 28, 46, 57.

20. "Principal Demons, Spirits, Apparitions," folder 25, box 119A, WJD Papers.

21. "OSS Plan to Fox Japs with Ghost Foxes Recalled," *Chicago Tribune*, March 21, 1948. On the various "fox" plans, see folder 25, box 119A, WJD Papers.

22. Franklin D. Roosevelt, "Annual Message to Congress," January 4, 1939, online by Gerhard Peters and John T. Woolley, the American Presidency Project, http://www.presidency.ucsb.edu/ws/?pid=15684. On the role of religion in American foreign policy, see Preston, *Sword of the Spirit*.

23. Donovan to FDR, May 5, 1942, box 149, President's Secretary's File; Archibald MacLeish to Steven Early, April 29, 1942, "Church Matters," box 3, President's Official File; Harold L. Ickes to FDR, January 6, 1942, box 128, President's Secretary's File, FDR Library.

Chapter 2. "Between Hope and Despair"

1. J. Edgar Hoover to the Attorney General, April 10, 1942, and Background Memo, Father Schulte, FBI file 65-1449, Rev. Paul Adam Adolph Schulte, box 116, Record Group 65 (hereafter cited as Schulte FBI file), NARA.

2. A. H. Johnson to Hoover, May 28, 1942, Francis Biddle to Secretary of State, June 13, 1942, Schulte FBI file, NARA. See also D. M. Ladd to E. A. Tamm, May 23, 1942, Schulte FBI file, NARA.

3. Ellery Huntington Jr. to Colonel Preston Goodfellow, "re: Schulte," April 7, 1942, frames 1054–1061, roll 105, M1642, RG 226, NARA.

4. November 14–15, 1934, Herman diary; Stewart W. Herman Jr. to family, January 9, 1934[5], box 20, Herman Papers.

5. Herman to family, January 14, January 16, and March 18, 1935, box 20, Herman Papers; March 17, 1935, Herman diary; Herman to family, March 25, 1935, box 20, Herman Papers. See also January 12–14, 1935, Herman diary.

6. Reinhold Niebuhr, *Moral Man and Immoral Society* (New York: Charles Scribner's Sons, 1932), xi, 179, 180.

7. November 5, 1935, Herman diary.

8. Herman to family, March 8, 1935, box 20, Herman Papers. For an excellent analysis of the war-era ecumenical movement, see Gene Zubovich, "For Human Rights Abroad, Against Jim Crow at Home: The Political Mobilization of American Ecumenical Protestants in the World War II Era," *Journal of American History* 105, no. 2 (2018): 267–290. On the international ecumenical movement, see Michael G. Thompson, *For God and Globe: Christian Internationalism in the United States Between the Great War and the Cold War* (Ithaca, NY: Cornell University Press, 2015).

9. Herman to family, February 17, 1935, box 20, Herman Papers.

10. Herman to family, September 30, 1935, box 20, Herman Papers.

11. Herman to family, October 3, 1935, box 20, Herman Papers.

12. Herman to family, October 22, 1935, box 20, Herman Papers.

13. Herman had significant reservations about Barth's theology and argued with the scholar's seminarian son about it. May 27, 1937, Herman diary.

14. Herman to family, October 29, 1935, box 20, Herman Papers; October 27, 1935, Herman diary.

15. Herman to family, November 10, 1935, box 20, Herman Papers.

16. Herman to family, November 10, 1935; November 10, 1935, Herman diary.

17. Clayton E. Williams to Herman, May 10, 1935, box 14; Herman to family, October 13, 1935, box 20, Herman Papers.

18. Herman to family, January 15, 1936, box 20, Herman Papers.

19. Herman to family, January 26, 1936, box 20, Herman Papers.

20. Herman to family, February 17, 1936, and November 17, 1935, box 20, Herman Papers.

21. Herman to family, February 23, 1936, box 20, Herman Papers; "Washington, Hitler Similarity Is Hinted," *New York Times*, February 23, 1936; February 22, 1936, Herman diary.

22. "Speech of Acceptance at American Church, February 23, 1936," box 20, Herman Papers; Stewart W. Herman Jr., *It's Your Souls We Want* (London: Hodder and Stoughton, 1943), x.

23. Herman to family, February 10, March 18, and November 30, 1936, box 20, Herman Papers. On Dodd, see Erik Larson, *In the Garden of the Beasts: Love, Terror, and an American Family in Hitler's Berlin* (New York: Crown, 2011).

24. Herman to family, March 31, 1936, box 20, Herman Papers; March 27 and November 23, 1936, Herman diary.

25. Herman to family, July 5, 1936, box 20, Herman Papers.

26. End-of-Year Memorandum and January 15 and May 29, 1938, Herman diary.

27. Herman to family, August 19, 1936, box 20, Herman Papers.

28. February 21, April 16, April 24, June 25, and July 2, 1937, Herman diary.

29. February 14 and July 30, 1938, Herman diary; Herman to family, June 21, June 28, and July 19, 1938, box 20, Herman Papers.

30. Herman to family, July 19, 1938, box 20, Herman Papers.

31. February 20 and December 17, 1940, Herman diary.

32. On American responses to escalating persecution of Jews in Europe, see Richard Breitman and Allan J. Lichtman, *FDR and the Jews* (Cambridge, MA: Belknap Press of Harvard University Press, 2013); and Preston, *Sword of the Spirit*.

33. June 21, 1938, Herman diary; Herman to family, July 19, 1938, box 20, Herman Papers; July 15, 1938, Herman diary.

34. Herman to family, November 14, 1938, box 20, Herman Papers.

35. Herman to family, March 2, 1938, box 20, Herman Papers.

36. November 18, 1938, Herman diary.

37. Herman to family, November 14, 1938, box 20, Herman Papers.

38. Herman to family, November 25, 1938, box 20, Herman Papers (ellipses in the original).

39. Herman to family, December 1 and December 8, 1938, box 20, Herman Papers.

40. Herman to family, August 25, 1939, box 20, Herman Papers.

41. September 3, 1939, Herman diary; Herman to family, September 5 and October 12, 1939, Berlin diary, 1939, 3, box 20, Herman Papers.

42. Herman to family, September 19 and November 3, 1939, box 20, Herman Papers.

43. Herman to family, July 19, 1941, box 20, Herman Papers; Herman to Ethelyn Cantrell, November 22, 1944, Herman letters; July 15, 1941, Herman diary.

44. Stewart W. Herman, "Memorandum on Conversation with Pastor Niemöller in Frankfurt on July 31, 1945," in *Die evangelische Kirche nach dem Zusammenbruch*, ed. Clemens Vollnhals (Göttingen: Vandenhoeck & Ruprecht, 1988); March 2, 1941, Herman diary.

45. Herman, *It's Your Souls We Want*, 160; Herman to family, October 3, 1940, box 20, Herman Papers.

46. December 6 and December 13, 1939, Herman diary.

47. April 3, 1941, Herman diary; "Berlin Americans Fear New Arrests," *New York Times*, April 4, 1941, "U.S. Aide's Arrest in Berlin Protested," *New York Times*, April 5, 1941; Herman to family, August 21, 1941, box 20, Herman Papers.

48. September 18, 1941, Herman diary; Herman to family, September 22 and October 6, 1941, box 20, Herman Papers.

49. Herman to family, October 17, 1941, box 20, Herman Papers.

50. Herman to family, October 24 and December 6, 1941, box 20, Herman Papers. See also Artemis Joukowsky, *Defying the Nazis: The Sharps' War* (Boston: Beacon Press, 2016).

51. Herman to family, December 6, 1941, box 20, Herman Papers.

52. Herman to family, December 22, 1941, box 20, Herman Papers.

CHAPTER 3. "A CONQUERING FAITH"

1. The only biography on Eddy is Thomas W. Lippman, *Arabian Knight: Colonel Bill Eddy USMC and the Rise of American Power in the Middle East* (Vista, CA: Selwa Press, 2008).

2. Eddy to Mary Garvin [Eddy], October 4, 1917, and Mary Eddy to J. A. Garvin, October 5, 1917, folder 6, box 5, Eddy Papers.

3. Eddy to Bill Jr., April 23, 1945, folder 4, box 3, Eddy Papers.

4. Eddy to Mary Eddy, December 1918, January 5, and January 14, 1919, box 5, folder 6, Eddy Papers.

5. William A. Eddy, "The Chaplain in Action," *New York Times*, February 11, 1923.

6. William A. Eddy, "Still a Moslem," *Christian Endeavor World*, November 26, 1931, 5.

7. William A. Eddy, "The Holy Land," *Holy Cross Magazine*, December 1940, 353.

8. William Alfred Eddy, "Can Mission Colleges Be Christian?," *Christian Century*, September 27, 1928. See also Eddy, "Still a Moslem," 5.

9. Stephen B. L. Penrose Jr., *That They May Have Life: The Story of the American University of Beirut, 1866–1941* (Princeton, NJ: Princeton University Press, 1941), 46.

10. William A. Eddy, "Hobart College and the Church," *Living Church*, March 23, 1938, 365–366.

11. Eddy to Rev. Condit M. Eddy, March 14, 1939, folder 5, box 9, Eddy Papers.

12. Francis B. Sayre to Eddy, December 14, 1938, folder 5, box 8, Eddy Papers.

13. Eddy to Paul Alling, March 1, 1939, folder 2, box 1, Eddy Papers.

14. William A. Eddy, "Democracy and Freedom," *Living Church*, July 5, 1939, 10, 11.

15. Eddy to Undergraduate Friends, August 23, 1941, folder 9, box 5, Eddy Papers.

16. Wallace Murray to Alexander Kirk, July 1, 1941, folder 6, box 11, Eddy Papers.

17. Eddy to Miss Brennan, July 16, 1941; Eddy to Mary Eddy, July 16, 1941; Eddy to Carmen Eddy, July 17, 1941, folder 11, box 5, Eddy Papers.

18. Eddy to Mary Eddy, July 21, 1941, folder 11, box 5, Eddy Papers.

19. Eddy to Bill, Marycita, and Jack Eddy, November 11, 1941, folder 9, box 5, Eddy Papers.

20. Eddy to Mary Eddy, October 19, 1941, folder 9, box 5, Eddy Papers.

21. Eddy to Mary Eddy, August 1 and September 4, 1941, folder 9, box 5, Eddy Papers.

22. Eddy to Bill, Marycita, and Jack Eddy, November 11, 1941; Eddy to Mary Eddy, October 2, 1941, folder 9, box 5, Eddy Papers.

23. Eddy to Mary Eddy, September 9, 1941, folder 9, box 5, Eddy Papers.

24. Eddy to Mary Eddy, July 17, 1935, folder 8, box 5, Eddy Papers.

25. Eddy to Mary Eddy, from München, n.d, folder 8, box 5, Eddy Papers.

26. Eddy to Bill, Marycita, and Jack Eddy, November 11, 1941, folder 9, box 5, Eddy Papers.

27. Eddy to Bill, Marycita, and Jack Eddy, November 11, 1941.

28. Eddy to Bill, Marycita, and Jack Eddy, November 11, 1941; Eddy to Mary Eddy, November 1, 1941, folder 9, box 5, Eddy Papers.

29. Eddy to family, November 17, 1941, folder 9, box 5, Eddy Papers.

30. Eddy to family, November 17, 1941; Eddy to Bill, Marycita, and Jack Eddy, November 11, 1941, folder 9, box 5, Eddy Papers.

31. James Forrestal to Eddy, December 11, 1941, and Donovan to Wallace Murray, December 29, 1941, folder 6, box 11, Eddy Papers.

32. Ernest Cuneo, "The OSS and BSC," Ernest Cuneo Papers, box 114, FDR Library.

33. Donovan to FDR, December 22, 1941, box 147, President's Secretary's File, FDR Library.

34. Mary Eddy to family, January 7, 1942, folder 2, box 3, Eddy Papers.

35. Donovan to Mary Eddy, January 9, 1942, folder 2, box 3; Eddy to Mary Eddy, January 6–19, 1942, folder 10, box 5, Eddy Papers.

36. Eddy to Mary Eddy, January 6–19, 1942, folder 10, box 5, Eddy Papers.

CHAPTER 4. "PROPHECIES YET TO BE FULFILLED"

1. George Birch Jr., Confidential Application; Ethel Ellis (Birch), Confidential Application, Board of Foreign Missions, Foreign Missionary Vertical File, RG 360, Presbyterian Historical Society, Philadelphia. On the rise of modern apocalyptic Christianity, see Matthew Sutton, *American Apocalypse: A History of Modern Evangelicalism* (Cambridge, MA: Belknap Press of Harvard University Press, 2014).

2. "Five New Missionaries Sent to China," *Fundamentalist*, March 8, 1940.

3. John Birch to Marjorie Tooker, May 15, 1945, folder 5, box 7, RG 197, Whittlesey Papers.

4. On Birch's childhood, see Terry Lautz, *John Birch: A Life* (New York: Oxford University Press, 2016).

5. Deposition of John Birch, March 9, 1939, Heresy trial.

6. Deposition of Birch, Heresy trial.

7. Reid Lunsford to Dr. Spright Dowell, March 31, 1939, Heresy trial; "Students Jeer Heresy Trial," *Mercer Cluster*, March 31, 1939, 1.

8. "Heresy Depositions and Letters," Heresy trial.

9. "Five New Missionaries Sent to China," *Fundamentalist*, March 8, 1940.

10. September 20, 1942, Herman diary.

11. World Fundamental Baptist Missionary Fellowship, Auditor's Report, July 1, 1940, folder 2003, box 44, collection 124, Norris Papers.

12. "Copy of Letter from John M. Birch," *Fundamentalist*, October 4, 1940.

13. Ernest Dale Johnson, *In Search of Ghosts: China Perspectives Past and Present* (Boise, ID: Jet, 1989), 129.

14. "Thrilling Account of How John Birch Escaped from the Japanese," "Letter from John Birch," *Fundamentalist*, February 8, 1942.

15. "John Birch Safe," *Fundamentalist*, January 30, 1942.

16. John Birch to the American Military Mission to China, Chungking, April 13, 1942, Carton 241, MSS 75/97c, Knowland Papers.

CHAPTER 5. "WHAT A FINE SCHOOLING YOU ARE HAVING"

1. V. R. Halsey to Gordon Loud, April 25, 1942, folder 3, box 5, Penrose Papers.

2. Penrose to mother and father, February 24 and May 1, 1942, folder 3, box 1, Penrose Papers.

3. Penrose to mother, May 8, 1942, folder 3, box 1, Penrose Papers.

4. Anne Mayer interview with Margaret (Peggy) Dale Penrose, May 14, 1987, folder 9, box 3, Penrose Papers.

5. Penrose to Virginia, February 25, 1931, folder 2, box 1, Penrose Papers.

6. Stephen B. L. Penrose Sr. to My Dear Binks, October 5, 1929, folder 2, box 1, Penrose Papers.

7. Stephen B. L. Penrose Sr. to My Dear Binks, October 31, 1930, folder 2, box 1, Penrose Papers.

8. Stephen B. L. Penrose Sr. to My Dear Binks, October 31, 1930.

9. Stephen B. L. Penrose Sr. to My Dear Binks, October 5, 1929, folder 2, box 1, Penrose Papers.

10. Stephen B. L. Penrose Sr. to My Dear Binks, January 30, 1933, folder 3, box 1, Penrose Papers.

11. Stephen B. L. Penrose Sr. to My Dear Binks, January 30 and June 1933, folder 3, box 1, Penrose Papers.

12. Extract from the letter of Senorita Perez, June 29, 1934, folder 3, box 1, Penrose Papers; Anne Mayer interview with Margaret (Peggy) Dale Penrose.

13. Albert Staub to W. A. Rowell, September 15, 1942, Near East College Association Records, folder 4, box 3, Burke Library, Columbia University, New York; Penrose to father, January 28, 1942, folder 3, box 1, Penrose Papers.

14. Anne Mayer interview with Margaret (Peggy) Dale Penrose.

CHAPTER 6. "CONVERTED TO OUR SERVICE"

1. Emory Ross to the president, February 3, 1942, and to Donovan, February 3, 1942, frames 698–699, roll 41, M1642, NARA; Donovan, Memorandum for the President, December 14, 1941; Donovan to Grace Tully, December 18, 1941, box 147, President's Secretary's File, FDR Library.

2. Penrose to Mr. Shapiro and Mr. E. B. Price, September 29, 1942, wn 14476, box 377, entry 210, RG 226, NARA.

3. "Expanded Job Descriptions," folder 12, box 5, Penrose Papers.

4. Penrose to Dulles, May 28, 1942, wn 14766, folder 7, box 370, entry 210, RG 226, NARA.

5. Carleton Coon, "The Question of Cover," Torch Anthology, folder 9, box 49, entry 99, RG 226, NARA.

6. Hugh R. Wilson to Dulles, May 28, 1942, folder 29, box 56, entry 92, RG 226, NARA.

7. Penrose to Dulles, May 28, 1942, wn 14766, folder 7, box 370, entry 210, RG 226, NARA.

8. Spencer Phenix to Loud, May 12, 1942, wn 221–225, box 62, entry 210, RG 226, NARA; Penrose to Herrick Young, August 29, 1942, Penrose to J. L. Dodds, June 18, 1942, declassified OSS records folder, box 5, Penrose Papers.

9. Dodds to Penrose, July 24, 1942, declassified OSS records folder, box 5, Penrose Papers.

10. "Report on a Trip Made to West African Coast by A. D. Hutcheson, July 25 to October 25, 1942," wn 22140, box 1, entry 217, RG 226, NARA; Mildred Black, *Laughter and Life in Africa* (Columbus, GA: Brentwood Christian Press, 2003). Jolly apparently got married and continued collecting OSS checks even though she stopped doing OSS work. R. Boulton, "Termination of Relations with Frances Jolly, March 31, 1943," wn 23743, box 14, entry 211, RG 226, NARA.

11. "OSS Undertaking in Liberia," October 26, 1942, wn 12644, folder 2, box 312, entry 210, RG 226, NARA; John McDonough to Peter Karlow, September 3, 1942, Memorandum regarding A. O. G. Missionaries Here and in West Africa, wn 210, box 62, entry 210, RG 226, NARA.

12. Penrose to Mr. Howland, November 12, 1942, declassified OSS records folder, box 5, Penrose Papers.

13. Penrose to John McDonough, June 18, 1942, wn 1534, box 71, entry 210, RG 226, NARA.

14. Penrose to F. M. Potter, June 18, 1942, declassified OSS records folder, box 5, Penrose Papers.

15. Penrose to F. M. Potter, June 22, 1942, declassified OSS records folder, box 5, Penrose Papers.

16. Penrose to Fred F. Goodsell, June 18 and September 5, 1942, declassified OSS records folder, box 5, Penrose Papers.

17. Fred F. Goodsell to Penrose, September 22, 1942; Penrose to Goodsell, December 1, 1942; Goodsell to Penrose, December 23, 1942; Penrose to Goodsell, December 18, 1942, declassified OSS records folder, box 5, Penrose Papers.

18. "Exhibit B," SI Operations, wn 2741, box 74, entry 210, RG 226, NARA; David Williamson to David Bruce, February 12, 1942, wn 14325, box 369, entry 210, RG 226, NARA; Penrose to Mr. Howland, November 12, 1942, declassified OSS records folder, box 5, Penrose Papers.

19. John McDonough to Penrose, June 25, 1942, wn 1533, box 71, entry 210, RG 226, NARA; Subject: Alfred Cookman Snead, November 10, 1942, wn 15030, box 392, entry 210, RG 226, NARA.

20. Penrose to Hugh Wilson, October 13, 1942, wn 14476, box 377, entry 210, RG 226, NARA.

21. Penrose to McDonough, June 18, 1942, wn 1534, box 71, entry 210, RG 226, NARA.

22. "Biographical Information on Glenn S. Rost, June 29, 1942," wn 14803, box 379, entry 210, RG 226, NARA.

23. Penrose to Dulles, June 4, 1942, folder 21, box 61, entry 92, RG 226, NARA (emphasis in the original).

24. Penrose to Dulles, June 4, 1942.

25. Penrose to Dulles, June 4, 1942.

26. Penrose to Robert E. Chandler, August 19, 1942; Penrose to Joe J. Mickle, September 28, 1942, declassified OSS records folder, box 5, Penrose Papers.

27. Eddy, "Manuscripts: 'Adventures in Arab Lands,'" folder 18, box 14, Eddy Papers.

28. Arthur J. Goldberg to Dulles, July 2, 1942, wn 1544, box 71, entry 210, RG 226, NARA. On Goldberg, see David L. Stebenne, *Arthur J. Goldberg: New Deal Liberal* (New York: Oxford University Press, 1996).

29. Donovan to FDR, February 18, 1942, frame 1059, roll 22, M1642, RG 226, NARA.

30. "No. 49, re: Father Morlion," May 23, 1942, Morlion FBI file.

31. Dulles to Robert van der Straten-Ponthos, July 3, 1942, folder 20, box 2, Brady Papers. The following year, the OSS again went to bat for Morlion, asking that the Belgian government renew his exemption from military service. The OSS described his work as of "increasing usefulness in the war effort." Officer John Hughes noted, "It would be quite impossible to find another of Father Morlion's experience and qualities." John C. Hughes to van der Straten-Ponthos, July 16, 1943, folder 22, box 2, Brady Papers.

32. "No. 162, re: Father Morlion," May 23, 1942; "Report, February 2, 1943," Morlion FBI file.

33. See, for example, "T. S. McDermott to Felix Morlion, March 4, 1944," folder 16, box 2, Brady Papers.

34. Memo from F. R. Dolbeare to A. M. Scaife, April 2, 1943, folder 2, box 414, entry 210, RG 226, NARA.

35. R. Boulton, "French West Africa," July 29, 1942, wn 12640, box 312, entry 210, RG 226, NARA; Donovan to FDR, April 20, 1942, frame 101, roll 23, M1642, RG 226, NARA.

CHAPTER 7. "SPIES AND LIES IN TANGIER"

1. Eddy to Mary Eddy, October 12, 1942, folder 10, box 5; Eddy, "Spies and Lies in Tangier," folder 24, box 13, Eddy Papers.

2. Eddy to Mary Eddy, January 27, 1942; Eddy to Jack Eddy, March 1, 1942, folder 10, box 5, Eddy Papers.

3. Eddy to Marycita Eddy, July 25, 1942, folder 8, box 10, Eddy Papers.

4. Eddy to Marycita Eddy, March 27, 1942, folder 10, box 5, Eddy Papers.

5. Eddy to Bill Eddy, March 24, 1942, folder 10, box 5; "The Plan of Attack," Das Reich, November 22, 1942, frames 554–556, roll 35, M1642, RG 226, NARA; Eddy to Marycita Eddy, March 8, 1942, folder 10, box 5, Eddy Papers.

6. Illegible to Eddy, February 25, 1942, frame 1144, roll 34, M1642, RG 226, NARA.

7. Eddy to Mary Eddy, May 13, 1942, folder 10, box 5, Eddy Papers.

8. Carleton Coon, Torch Anthology, section 22, folder 8, box 49, entry 99, RG 226, NARA; Eddy to Marycita Eddy, May 16, 1943, folder 12, box 5; Eddy, "Manuscripts: 'Adventures in Arab Lands,'" folder 18, box 14, Eddy Papers. See also Carleton S. Coon, A North Africa Story: The Anthropologist as OSS Agent, 1941–1943 (Ipswich, MA: Gambit, 1980); and David H. Price, Anthropological Intelligence: The Deployment and Neglect of American Anthropology in the Second World War (Durham, NC: Duke University Press, 2008).

9. "Basic Report, British West Africa, March 29, 1943," wn 786, box 64, entry 210, RG 226, NARA. On the CMA, see also "Memorandum of Interview with Mrs. Kurlak, January 12, 1943; Walter Lord to Edwin Merrill, April 14, 1943; and A. E. Snead to J. J. McDonough, January 22, 1943, wn 15030, box 392, entry 210, RG 226.

10. Carleton Coon, "Dramatis Personnae," Torch Anthology, wn 2525, box 63, entry 210, RG 226.

11. Coon, "Dramatis Personnae."

12. Coon, "Dramatis Personnae."

13. Eddy, "Spies and Lies in Tangier."

14. Eddy, "Manuscripts: 'Adventures in Arab Lands.'"

15. Eddy, "Manuscripts: 'Adventures in Arab Lands.'"

16. Coon, "Dramatis Personnae."

17. Coon, "Dramatis Personnae."

18. Coon, "Dramatis Personnae."

19. Eddy to Jack Eddy, September 27, 1942, folder 8, box 10, Eddy Papers.

20. Eddy to Donovan, March 11, 1942, frame 1036, roll 34, M1642, RG 226, NARA; Robert Murphy, Diplomat Among Warriors (Garden City, NY: Doubleday, 1964), 82.

21. Eddy to Donovan, March 11, 1942, frame 1036, roll 34; and March 19, 1942, frame 1001, roll 34, M1642, RG 226, NARA.

22. Memo, frame 1111, roll 34, M1642; Donovan to FDR, April 13, 1942, frame 146, roll 34, M1642, RG 226, NARA; Donovan to Eddy, April 23, 1942, folder 1, box 46, Robert D. Murphy Papers, Hoover Institution Archives, Stanford University, Stanford, CA.

23. Eddy to Mary Eddy, March 13, 1942; and n.d. [1942?], folder 8, box 10, Eddy Papers.

24. Eddy to Marycita Eddy, May 17, 1942, folder 8, box 10, Eddy Papers.

25. Eddy to Marycita Eddy, September 14, 1942, folder 10, box 5, Eddy Papers.

26. Eddy to Marycita Eddy, April 29, 1942, folder 10, box 5; Eddy to Bill, Mary, and Jack Eddy, September 25, 1941, folder 9, box 5, Eddy Papers.

27. Eddy to Mary Eddy, July 8, 1942, folder 8, box 10, Eddy Papers.

28. Stewart Alsop and Thomas Braden, *Sub Rosa: The O.S.S. and American Espionage* (New York: Reynal & Hitchcock, 1946), 87.

29. Memorandum of Meeting at the St. Regis Hotel, August 21, 1942, wn 12641, box 312, entry 210, RG 226, NARA.

30. Eddy, "Manuscripts: 'Adventures in Arab Lands.'"

31. Memorandum of Meeting at the St. Regis Hotel.

32. Memorandum of Meeting at the St. Regis Hotel.

33. Eddy to Donovan, September 23, 1942, "The Situation Regarding the Possible Use of Moorish Personnel in Military Operations," folder 8, box 43, entry 99, RG 226, NARA.

34. Eddy to Donovan, September 23, 1942.

35. Eddy to Donovan, September 23, 1942.

36. Eddy to Donovan, September 23, 1942. See also Coon to Donovan, October 1, 1942, frames 297ff, roll 35, M1642, RG 226, NARA.

37. Eddy to Donovan, September 23, 1942. Another pamphlet explained of the US soldiers, "They are not as other Christians, for they are friends of the Muslim; They do not wish to destroy our religion nor to trample us underfoot; they do not wish to take our lands or our property, nor to treat us as slaves. They are the lovers of freedom and they are our allies and our friends." Coon to Donovan, "Nationalist Leaflet," October 1, 1942, frame 305, roll 35, M1642, RG 226, NARA.

38. Coon, Torch Anthology, September 6, 1944, folder 6, box 49, entry 99, RG 226, NARA.

39. Donovan to Mary Eddy and Eddy to Mary Eddy, November 9, 1942, folder 10, box 5, Eddy Papers; Eddy to Donovan, February 6, 1943, frame 8, roll 83, M1642, RG 226, NARA; Eddy to Mary Eddy, November 20, 1942, folder 10, box 5, Eddy Papers.

40. Eddy to Jack Eddy, December 6, 1942, folder 10, box 5; Eddy to Mary Eddy, January 29, 1943, folder 12, box 5, Eddy Papers; Eddy to Donovan, February 6, 1943, frame 8, roll 83, M1642, RG 226, NARA; Eddy to Bill Eddy, March 14, 1943, folder 12, box 5, Eddy Papers.

41. Coon, Torch Anthology, September 6, 1944, folder 6, box 49, entry 99, RG 226, NARA.

42. Coon, "Dramatis Personnae"; Donovan to Adjunct General, War Department, July 21, 1945, frames 197–198, roll 45, M1642, RG 226, NARA. See also W. Stafford Reid to History Office, May 23, 1945, folder 3, box 45, entry 99, RG 226, NARA.

43. Eddy, "Manuscripts: 'Adventures in Arab Lands.'"

44. Eddy to Bill Eddy, February 8, 1943, folder 12, box 5, Eddy Papers.

CHAPTER 8. "THE DOUBLE OPPORTUNITY TO SERVE GOD AND COUNTRY"

1. James H. Doolittle with Carroll V. Glines, *I Could Never Be So Lucky Again* (New York: Bantam Books, 1991), 256; Henry A. Potter interview by James C. Hasdorff, June 8–10, 1979, 109, United States Air Force Oral History Program, Albert F. Simpson Historical Research Center.

2. John Birch interview by Fourteenth Air Force Historical Office staff, March 20, 1945, "The Battle of Changteh," Air Force Historical Research Agency, Maxwell Air Force Base, AL, 4.

3. Birch to mother and father, April 27 and May 4, 1942, Knowland Papers. A few weeks later, Doolittle sent off a letter to Norris about "Johnny Birch." Without mincing words, he explained how difficult conditions were for Birch and his fellow missionaries. He warned Norris that missionaries in China needed better support from their agencies. Norris used Doolittle's "rebuke" to try to drum up new support for his fledgling missionary agency. "Personal Letter from General Doolittle," *Fundamentalist*, June 5, 1942.

4. Doolittle, *I Could Never Be So Lucky Again*, 257–258.

5. Birch to mother and father, June 24, 1942, Knowland Papers.

6. Birch, "The Battle of Changteh," 6; "Application for Appointment," "Personal History Statement," Service Documents File, Official Military Personnel File of John M. Birch, NARA-STL.

7. Birch to mother and father, June 24, 1942, Knowland Papers.

8. Arthur H. Hopkins Jr. to Mrs. Birch, n.d., Knowland Papers. Marjorie Tooker also noted that Birch blended into his surroundings, disguising himself as "a Chinese laborer." Marjorie Tooker Whittlesey, "J. B.," unpublished manuscript, folder 10, box 8, Whittlesey Papers. On chaplains in the war, see Ronit Y. Stahl, *Enlisting Faith: How the Military Chaplaincy Shaped Religion and State in Modern America* (Cambridge, MA: Harvard University Press, 2017).

9. "The Reminiscenses of Paul Frillmann, 1963," 299, Oral History Research Office, Butler Library, Columbia University, New York; Thomas G. Trumble, "WWII Biography," http://www.usshawkbill.com/tigers/trumble.htm; Claire Chennault interview with Mrs. George S. Birch, December 10, 1945, Knowland Papers. Robert Lynn later worked for the OSS and recruited another missionary for the OSS, Merrill S. Ady. See the Merrill and Lucille Ady Papers, RG 138, Yale Divinity School, New Haven, CT. Another missionary who did substantial work for the OSS in China was Oliver J. Caldwell. See Oliver J. Caldwell, *A Secret War: Americans in China, 1944–1945* (Carbondale: Southern Illinois University Press, 1972).

10. On Landon and his work for the OSS, see Hollinger, *Protestants Abroad*.

11. Claire Lee Chennault, *Way of a Fighter* (New York: G. P. Putnam's Sons, 1949), 259.

12. Birch, "The Battle of Changteh," 8; Chennault, *Way of a Fighter*, 259.

13. J. C. Williams to Mrs. Geo. S. Birch, March 22, 1946, Knowland Papers.

14. Doolittle, *I Could Never Be So Lucky Again*, 258.

CHAPTER 9. "IT'S YOUR SOULS WE WANT"

1. Herman to family, December 22, 1941, box 20, Herman Papers.

2. Berlin diary, 1939, 78, 117, box 20, Herman Papers.

3. On the internment, see Charles B. Burdick, *An American Island in Hitler's Reich: The Bad Nauheim Internment* (Menlo Park, CA: Markgraf, 1987).

4. End-of-Year Memorandum, 1941, Herman diary.

5. Herman to family, June 2, 1937, box 20; June 8, 1937, Herman diary; Herman to family, April 29, 1937, box 20, Herman Papers. On Martha Dodd, see Larson, *In the Garden*.

6. Herman to family, June 14, 1937, box 20, Herman Papers; June 6, 1937, Herman diary.

7. Herman to family, November 11, 1936; Herman to family, February 14, 1939, box 20, Herman Papers; February 15, 1935, Herman diary.

8. July 30, August 4, December 1, 1942, Herman diary.

9. Stewart W. Herman Jr., "Hitler Can't Do Business with the Church," *Saturday Evening Post*, September 26, 1942, 100; Stewart W. Herman Jr., "The Church in Germany Today," *Christianity and Crisis*, July 26, 1943, 11.

10. Herman, "Christian Church Is German Government's 'Loyal Opposition,'" unpublished manuscript, fall 1942, box 3, Herman Papers.

11. Douglas Miller, "The Nazis Versus God," *New York Times*, March 14, 1943.

12. Herman, *It's Your Souls We Want*, 209, 263.

13. December 15, 1942, Herman diary.

14. End-of-Year Memorandum, 1942, Herman diary.

15. End-of-Year Memorandum, 1942, Herman diary.

16. Ethelyn Cantrell to Herman, November 1, 1943, Herman letters; October 17, 1943, Herman diary.

17. Ethelyn Cantrell to Herman, November 28 and December 17, 1943, Herman letters.

18. "Peacemakers at Princeton Launch a Plan," *Life*, July 26, 1943.

19. Herman to J. R. Lovell, July 7, 1943, and J. R. Lovell to General Kramer, July 12, 1943, box 14, Herman Papers.

20. July 17, 1943, Herman diary; Herman to family, September 13, 1943, box 20, Herman Papers.

21. Stewart Herman Personnel File, box 330, entry 224, RG 226, NARA.

22. June 12, 1936, Herman diary; F. L. Mayer to Security Office, August 24, 1943, folder 1775, box 88, entry 92A, RG 226, NARA.

23. August 17 and August 19, 1943, Herman diary.

24. August 16–17, 1943, Herman diary.

25. Donovan to E. E. Flack, August 23, 1943; Flack to Donovan, August 30, 1943, folder 1775, box 88, entry 92A, RG 226, NARA.

26. End-of-Year Memorandum, 1943, Herman diary.

27. November 5 and November 7, 1943, Herman diary.

28. End-of-Year Memorandum, 1943, Herman diary.

29. End-of-Year Memorandum, 1943, Herman diary; Herman to family, November 28, 1943, box 20, Herman Papers; February 15, 1944, and December 23, 1943, Herman diary.

30. Herman to Cantrell, January 4, 1944, Herman letters.

31. January 10 and January 11, 1944, Herman diary; Herman to Cantrell, Wednesday [February 16], 1944, Herman letters; Herman to family, February 15, box 20, Herman Papers.

32. Herman to Cantrell, March 21 and February 25, 1944, Herman letters.

33. Cantrell to Herman, August 17 and February 21, 1944, Herman letters.

34. Herman to Cantrell, February 25, 1944; Cantrell to Herman, March 6 and March 9, 1944, Herman letters.

35. Cantrell to Herman, March 12, 1944; Herman to Cantrell, March 1, 1944, Herman letters.

36. "History of the London Office of the OSS, 1942–1945," frame 975, roll 9, M1623, RG 226, NARA; January 22, 1944, Herman diary.

37. Herman to family, March 21, 1944, box 20, Herman Papers; March 7, 1944, Herman diary.

38. "In Bombed Berlin," *New York Times*, December 10, 1943; December 17, 1943, Herman diary. There is some ambiguity as to whether the picture depicting what editors identified as the ruins of the American Church in Berlin was actually the American church, but the paper correctly noted that the church was reduced to rubble that week.

CHAPTER 10. "THE NEXT JUMP"

1. On the role of the Mediterranean in the war, see Andrew Buchanan, *American Grand Strategy in the Mediterranean During World War II* (Cambridge: Cambridge University Press, 2014).

2. "Report from Algiers," folder 1, box 45, entry 99, RG 226, NARA.

3. Eddy to Jack Eddy, February 28, 1943, "SGS Censorship," roll 70, box 294, entry AFHQ microfilm, RG 331, NARA.

4. Max Corvo, *The O.S.S. in Italy, 1942–1945: A Personal Memoir* (New York: Praeger, 1990), 62; Mary Eddy to Bill and Marycita Eddy, July 13, 1943, folder 12, box 5, Eddy Papers.

5. Eddy to Carmen Eddy, February 28, 1943, and Eddy to Mary Eddy, February 28, 1943, in "SGS Censorship," roll 70, box 294, entry AFHQ microfilm, RG 331, NARA.

6. Lowell W. Rooks, "Violation of Censorship," March 13, 1943, "SGS Censorship," roll 70, box 294, AFHQ microfilm, RG 331.

7. Eddy to Marycita Eddy, May 16, 1943, folder 12, box 5; Eddy to Mary Eddy, April 20, 1943[?], folder 13, box 5; Eddy to Marycita Eddy, May 30, 1943, folder 12, box 5; Eddy to family, September 10, 1943 [page 2], folder 12, box 5, Eddy Papers.

8. Eddy to family, September 10, 1943 [page 2]; Eddy to Marycita Eddy, July 4, 1943, folder 12, box 5, Eddy Papers.

9. Eddy to Marycita Eddy, June 21, 1943, folder 12, box 5, Eddy Papers.

10. Mary Eddy to Bill and Marycita Eddy, July 13, 1943, folder 12, box 5, Eddy Papers; C. A. Bane to Edward Glavin, February 1, 1946, frame 192, roll 45, M1642, RG 226, NARA.

11. Eddy to R. A. Winnacker, August 18, 1943, folder 990, box 93, entry 144, RG 226, NARA; J. Ray Olivera to Chief, West European Division, May 6, 1943, wn 14225, box 377, entry 210, RG 226, NARA.

12. Eddy to Assistant Chief of Staff, September 18, 1943, frame 658ff, roll 34, M1642, RG 226, NARA.

13. Corvo, *O.S.S. in Italy*, 99.

14. Eddy to Donovan, September 11, 1943, folder 986, box 93, entry 144, RG 226, NARA.

15. Ellery Huntington Jr. to Eddy, October 23, 1943, folder 988, box 93, entry 144, RG 226, NARA.

16. H. H. Newman to William Eddy, October 18, 1943, folder 7, box 11, Eddy Papers; Ellery Huntington Jr. to Eddy, October 23, 1943, folder 988, box 93, entry 144, RG 226, NARA; Edward Stettinius Jr. to Donovan, November 9, 1943, frame 174, roll 45, M1642, RG 226, NARA.

Chapter 11. "A Great Hodge-Podge of Conflicting Loyalties"

1. "History of the Near East Section, O.S.S. Cairo, May 15 1943–15 September 1944," wn 11384, box 261, entry 210, RG 226, NARA.

2. On US intelligence operations in the Middle East, see Osamah F. Khalil, *America's Dream Palace: Middle East Expertise and the Rise of the National Security State* (Cambridge, MA: Harvard University Press, 2016).

3. Cordell Hull to Ambassador Winant, August 27, 1942, in FRUS, *1942: The Near East and Africa* (Washington, DC: Government Printing Office, 1942), vol. 4, document 20.

4. Harold Hoskins, "The Present Situation in the Near East, Part I, April 20, 1943," frame 747, roll 79, M1642, RG 226, NARA.

5. Penrose to Mr. Shepardson, January 26, 1943, frame 701, roll 79, M1642, RG 226, NARA.

6. "Outline of SI, OSS/Cairo, History," folder 1, box 55, entry 99, RG 226, NARA.

7. Sterling Hayden, *Wanderer* (New York: Alfred A. Knopf, 1963), 310; Penrose to Peggy Penrose, May 18, 1943, Dale Penrose Papers.

8. "Outline of SI, OSS/Cairo, History," folder 1, box 55, entry 99, RG 226, NARA; "History of the Near East Division, S.I., April 1942–September 1944," folder 44, box 75, entry 190, RG 226, NARA; Cairo History, folder 2, box 55, entry 99, RG 226, NARA.

9. Muggeridge, *Chronicles of Wasted Time*, 447; "Outline of SI, OSS/Cairo, History."

10. "Memorandum for General Roberts, Subject: US Policy on Iran, October 31, 1944," "Iran," box 222, entry 421, RG 165, NARA. On the OSS in Persia, see Adrian O'Sullivan, *Espionage and Counterintelligence in Occupied Persia (Iran)* (New York: Palgrave Macmillan, 2015).

11. "Preliminary Report of Trip of S. B. L. Penrose, Jr., Aug–Sept., 1943," wn 25969, box 3, entry 215, RG 226, NARA.

12. Penrose to John McDonough, August 11, 1942, wn 1531, box 71, entry 210, RG 226, NARA; B. J. Maunsell to US Liaison, August 12, 1943, wn 11223, box 260, entry 210, RG 226, NARA.

13. Oral history interview with Edwin M. Wright by Richard D. McKinzie, July 26, 1974, Truman Library, https://www.trumanlibrary.org/oralhist/wright.htm.

14. On the Soviet intelligence apparatus, see Hastings, *Secret War*.

15. Floyd S. Fierman, "Nelson Glueck and the OSS During World War II," 1, Fierman Papers. On Glueck, see also Jonathan M. Brown and Laurence Kutler, *Nelson Glueck: Biblical Archeologist and President of Hebrew Union College–Jewish Institute of Religion* (Detroit: Hebrew Union College Press, 2005).

16. David Williamson to David Bruce, February 12, 1942, wn 14325, box 369, entry 210, RG 226, NARA.

17. Nelson Glueck to Wallace B. Phillips, December 12, 1941; Glueck, Curriculum Vitae; Williamson to Bruce, February 24, 1942, wn 14334, box 369, entry 210, RG 226, NARA.

18. Helen Glueck to Floyd S. Fierman, November 17, [year?], Fierman Papers; Nelson Glueck, report on work in the field, August 20, 1945, wn 14334, box 369, entry 210, RG 226, NARA; Nelson Glueck, "Report on Field Conditions, August 17, 1945," wn 14334, box 369, entry 210, RG 226, NARA.

19. Williamson to Bruce, Hutcheson, and Rehm, February 28, 1942, wn 14334, box 369, entry 210, RG 226, NARA.

20. Penrose to Loud, July 10, 1943, folder 70, box 76, entry 190, RG 226, NARA.

21. Penrose to Loud, July 10, 1943.

22. Penrose to Loud, August 5, 1943, folder 70, box 76, entry 190, RG 226, NARA.

23. Penrose to Ernest O. Holland, January 1, 1943, wn 14476, box 377, entry 210, RG 226, NARA.

24. David Ben-Gurion to Donovan, December 5, 1941, frame 238, roll 61, M1642, RG 226, NARA; John C. Wiley to Donovan, May 27, 1942, frame 543–544, roll 1, M1642, RG 226, NARA.

25. Advertisement: "A Proclamation," *New York Times*, December 7, 1942.

26. Penrose to Holland, December 10, 1942, wn 14476, box 377, entry 210, RG 226, NARA.

27. Penrose to mother and father, May 1, 1942, folder 3, box 1, Penrose Papers.

28. Penrose to John G. Kelly, February 4, 1943, folder 61, box 23, entry 92, RG 226, NARA; Penrose to Major Bruce, January 14, 1943, folder 70, box 76, entry 190, RG 226, NARA.

29. Cairo History, folder 2, box 55, entry 99, RG 226, NARA.

30. Penrose to Loud, July 31, 1943, folder 70, box 76, entry 190, RG 226, NARA.

31. J. A. Brown to Dulles, July 24, 1942, wn 1532, box 71, entry 210, RG 226, NARA; Dulles to Penrose, July 16, 1942, folder 50, box 102, entry 92, RG 226, NARA; Penrose to Whitney H. Shepardson, December 19, 1944, folder 13, box 72, entry 190, RG 226, NARA; Donovan to FDR, October 13, 1944, box 150, President's Secretary's File, FDR Library.

32. Penrose to Loud, July 28, 1943, wn 25970, box 3, entry 215, RG 226, NARA.

33. Penrose to Loud, July 21, 1943, folder 4, box 5, Penrose Papers; Nelson Glueck, newsletter no. 1, January 3, 1943, American School of Oriental Research, "Nelson Glueck," box 10, entry 169, RG 226, NARA.

34. Archie S. Crawford to Loud, August 19, 1943, wn 25974, box 3, entry 215, RG 226, NARA; Penrose to Major Keep, March 24, 1944, wn 22959, box 4, entry 211, RG 226, NARA.

35. Loud to Penrose, July 27, 1943, folder 70, box 76, entry 190, RG 226, NARA; Penrose to Loud, July 28, 1943, wn 25970, box 3, entry 215, RG 226, NARA.

36. "Near East Section Report, April 15, 1944," wn 11383, box 261, entry 210, RG 226, NARA; "Preliminary Report of Trip of S. B. L. Penrose, Jr., Aug–Sept., 1943," wn 25969, box 3, entry 215, RG 226, NARA.

37. Penrose to Peggy Penrose, April 28, 1944, Dale Penrose Papers.

CHAPTER 12. "THE ANGRY SAINT WHO KEPT A SOLDIER'S FAITH"

1. James Hart to Mr. and Mrs. Birch, March 7, 1947, Knowland Papers.
2. Birch to Dear folks, September 21, 1943, folder 152, box 4, Norris Papers.
3. Paul W. Frillmann to Mrs. Birch, n.d., Knowland Papers.
4. Arthur H. Hopkins Jr. to Mrs. Birch, n.d., Knowland Papers; Birch, "The Battle of Changteh," 12.
5. Chennault, *Way of a Fighter*, 259; Birch, "The Battle of Changteh," 13.
6. Birch, "The Battle of Changteh," 11; Wilfred Smith to Mrs. Birch, June 18, 1947, Knowland Papers.
7. Birch, "The Battle of Changteh," 11.
8. Birch, "The Battle of Changteh," 12; Birch to Dear folks, September 21, 1943, folder 152, box 4, Norris Papers.
9. Birch to folks, April 20, 1943, Knowland Papers; Arthur H. Hopkins Jr. to Mrs. Birch, n.d., Knowland Papers; Claire Chennault interview with Mrs. George S. Birch, December 10, 1945, Knowland Papers; Birch to mother, December 30, 1943, folder 152, box 4, Norris Papers.
10. John Birch, "The Fundamental Baptist Bible Institute: A Student Testimony," *Fundamentalist*, June 7, 1940; Wilfred Smith to Mrs. Birch, June 18, 1947, Knowland Papers.
11. Lieutenant Colonel Fred P. Manget to Mr. and Mrs. Birch, October 30, 1943, folder 152, box 4, Norris Papers.
12. Birch to J. Frank Norris, April 6, 1944; Birch to Dear folks, September 21, 1943, folder 152, box 4, Norris Papers.
13. "Reminiscenses of Paul Frillmann," 323; Paul Frillmann and Graham Peck, *China: The Remembered Life* (Boston: Houghton Mifflin, 1968), 186; Birch to Norris, April 6, 1944, folder 152, box 4, Norris Papers; Wilfred Smith to Mrs. Birch, June 18, 1947, Knowland Papers.
14. Birch to mother, December 30, 1943, folder 152, box 4, Norris Papers; Birch to Dear Aunt May, March 1944, Knowland Papers.
15. James Tull to Mr. Birch, n.d.; Arthur H. Hopkins Jr. to Mrs. Birch, n.d., Knowland Papers.
16. Birch to mother, December 30, 1943, folder 152, box 4, Norris Papers.
17. Birch quoted in Lautz, *John Birch: A Life*, 107.
18. Birch quoted in Lautz, *John Birch: A Life*, 108.
19. Birch quoted in Lautz, *John Birch: A Life*, 109.
20. Birch to Norris, April 6, 1944, folder 152, box 4, Norris Papers.
21. Birch to Norris, April 6, 1944; "John Birch Promoted to Three High Honors," *Fundamentalist*, March 26, 1943.
22. Birch quoted in Lautz, *John Birch: A Life*, 109, 110.

CHAPTER 13. "THE THOROUGH BEATING THEY SO RICHLY DESERVE"

1. March 21, 1944, Herman diary.
2. Kermit Roosevelt, *The Overseas Targets: War Report of the OSS* (New York: Walker, 1975), 2:305.

3. T. G. Early to Colonel Glavin, "Establishment of a Central European Desk," May 24, 1944, folder 533, box 31, entry 97, RG 226, NARA.

4. Herman to family, April 16, 1944, box 20, Herman Papers; Herman to Cantrell, May 19, 1944, Herman letters; Herman to family, May 28, 1944, box 20, Herman Papers.

5. October 16, 1944, Herman diary. On Berg, see Nicholas Dawidoff, *The Catcher Was a Spy: The Mysterious Life of Moe Berg* (New York: Vintage Books, 1994).

6. Cantrell to Herman, March 15, 1944, Herman letters.

7. Herman to Cantrell, June 11 and June 17, 1944; Cantrell to Herman, June 23, 1944, Herman letters.

8. Herman to Cantrell, June 11 and June 27, 1944, Herman letters.

9. Herman to Joseph F. Haskell, "Mid-Monthly Report of Central European Section, August 14, 1944," folder 6, box 2, entry 99, RG 226, NARA; "History of the London Office of the OSS, 1942–1945," frame 981, roll 9, M1623, RG 226, NARA.

10. Francis Pickens Miller, *Man from the Valley: Memoirs of a 20th-Century Virginian* (Chapel Hill: University of North Carolina Press, 1971), 56.

11. Herman to family, May 7, 1944, box 20, Herman Papers.

12. Waller, *Wild Bill Donovan*.

13. Herman to family, June 7, 1944, box 20, Herman Papers; Herman to Cantrell, August 24, 1944, Herman letters.

14. Herman to family, June 14 and June 21, 1944, box 20, Herman Papers; Cantrell to Herman, October 28, 1944, Herman letters; June 2, 1944, Herman diary.

15. Herman to Joseph F. Haskell, "Mid-Monthly Report of Central European Section, August 14, 1944," folder 6, box 2, entry 99, RG 226, NARA; Herman to Joseph F. Haskell, "Progress Report of Central European Section, August 1944," folder 5, box 2, entry 99, RG 226, NARA; September 25, 1944, Herman diary.

16. Herman to Dulles, October 13, 1944, "Personnel Survey of Possible Candidates for Staff of Austrian Operations," folder 66, box 333, entry 190, RG 226, NARA.

17. Hastings, *Secret War*, 8.

18. On Hall, see Elizabeth P. McIntosh, *Sisterhood of Spies: The Women of the OSS* (New York: Dell, 1998).

19. On Herman's work with Hall, see folder 55, box 332, entry 190, RG 226, NARA.

20. Alsop and Braden, *Sub Rosa*, 37; "Report on the Cover and Documents Branch of the G-2 Strategic Services Section, May 8, 1945," wn 98, box 3, entry 210, RG 226, NARA.

21. Minutes of Meeting, April 17, 1944, wn 912, box 45, entry 210, RG 226, NARA; Herman to Joseph F. Haskell, "Mid-Monthly Report of Central European Section, September 13, 1944," folder 1, box 3, entry 99, RG 226, NARA. See also "Report of the Activities of Jack Smith, September 1, 1944–April 9, 1945," wn 912, box 45, entry 210, RG 226, NARA; and Arthur Goldberg to Mortimer Kollender, June 21, 1944, folder 553, box 32, entry 97, RG 226, NARA.

22. Joseph Haskell to Donovan, August 8, 1944, frame 41, roll 81, M1642, RG 226, NARA; "History of the London Office of the OSS, 1942–1945," frame 1007, roll 9, M1623, RG 226, NARA; Donovan to FDR, Memorandum for the President, September 2, 1944, box 153, President's Secretary's File, FDR Library.

23. Herman to Gerald E. Miller, September 15, 1944, folder 69, box 333, entry 190, RG 226, NARA. Herman was undoubtedly influenced by the interwar ecumenical movement in the United States, which focused on postwar planning. See Gene Zubovich, "The Global Gospel: Protestant Internationalism and American Liberalism, 1940–1960" (PhD diss., University of California, Berkeley, 2015).

24. Cantrell to Herman, May 9, 1944, Herman letters.

25. "History of the London Office of the OSS, 1942–1945," frame 985, roll 9, M1623, RG 226, NARA; "Suggested Rumors Prepared by Central European Section," folder 54, box 332, entry 190, RG 226, NARA; Herman to Joseph F. Haskell, "Mid-Monthly Report of Central European Section, August 14, 1944," folder 6, box 2, entry 99, RG 226, NARA; Herman to Joseph F. Haskell, "Progress Report of Central European Section, August 1944," folder 5, box 2, entry 99, RG 226, NARA.

26. Herman to Planning and Operations Committee, September 28, 1944, folder 69, box 333, entry 190, RG 226, NARA.

27. "Note on Broadcasts for Psychological Warfare in Religious Circles of Occupied Europe," folder 312, "Catholic Intelligence," box 62, entry 106, RG 226, NARA.

28. Herman to family, July 13 and August 19, 1944, box 20, Herman Papers.

29. Herman to Herbert Pell, June 5, 1944, box 14; Herman to family, April 22 and August 19, 1944, box 20, Herman Papers.

30. Herman to family, July 25, 1944, box 20, Herman Papers.

31. Herman to family, October 4, 1944, box 20, Herman Papers.

32. August 18, 1944, Herman diary; Herman to Cantrell, November 2, 1944, Herman letters.

33. Herman to Cantrell, July 10, 1944, Herman letters.

34. Herman to Cantrell, October 7 and August 6, 1944; Cantrell to Herman, August 24, 1944, Herman letters.

35. Herman, "CES-SO Interest in Recruitment and Use of P/Ws," November 21, 1944, folder 163, box 340, entry 190, RG 226, NARA.

36. Herman to Charles Eubank, February 6, 1945, folder 1775, box 88, entry 92A, RG 226, NARA.

37. End-of-Year Memorandum, 1944, Herman diary. Herman was referring here to what would later be called the "Battle of the Bulge."

CHAPTER 14. "AMERICA'S ONE PRIORITY IN THE ARAB WORLD"

1. Eddy to Director, Naval Intelligence, September 10, 1941, folder 6, box 11, Eddy Papers.

2. John A. Wilson to Donovan, July 8, 1942, Fierman Papers.

3. "Memorandum of Conversation, by Lieutenant Colonel Harold B. Hoskins, September 27, 1943," FRUS, Diplomatic Papers, 1943: The Near East and Africa, vol. 4, document 850.

4. Secretary of State to Eddy, January 28, 1944, folder 7, box 11, Eddy Papers.

5. Eddy to Mary Eddy, March 16 and March 21, 1944, folder 13, box 5, Eddy Papers.

6. Eddy to Mary Eddy, March 16, 1944, folder 13, box 5, Eddy Papers.

7. Eddy to Mary Eddy, March 24, 1944, folder 13, box 5; September 5, 1944, folder 3, box 3, Eddy Papers.

8. Eddy to Mary Eddy, March 21 and March 25, 1944, folder 13, box 5, Eddy Papers.

9. Eddy to family, April 27, 1944, folder 13, box 5, Eddy Papers.

10. Gustav, Cairo to Donovan, Official Dispatch, March 18, 1944, frame 184, roll 45, M1642, RG 226, NARA.

11. Cordell Hull to FDR, Memorandum for the President, May 31, 1944, OF 5552, President's Official File, FDR Library.

12. Memorandum to the Officer in Charge, June 30, 1944, frame 171, roll 45, M1642, RG 226, NARA.

13. Eddy to Mary Eddy, September 5 and September 14, 1944, folder 3, box 3, Eddy Papers.

14. Eddy to Mary Eddy, September 8, 1944, folder 3, box 3; August 28, 1944, folder 13, box 5; September 14, 1944, folder 3, box 3; October 19, 1944, folder 13, box 5, Eddy Papers.

15. Mary Eddy to family, March 28 and March 10, 1945, folder 4, box 3, Eddy Papers.

16. Mary Eddy to Marycita, November 7, 1944, folder 3, box 3, Eddy Papers.

17. Eddy to Carmen Eddy, January 23, 1945; Eddy to Bill Eddy, January 3, 1945, folder 4, box 3, Eddy Papers.

18. Eddy to Mary Eddy, September 5, 1944, folder 3, box 3, Eddy Papers.

19. "Saudi Arabia," wn 1424, box 56, entry 210, RG 226, NARA; Penrose to Eddy, December 28, 1944, folder 70, box 76, entry 190, RG 226, NARA.

20. "Meeting with Colonel Eddy," n.d., wn 10240, box 235, entry 210, RG 226, NARA.

CHAPTER 15. "TOP-NOTCH AND ABSOLUTELY FEARLESS"

1. "History of OSS Cairo," folder 1, box 54, entry 99, RG 226, NARA.

2. Hart interview.

3. Penrose to Peggy Penrose, May 17, 1944, Dale Penrose Papers.

4. Penrose to Peggy Penrose, August 6 and August 25, 1944, Dale Penrose Papers; Hart interview.

5. Penrose to W. T. M. Beale Jr., October 7, 1944, folder 8, box 5, Penrose Papers.

6. Hart interview.

7. Penrose to Peggy Penrose, July 16, 1944, Dale Penrose Papers.

8. Penrose to Peggy Penrose, December 18, 1944, Dale Penrose Papers; Penrose to Shepardson, November 21, folder 8, box 5, Penrose Papers.

9. Penrose to Shepardson, August 10, 1944, folder 7, box 5, Penrose Papers; Penrose to Robert P. Joyce, August 5, 1944, wn 11112, box 255, entry 210, RG 226, NARA. See also Penrose to Lt. Kennedy, August 8, 1944, wn 11111, box 255, entry 210, RG 226, NARA.

10. Wilford, *Mighty Wurlitzer*, 19–20. See also Peter Grose, *Operation Rollback: America's Secret War Behind the Iron Curtain* (Boston: Houghton Mifflin, 2000); and Evan Thomas, *The Very Best Men: Four Who Dared—the Early Years of the CIA* (New York: Simon & Schuster, 1995).

11. Penrose to Horace Andrews, September 20, 1944, folder 8, box 5, Penrose Papers.

12. On Keszthelyi's relationship and mission, see Sonya N. Jason, *Maria Gulovich, OSS Heroine of World War II* (Jefferson, NC: McFarland, 2008).

13. On the Keszthelyi mission, see "Dawes Team," War Crimes Office, June 8, 1946, file no. 8–9, box 116, entry 143, RG 153, NARA; "Operational History, Dawes and

Associated Teams, January 27, 1945," folder 1, box 22, entry 190, RG 226, NARA; Keszthelyi file, folder 1022, box 58, entry 92A, RG 226, NARA; and Keszthelyi Personnel File, box 402, entry 224, RG 226, NARA.

14. Penrose to Peggy Penrose, December 31, 1944, Dale Penrose Papers; Hart interview.

15. Penrose to Dale Penrose (Harrell), June 25, 1944; Penrose to Peggy Penrose, April 28, 1944, Dale Penrose Papers.

16. Penrose to Peggy Penrose, April 28, May 17, and October 16, 1944, Dale Penrose Papers.

17. Robert K. Enders to H. L. Robinson, October 27, 1943, wn 14334, box 369, entry 210, RG 226, NARA.

18. Nelson Glueck, "On the Trail of King Solomon's Mines," *National Geographic*, February 1944.

19. Loud to Shepardson, February 2, 1943, Fierman Papers; Lewis Leary to Bill Hicks [Nelson Glueck], March 1, 1944; Hicks [Glueck] to Leary, June 16, 1944, wn 14335, box 369, entry 210, RG 226, NARA.

20. Leary to Hicks [Glueck], March 1, 1944, and March 27, 1945, wn 14335, box 369, entry 210, RG 226, NARA.

21. Leary to Hicks [Glueck], April 26, 1944; Hicks [Glueck] to Leary, March 7, 1944, wn 14335, box 369, entry 210, RG 226, NARA; Leary to Penrose, June 23, 1944, wn 14335, box 369, entry 210, RG 226, NARA.

22. Leary, "File Memorandum, September 12, 1944," wn 14334, box 369, entry 210, RG 226.

23. Leary to Loud, May 24, 1944, wn 14335, box 369, entry 210, RG 226, NARA; Penrose to Loud, September 14, 1944, wn 11219, box 260, entry 210, RG 226, NARA.

24. Leary to Loud, May 24, 1944; Penrose to Loud, September 14, 1944; Leary, "William Hicks [Nelson Glueck] Performance Review," wn 14334, box 369, entry 210, RG 226, NARA; "Objectives of Hicks Mission, September 7, 1944," wn 14335, box 369, entry 210, RG 226, NARA.

25. Hicks [Glueck] to Leary, March 30, 1944; Hicks [Glueck], "Suggestions for Future Work," June 21, 1944, wn 14335, box 369, entry 210, RG 226, NARA.

26. "Propositions by Mr. Schachter of the Jewish Agency for Supply of Agents to the O.S.S.," folder 1281, box 172, entry 190, RG 226, NARA.

27. Howard M. Chapin to Penrose, July 24, 1944, folder 1281, box 172, entry 190, RG 226, NARA; "Propositions by Mr. Schachter of the Jewish Agency for Supply of Agents to the O.S.S."

28. C. T. S. Keep to Penrose, June 13, 1944, folder 1281, box 172, entry 190, RG 226, NARA.

29. Penrose to Chapin, August 1, 1944, folder 1281, box 172, entry 190, RG 226, NARA.

30. Penrose to Chapin, August 1, 1944; Penrose to Frank G. Wisner, August 24, 1944, wn 10250, box 235, entry 210, RG 226, NARA.

31. Carl Devoe to Penrose, September 16, 1944, folder 32, box 73, entry 190, RG 226, NARA.

32. Penrose to Devoe, September 22, 1944, folder 32, box 73, entry 190, RG 226, NARA; Leonard Appel to Goldberg and Devoe, December 20, 1944, wn 11125, box 260, entry 210, RG 226, NARA.

33. "History of the Labor Section, SI-ME, to 15 September 1944," wn 11132, box 260, entry 210, RG 226, NARA.

34. John E. Toulmin to Commanding General, November 11, 1944, Penrose Personnel File, box 595, entry 224, RG 226, NARA.

35. Penrose to Peggy Penrose, December 18, 1944, Dale Penrose Papers.

CHAPTER 16. "THE BEGINNING OF THE END OF JAPAN'S UNGODLY POWER"

1. On the OSS in China, see Maochun Yu, OSS in China: Prelude to Cold War (New Haven, CT: Yale University Press, 1996).

2. On Moran, see Hollinger, Protestants Abroad.

3. Donovan to FDR, June 5, 1943, folder 42, box 119B, Donovan Papers. See also "Dalai Lama, The," folder 8108, President's Personal File, FDR Library; and Ilia Tolstoy, "Across Tibet from India to China," National Geographic, August 1946.

4. Alsop and Braden, Sub Rosa, 199. See also "Report by Father Stewart on the Help Given 'Merrill's Marauders' by the Kachins," folder 14, box 71, entry 99, RG 226, NARA.

5. Chief, SI, to Director, OSS, memorandum, February 21, 1945, frame 849, roll 82, M1642, RG 226, NARA. The OSS recruited numerous missionaries for fieldwork, including Horace B. Underwood, who then helped the agency identify additional missionaries for the OSS who had served in Asia. See wn 18685 and wn 18687, box 507; wn 18812, box 508; wn 18669, wn 18291, wn 18292, and wn 18651, box 513, entry 210, RG 226, NARA.

6. Special Orders Number 118, May 25, 1944; "Birch, John M." [service card], February 2, 1943, folder 48 (John Birch), box 57, entry 224, RG 226, NARA; Chennault, Way of a Fighter, 260; Birch, "The Battle of Changteh," 19, 20; Wilfred Smith to Mrs. Birch, June 18, 1947, Knowland Papers.

7. "C.B.I. Report," September 1944, folder 13, box 71, entry 99, RG 226, NARA.

8. Chennault, Way of a Fighter, 260; Johnson, In Search of Ghosts, 131.

9. Birch to father and mother, May 7, 1944, folder 152, box 4, Norris Papers.

10. "C.B.I. Report," September 1944; Drummond to Coughlin, October 20, 1944, folder 3, box 76, entry 99, RG 226, NARA.

11. Birch, "The Battle of Changteh," 17.

12. T. C. Gleysteen memo, August 24, 1944, folder 180, box 34, entry 182, RG 226, NARA; Birch, "The Battle of Changteh," 23; Birch to mother, August 8 and August 5, 1944, folder 152, box 4, Norris Papers.

13. Birch, "The Battle of Changteh," 23; Birch to little sister, n.d., folder 152, box 4, Norris Papers.

14. Whittlesey, "J. B."

15. Whittlesey, "J. B."

16. Whittlesey, "J. B."

17. Whittlesey, "J. B."

18. Whittlesey, "J. B."

19. Whittlesey, "J. B."

20. Birch to Tooker, March 21, 1945, folder 5, box 7, Whittlesey Papers.

21. Whittlesey, "J. B."

22. Whittlesey, "J. B."

23. Birch to Tooker, March 21, 1945, folder 5, box 7, Whittlesey Papers; Whittlesey, "J. B."

24. Birch to Tooker, March 21 and May 15, 1945, folder 5, box 7, Whittlesey Papers.

25. Whittlesey, "J. B."

26. Whittlesey, "J. B."

27. "C.B.I. Report," September 1944.

28. "Awards of the Legion of Merit, July 17, 1944," Service Documents File, Official Military Personnel File of John M. Birch, NARA-STL; Birch to mother, September 22, 1944, folder 152, box 4, Norris Papers.

29. Birch to mother, September 22, 1944, folder 152, box 4, Norris Papers; Chennault, *Way of a Fighter*, 259.

30. Office Memo, September 30, 1944, John Birch folder, box 2, entry 197, RG 226, NARA; Arthur H. Hopkins Jr. to Mrs. Birch, n.d., Knowland Papers.

31. William Drummond dictated to Mrs. George S. Birch, December 31, 1945; Claire Chennault interview with Mrs. George S. Birch, December 10, 1945, Knowland Papers.

32. Johnson, *In Search of Ghosts*, 125, 127, 130.

33. Frillmann and Peck, *China: The Remembered Life*, 186.

34. Wilfred Smith to Mrs. Birch, June 18, 1947, Knowland Papers.

35. William Drummond dictated to Mrs. George S. Birch, December 31, 1945, Knowland Papers.

36. Donovan to FDR, Memorandum for the President, December 23, 1944, folder 8108, box 151, President's Secretary's File, FDR Library.

37. Birch to Dear folks, December 14, 1944, folder 152, box 4, Norris Papers

38. Birch to Dear folks, December 14, 1944; Birch to Dear Aunt May, March 1944, Knowland Papers.

CHAPTER 17. "PILGRIM'S PROGRESS"

1. Donovan to FDR, Memorandum for the President, July 3, 1944, box 149, President's Secretary's File, FDR Library. Michael Graziano has an excellent article on the OSS and the Catholic Church. See "William Donovan, the Office of Strategic Services, and Catholic Intelligence Sources During World War II," *US Catholic Historian* 33, no. 4 (2015): 79–103.

2. On Nazi efforts to spy on the Catholic Church, see David Alvarez, *Spies in the Vatican: Espionage and Intrigue from Napoleon to the Holocaust* (Lawrence: University Press of Kansas, 2002).

3. On the pope's work in supporting anti-Hitler espionage, see Mark Riebling, *Church of Spies: The Pope's Secret War Against Hitler* (New York: Basic Books, 2015).

4. Lovell, *Of Spies and Stratagems*, 92.

5. Frederic R. Dolbeare to Alan M. Scaife, December 29, 1943, wn 15556, box 414, entry 210, RG 226, NARA.

6. Hugh R. Wilson to Frederic R. Dolbeare, December 4, 1943, wn 14614, box 297, entry 210, RG 226, NARA.

7. Huntington Harris, "Field Report on the 'Pilgrim's Progress Project,'" November 15, 1945, wn 24939, box 3, entry 216, RG 226, NARA.

8. See folder 16, box 2, Brady Papers.

9. Hughes to van der Straten-Ponthos, July 7, 1944, folder 24, box 2, Brady Papers.

10. Zsolt Aradi to Chief SI, November 27, 1944, "Intelligence Through the Vatican"; Aradi to Chief SI, December 16, 1944, "Vatican Contacts," wn 13380, box 327, entry 210, RG 226, NARA.

11. Grey to Frederic R. Dolbeare, November 26, 1944, wn 11890, box 311, entry 210, RG 226, NARA; Dolbeare to Dulles, November 9, 1944, wn 15556, box 414, entry 210.

12. Some sources are identified in wn 11890, box 311, entry 210, RG 226, NARA.

13. Robert DeVecchi to Ferdinand L. Mayer, December 7, 1944, wn 15556, box 414, entry 210, RG 226, NARA.

14. Mayer to DeVecchi, December 4, 1944, wn 15556, box 414, entry 210, RG 226, NARA; Mayer to Dolbeare, January 5, 1945, wn 15556, box 414, entry 210, RG 226, NARA; M. B. Ogle Jr. to Lester C. Houck, April 4, 1945, wn 15557, box 415, entry 210, RG 226, NARA; Houck to Shepardson, July 23, 1945, wn 15557, box 415, entry 210, RG 226, NARA. See also Hughes to Shepardson, February 3, 1945, folder 98, box 7, entry 92A, RG 226, NARA.

15. Penrose to Dorothy Wentworth, October 17, 1945, wn 15557, box 415, entry 210, RG 226, NARA.

16. John Magruder to Caserta, January 6, 1945, frame 3, roll 119, M1642, RG 226, NARA.

17. Magruder to Caserta, March 3, 1945, folder 72, box 6, entry 90, RG 226, NARA; Donovan, Memorandum for the President, February 16, 1945, box 153, President's Secretary's File, FDR Library.

18. On the role of famed CIA spy hunter James Jesus Angleton in the Vessel operation, see Timothy J. Naftali, "ARTIFICE: James Angleton and X-2 Operations in Italy," in *The Secrets War: The Office of Strategic Services in World War II*, ed. George C. Chalou (Washington, DC: National Archives and Records Administration, 1992).

CHAPTER 18. "GOD HELP US!"

1. Hugh Wilford's excellent *America's Great Game: The CIA's Secret Arabists and the Shaping of the Modern Middle East* (New York: Basic Books, 2013) details the role of Penrose and others in the postwar State Department.

2. Penrose to Leary, February 7, 1945, folder 9, box 5, Penrose Papers; Leary to Penrose, February 7, 1945, "S.B.L.P. Jr. Correspondence," folder 67, box 76, entry 190, RG 226, NARA.

3. Hicks [Glueck] to Leary, April 14, 1945, wn 14335, box 369, entry 210, RG 226, NARA.

4. Hicks [Glueck] to Leary, January 11 and May 17, 1945, wn 14335, box 369, entry 210, RG 226, NARA.

5. Penrose to Dulles, February 23, 1945, wn 25837, box 7, entry 214, RG 226, NARA; Dulles to Penrose, April 21, 1945, folder 132, box 15, entry 165, RG 226, NARA.

6. Irving Sherman to Dulles, January 17, 1945, wn 9446, box 223, entry 210, RG 226, NARA.

7. Penrose to Irving Sherman, March 10, 1945, wn 9439, box 223, entry 210, RG 226, NARA.

8. Official Dispatch, #198, SAINT, February 12, 1944, wn 14601, box 297, entry 210, RG 226, NARA; Edward P. Barry, "Translation of Notes found on a prominent member of the Jewish Agency," June 13, 1944; Penrose to Chapin, August 1, 1944, folder 1281, box 172, entry 190, RG 226, NARA.

9. Leary to Penrose, February 27, 1945, folder 67, box 76, entry 190, RG 226, NARA.

10. Penrose to Dulles, March 22, 1945, wn 18697, box 507, entry 210, RG 226, NARA.

11. Leary to Shepardson, March 6, 1945; Penrose to Leary, March 20, 1945, folder 1281, box 172, entry 190, RG 226, NARA.

12. Penrose to Leary, March 20, 1945, folder 1281, box 172, entry 190, RG 226, NARA.

13. Penrose to Thomas G. Cassady, March 28, 1945, wn 18811, box 508, entry 210, RG 226, NARA; European-Mediterranean Pouch Review, April 4, 1945, folder 1, box 12, entry 99, RG 226, NARA; Penrose to Dulles, March 30, 1945, wn 18813, box 508, entry 210, RG 226, NARA.

14. Leary to Chapin, April 4, 1945, folder 1281, box 172, entry 190, RG 226, NARA; Leary to Loud, April 6, 1945, wn 25994, box 3, entry 215, RG 226, NARA.

15. Leary to Penrose, May 4, 1945, "S.B.L.P. Jr. Correspondence," box 76, entry 190, RG 226, NARA.

16. Leary to Hicks [Glueck], April 6 and May 5, 1945, wn 14335, box 369, entry 210, RG 226, NARA.

17. Louis E. Frechtling to William Langer, June 30, 1945, folder 11, box 22, entry 54, RG 226, NARA; Leary to Penrose, August 12, 1945, "S.B.L.P. Jr. Correspondence," box 76, entry 190, RG 226, NARA.

18. "The Jewish Agency of Palestine," in "Outline of SI, OSS/Cairo, History," folder 1, box 55, entry 99, RG 226, NARA.

19. John Magruder to Adjunct General, War Department, August 10, 1945, Penrose Personnel File, box 595, entry 224, RG 226, NARA.

CHAPTER 19. "AN UNUSUAL OPPORTUNITY"

1. Dulles to Donovan, October 7, 1944, wn 9322, box 180, entry 210, RG 226, NARA.

2. Herman to family, September 11, 1944, box 20, Herman Papers.

3. Herman to Henry Leiper, September 7, 1944, box 14, Herman Papers. Some FCC leaders, including Samuel McCrea Cavert, had done some earlier wartime work with the OSS. See ECR to Osborne, November 26, 1942, wn 13243, box 327, entry 210, RG 226, NARA.

4. Herman to Dulles, October 17, 1944, box 19, Herman Papers.

5. Herman to Leiper, October 13, 1944, box 14, Herman Papers.

6. October 12 and October 13, 1944, Herman diary.

7. Dulles to Lester Armour, October 31, 1944, wn 9322, box 180, entry 210, RG 226, NARA. In 1943 the OSS had recruited another church leader, Carl Hermann Voss, whom leaders thought they might use on a similar mission. See folder 62, box 141, entry

92, RG 226, NARA. On the breadth of Voss's religious work, see Wolfgang Saxon, "Carl H. Voss," *New York Times*, March 18, 1995.

8. See Warnshuis file, folder 8914, President's Personal File, FDR Library; A. L. Warnshuis to Leslie B. Moss, November 9, 1944, folder 128, Warnshuis Papers.

9. Herman to family, November 21, 1944, box 20, Herman Papers; A. L. Warnshuis to Margaret Warnshuis, November 17, 1944, folder 128, Warnshuis Papers.

10. Dulles to Hughes, December 7, 1944, wn 9322, box 180, entry 210, RG 226, NARA.

11. John D. Wilson to Hughes, December 13, 1944; Hughes to Wilson, December 14, 1944, wn 9322, box 180, entry 210, RG 226, NARA; Herman to Charles Eubank, February 6, 1945, folder 1775, box 88, entry 92A, RG 226, NARA.

12. A. L. Warnshuis to Herman, January 8, 1945, box 14, Herman Papers; Herman to Eubank, February 6, 1945, folder 1775, box 88, entry 92A, RG 226, NARA.

13. Dulles refers to his work with Visser 't Hooft in various cables. See, for example, April 19, May 22, and May 23, 1945, folder 128, box 14, entry 165, RG 226, NARA.

14. W. A. Visser 't Hooft, *Memoirs* (Philadelphia: Westminster Press, 1973), 136, 144.

15. Visser 't Hooft, *Memoirs*, 149.

16. January 15, 1945, Herman diary; Herman to Cantrell, March 2, 1945, Herman letters.

17. Cantrell to Herman, March 6 and March 27, 1945, Herman letters.

18. Eubank to B. W. Antell, February 17, 1945, folder 1775, box 88, entry 92A, RG 226, NARA; Eubank to the Director, February 23, 1945, Stewart Herman Personnel File, box 330, entry 224, RG 226, NARA.

19. Eubank to the Director, February 23, 1945, Stewart Herman Personnel File, box 330, entry 224, RG 226, NARA.

20. April 5 and November 3, 1945, Herman diary.

21. Herman orders, August 4, 1945, box 32, Herman Papers; Warren J. Tarrant to Herman, August 4, 1945, box 32, Herman Papers; August 20, 1945, Herman diary.

22. Many of Herman's reports are included in Clemens Vollnhals, ed., *Die evangelische Kirche nach dem Zusammenbruch* (Göttingen: Vandenhoeck & Ruprecht, 1988).

23. Herman's many meetings with religious and military leaders are noted in his summer 1945 diaries.

24. August 1, 1945, Herman diary.

25. For Herman's analysis of this reaction, see Stewart Herman, "Report on German Reaction to the Stuttgart Declaration," December 14, 1945, folder 4, box 13, World Council of Churches Records, Burke Library, Columbia University, New York.

26. World Council of Churches, "Report on the Visit of a Delegation from the World Council of Churches to Germany," October 1945, box 3, Herman Papers; Herman to John Foster Dulles, November 10, 1945, box 3, Herman Papers; Herman to Dulles, September 1, 1945, box 3, Herman Papers.

27. End-of-Year Memorandum, 1945, Herman diary.

28. Niemöller to Herman, February 28, 1948, box 16, Herman Papers; Personnel Orders, November 28, 1945, box 14, Herman Papers; "Report by Dr. Stewart Herman on Trip to Poland, June 1946," October 15, 1946, wn 16231, box 448, entry 210, RG 226, NARA.

CHAPTER 20. "THE HIGH POINT OF MUSLIM ALLIANCE"

1. Mary Eddy to family, February 23, 1945, folder 4, box 3, Eddy Papers.

2. Mary Eddy to family, February 23, 1945.

3. William A. Eddy, *F.D.R. Meets Ibn Saud* (New York: American Friends of the Middle East, 1954), 25, 26.

4. Eddy, *F.D.R. Meets Ibn Saud*, 31–32.

5. "Memorandum of Conversation Between the King of Saudi Arabia (Abdul Aziz Al Saud) and President Roosevelt, February 14, 1945, Aboard the U.S.S. Quincy," FRUS, *Diplomatic Papers, 1945: The Near East and Africa,* vol. 8, document 2; Eddy, *F.D.R. Meets Ibn Saud,* 34.

6. "Memorandum of Conversation Between the King of Saudi Arabia (Abdul Aziz Al Saud) and President Roosevelt."

7. Eddy, *F.D.R. Meets Ibn Saud,* 42.

8. Eddy, *F.D.R. Meets Ibn Saud,* 40; Eddy to Marycita Eddy, March 16, 1945; Eddy to Jack Eddy, February 23, 1945, folder 4, box 3, Eddy Papers.

9. Winston Churchill, "Triumph and Tragedy," *Life,* November 9, 1953, 94.

10. "The Minister in Saudi Arabia (Eddy) to the Secretary of State, February 22, 1945," FRUS, *Diplomatic Papers, 1945: The Near East and Africa,* vol. 8, document 671.

11. William A. Eddy, "King Ibn Saud," *Middle East Journal* (Summer 1963): 257.

12. "The Minister in Saudi Arabia (Eddy) to the Secretary of State, Jidda, August 8, 1945," FRUS, *Diplomatic Papers, 1945: The Near East and Africa,* vol. 8, document 921.

13. Eddy to Jack Eddy, February 23, 1945, folder 4, box 3, Eddy Papers.

14. Eddy to Bill Eddy, April 23 and May 25, 1945, folder 4, box 3, Eddy Papers.

15. Mary Eddy to Jack, Bill, Marycita, and Carmen Eddy, April 13, 1945, folder 4, box 3; Eddy to Marycita Eddy, April 25, 1945, folder 1, box 6, Eddy Papers.

16. Eddy to Bill Eddy, January 3 and May 25, 1945, folder 4, box 3, Eddy Papers.

17. Eddy to Mary Eddy, July 23, 1945, folder 1, box 6, Eddy Papers; Eddy to Frederick B. Lyon, September 16, 1946, "Postwar Intelligence Plans," box 1, entry 1491, RG 59, NARA.

18. Eddy to Bill and Jack Eddy, July 23, 1945, folder 1, box 6, Eddy Papers.

19. Eddy to Bill, Marycita, Jack, and Carmen and Mother, August 9, 1945; Eddy to Mary Eddy, August 12, 1945, folder 1, box 6, Eddy Papers.

20. Eddy to Mary Eddy, August 30 and September 18, 1945, folder 1, box 6, Eddy Papers.

CHAPTER 21. "BETWEEN A STRIFE-TORN EARTH AND WRATH-DARKENED HEAVENS"

1. Wilfred Smith to Mrs. Birch, June 18, 1947, Knowland Papers.

2. John Birch, "A.G.F.R.T.S. Activities in North China," January 1, 1945, folder 2964, box 171, entry 154, RG 226, NARA; Birch, "The Battle of Changteh," 23.

3. On Birch and Korea, see Robert S. Kim, *Project Eagle: The American Christians of North Korea in World War II* (Lincoln: University of Nebraska Press, 2017).

4. Revised Copy of Crow Plan, August 1, 1945, folder 102 (Crow), box 7, entry 148, RG 226, NARA.

5. OSS X-2 Branch Report No. YKX 2290, May 14, 1945, folder 52, box 17, entry 182, RG 226, NARA.

6. Birch to Tooker, March 21, 1945, folder 5, box 7, Whittlesey Papers.

7. Wilfred Smith to Mrs. Birch, June 18, 1947; Birch to mother, July 4, 1945, Knowland Papers.

8. Birch to Tooker, May 15, 1945, folder 5, box 7, Whittlesey Papers.

9. Birch to Tooker, July 4, 1945, folder 5, box 7, Whittlesey Papers.

10. Birch to Betty Birch, March 22, 1945, Knowland Papers; Birch to Tooker, July 4, 1945, folder 5, box 7, Whittlesey Papers.

11. Birch to mother, July 4, 1945; Birch to folks, August 13, 1945, Knowland Papers.

12. Birch to Tooker, August 11, 1945, folder 5, box 7, Whittlesey Papers; Birch to folks, August 13, 1945, Knowland Papers. On the end of the war, see Tsuyoshi Hasegawa, *Racing the Enemy: Stalin, Truman, and the Surrender of Japan* (Cambridge, MA: Belknap Press of Harvard University, 2005).

13. Birch to folks, August 13, 1945, Knowland Papers.

14. Birch to Tooker, August 11, 1945, folder 5, box 7, Whittlesey Papers.

15. Birch to Tooker, August 11, 1945.

16. Birch to Tooker, August 11, 1945.

17. "Re: Captain John M. Birch," March 23, 1946, folder 225, box 16, entry 168, RG 226, NARA.

18. Birch to Tooker, August 11, 1945, Whittlesey Papers; "Re: Captain John M. Birch"; Claire Chennault interview with Mrs. George S. Birch, December 10, 1945, Knowland Papers. On Birch and post-traumatic stress disorder, see Lautz, *John Birch: A Life*, 145.

19. "Inventory of Effects," Service Documents File, Official Military Personnel File of John M. Birch, NARA-STL; "The Birch Case: Testimony of Tung Fu Kuan [Dong Qinsheng]," October 6, 1945, folder 225, box 16, entry 168, RG 226, NARA.

20. "Birch Case: Testimony of Tung Fu Kuan."

21. "Birch Case: Testimony of Tung Fu Kuan."

22. "The Birch Case: William Miller to Albert Wedemeyer, September 1, 1945," folder 225, box 16, entry 168, RG 226, NARA; Jeremiah J. O'Connor, "Death of Captain John Birch, November 13, 1945," folder 2, box 87, Wedemeyer Papers.

23. "Birch Case: William Miller to Albert Wedemeyer, September 1, 1945."

24. John Thomson to Mrs. Birch, January 8, 1946, Knowland Papers; "The Birch Case: John Thomson to Major Gustav J. Krause, re: Account of the Death of Captain John Birch, September 14, 1945," folder 225, box 16, entry 168, RG 226, NARA; Major General Charles B. Stone III to Mr. Birch, September 28, 1945, Knowland Papers; "Birch, John M." [service card], folder 48 (John Birch), box 57, entry 224, RG 226, NARA. See also Major General Edward F. Witsell to Mrs. George Birch, September 12, 1945, Knowland Papers.

25. "Minutes of Meeting Held at Ambassador Hurley's Home, August 30, 1945," folder 6, box 87, Wedemeyer Papers.

26. O'Connor, "Death of Captain John Birch."

27. "Award of the Legion of Merit," "Birch, John M." folder 48 (John Birch), box 57, entry 224, RG 226, NARA; Chennault, *Way of a Fighter*, 260.

28. "Reminiscenses of Paul Frillmann," 406.

CHAPTER 22. "THE CIA HOLDS NOTHING SACRED INCLUDING THE SACRED"

1. Ferdinand L. Mayer to Donovan, July 17, 1945, wn 13278, box 338, entry 210, RG 226, NARA.

2. Kermit Roosevelt, *War Report of the OSS* (New York: Walker, 1976), 1:115.

3. Arthur Krock, "In the Nation: The Intelligence Unit of the State Department," *New York Times*, August 2, 1946.

4. Eddy, "Memorandum for the Director of Central Intelligence, October 18, 1946," folder 12, box 22, entry 36, RG 263, NARA; "Memorandum from the Secretary of State's Special Assistant for Research and Intelligence (Eddy) to the Acting Assistant Secretary of State for Administration (Peurifoy), January 27, 1947," FRUS, *Emergence of the Intelligence Establishment, 1945–1950*, document 92; "Memorandum from the Acting Assistant Secretary of State for Administration (Peurifoy) to the Under Secretary of State (Acheson) and Secretary of State Marshall, January 31, 1947," FRUS, *Emergence of the Intelligence Establishment, 1945–1950*, document 94.

5. "Presidential Directive on Coordination of Foreign Intelligence Activities," January 22, 1946, FRUS, *Emergence of the Intelligence Establishment, 1945–1950*, document 71. See also Michael Warner, "The Creation of the Central Intelligence Group," *Studies in Intelligence* 39, no. 5 (1996).

6. "Memorandum from the Secretary of State's Special Assistant for Research and Intelligence (Eddy) to the Under Secretary of State (Acheson), February 28, 1947," FRUS, *Emergence of the Intelligence Establishment, 1945–1950*, document 188.

7. "Memorandum from the Secretary of State's Special Assistant for Research and Intelligence (Eddy) to Secretary of State Marshall, February 15, 1947," FRUS, *Emergence of the Intelligence Establishment, 1945–1950*, document 186.

8. Penrose to W. J. McNeil, memo regarding Proposed Joint Congressional Committee on Intelligence, April 29, 1948, CREST, CIA-RDP86B00269R000500050048-9, NARA.

9. "The Consequences of the Petition of Palestine, November 28, 1947," https://www.cia.gov/library/readingroom/docs/DOC_0000256628.pdf; Eddy, *F.D.R. Meets Ibn Saud*, 37.

10. Eddy, "Manuscripts: 'Adventures in Arab Lands.'"

11. Eddy, "Manuscripts: 'Adventures in Arab Lands.'" On ARAMCO and Eddy, see Darren Dochuk, *Anointed with Oil: How Christianity and Crude Made Modern America* (New York: Basic Books, 2019).

12. "Letter from the Secretary of Defense's Special Assistant (McNeil) to Mathias F. Correa, February 2, 1948," enclosure: Stephen Penrose, "Report on CIA, January 2, 1948," FRUS, *Emergence of the Intelligence Establishment, 1945–1950*, document 338; Penrose to Dulles, January 16, 1948, folder 5, box 1, Penrose Papers.

13. James Forrestal to Penrose, May 13, 1948, folder 6, box 1, Penrose Papers.

14. Peggy Penrose to family, November 4, 1948, folder 7, box 1, Penrose Papers.

15. "Report by Dr. Stewart Herman on Trip to Poland, June 1946" and "Report on Trip to Hungary," folder 4, box 71, World Council of Churches Records, Burke Library, Columbia University, New York; "Report by Dr. Stewart Herman on Trip to Poland, June 1946," wn 16231, folder 5, box 448, entry 210, RG 226, NARA.

16. "Foreign Aid Urged on Spiritual Basis," *New York Times*, November 19, 1947.

17. Stewart W. Herman, "Why We Marched in Alabama," *Lutheran*, April 7, 1965.

18. "Goldwater's 1964 Acceptance Speech," *Washington Post*, https://www.washingtonpost.com/wp-srv/politics/daily/may98/goldwaterspeech.htm?noredirect=on.

19. On Donovan's postwar career, see Waller, *Wild Bill Donovan*.

20. For an excellent analysis of Truman's use of religion during the Cold War, see Inboden, *Religion and American Foreign Policy*.

21. "Version D of a Report on the History of the Division of Oral Intelligence, ca. January 1945," wn 780, box 64, entry 210, RG 226, NARA; "Personnel, Missionaries," Plan for Post War Secret Intelligence Operations in the Far East, January 1946, wn 18742, box 513, entry 210, RG 226, NARA.

22. "Black Letter from the 'Preparatory Committee for an Organization of the Militant Godless,' HUL-A-875," box 8B, entry 41: Records Relating to Activities in Guatemala, RG 263, NARA.

23. "How C.I.A. Put 'Instant Air Force' into Congo," *New York Times*, April 26, 1966; Leon Howell, "Growing Up in America," *Christianity and Crisis*, March 20, 1967, 50. See also "The C.I.A. Caper," *Christian Century*, March 8, 1967, 301.

24. Victor Marchetti and John D. Marks, *The CIA and the Cult of Intelligence* (New York: Alfred A. Knopf, 1974), 255; "Q and A: John Marks Talks About the CIA," *Washington Star*, May 13, 1975.

25. Richard L. Rashke, "CIA Funded, Manipulated Missionaries," *National Catholic Reporter*, August 1, 1975; Seymour M. Hersh, "Huge C.I.A. Operation Reported in U.S. Against Antiwar Forces, Other Dissidents in Nixon Years," *New York Times*, December 22, 1974. See also "Bishop Said Paid by CIA," *Washington Post*, July 25, 1975.

26. *Foreign and Military Intelligence, Book I, Final Report of the Senate Select Committee to Study Governmental Operations with Respect to Intelligence Activities* (Washington, DC: Government Printing Office, 1976), 202.

27. *Foreign and Military Intelligence, Book I, Final Report*, 201.

28. Senator Mark O. Hatfield, "Prohibiting Federal Intelligence Agency Involvement with the Clergy," *Congressional Record—Senate*, December 15, 1975, 40434.

29. Mark O. Hatfield to President Gerald Ford, September 19, 1975; Philip W. Buchen to Hatfield, November 5, 1975, box 17, White House Congressional Mail Files, 1974–77, Gerald R. Ford Presidential Library, Ann Arbor, MI.

30. On the ecumenical-evangelical divide, see Hollinger, *Protestants Abroad*.

31. Senator Mark O. Hatfield, "Prohibiting Federal Intelligence Agency Involvement with the Clergy," *Congressional Record—Senate*, December 15, 1975, 40432, 40433.

32. Garry Wills, "Church-State Relations Don't Need CIA Meddling," *Washington Star*, August 13, 1975; Michael Novak, "CIA War Preferable to Nuclear War," *National Catholic Reporter*, August 1, 1975. See also Marjorie Hyer, "Clergy Wary of CIA Approaches," *Washington Post*, August 5, 1975.

33. Senator Mark O. Hatfield, "CIA Issues New Regulation on Contact with Missionaries Abroad," *Congressional Record—Senate*, May 25, 1976. See also Nicholas M. Horrock, "C.I.A. to Stop Enlisting Agents from the Press and the Church," *New York Times*, February 12, 1976.

34. Stansfield Turner to Royal L. Tinsley, July 18, 1977, CREST CIA-RDP79M 00983A001800030003-4.

35. "CIA's Use of Journalists and Clergy in Intelligence Operations," *Hearing Before the Select Committee on Intelligence of the United States Senate, One-Hundred and Fourth Congress* (Washington, DC: Government Printing Office, 1996), 7. See also "CIA Use of Missionaries Resisted," *Christianity Today*, April 29, 1996, 59; "CIA Recruitment and the Church," *Christian Century*, March 13, 1996, 285; and "CIA Wants Option of Recruiting Clergy," *Christian Century*, September 11–18, 1996, 844.

36. Hatfield to John Deutch, February 28, 1996, "CIA's Use of Journalists and Clergy in Intelligence Operations," 38.

37. "AR 2-2 (U) Law and Policy Governing the Conduct of Intelligence Activities (Formerly HR 7-1), May 10, 2013," CIA Reading Room document 0006235713 https://www.cia.gov/library/readingroom/docs/DOC_0006235713.pdf.

INDEX

Credit: Julia Lampe

Matthew Avery Sutton is Edward R. Meyer distinguished professor of history at Washington State University. The author of award-winning books, including *American Apocalypse*, he lives in Pullman, Washington.